Police and State in Prussia, 1815–1850

Cet ouvrage est publié dans le cadre de l'accord de co-édition passé en 1977 entre la Fondation de la Maison des sciences de l'homme et le Press Syndicate of the University of Cambridge. Toutes les langues européennes sont admises pour les titres couverts par cet accord, et les ouvrages collectifs peuvent paraître en plusieurs langues.

Les ouvrages paraissent soit isolément, soit dans l'une des séries que la Maison des sciences de l'homme et Cambridge University Press ont convenu de publier ensemble. La distribution dans le monde entier des titres ainsi publiés conjointement par les deux établissements est assurée par Cambridge University Press.

This book is published as part of the joint publishing agreement established in 1977 between the Fondation de la Maison des sciences de l'homme and the Press Syndicate of the University of Cambridge. Titles published under this arrangement may appear in any European language or, in the case of volumes of collected essays, in several languages.

New books will appear either as individual titles or in one of the series which the Maison des sciences de l'homme and the Cambridge University Press have jointly agreed to published. All books published jointly by the Maison des Sciences de l'Homme and the Cambridge University Press will be distributed by the Press throughout the world.

Police and State in Prussia, 1815–1850

ALF LÜDTKE
Max-Planck-Institut für Geschichte, Göttingen

TRANSLATED BY PETE BURGESS

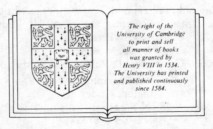

The right of the University of Cambridge to print and sell all manner of books was granted by Henry VIII in 1534. The University has printed and published continuously since 1584.

CAMBRIDGE UNIVERSITY PRESS
CAMBRIDGE
NEW YORK PORT CHESTER MELBOURNE SYDNEY
EDITIONS DE
LA MAISON DES SCIENCES DE L'HOMME
PARIS

Published by the Press Syndicate of the University of Cambridge
The Pitt Building, Trumpington Street, Cambridge CB2 1RP
40 West 20th Street, New York, NY 10011, USA
10 Stamford Road, Oakleigh, Melbourne 3166, Australia
and Editions de la Maison des Sciences de l'Homme
54 Boulevard Raspail, 75270 Paris Cedex 06

Originally published in German as
'Gemeinwohl', Polizei und 'Festungspraxis': Staatliche Gewaltsamkeit und innere Verwaltung in Preussen, 1815–1850
by Vandenhoeck and Ruprecht, Göttingen 1982

First published in English by Editions de la Maison des Sciences de l'Homme and Cambridge University Press 1989 as *Police and State in Prussia, 1815–1850*

Printed in Great Britain by
Redwood Burn Ltd, Trowbridge, Wiltshire

British Library cataloguing in publication data

Lüdtke, Alf
Police and State in Prussia, 1815–1850
1. Prussia. Police. Role. Political aspects,
1800–1900
I. Title II. ['Gemeinwohl', Polizei und
'Festungspraxis'. *English*]

Library of Congress cataloguing in publication data

Lüdtke, Alf, 1943–
['Gemeinwohl', Polizei und 'Festungspraxis'. English]
Police and State in Prussia, 1815–1850/Alf 'Lüdtke:
translated by Pete Burgess.
p. cm.
Translation of: 'Gemeinwohl', Polizei und 'Festungspraxis'.
Bibliography.
Includes index.
ISBN 0–521–30164–5
ISBN 0–521–30164–5
1. Prussia (Germany) – Politics and government – 1815–1870.
2. Bureaucracy – Prussia (Germany) – History – 19th century.
3. Property – Prussia (Germany) – History – 19th century. I. Title.
JN4447. L8313 1989
321.9'0943 – dc19 88–30183 CIP

ISBN 0 521 30164 5
ISBN 2 7351 0282 1 (France only)

WV

Contents

Illustrations

Plates 1, 2, 3 and 6 are taken, respectively, from W. Abegg (ed.), *Die Polizei in Einzeldarstellungen* (Berlin, 1926), vol. 10, pp. 48, 47 and 47, and vol. 1, p. 75; Plates 4, 5 and 7 from *Fliegende Blätter*, Munich 3 (1846), 80, 4 (1847), 96, and 6 (1848), 150; and Plates 8 and 9 from *Kladderadatsch*, Berlin 2 (1849), 148, and 3 (1850), 172.

Preface

Lieutenant Elard von Oldenburg-Januschau incarnated the classical idea of the Prussian *Landjunker* in the Wilhelmine Reich. A retired soldier and East Elbian estate owner he was also for a while a member of the Reichstag and the Prussian House of Deputies. During the first days of the 1918 November Revolution he sought to the last to organise a military counter-revolution in Berlin. When nothing immediately came of his efforts he returned, in the middle of November, to Oldenburg-Januschau, his patrimonial estate. His aim: 'to provide for order and discipline at least within the boundaries assigned to me'. His autobiography recalls:

> In Januschau I was greeted by my old servant with the message that the spirit of revolt had also raised its head here. One of my hands had declared himself master of Januschau and not without issuing threats against my own person. Realising that here on my land and soil this called for swift, personal and vigorous action, I took a solid stick and ventured out into the field where the aforementioned hand was at work. I approached him, took him by the ear and asked him 'Who governs here in Januschau?' When he gave no answer I yelled at him, 'I'll smash you so hard in the mouth you won't know what hit you.' This language he understood. His courage left him and he acknowledged me as his master. Our mutual relationship of trust had been restored.[1]

Historical processes, their rhythms and continuities, contradictions and interruptions, cannot be reduced to individuals. The phenomenon of one palpably violent estate owner, such as Oldenburg-Januschau, though providing us with some pointers, cannot furnish anything resembling a proper explanation. This is all the more true for the pseudo-continuity of Prussian history wielded for propagandistic purposes: the well-known line from Luther, through Frederick II, Bismarck, Wagner, and Nietzsche and finishing with Hitler. Such a cavalcade of stars has nothing to do with historical explanation or historical understanding. The same can be said of approaches which hinge on alleged national characteristics.

Interest in Prussia is often focused on the continuity of the Prussian state. Central in this are the consequences of 'Prussianism'. Did the Prussian state, Prussian society, make a special contribution to the emergence of National Socialism in Germany? Leaving aside the diversity of positions involved, both contemporaries and later observers have argued that this was the case, a contention culminating in the legitimation for the dissolution of the Prussian state. The resolution of the Allied Control Commission in Germany in February 1947, for example, reads: 'Prussia has long been the bearer of militarism and reaction in Germany.'

Any debate on the continuity of Prussia, the Prussian system and Prussianism understood as a social process critically turns on the issue of the *Sonderweg*, Germany's singular historical path – a term rooted in the idea of a unique discrepancy between economic modernity and social and political backwardness. This thesis, the germ of which was already evident in the nineteenth century, has been the object of renewed attention throughout the two decades or so of critical debate over the nature of the Bismarckian and Wilhelmine Reich of 1871. Historical social scientists have argued that the development of capitalism in the countryside, especially in the East Elbian estate economy (the *Gutswirtschaft*) and even more so in the tempestuous progress of industrial capitalism after the 1850s, did not unseat the 'traditional power elites'. Neither, so the thesis has it, were their 'pre-industrial values' supplanted or revised.[2] These 'traditional' forces and attitudes were able to persist because of the absence, or more properly speaking the defeat, of 'bourgeois revolution' in Germany, and in particular in Prussia.

For Germany, David Blackbourn and Geoff Eley[3] have cast fundamental doubts on the assumption that there must be some correspondence, at the least over the long term, between economic growth, social change, and the forms of political rule and participation – a uniform rhythm of transformation. In fact, closer examination of social and economic development in continental Europe, and elsewhere in the world, reveals no 'norm'. And, in particular, there are no grounds for believing that development in the United States, England or France represents such a norm, let alone an ideal. In fact it is England, the capitalist pioneer, which would be better thought of as 'peculiar'.

Geoff Eley, in common with most other historians, does at least agree that the development of bourgeois society in Germany did exhibit a 'particular form'.[4] The advance of the capitalist mode of production in Prussia-Germany was spurred on not by political revolt by the bourgeoisie but by an aristocratic-bureaucratic 'revolution from above' which had fostered capitalist economic processes – the core of bourgeois revolution – in a number of different stages since the late eighteenth century. The Prussian state plays a key role here. In Germany, the historical points were set by the 'civil' and 'military bureaucracy'.[5] The process through which the state and bureaucracy determined the conditions for capitalist growth culminated in the unification of the *Kleindeutsch* Reich of 1871, pursued and imposed by Prussia through military force.

On this view, social relations and structures were characterised not by a clear line between their component elements but by a patchwork pattern of interfusion and admixture. Social formations were characterised by interests and modes of conduct which had developed 'unevenly'. Blackbourn and Eley's critique represents a major contribution to the analysis of the seminal issue of the synchronicity of change and continuity – that is, the contradictory character of historical processes.

Any attempt to delineate and define Prussia's 'asynchronicities' and social 'patchwork' must begin with the works of Hans Rosenberg. His short essay on the Prussian 'estate-owning class', published in 1958,[6] illustrates an acute awareness of the abstractness and hence inadequacy of the stereotype of the 'traditional power elite'. The question is not simply that the estate owners absorbed, in fact had to absorb, bourgeois in large numbers into their circles from the late eighteenth century – a process in which the Junker, at least in the 'open country', continued to set the standard of conduct and political predilection – but that these capitalist Junkers, from at the latest the middle of the nineteenth century, availed themselves of all the 'bourgeois' techniques of political mass mobilisation. And their success was considerable: small landowners and also their 'own' agricultural workers and dependent servants overwhelmingly voted conservative. This was the principal popular basis of Bismarck's support. The unique Prussian 'relationship of trust' between master and servant – both as estate owner and factory master – remained intact. The 'pliancy' of the ruled in the given order could be restabilised.

Rosenberg's essay marked a major step in more precisely defining the notion of Bonapartism. The combination of the traditional authority and force of the police and the state with 'modern forms' of mass appeal has been a subject of debate since the rule of Napoleon Bonaparte III.

In his analysis of the Prussian military reforms of the 1860s Friedrich Engels accused the bourgeoisie of a 'notable lack of courage'.[7] After 1848–9 social peace was bought at the price of political subservience. A number of variants of this accusation, often self-accusation, can be found in debates extending back to the middle of the last century. When in doubt – and in view of the growing 'red menace' this was increasingly the case – bourgeois strata and groupings fell back on the 'strong arm' of the state.

Such a moralistic critique of the political timidity and hesitancy of the bourgeoisie would, however, be quite misplaced, as David Blackbourn argues.[8] Economic success and the gradual permeation of bourgeois norms and modes of conduct made it less urgent to seek direct political rule. Moreover, direct control over the apparatus of government did not seem necessary given the administration's policy of modernisation. Certainly, there was no particular urgency for the bourgeoisie to unseat the aristocracy and bureaucracy from their political positions.

However, the form and intensity of political rule in Prussia are not reducible solely to the control exercised by the government and bureaucracy. Domination in Prussia was clearly inseparable from servility. Military discipline was perfectly compatible with the industrial control and organisation of labour. This link between an authoritarian order and self-disciplined zealousness on the part of the dominated throws up the issue of the development of the state and society in Prussia after the late eighteenth century. State and 'civil society' remained separate but interrelated.

In Hegel's *Philosophy of Right* – written in Berlin in the 1820s – 'civil society' constituted the 'system of needs'. Civil society was the 'battleground' of the individual private interest of all against all. Individual interests were defined through a pre-given 'general interest' expressed and embodied in the state, which mediated the individual social spheres and the overall structure. The 'general interest' was the state's province.

In Prussia, the reform legislation of 1807–12 proclaimed the free activity of individual subjects. Motivated not least by fiscal considerations, the reform bureaucracy set about the development of capitalist production in both industry and agriculture. The new commercial society was based, naturally, on the 'rule of law' (*Rechtsstaat*). This meant two things. First, the forms of intercourse of the commercial 'bourgeois' were based on legal instruments. Secondly, officials, as the only 'universal estate', laid claim to the manipulation of these legal forms. This led to a double legitimation for officials: first and foremost they felt responsible for the 'common good'; at the same time, they saw themselves as the protectors of the lawfulness of both social and state relations.

However, the 'rule of law' was far from implying equality before the law. In fact, the Prussian Legal Code of 1794 had confirmed the inequalities between the various estates. Rather, instead of being arbitrary, state interventions, exactions or controls were now to be calculable, checkable and, if necessary, actionable. From this standpoint the rule of law under the bureaucracy might be seen as the apotheosis of the constitution – before any constitutional forms had been attempted for the participation of all in the political process.

The 'rule of law' as the precondition and context of civil society gave as much weight at least to 'rule' as it did to legality. Subjects remained merely 'bourgeois': there was no need for *citoyens*. For officials, who – as the 'universal estate' – participated directly in the state, this construction provided scope to advance their own definitions and interests. At the same time their position and legitimation allowed them to derive that 'inner freedom' which Theodor Fontane characterised at the end of the century as the 'Prussian idea'.

More recently, Thomas Nipperdey has referred to the 'Janus head' of the post-1815 Prussian state. Governmental and social reform was never regarded as being in any way antithetical to extensive control over minds and bodies.[9] And the spectrum of repression was wide indeed: the censorship of science and journalism, and police obsession with countless possible misdemeanours not only in streets and public places but also within the home.

There were, of course, alternative paths and critical junctures. The question of continuity would be misplaced were it to turn solely on the search for a one-way street. Gordon Craig has recently indicated some of the possible alternatives in his *The End of Prussia*.[10] For the period of the governmental and administrative reforms after 1807 Craig sees the antithesis and possible alternative paths of development embodied, on the one hand, in Freiherr vom Stein, and on the other in the Mark-Brandenburg *Landjunker*, August Ludwig von der Marwitz. And for the period in which the 'social question' – that is, the activity of the plebeian and proletarian masses in the industrial centres – became the mainspring of both Junker and bourgeois politics of containment, Craig points on the one hand to Bismarck, and on the other to the socially critical author of the 1840s, Bettina von Arnim. Marwitz and Bismarck prevailed. In the case of Marwitz, as the enemy of all things new; in the case of Bismarck, as the sophisticated political tactician, both Junker and Bonapartist.

Craig's continuing commitment to the *Sonderweg* is of less importance here. What is problematic, however, is that his acute personalisation of history pushes the social context too much into the background. And, critically, he leaves out of account the rise and power of the bureaucracy from the eighteenth century. Ultimately was it not the bureaucracy which prevailed – over Stein *and* Marwitz? Certainly the bureaucracy was by no means merely an instrument in Bismarck's policies, especially his interior policy. And was it not the regulation of social life by bourgeois, but also numerous aristocratic and Junker bureaucrats which made possible the retention of Junkerdom's privileges on such an extensive scale?

Governance does not necessarily entail loyalty. What is indispensable, though, is a minimum of acceptance by the ruled. Oldenburg-Januschau's reference – nothwithstanding his violent intervention – to a 'relation of trust', a relationship promptly 'restored', certainly testifies to the arrogance of power. But his phrase was not merely cynical verbiage. It denoted a ruling claim which distinguished between conscious assent and blind obedience.

How was this equation practised? How could assent, acceptance and obedience be so closely linked? Was the reason really the oft-cited Prussian form of *égalité* – universal conscription? During their three-year military service, reduced to two after 1837, the majority of young men were pledged to the 'King' and 'Flag' in the everyday routinised drill of a monarchic and aristocratic institution. But what role was played by civil officials? What was the significance of the bureaucracy for the characteristically Prussian form of domination?

Critics of the pre-1848 bureaucracy already had bitter experience of its 'commanding tone'. There are even occasional self-critical remarks by officials themselves – albeit a minority. The extent to which conduct in civil society, and in particular in the bureaucracy, was impregnated by military norms is strikingly illustrated by the case of the imposter 'Captain' of Köpenick in which a discharged prisoner, in fact a tailor by the name of Wilhelm Voigt, seriously rattled the civil authority in the town of Köpenick near Berlin in 1906, equipped only with a uniform and commanding manner. The episode dramatically revealed that, even in a capitalist society, Prussia's military bent was by no means confined to officer casinos or aristocratic clubs. Rather, the military style and demeanour cohabited quite happily with the rationality of bourgeois life, both in business and in the administration. No doubt the emphasis shifted. The servile 'subject' (Heinrich Mann, *Der Untertan*) increasingly figured as a subject of criticism and irony: however, he remained a millionfold reality.

The German tradition of the philosophy of the state viewed civil society as subject to state control from above. Order, and its maintenance, was to be and remain the fulcrum of action for every citizen. Hardly surprising then that, in practice, the hoped-for 'trust' in authority and the state inevitably manifested itself as the acceptance of domination and its various injunctions.

The present book seeks to sketch out some of the central lines of development for the first half of the nineteenth century.

The German manuscript for this book was completed in the early part of 1981 and published in 1982 under the title *'Gemeinwohl', Polizei und 'Festungspraxis': Staatliche Gewaltsamkeit und innere Verwaltung in Preußen, 1815–1850* (Vandenhoek & Ruprecht: Göttingen). Some small changes have been made for the English edition: Chapter 4 has been cut in some places. The excurses and appendices contained in the German edition have been dropped and replaced by extracts from a number of original texts which it is hoped will prove informative and illustrative for a readership probably less acquainted with the continental European or Prussian-German police context. The body of the text itself has not been amended to any great degree. I have also dispensed with a detailed treatment of literature published since the German date of publication. In my view nothing which has been published since then would require any fundamental revision of my argument here. The only exceptions would be some work on the origins of the modern state and the emergence of the police in England. I turn to these briefly below.

Klaus Eder's extensive study raises a number of issues on the development of the state in the modern period.[11] Working on the basis of Habermas's theories, he proposes that the pre-bourgeois model of order of hierarchy and the justification of norms by traditions have been replaced by 'equality' and 'discursiveness'. Bourgeois society and the bourgeois state have, accordingly, followed the principle of the legitimation of norms and values via argumentation. This is translated into practice in communication between theoretically equal subjects. Equality and discursiveness are also, in Eder's view, the guiding principles of juridical procedure. These principles have been adopted, used and increasingly applied by the bureaucracy and officialdom. However, their efficacy, at least for the Prussian-German case, was obstructed. This 'pathogenesis' of the bourgeois state is rooted in the 'autonomy of administrative practice' which, especially in Prussia, subverted these principles of civil order.

This seems to me to pass over one key point: bureaucracy not only sought control over civil society, as Eder contends. More crucially, administrative practice constantly embraced the application or threat of direct physical force. Violent assertion, not domination-free communication, was integral to the basic pattern of officials' conduct. And where the 'common good' demanded it, the ultimate resort to the 'strong arm' of the state seemed entirely legitimate.

The work of Clive Emsley on the development of the police in England raises two points of importance for the brief comparative section at the end of Chapter 6 below. Emsley shows convincingly that police practice 'on the ground' in eighteenth-century England was by no means as casual, easy-going and ineffective as has been broadly imagined. The London 'new police' of 1829 thus marked a much less dramatic change than previously supposed. Emsley also confirms Robert Storch's position, already discussed here: the 'new police' were particularly concerned to assuage the fears of the 'propertied classes'. However, Emsley poses an intriguing simultaneity: the policeman might appear not only as a dreaded official but also at times as 'the individual to whom resort could be made in a variety of troubles'. These effects of the 'new police', unintended as they largely were, stimulated acceptance of the new state organ amongst those who were its primary targets. This is certainly a major point. The image of subjects cooperating with the police, even invoking its action, is very different to one of strictly maintained distance or open hostility. Nevertheless, despite raising this issue Emsley does not explore just how closely related surveillance of and aid to the poor and destitute were. Reliance on the police by the policed enhanced the primary role of these agents of authority – that of controlling the 'dangerous classes' of the proletariat. Thus the containment of the disorderly and suspicious continues to hold good as the real 'sub-text' of all attempts to combat crime and safeguard order, not only in Prussia or France but also in nineteenth-century England.

I am indebted to my colleagues and friends at the Max-Planck-Institut für Geschichte, Göttingen, for the many stimulating discussions which formed the backdrop to this present work and in particular to the generous support of its director, Professor Rudolf Vierhaus, who made possible the present English edition. I also wish to express my gratitude to Robert Berdahl (University of Illinois, Urbana-Champaign), David W. Sabean (Cornell University) and Gerald Sider (CUNY) who never hesitated to share their thoughts on issues of police and *Herrschaft* with me. I remain, of course, responsible for what is flawed in this text.

The English edition of this book would not have been possible without the strenuous efforts, patient support and friendly cooperation of the translator, Pete Burgess. To him I extend particular thanks.

Translator's note

Readers are referred to the glossary for explanation and translation of terms used within the Prussian administrative bureaucracy.

In order to avoid the 'his/her' formulation, the translator has used 'their/them' to refer to the gender-neutral 3rd person singular.

Abbreviations

ALR	*Allgemeines Landrecht*
APP	Archiwum Państwowe we Poznaniu
APW	Archiwum Państwowe we Wrocławiu
BA	Bundesarchiv Koblenz
GG	*Geschichte und Gesellschaft*
GS	*Gesetzsammlung für die Königlichen Preußischen Staaten*
GStA/PK	Geheimes Staatsarchiv Preußischer Kulturbesitz Berlin
HistA Köln	Historisches Archiv der Stadt Köln
HStAD	Hauptstaatsarchiv Düsseldorf
HZ	*Historische Zeitschrift*
JbWG	*Jahrbuch für Wirtschaftsgeschichte*
KA	*(Kamptz') Annalen der preußischen inneren Staatsverwaltung*
KO	Kabinetts-Ordre
KZSS	*Kölner Zeitschrift für Soziologie und Sozialpsychologie*
MdI	Ministerium des Innern
MEW	*Marx-Engels-Werke*
NCC	*Novum Corpus Constitutionum*
NPL	*Neue politische Literatur*
Reg.-Bez.	Regierungsbezirk
RP	Regierungspräsident
RR	Regierungsrat
Sgr	Silbergroschen
SOWI	*Sozialwissenschaftliche Informationen für Unterricht und Studium*
StADT	Staatsarchiv Detmold
StadtA AC	Stadtarchiv Aachen
StadtA DO	Stadtarchiv Dortmund
StadtA IS	Stadtarchiv Iserlohn
StadtA TR	Stadtarchiv Trier
StAK	Landeshauptarchiv Koblenz
StAMS	Staatsarchiv Münster
Tlr	Taler
VSWG	*Vierteljahrschrift für Sozial- und Wirtschaftsgeschichte*
ZfG	*Zeitschrift für Geschichtswissenschaft*
ZfS	*Zeitschrift für Soziologie*
ZStA II	Zentrales Staatsarchiv der DDR, Merseburg

Glossary

Allgemeines Landrecht (ALR)	Prussian Legal Code, promulgated in 1794. However, it was not applicable in every Prussian Province: large parts of the Rhine Province – all areas to the west of the Rhine and the area around Düsseldorf and Elberfeld – fell under the Napoleonic Code.
Bezirksregierung	District Government: part of the post-1808 Prussian provincial administrative structure. They comprised a number of officials with life-tenure (*Beamte*) (specific officials are referred to individually). The *Bezirksregierung* administered a Government District (*Regierungsbezirk*).
Gesinde	Servants bound by the provision of the Servants Ordinance (*Gesindeordnung*, 1810).
Gutsbezirk	Independent estate district: a unit of administration in which jurisdiction was exercised by the Junker estate owners.
Gutsherrschaft	Mode of domination within an independent estate district (*Gutsbezirk*) constituted by the simultaneity of administrative–political and economic control. The Junker estate owner (*Gutsherr*) was entrusted with first instance jurisdiction, although the court may have been presided over by a justiciary, and also exercised local policing (*gutsherrliche Polizeigewalt*).
Gutswirtschaft	Estate economy of East Elbia (*Gut*=an estate), based on the extraction of a surplus from unfree labour.
Häusler, Heuerlinge, Kossäten	Cottagers or small peasants with little or no land: often called on to perform labour for the landowner, and rewarded in cash or kind, including lodgings.
Instmann (pl. *Instleute*)	A type of cotter, working on the East Elbian estates, living in their own households but also sometimes housed in barracks. Paid in cash and kind, they were subject to the Servants Ordinance.
Justitiar	Legal officer of a District Government.

Kaufsystem	'Merchant system', where the producers own the means of production but sell their product to a merchant.
Kreistag	Body responsible for electing the *Landrat*.
Landrat	Elected official responsible for administration in a 'county' (*Kreis*). Oversaw the mayors of the towns (*Bürgermeister*) and villages (*Amtmänner* and *Dorfschulzen*).
Landsturm	Home Guard.
Landwehr	Militia.
Oberpräsident	Permanent commissioners of the Ministries responsible for the 'administrative conduct' and 'state of welfare' of the provinces to which they were assigned.
Oberregierungsrat	Senior executive official ('senior councillor'). Two in each District Government would be subordinate to the *Regierungspräsident*. As an *Abteilungsdirigent* each was responsible for one of the two Departments in each District Government.
Offiziant	Lower 'executive' police officers.
Präsidium	Comprised the President and heads of the two Departments of a District Government. They organised administrative procedures and were responsible for discipline and appointments.
Regierung	*Bezirksregierung* (see above).
(*Regierungs-*)*Assessor*	Junior official of a District Government (after three years as *Regierungsreferendar*)
Regierungspräsident	The senior offical of a District Government.
Regierungspräsidium	Synonym for *Regierung*.
Regierungsrat	Official ('councillor'). From six to eight in each District Government. Together with an *Assessor* they were responsible for one branch of administrative activity.
Regierungsreferendar	Administrative trainee. Obtained their post after three years as an *Auskultator*.

Staatsrat — Council of State: advisory body to the crown. Established in 1817, it comprised members of the royal family, central government ministers, heads of the main central agencies (e.g. the mint), senior military, and the senior officials of the provinces (*Oberpräsident*). A member of the Council of State was also termed a *Staatsrat*.

Verlagssystem — Putting-out system, where the direct producer works under contract to a putter-out (*Verleger*) who may supply some of the means of production.

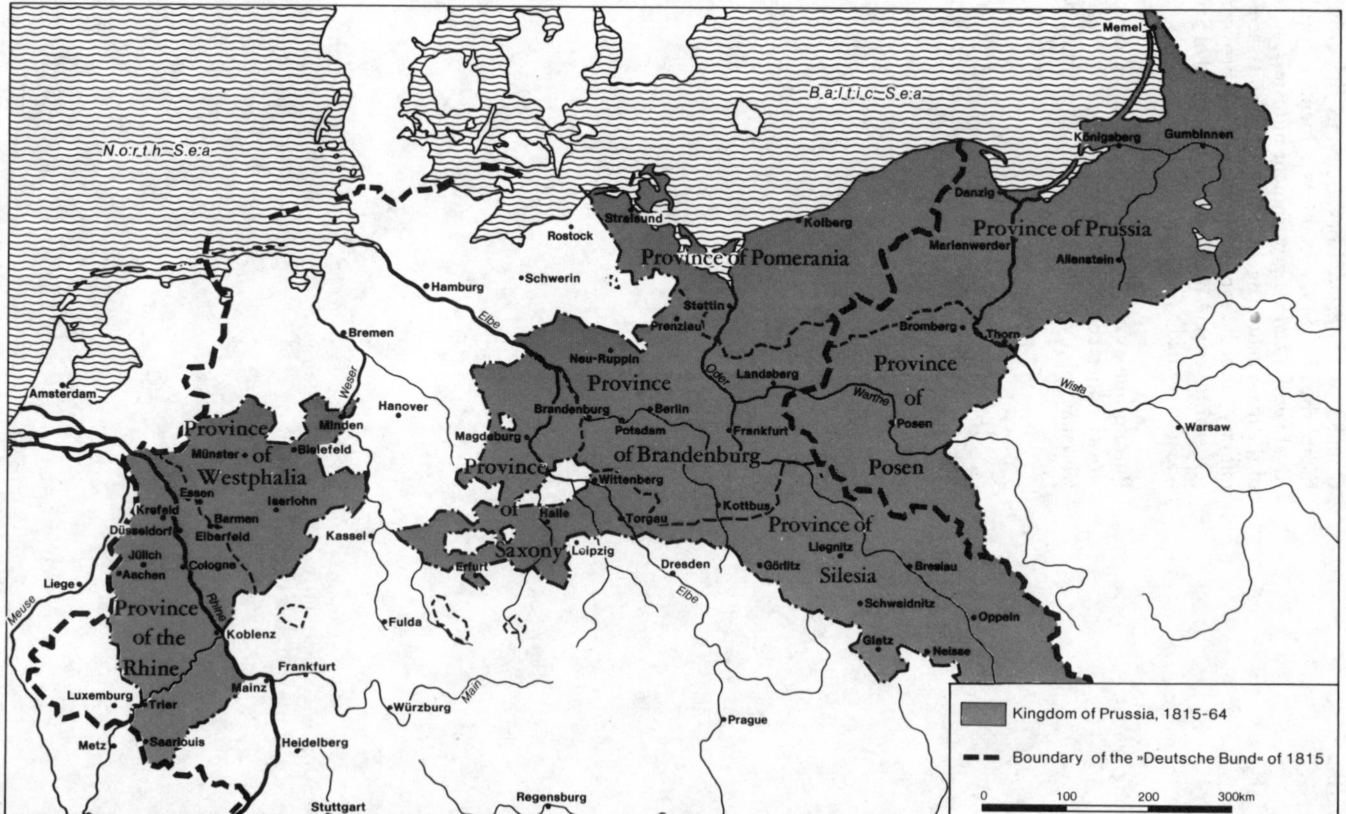

North Sea
Baltic Sea
Province of Prussia
Province of Pomerania
Province of Posen
Province of Brandenburg
Province of Silesia
Province of Saxony
Province of Westphalia
Province of the Rhine
Memel
Königsberg
Gumbinnen
Danzig
Marienwerder
Allenstein
Kolberg
Stralsund
Rostock
Schwerin
Hamburg
Stettin
Prenzlau
Bromberg
Thorn
Landsberg
Posen
Warsaw
Bremen
Neu-Ruppin
Amsterdam
Hanover
Minden
Brandenburg
Berlin
Potsdam
Frankfurt
Magdeburg
Münster
Bielefeld
Wittenberg
Essen
Iserlohn
Halle
Torgau
Kottbus
Krefeld
Barmen
Elberfeld
Düsseldorf
Kassel
Jülich
Aachen
Cologne
Leipzig
Dresden
Görlitz
Liegnitz
Breslau
Erfurt
Liege
Schweidnitz
Fulda
Koblenz
Oppeln
Glatz
Neisse
Mainz
Luxemburg
Trier
Würzburg
Prague
Metz
Saarlouis
Heidelberg
Regensburg
Stuttgart
Elbe
Oder
Warthe
Wisła
Weser
Rhine
Meuse
Main
Kingdom of Prussia, 1815-64
Boundary of the »Deutsche Bund« of 1815
0
100
200
300km

1

State domination in the transition to industrial capitalism

The synchronism of symbolic and physical force

The formation of the 'modern' state was a topic which repeatedly engaged the attention of Max Weber. In his sceptical look at the secular advance of 'occidental rationalism' he noted two, related, tendencies:

> The spread of pacification and the expansion of the market thus constitutes a development which is accompanied, along parallel lines, by (1) that monopolisation of legitimate violence by the political organisation which finds its culmination in the modern concept of the *state* as the ultimate source of every kind of legitimacy of the use of physical force; and (2) that rationalisation of the rules of its application which has come to culminate in the concept of the legitimate legal order.[1]

Weber's own sceptical reticence deterred him from asserting generalised causal relations; developments parallel in time sufficed. The long-term process of the advance of market relations was accompanied by the politically organised monopolisation of 'violence' (*Gewaltsamkeit*), the legitimacy of which was inseparable from the formation of the political system, from the state. What was central here was not the state as apparatus, as material substrate: rather, the guarantee of the legitimacy of the conduct of the state, and especially state violence, lay in the latent and manifest concept of 'the state' itself. And with this legitimate violence went the formulation and development of socially accepted rules of procedure, the 'legitimate legal order' through which the force monopolised by the state would be applied.

A complementary relationship therefore exists between 'capitalisation', the increasingly commodity form of social relations – which, although not disregarded by Weber, tends to be swallowed up in the idea of the 'market' – and the transformation of the procedures by which power is wielded and secured. As fundamental as this characterisation may be, however, it concentrates solely on *form*, excluding both the substance of social transformation in its uneven regional and cyclical dynamics (these, as it were, prior to the more general labels of commercial, agrarian, and industrial capitalisation and forms of proletarianisation) and the interaction between this substance and the formation of centralised political authority. The social foundations of state power and the state apparatus, their functions and dysfunctions for social transformation, for both the dominant as well as the revolutionary or oppressed classes, remain unspecified. In fact, Weber explicitly avoids any such imputation of content: political associations or states are not constituted by virtue of any unique substance or tasks ascribed to them.[2]

Nevertheless the pivot of this characterisation of the state is not 'merely formal'. The decisive criterion adopted by Weber is the *means* through which the state acts. And by choosing the level of 'means', considerable scope for concretisation is provided which is indispensable when dealing with questions of power, domination and force as they affect relationships between people rather than abstract entities. Weber's reluctance to reconstruct state functions from the 'logic' of social modes of production in fact proves to be an advantage: he obtained his characterisation from extensive historical and ethnographical material. And it was on this basis that he was able to expound the thoroughly descriptive definition quoted above.

For Weber, the specific 'means' used by the state, although not its sole means, was its capacity for physical violence (*Gewaltsamkeit*),[3] and Weber here refers to *legitimate* violence, a fact which he usually explicitly adds. It is therefore assumed that the dominated regard the state's capacity for violence and its actual exercise of violence as legitimate. The condition and the possibility of such legitimacy is a fundamental consensus between rulers and ruled. The *possibility* of power and domination,[4] the suppression of the needs of the 'governed', is consequently traced back to a 'belief in legitimacy'. This does not of course mean the disappearance of non-consensual and non-normative sources of such consent. Alvin Gouldner has noted that for Weber the process of assent to domination represents a 'datum' and not a problem: 'for Weber, authority was given assent *because* it was legitimate, rather than being legitimate because it evoked assent' (emphasis in original).[5] In Weber, precisely which modes of behaviour by the governed are to be subsumed under their belief in legitimacy, to what extent ascribing such belief can ever be consensual given unequal access to social resources, and whether agreement is nothing more than a pious hope or, at best, an illusion on the part of the rulers or analysts, represent questions which are simply not raised. Whether violence requires any justification at all is simply passed over.

Weber's approach not only left aside the conditions for the possibility of state domination: it also excluded the practice of domination. This is a very serious and fateful analytic omission – one not confined to Weber alone: numerous interpretations, some sympathetic and some competing, exhibit the same deficiency. In particular, this lacuna is a meeting ground for theories both of social development and of 'modernisation' which draw on Weber's concept of rationalisation and on the 'critique of political economy'.

Those theories based on the principle that the characteristic feature of modern societies is the self-regulating market system[6] tend to regard the physically violent assertion of state power or state-supported claims to power as an atavistic throw-back[7] – or at most an exception wielded only in times when crisis threatens to overwhelm the system itself. In societies of this type direct coercion is merely a subsidiary means of domination. Such a perspective also corresponds to one central strand in the 'critique of political economy'; the oft-quoted 'silent compulsion of economic relations'[8] also extends into the 'juridic form'[9] which pervades all social relations and divests 'extra-economic' coercion of the violence characteristic of pre-capitalist societies.

Both arguments focus their attention on the question: how do either production and market mechanisms or (and possibly simultaneously) cultural and ideological systems facilitate the smooth reproduction of power and domination? Or, alternatively: how in 'modern' societies is the apparent spontaneous acceptance of superior power by the 'governed' possible? Acts of directly perceptible oppression do not seem of great consequence in such societies. Rather, the problem seems to lie in understanding how the 'rules of the game' are determined and formulated, and further how they become acceptable: what are the 'filters' which allow needs to be articulated, and hence problems and conflicts to be perceived, formulated and represented, and additionally acted out and resolved.

Not surprisingly, such interpretations take for granted those institutions which maintain and uphold the law, that is the *police* and the *judiciary*. This also applies to those theories which neglect the 'hegemony' or the 'intellectual and moral leadership of a group', class or class formation, as developed by Gramsci.[10] Nicos Poulantzas's position is not untypical. For Poulantzas, contemporary French experience provides sufficient demonstration of the fact that repression, that is physically violent domination, is a regular practice within developed industrial-capitalist societies. It constitutes one amongst a number of means for safeguarding the core areas – to be defined – of capitalist commodity production, and in particular for any periodically necessary disciplining of the sellers of labour-power.[11] Essentially, however, this position holds that it is not violence – irrespective of its specific form – but rather that 'illusory "general" interest in the form of the state', whose socially necessary ambiguity was pinpointed by Marx and Engels, which guarantees the perpetuation of even unequal social relations.[12] According to Poulantzas, the translation of this interest into reality depends on the state of class struggle between the rulers and ruled, and in particular on the strategy of power blocs.

In contrast, theories which emphasise system functions and mechanisms, rather than the practice of the actors, accentuate the dual meaning of those ideological and welfare provisions which supposedly generate legitimacy. These not only regulate the unequal perception and satisfaction of the needs of the ruled, but also 'continuously and permanently deny that such a selectivity takes place'.[13] Offe is thinking here of payments to compensate for social and economic distress, such as state provision of social services or forms of 'legitimation through procedure' (Luhmann, *Zweckbegriff und Systemrationalität*) either in the form of elections or in an extensive network of juridical forms.

To propose that the assertion and concealment of domination are two moments in an identical process is not, of course, to be committed to one specific theoretical approach. This thesis is fully elaborated only when it is no longer confined to political apparatuses and their procedures, but rather embraces the totality of everyday life,[14] the 'production and reproduction of immediate life' (Engels, letter to J. Bloch, September 1890. Two considerations developed by Pierre Bourdieu in the context of his studies of the pre-industrial Kabylia society in Algeria might take us a little further here. One is associated with the concept of 'gentle violence' ('violence douce') the other with the notion of 'habitus'.[15]

For capitalist societies 'gentle violence' not only means the symbolic representation of physical power and domination, both state and private. Primarily it raises questions of the dual meaning and function of mechanisms and institutions which, precisely by virtue of their unique service for the reproduction of society and its individuals, systematically reproduce both social inequality *and* state power and domination *simultaneously*, ranging from the 'veil of money' to social standards of education and cleanliness.[16] For Bourdieu, their 'gentle violence' is effective because their function in stabilising power relations and unequal life-chances is masked in the everyday compliance with these standards. For example, the socially accepted necessity for cleanliness and a certain level of knowledge for individual well-being and survival is an expression of a form of self-discipline not only presupposed by such standards but constantly etched into those subject to them in their observance.

'Gentle violence' suggests a dissolution of the analytical – yet emancipatory – distinction between those forms of social intercourse prescribed from above, which are actually given, and social relations free of such domination which might, or should, be possible in the future. It renders this historical 'not yet' a matter which already appears settled, as if the first phases, at least, of Marx's 'realm of freedom' were already a reality. 'Hegemony' in the form of 'gentle violence' thus goes beyond the direct bribery which buys consent 'against one's better judgement'. In developed bourgeois society, 'gentle violence' is imparted through both schools and families, in both public and private institutions, although the distinction between public and private is to some degree transcended in the reproduction of social relations. This form of coercion is effective because it is a constitutive moment in *all* social relations; for example, the monetarised exchange of commodities for the capitalist mode of production. It impregnates the everyday practice of *all* members of society, although to varying degrees. The self-activity of individuals always reflects and confirms the patterns which serve the production and unequal distribution of social wealth and social esteem: 'gentle violence' allows the dominated the illusion of non-coercive assent to their status – to inequality and domination.

One of the particular advantages of this approach is the logic inherent in its insistence on the microscopic point of view. Situations and interactions do not count as mere 'manifestations': yet analysis is not exhausted in the simple description of their details. The 'truth' of processes as perceived does not lie within themselves (Bourdieu, pp. 188–9). What is problematic, however, is the bivalent logic, the 'either–or' of the tendency held to characterise social development. The fascination induced by the principle of the market system makes it appear as if the transformation of the social mode of production is total: asynchronous or anomalous events are either eliminated in advance or treated merely as trifles:

> The greater the extent to which the task of reproducing the relations of domination is taken over by objective mechanisms, which serve the interests of the dominant group without any conscious effort on the latter's part, the more indirect, and, in a sense, impersonal, become strategies objectively oriented towards reproduction: it is not by lavishing generosity, kindness or politeness on his charwoman . . . but by choosing the best investment for his money, or the best school for his son, that the possessor of economic or cultural capital perpetuates the relationship of domination which objectively links him with his charwoman and even her descendants.[17]

In contrast, in non, or not-yet capitalised societies, the rulers are obliged,

> to work directly, daily, personally, to produce and reproduce conditions of domination which are even then never entirely trustworthy . . . they are obliged to resort to the most elementary forms of domination . . . thus this system contains only two ways . . . of getting and keeping a lasting hold over someone: gifts or debts, the overtly economic obligations of debt, or the 'moral', 'affective' obligations created and maintained by exchange, in short, overt (physical or economic violence), or symbolic violence, censored, euphemised, i.e. unrecognisable, socially recognised violence.

Bourdieu, crucially, asserts no contradiction between each type of violence within pre-capitalist societies; in fact, under such social relations, the 'co-existence of overt physical and economic violence and of the most refined symbolic violence' is limitless. The establishment of 'objective mechanisms . . . which serve the interests of the dominant group *without any conscious effort on the latter's part*' (emphasis added) is, accordingly, a product of the unfolding of bourgeois capitalist society.

Thus, whereas the rationalisation or capitalisation approach identified a reduction in physical coercion as a key hallmark of social development, for Bourdieu, the (in-) activity of the rulers constitutes an additional difference. In capitalist society the automatism of reproductive mechanisms replaces the unremitting *labour* of domination. Not only does direct repression take on a secondary importance: the 'do-it-yourself' element in the enforcement of domination by the dominant group is also rendered superfluous.

Admittedly, Bourdieu does not consider the possibility of crisis in, threat to, let alone breakdown of this supposedly automatic mechanism of social reproduction and universal dominant (self-) control force. His analysis of the everyday mechanisms of domination also exhibits a further deficiency, in a unique inversion reflecting the weakness of the politico-economic type of analysis.

Although physical repression is not the decisive means of domination for the latter, it is none the less effective 'in the last instance': and its social origins can be determined. What is omitted is any consideration of the mediations with other forms of domination and violence. In contrast, Bourdieu's analysis, by definition, excludes the social locus of violence and the agents of violence – violence is *omnipresent*. This neglect of unmediated violence leads to the omission of the relations between 'euphemised' and directly physical forms of violence.

Thus far we have concentrated our attention on those means of domination and forms of violence which are intended to guarantee domination. The significance of such strategies and such arrangements of social mechanisms designed by rulers to foster domination – their 'internal face' – has only been hinted at. Studies which emphasise the 'self-restraint' (*Selbstzwang*) (Elias) of socialised individuals, their 'discipline' (Foucault), the disposition to acquiesce in the face of exactions and coercion in the 'habitus' (Bourdieu) all attempt to find a vocabulary in which to discuss the processes by which the exactions of the rulers are appropriated, yet, at the same time, redefined by the ruled 'in their own terms'.

Norbert Elias was one of the first to recognise that the rise of bourgeois society was not merely the consequence of changed relationships at the level of society as a whole. The main focus of his studies on the 'civilising process' was on the conditions and consequences of the monopolisation of violence in the forms of everyday social intercourse.[18]

His work provides impressive demonstration, in particular in the example of eating rituals, of the considerable extent to which 'self-coercion' constitutes the precondition and foundation of centralised political organisation – the modern state, as defined by Weber. Of particular relevance in our context is Elias's view that the development of 'the apparatus of self-restraint is very closely linked to the formation of institutions monopolising physical violence and the growing stability of the central organs of society'. 'Self-restraint' is not only, therefore, a symbol of the possible, or actual, use of physical violence by the rulers or their organs; it also represents a focus around which the concrete experiences of suffering at the hands of the violence of the rulers accumulate. But how 'the physical act of violence works together with the force of habit' is left open: we are not told how this mediation appears concretely.

Fleshing this out obliges us to extend our vision to encompass the entire spectrum of 'corrective' activities and institutions; the enforcement of labour and time discipline not only in manufacturing workshops and factories, but also in prisons, workhouses and reform 'institutions', in which the policing and enforcement of 'discipline' and 'care' by an absolutist administration is expressed symbolically, and through physical violence.[19] The 'complete household' (*ganzes Haus*) of both the noble-aristocratic as well as the (mainly large-) bourgeois variety also naturally contributed to this social and psychological abuse, in particular of the direct producers. The experiences of maidservants and farmhands at the hands of their 'overlords' were part of the immediate everyday reality of the 'propertyless' and 'property-poor' in both town and country. And, although the supposed protection of the bourgeois small family may have displaced, replaced or complemented the multi-limbed household economy, it nevertheless retained violent patriarchal authority. The bourgeois family continued to be the parade ground for the forced internalisation of discipline and oppression, both of itself and of others. One clue to the connections and mediations of the forms of violence is alluded to here: both institutional and familial discipline reveal the permanence, the continuing functional contribution, of 'extra-economic' forms of coercion stemming from pre-capitalist and agrarian societies to the regulation of capitalist production and bourgeois society.

This synchronicity is also apparent in systems of education and hygiene, the advance of which is a hallmark of developed bourgeois societies. School learning in the German states of the eighteenth, and even more so the nineteenth centuries, not only wore legal attire in the form of compulsory attendance, but was additionally enforced through the brutal violence of 'authority'.[20] Running parallel to this, the attentions of the police or more long-term institutional discipline could (and can) be expected for any neglect of hygiene regulations.[21]

This would lend support to the supposition that the direct application of violence, immediate physical suffering, is the prime basis for that experience of domination which is the precondition for the possibility or probability of the willingness to accept, or at least the actual acceptance, of the impositions of political and social authority.

Such acceptance will then appear to be the free acknowledgement of the legitimacy of authority, moved by the 'silent compulsion' of the economy or socio-cultural 'hegemony' – an all-pervading 'habitus' seemingly automatically reproducing submissiveness – when looked at from a distance.

The notion of 'habitus' seeks to break away from the motives, interests, strategies and decisions of actors as the parameters of analysis. Instead it concentrates on the principles by which patterns of behaviour are generated:

> . . . habitus, systems of durable, transposable dispositions, structured structures predisposed to function as structuring structures, that is, as principles of the generation and structuring of practices and representations which can be objectively 'regulated' and 'regular' without in any way being the product of obedience to rules, objectively adapted to their goals without presupposing a conscious aiming at ends or an express mastery of the operations necessary to attain them and, being all this, collectively orchestrated without being the product of the orchestrating action of a conductor.[22]

Such a proposal holds out one prospect for advancing beyond the, by now, ritual theatre between subjectivist and objectivist interpretations of social processes. Based neither solely nor overwhelmingly on the needs and interests of competent actors, nor on a reduction of the entire issue to the objective requirements of the system, habitus represents acquired dispositions, in which patterns embedded into individuals are simultaneously seen as specific to social groups: it constitutes the mediation between objective regularities and directly observable behaviour. It therefore denotes the dialectical link between practical action and the given conditions – which, in turn, are (re-) produced through such action.

Of course, the intention behind this approach and its implementation are not one and the same thing. Bourdieu's *Outline of a Theory of Practice* makes repeated reference to the 'work of inculcation and appropriation' inherent in the habitus to some degree. But the concrete form, the actual performance of this work, goes unmentioned. As a consequence, the complex structure of self-activity and external control, of conscious and non-conscious processes, is reduced to a hermetic social mechanism. 'Self-coercion', a process in which psychic repression collaborates with political and institutional sanctions, is sacrificed to the idea of a self-generating behavioural matrix – the 'habitus'. And, despite all the subtlety of Bourdieu's reconstruction, the 'forms of the habitus' crucially are essentially or almost exclusively assembled and operative 'behind the backs' of the subjects. As was the case with 'gentle violence', the agencies of mediation under consideration are the structures of social reproduction, and in particular the processes and institutions of education. And here too the *forms* of the historical advance of those processes and institutions are, for the most part, ignored. Despite Bourdieu's orientation to practice, the actual course of events (of those affected) is obscured by the structure of his logic. Despite the fact, and palpability, of the act of physical violence in everyday life – even in developed societies – it is a fact which escapes Bourdieu; it is as if his intense preoccupation with such an alien society as the Kabylic simultaneously estranged him from specific aspects of his own society.

In contrast to the positions outlined above, the thesis advanced here is directed at the *simultaneity* of the physically violent character of the 'modern state' and the symbolic presence of this violence – including within the forms of social reproduction. This thesis has a methodological obverse: we have to reconstruct the state's mode of action,[23] and the characteristic forms of 'habitus' of its subjects. In other words: the domination and violence exercised or mediated by the state are to be understood as social relations and social practice.

Such a concentration on social practice points the way towards a position which, although on the face of it similar to the position outlined above, presupposes the continuing necessity of extra-economic force for the safeguarding of the production process (and social reproduction) both demonstratively and in the abstract.[24] A number of studies of individual spheres of state activity, in particular planning, infrastructural and economic policy, indicate that general formulae which characterise the state as a 'committee of the bourgeoisie' and point to the growing instrumentalisation of 'state power as a machine of class domination' apply only to the 'state in general'.[25] Evidently, the function of the state, or its apparatuses, as an instrument of the ruling class – more precisely the ruling class configuration – does not fit neatly together with the exigencies of guaranteeing and promoting the further advance of the industrial-capitalist mode of production. The interests of individual capitals, groupings of capitals and the 'average' interests of 'the aggregate capital' were (and are) not self-evident or self-explanatory. The 'limits of activity' for the agents and occupiers of positions of power are not always, or necessarily, coterminous with the 'limits of the system'. The difference between them provides the space for the 'relative autonomy'[26] of state bureaucracies – in fact, it demands it. Determining the function, degree and meaning of this autonomy requires not only detailed study of individual decision-making processes and structures of motivation: it also crucially depends on establishing the systematic relationship between forms of behaviour of political agencies and political agents. These display characteristic differences. Standards and criteria applied in establishing conditions of production (both general and specific) do not coincide with those exercised in upholding the law and maintaining 'civil order': state agencies act differently in different political arenas.[27] One especially notable example for the Prussian 'case' is the simultaneity observable in the 1840s: swift application of violence by the organs of the state against the 'tumultuous movements' of railway construction workers on the one hand, with solicitous and circumspect temporising by the same authorities and officials as regards the financing of the same railway on the other.

Our aim in this study is to reconstruct the physical violence within the exercise of state power and domination. Setting out the functions of the state, the arenas in which political processes are acted and fought out and the forms of conduct considered appropriate in each, the class- and group-interests of those under scrutiny here – and in particular the bureaucracy – is simply the first step in this task. Merely advancing beyond a bird's-eye view of society, and not reducing actors, and their actual and contradictory actions, to a set of 'results' is also inadequate for our purpose. Establishing the relationship between the emergence and formation of 'modern' state authority and the perceptions and sufferings of those at the receiving end of this authority requires an investigation into how the imperatives of the state and the bureaucracy are translated into everyday practice. The situation of the victims will also then cease to count merely as a 'cost factor' in the calculations of the dominators. And such a perspective might also point to the possibilities of developing non- (or, at least as yet un-) bureaucratised forms and potentials for resistance and alternative patterns of social organisation.

Functions and *modus operandi* of state bureaucracies: the case of Prussia

Adam Smith summed up the experience in England, the industrial-capitalist pioneer, in the brief formula that the acquisition of valuable and extensive property indispensable for an expanding economy, 'therefore necessarily requires the establishment of civil government'. He added, 'civil government, so far as it is instituted for the security of property, is in reality instituted for the defence of the rich against the poor, or of those who have some property against those who have none at all'.[28]

In the relatively developed 'society of free acquisition' (Lorenz Stein, *Geschichte der sozialen Bewegung in Frankreich*) of eighteenth century England, one of the central functions of state activity was therefore the safeguarding of private property. Redistributive policies, or steps to redistribute power of disposition over resources, could not be allowed to go so far as to jeopardise the system's organising principles. Smith's sober formulation should be taken as testimony to the real process taking place in England as well as in other societies engaged in the transition to a capitalist mode of production: expanding commodity production and exchange needed state guarantees. And this entailed maintaining the primacy of the private power of disposition over labour-power and its products by administrative or judicial means on an everyday basis. The programme of action pursued by the local powers, as well as centralised administrative and judicial bureaucracies, was that of 'quiet and order'. The policing of the public domain was not detached from the state's, and private, interests in securing the maximum use of means of production to the benefit of their owners, or, in continental Europe, to the benefit of the 'fiscal state'.[29]

Since the eighteenth century, state guarantees for property in England had taken the specific form of the 'rule of law'. Nevertheless, this symbolic yet physically ruthless blend of arbitrariness, paternalistic beneficence and ruling calculus did not necessarily reduce the brutality of its rulers. As Douglas Hay has shown, for the penalties imposed for crimes against property, even the most trivial misdemeanours by the propertyless incurred draconian punishments.[30] At the same time, 'the rhetoric and the rules of a society are something a great deal more than sham' (E. P. Thompson). In Thompson's view – and depending on the context – 'the form and rhetoric of law can restrain the use of power and provide the powerless with a certain protection'.[31] Nevertheless, it may also be the case that the 'rule of law' during this period of transformation favoured a predominantly violent form of domination, with the spurious justification that draconian means had to be applied to permit any kind of judicial resolution of interests at all. At the same time, the everyday social selectivity inherent in any legal system intended to function within an entrepreneurial bourgeois society may have been overshadowed by a concomitant product of this system: namely the right of every individual to resist blatantly arbitrary treatment.

In contrast to England, economic activity in Prussia – meaning not simply production but also circulation and consumption[32] – was dominated by the agrarian cycle until well into the 1850s. At the same time, market relations and dependencies were also clearly intensifying, both sectorally and regionally. On the land these changed market conditions – and in particular the secular rise in grain prices after 1750 – were reflected in the increase in the number of large estates run under landlord administration.

However, the expedient of simply stepping up the level of exploitation of the dependent peasantry in the East Elbian agrarian regions was no longer sufficient to guarantee the required increases in the productivity of labour. Higher labour rents might provoke insubordination or open protest. Estate owners therefore preferred to use 'landpoor and landless producers' (Harnisch, *Kapitalistische Agrarreform*) who worked on contracts as *Einlieger* or *Häusler* (lodgers and cotters). This trend in the recruitment of agricultural labour-power was mirrored in a rapid expansion in the number of such agrarian 'direct producers'.

The, on the whole, gradual transition from the essentially feudal *Gutsherrschaft* based on the 'extra-economic coercion' of dependent labour-power to the capitalist *Gutswirtschaft* estate economy[33] created pauperism on an unprecedented scale. The chief victims were the small landholders and the landless. Parallel changes in the structure of proto-industry, the domestic industrial trades[34] and manufacturing also generated 'new poverty'.[35] These changes were very evident in the textile and metal-working districts west of the Rhine and north of the line between Cologne and Eupen. Putters-out, merchants (*Kaufleute*) and the owners of manufactories sought to fight off English factory competition by setting up their own factories – that is by employing machinery and a greater division of labour. Similar changes were also taking place in the small-scale iron-working trades of the uplands of the Wupper valley and in the adjacent Westphalian Mark to the north east (Hagen, Iserlohn, Altena), amongst the textile producers of East Westphalia and Mid-Silesia, and in the textile and metal-working trades in and around Berlin. This complex process of social and economic transformation culminated in the deep economic crisis of the 1840s, one manifestation of which was the contraction, and locally the elimination, of domestic industrial production in these areas. Weavers and spinners in the Minden-Ravensberg and Mid-Silesian mountain districts were especially hard hit. The main outcome was the transformation of pauperised producers from domestic industry into an initially virtually inexhaustible reservoir of cheap labour-power for the factories which had been expanding since the 1830s.

Nevertheless, despite their parlous state, the immediate circumstances of direct producers in domestic industry were still more 'open' than those of day-labourers on estates or wage-labourers in factories.[36] Although dependent on the market, domestic industrial producers often owned their means of production. Most important of all, they had almost complete control over the labour process and the resources of the family economy – constantly on hand for 'self-exploitation'. Although confined to the most meagre elements of subsistence, this power over everyday life permitted some opportunities for a relatively autonomous articulation and satisfaction of needs and interests. Such 'dissipation' on articles of conspicuous consumption must have seemed irrational, to say the least, to the merchants and putters-out who established and embodied market relations. The excessive drinking and smoking which marked the receipt of the purchase price militated against saving for periodic episodes of hardship and mocked the otherwise clear line of class demarcation between 'above' and 'below'. In this respect, the independence of weaver families (or of the smiths in the small-iron trades) threatened the 'order' of the exploitative, or more accurately the *profit-based*, system of production in general.

Although the uneven process of expanding commodity production and capitalisation in Prussia took place under conditions of 'relative economic backwardness' (Gerschenkron, *Economic Backwardness*), the Prussian path was by no means exceptional within Europe – at least, not at this level of generality. However, such global schemas are inappropriate for an examination of the 'intrinsic connection between form, function, mode of articulation and conditions for the appearance and transformation of these social relations and . . . ways of thinking'.[37] In the case of Prussia, this embraced – alongside the unique character of the East Elbian estate economy – the existence of a bureaucratic 'state machine'. In company with its eudaemonistic aims, this hierarchical organisation also possessed a unique 'rhetoric' which appeared to legitimate a 'police' practice not only intrinsically violent in character but – in contrast to England – permanently striving to encompass and regulate the totality of the everyday life of those it 'administered'. The social substrate of this administrative practice consisted of the state or royal officialdom (*Beamtenschaft*).[38] This had insinuated itself between the powers exercised by the feudal estates from the close of the seventeenth century, and overlapped or superseded them entirely.

The social precedence enjoyed by the East Elbian nobility lent a particular flavour to the standards of perception and conduct of these 'royal' or 'state servants'. Although the state's promotion and utilisation of manufacturing workshops and petty or proto-industrial commodity production were subject to the primacy of fiscal and military objectives,[39] this did not encroach on the prime purpose and basic operation of state institutions, which remained the preservation and multiplication of the rural landowners' opportunities to increase their wealth and acquire status.[40] Even the state reforms implemented between 1807 and 1817 under the pressures of the need to mobilise against revolutionary France did little to change this situation. The drive towards the formation of an 'absolute bureaucracy'[41] associated with the more effective organisation of the administration, and even the push for the development of trade and industry could not alter the primary function of the state's judicial and enforcement apparatuses: the maintenance of inequalities of power, within which the production and distribution of social wealth was structured to endow the Junker-bourgeois estate-owning class with its particular privileges.[42] The creation of a 'free' market in land after 1807 without serious detriment to the interests of this class provides a notable example.[43]

Two factors should be borne in mind when looking at the numerous supports provided by the state and state bureaucracy for the social and political privileges enjoyed by the landlord class. First, the mode of production on the estates underwent the profound change outlined above: the capitalisation of agriculture was therefore tied to the pattern of exploitation and domination which had characterised the preceding feudal society. At the same time, the long-term beneficiaries of state policy were not merely the industrial and commercial small- and medium-scale bourgeoisies, but principally – once the bureaucracy had set about abolishing or reducing local monopolies and other obstacles to the mobility of capital, labour-power and goods – the growing numbers of putters-out, merchants and manufacturers. In particular, both the estate economy and the urban and rural industries remained dependent on the discipline and controls exercised by the state agencies to ensure a supply of 'willing' labour-power.

Up until the middle of the nineteenth century, therefore, these forms of production not only coexisted but were subject to a 'reciprocal penetration of modes of production within the social formation'[44] which, although uneven, was none the less effective. This was also evident in the case of France under the *ancien régime*: the 'state' simultaneously represented the aristocracy and the bourgeoisie – two classes and two modes of production with only partially identical and often antagonistic interests. In contrast, in Prussia – a society with an only rudimentary entrepreneurial class – the central point of reference for the bureaucracy remained the commercially active nobility, and its aim was either to dominate the incipient industrial and commercial bourgeoisie or, at the least, to make sure that the process of capitalisation took place in the interests of the East Elbian estate owners, the Junkers. Transformations in the mode of production were, therefore, by no means excluded from the scope of the bureaucracy – as long as 'callous "cash payment" ' never became the sole 'nexus between man and man'.[45]

It was less the antagonism between classes than tensions and conflicts within them which required the state bureaucracy to possess a degree of autonomy. The propertied section of society was riven by a multiplicity of regional and factional divisions: between Silesian, Brandenburg-Pomeranian and East Prussian aristocratic estate owners on one hand, or putters-out and manufacturers in Cleves and in Westphalia, or Magdeburg and Berlin on the other.[46] It was vital for such differences to be mediated via the state. Most crucially of all, those localised tentative steps towards the development of capitalist factory industry remained in no small measure dependent on the absolutist bureaucracy, at least into the 1840s.

In France, the conflicts inherent in the tenacious adhesion of both aristocratic and bourgeois classes to the state produced an evident 'permanent disequilibrium' (Robin, 'Der Charakter des Staates') between contradictory demands and limited powers and resources. In contrast, the 'Prussian path' of capitalisation plus social compromise enjoyed obvious success in its ability to safeguard the status quo. No total social transformation took place.[47]

This poses two problems: on the one hand, that of the particular interests and the forms in which they were articulated which gave the East Elbian landowning nobility its special stamp as *Junkerdom*. This central element in the Prussian situation is not dealt with systematically or in detail here, but is considered from the aspect of its impact on the character of political domination. Our main concern here is with the second of these problems: 'state authority' as shaped by the bureaucracy and mediated as the bureaucratic domination of everyday life, within which the actions (or absence of action) of the administration serve to realise the complex, socially determined 'impure' character of the state.[48] For the dominated, domination in the shape of the 'state' became an everyday reality via the conduct and actions of 'royal officials'. The object of our analysis is therefore the activity of the state, not in its general function for social reproduction, but as the practice of domination. By looking at the practice of domination, we can explore the links between the broader maintenance of the status quo and the 'overpowering' of the suppliers of labour-power, the propertyless and the direct producers. But primarily, such an approach provides a point of access to the genesis of the social forms of the 'habitus', both the acceptance of domination, but also the resistance and refusal of the dominated.

The maintenance of state security and social order: 'citadel practice' as the model for official conduct

In late-eighteenth- and early-nineteenth-century Prussia, the practice of domination – the perception of, response to and influencing of social and economic processes and exigencies – was marked by the need for the state to respond to two parallel but not completely conjoined phenomena: on the one hand, the processes of commercialisation and capitalisation, and on the other the French revolution – or, more to the point, the fear that it might 'infect' Germany. These processes imposed particular pressures on a bureaucracy which increasingly posed as the embodiment of the 'intelligentsia' after the turn of the century.

In 1823 Johann Gottfried Hoffmann, the leading Prussian statistician, member of the Council of State, and Professor of State Economy at the University of Berlin, identified three 'fundamental changes' in the activity of the state and 'police and financial legislation'.[49] 'No country has been able to escape them.' In his short monograph intended for the training of future senior officials, Hoffmann set out those 'events of the foregoing thirty years' which he regarded as the cause and trigger of these 'innovations':

> Complete transformations in accustomed ways of commerce arising from the new outlook on industrial policy and the tax system, security measures against foreigners previously only customary in time of war, state borrowing on an undreamt-of scale, and the institutions associated with it for servicing the interest, have in no small measure also appeared in those states in which the most prudent retention of the existing order is not only the guiding principle of government and administration, but also of their corporations and communes, in fact of the totality of public life.

In addition to the creation of a market in productive forces for market exchange and fiscal rationalisation, Hoffmann also noted that one of the main tasks of state administration was the repressive enforcement of the existing order. However, he gave little detailed consideration to the origins of these phenomena, nor did he concern himself with the issue of how the tasks he had identified were to be fulfilled. Instead, he abandoned himself to the temptations of his proto-Weberian search for subjectless market mechanisms by means of international comparisons.

Hoffmann also stressed – clearly with a practical didactic aim in mind – how little the changes noted by him had been linked with any revolutionary leanings on the part of the political agencies involved, or any correspondingly revolutionary social order. In fact, so Hoffmann's argument ran, not only did non-revolutionary regimes have to resolve the problems of stimulating economic activity, stabilising state revenues, and maintaining strict control over internal and external 'aliens', but they were in fact those regimes most acutely affected by these exigencies.

For Hoffmann, the extent to which the exercise and pursuit of these aims and functions required the domination of the 'administered' did not constitute a problem. Even the threat of physical violence implied in his reference to 'disciplinary measures for the maintenance of security' disappeared behind this label, which gave a clear indication of the real nature of officialdom's concern for the 'common good'. Any supposed consensus over the purposes of the state inevitably endowed the means employed to enforce them with a particular legitimacy. For such a police mentality, the conflicts and sufferings of the 'subjects' were merely the product of their own intransigence and maliciousness: the disinterested aims and means of the 'servants of the state' appeared irreproachable in comparison.

However, the 'gentle violence' which underpinned the state's justification of its all-embracing policing of society could sometimes be exposed. In 1831, an anonymous writer drafted a general outline of the logic of the police practice of domination: the self-defined necessity for preventive repression easily led on to the conclusion that civil freedoms and the 'powers' of the institution for their protection had to exist in mutally appropriate proportions. 'The greater the civil and political liberty of the citizen . . . the stronger and more powerful must be the institutions for their protection.'[50]

Regierungsrat Maximilian Karl Friedrich Wilhelm Grävell, a senior official later suspended because of his unseemly interest in constitutional matters, illustrated these perceptions and legitimations both more concretely and as an insider. His 1820 treatise on policing provides a clear demonstration of the manichean uni-dimensionality of this essentially traditional concept of 'good' – that is, all-embracing – 'policing'. Grävell based his argument on a constitutional-legal syllogism. Given 'civil order', the activity of the state or police is constrained by procedural and legal regulations.[51] Or, to invert the argument, the existence of social processes and situations repugnant to the police signal the absence of *any* civil order. Such circumstances therefore demand the unrestrained application of every means available:

> However, a completely different situation arises when the police either struggle with the forces of nature and are supposd to put a halt to their destruction, or if they have to overcome the resistance of people who oppose their esteem and authority with *force*. Just as it would be ridiculous to seek to instruct a general where and how to join battle, it is no less ridiculous to seek to prescribe to the police what they must do to stop the spread of a conflagration or extirpate the resistance of a band of robbers or an enraged mob.

Interestingly, Grävell quite happily equates an 'enraged mob' with acts of nature, and makes no distinction between such a group and 'common criminality'. However the crux of his argument lies in what was evidently for him the self-explanatory congruence between the military and civil police. The rules of conduct and procedure of both are brought together in the 'mos militare'. Against such a background, the latent difficulties between the civil and military authorities, which became more open after 1807, would appear to be no more substantial than slight differences of style and demeanour. Grävell proceeds accordingly. 'The general and the police officer represent the laws and authority of the state against its enemies . . . and just as any individual person has the right to resist violence, to overcome their enemy, so too the moral person of the state and its representatives.' Faced with such an all-embracing claim to self-defence, with its fixation on the existence of a permanent state of emergency, any social and political difficulties between the military and civil officials are no more than minor irritations. The 'violence' of a tumult, be it a rebellious movement against unjust prices for bread or the product of 'injured honour' (such as lack of appropriate ceremony in burying the plebeian victims of a cholera epidemic in Königsberg in 1831 – see p. 162 below) expunged the need for any further investigation: the cause or motivation behind popular outrage was of no relevance.

These quotations from Grävell get to the heart of that characteristic bureaucratic practice of domination in Prussia which we look at below under the term 'administrative citadel practice'. This not only embraces the extensive, and usually highly codified, military power of definition, which always proved decisive 'on the ground'. More importantly, it illustrates the development, or more accurately, the re-inculcation of one interpretation of the aims of policing amongst civil officials. 'Citadel-like' rules of perception and conduct gave a unique character to police activities. The 'highest and most sacred duty of officials' was the 'maintenance of public quiet'. And the optimal means for achieving this was self-evidently seen as military-style threats, and where necessary the use of direct force on the principles of 'short shrift'.

Rooted in the assumption that the state was a citadel under permanent threat, the practice of executive officials combined doggedness with brutal violence in their defence of the state against its innumerable enemies. From the heights of the police citadel, the motives, reasons and causes of the insubordination or rebelliousness of the incalculably 'dangerous classes' were no longer discernible. At best, the manner of administration and policing deemed appropriate to the 'administered' was set out in the general sections of manuals issued for the guidance of officials. Public quiet and order had absolute priority wherever there was doubt – at least in all public places. And in emergencies this implied the virtual daily use of brute force to eliminate or surmount any lack of cooperation on the part of the subject population.

2

Bureaucracy as an apparatus of domination

The structures of power and officialdom after 1815

The administrative reforms of 1808–25[1] represented a turning point for the Prussian bureaucracy. Although the reorganisation of the state apparatus along departmental rather than geographical lines (the *Fachministerium* replacing the *Provinzialministerium*) were part and parcel of wider efforts to stimulate economic activity, our concern here is with those developments within governmental institutions and the general rules of conduct prescribed for officials: some consideration of the steps taken in the areas of agrarian, financial, and trade reform can be found in Chapter 3 below. The key changes in the establishment of a new body of administrative institutions were effected by the Edicts and Orders of 1808, some of which were subsequently modified in 1815, 1817 and 1825. Below ministerial level, the main purpose of the reforms was to separate the administration of justice from the 'police' authorities. (A number of 'specialised' administrative agencies were also set up at the same time. However, we do not deal here with those concerned with taxation, the General Commissions responsible for property disputes, the commutation of services, land apportionment and compensation set up after 1811 in the wake of the agrarian reforms.)

The *Regierungen* of the eighteenth century were mainly, although not exclusively, judicial bodies. After 1808 their title was transferred to the intermediate regional tier of internal administration, which took over the powers – and personnel – of the *ancien régime*'s Chamber of War and Domains. These new District Governments were not only entrusted with the implementation of ministerial Directives and Orders (ministries were now organised along departmental lines): their members, the *Regierungsräte*, were also expected to represent those they administered before the central authorities. This mediating function had its counterpart in a particular organisational form: decisions made by the District Governments – both at departmental and plenary level (the *Räte* in company with their juniors, the *Assessoren*) – were taken according to the principles of collegiate responsibility. 'All members of the agency involved took part in the discussion of every major question to come before their college, and all shared legal responsibility for the collective decision.'[2] Although the three member *Präsidium* retained a right of veto[3] – after 1825 confined to the *Regierungspräsident* – in theory, at least, these collegial bodies together with the higher and lower levels of administration, which were structured along *Préfecture* lines, were to combine the cautious 'deliberation' of the colleges with the decisiveness of individual office holders, yielding the optimum form of state organisation – with its proclaimed aim, the furtherance of 'the common good'.[4]

The 'higher' officials in this administrative bureaucracy consisted mostly – and after 1817 solely – of university educated jurists with proven financial 'means'.[5] In addition to the departmental ministries and all-embracing District Governments, this professional and status-group, in theory, also staffed the offices of the *Landräte*, the tier of administrative authority below that of the District Governments. And they additionally invariably provided the personnel for the unique intermediate position of provincial *Oberpräsident*. The *Landrat*'s office and that of *Oberpräsident* – President of the Province – were 'bureaucratic' rather than collegial organs. The *Landrat*, appointed on the suggestion of the *Kreisstände* – a local assembly of notables – represented an exemplary symbol of the sought-for fusion between the state and 'society', the latter being confined to reputable 'subjects', and more specifically the local landowners from whose ranks the position had to be filled. The office of *Landrat* also marked the perceptible boundary in another respect. In contrast to the *Räte* in the District Governments, who shared the same rank, *Landräte* did not have to pass through a three-stage process of education and training. (For the *Räte* this involved three years as *Auscultator* after completion of university, four years as *Referendar* following an examination, and then, after a further examination before the *Ober-Examinations-Kommission*, appointment as *Assessor*, the first salaried position.) By contrast, applicants for the post of *Landrat* were not required to undergo a written and oral examination until 1838. In many instances, the *Regierungsräte*, who conducted the examination anyway, decided the results on political grounds.

The roughly 540 *Oberregierungsräte* and *Assessoren*,[6] with their professional training and many years of vocational socialisation, who staffed the twenty-five District Governments (twenty-three after 1825) responsible for overseeing the *Landräte*, were entrusted with the extensive yet diffuse task of furthering the best interests of the 'common good'. In this they were expected to transcend the particular interests which the ten to fifteen *Landräte* for which they were responsible were suspected of harbouring. (In 1828 there was a total of 313 *Landräte*, some of whom also served as mayor in boroughs such as Aachen, Cologne or Koblenz.)[7] The supervision (and first instance jurisdiction over complaints raised by the 'administered') exercised by the *Regierungsräte* also had a corresponding internal facet: to observe the rules of respectful etiquette and distance, and hence establish the 'honour' of the administration within their own circle.[8]

Ten *Oberpräsidenten* were initially appointed; this fell to eight following the merger between the two provincial presidencies of the Rhine in 1822 and the incorporation of the *Oberpräsident* in West Prussia into East Prussia in 1824. As commissary representatives of the ministries, the *Oberpräsidenten* possessed a vaguely defined responsibility for 'all matters' within their territory, and in 1825 were also assigned unspecified powers of 'superintendence' over all the authorities in their province. Institutions and projects which crossed District Government boundaries, such as road building, also came within their brief,[9] and they exercised part-jurisdiction over schools, church affairs and all matters concerned with the Estates (*Stände*). The *Oberpräsident* also had to mediate between the military and the civil authorities at regional level. Despite their enhanced powers they could not give direct orders to the District Governments after 1825, except where acting as the court of first instance in conflicts involving a number of collegial bodies on matters affecting appointments and discipline. The sensibilities and interests of both parties provided frequent occasion for the bypassing of the *Oberpräsidenten* by District Governments,[10] who reported directly to the relevant minister. The problems of status and power which this gave rise to could be aggravated by the fact that the *Oberpräsident* often also held office within the *Präsidium* of the District Government: von Merckel, the *Oberpräsident* in Silesia, headed the *Regierungspräsidium* in Breslau, and von Vincke, *Oberpräsident* in Westphalia, the *Regierungspräsidium* in Münster. However, they customarily assigned their tasks at District Government level to a Vice-President. In the 1820s, for example, von Ingersleben in Koblenz assigned this job to *Oberregierungsrat* and Vice-President Fritzsche. Von Vincke appointed du Vignau, also Vice-President, between 1836 and his death in 1844.

Reports from the *Landräte*, District Governments (or their Presidents) and *Oberpräsidenten* were received and evaluated by the ministries in Berlin – not least to provide material for the preparation of new Directives, Instructions, Rescripts and Decrees, and of course General Orders (*Verordnungen*) and statutes, differences between which were of little political or legal relevance. The final category (Order, etc.) frequently required consultations with ministerial colleagues or examination by the Council of State (*Staatsrat*). The Council was established in 1817. Detached from the administration itself by virtue of its own constitution, this 'intra-administrative parliament' was entrusted with the task of discussing all laws and the basic planning of the entire administration.[11]

The actual implementation of ministerial Orders or Instructions from the District Governments, from *Landräte* and from municipalities was undertaken by 'executive officials'. The actual 'labour of domination' entailed by the internal administration, or – to use the terminology of the time – the 'police authorities', was carried out by 'lower' officials. Their task was to represent the demands of the bureaucracy and the state – concretised in their superiors' expectations – whose symbol they were, on the ground on an everyday basis. At the same time, they had to balance these demands against their own interests and those of the 'administered'. For these subordinate officials, therefore, any executive act was fraught with the possibility of sanctions from a large number of quarters – both their superiors and the 'subject' population – and within this latter group both notables and the 'lower popular classes' and their communal and social loyalties and solidarity. Since the status and number of these executive officials varied considerably from locality to locality, it is virtually impossible to make broad generalisations about them (see pp. 70–7 below on 'police servants' in the Government Districts of Arnsberg and Trier).

As far as the more senior officials were concerned, data on the institutional structure and staffing can be supplemented by data on social origins.[12] Approximately three-quarters of the *Regierungsräte* in the District Governments were of bourgeois origin, a proportion which tended to fall after 1818. In contrast, three-quarters to four-fifths of the *Landräte* were from aristocratic families: the only exceptions were those in the provinces of Prussia, Westphalia and Rhineland – the latter quite markedly so. In Prussia and Westphalia almost a third of these local representatives of state power in rural areas with at least some professional knowledge and experience were bourgeois, and in the Rhineland more than half.

However, all in all, such institutional and structural features of the bureaucracy offer little in the way of explanation. Given the intense professional socialisation undergone by officials, considerable caution has to be exercised in using such sociological data to yield predictions or hypotheses as to their perceptions and conduct – that is, the actual practice of domination. Similar considerations apply to the use of group and religious affiliations, a subject of discussion in the Rhine province in particular.[13]

Our priority here is to examine the extent to which the 'stipulations' laid down by the upper echelons of government were able to shape and redefine the well-established routines and standards of executive officials; or whether, conversely, these stipulations were simply accommodated to the existing practice of lower-level officials. In either case, the real 'costs' of domination were borne by the dominated.

Modes of interpretation within the bureaucracy

The actual conduct of officials such as the Prussian *Landräte* rarely matched the prescription that it should be 'free and in full accordance with the law'.[14] Rather than setting out from such an unrealistic premise, we pursue the more promising approach of examining when and under what circumstances officials made use of their 'power of rapid execution', and to what extent their 'acquittal of their business' was conducted with that 'ease of direct observation and efficacy' required by their superiors. In turn, such a detailed consideration of how officials responded to and implemented the regulations issued by the higher authorities may provide an initial impression of the modes of interpretation which characterised the individuals and groups concerned.

Analytically, this cannot mean merely pairing off the interests associated with a particular position in the apparatus of domination with a particular perception of those interests, and the related action, as if interests and sociocultural modes of interpretation can be counterposed – the former part of the mechanism of society, the latter the reflection of personal identity and agency. The question is rather one of complementary dimensions of social interaction. *Interests* can be defined in relation to actions intended to change or maintain situations;[15] socio-cultural modes of interpretation refer to the perception which actually creates and 'colours' such situations, within which social relations, including relations of domination, can take on a practical relevance for those immediately party to them. The typical interest of officials in preserving their positions and careers, and the interests of the state proclaimed and represented by them each permitted identical interpretations of divergent conflicts and concrete situations. For example, the interpretation of a hunger riot in which 'civil order' was threatened could easily be transferred to other situations, such as confrontation with individual plebian 'impudence' (as in the complaints of the *Landrat* in Paderborn in 1836: see pp. 45–8 below) or the combating of the collective insubordination manifested in wage struggles (as in Iserlohn in 1840).[16] At any event, such a technique of interpretation could continue to be applied as long as errors made on the basis of such stereotypical judgements could be covered or corrected by the threat or use of force – with the costs of any such error ultimately borne by the dominated classes.

However, actions guided and motivated by interests, such as the restoration of 'quiet and order', do not necessarily exhaust their meaning for actors through the direct effect of the action. For example, the interest of Prussian *Landräte* and *Regierungsräte* in maintaining 'quiet and order' rested on an interpretation of situations[17] which defined any mobile group in the population as 'a threat' from the very outset. For officials, police intervention did not mean simply fending off any real or supposed danger: it also allowed the symbolic celebration of 'justice' and provided an opportunity for officials to establish their identity *vis-à-vis* superiors and colleagues by acting 'honourably'.

Parallels can be drawn between modes of interpretation and the concept of habitus and its forms discussed in Chapter 1. Habitus is the more comprehensive concept however. Whereas modes of interpretation constitute 'theories of everyday life', forms of habitus point to more basic and antecedent 'structuring structures'. In addition – at least in the present context – modes of interpretation not only allow actors to make sense of situations in which they are required to act, and in turn guide action, but are also the result of such situations. Modes of interpretation constitute a résumé of experience and exhibit some degree of consistency: at the same time, they are also shaped by breaks in and cycles of experiences.

The formulation and pursuit of interests are not a linear function of imputed systemic needs, either of a bureaucratic organisation or a social class, or even of more general social 'imperatives'. And, as with the articulation of interests, the *perception* of such exigencies is possible only via a mediating 'hierarchy of structures of meaning'.[18]

The first step in identifying the actual 'rules of behaviour' governing official conduct – that is, establishing the forms and degrees of distance from both formal and informal expectations, together with the necessity and scope for new definitions of the demands placed on them – firstly requires an examination of the explicit aims of the bureaucracy. And, since our concern here is with the 'inner' or 'police' administration, we are immediately confronted with the conceptual problem of what this bureaucracy, with its 'police' role, represented.

Police I: The unity of security and welfare

Any first approximation to the rules and standards which regulated the actual conduct of the police would have to provide the explicit definitions or descriptions given by officials themselves about their task. However, such an attempt at reconstruction immediately runs into difficulties: the rules involved consist of terse yet empty formulae – themselves in need of interpretation – together with occasional complaints as to deficient or absent instructions from their superiors. The acerbity of a report on police legislation drafted by a senior ministerial official in 1808 gives some indication of the extent to which the administrative labour of domination was beset with such conceptual deficiencies. *Staatsrat* Friese noted in his internal memorandum:

> The police portion of our legislation is undeniably the most backward. We have innumerable police Edicts, Orders, Regulations, Instructions, Public Announcements, and all the other titles which they have been given, but they are completely lacking in system, order, context and connection, without any regard for general fundamental principles. We do not even have a legal definition of the notion of police authority; or, at least, the definition provided by the law does not accord with the constitution . . . Whenever some Chamber feels that a police order is necessary, it usually decrees it. This is regarded as the end of the matter, irrespective of whether the change is observed or not. This practice has produced such an accumulation and scattering of provisions that even someone from the department finds it extremely difficult to establish whether a provision already exists or does not exist for a particular instance. Consider then the plight of the invalided sergeant or master of the watch whose destiny has called him to be a *Polizeibürgermeister*, let alone the private individual who is expected to obey them.[19]

Friese stressed two things: on the one hand, the 'notion of police authority' was neither specified nor established. At the same time – and this was the disadvantage for him as far as everyday administration on the streets or in offices was concerned – the police administration had to deal with an incomprehensibly large number of orders. The inference was clear; no one should be surprised if even the best intentions towards public welfare and safety never became anything more than pious hopes.

Friese's wholesale criticism of legislative practice on police matters was confined to its dysfunctional consequences – that is, those particularly troublesome to the 'executive officers'. No consideration was given to the question as to whether the scope for the independent exercise of bureaucratic power and power of definition which this practice created might be useful or even necessary. Friese may have been apprehensive that greater local powers would have limited ministerial authority, and that the 'invalided sergeants' might begin acting in ways unbecoming to their office. But we first have to clarify what we are able to establish – beyond mere empty phrases – about the 'notion of police authority'.

Typical of the form and structure of the aims prevailing in administrative-police practice was the rule set out in one of the most commonly used manuals, Ludwig von Rönne's *Staatsrecht der preussischen Monarchie*.[20] As late as the third edition published in 1872 (the first was in 1856), the author, a professor of constitutional law[21] and national liberal parliamentarian, offered the following formulation of the 'task and essence of the police': 'official attendance to the everyday requirements of public safety and welfare'.[22] Rönne added that a distinction was often drawn between the security aspects and welfare aspects of policing. For him, however, this was a mere definitional dispute since 'in practice no such strict distinction can be made between the two tendencies; police activity operates simultaneously in both spheres'. The author drew the consequence from this evidently unproblematic maxim that 'such a division of the organism of the police is neither appropriate nor capable of implementation within the state'. He added laconically, 'and no such distinction exists in the Prussian state'. In Prussia the police were both 'negative and conserving', inasmuch as they 'fended off impending dangers and overcame obstacles to free movement', and 'positive and productive'. They 'aspired to advance the common good' in both respects.

Such an exiguous formulation was bound to win the applause of officials. The significance – better, the explosive potential – of the all-embracing duties assigned to the police which it implied becomes evident to the reader if he or she considers the debate on the police and police powers which began, with some vehemence, in the last thirty years of the nineteenth century. The question of the extent of police powers first became a burning issue, although predominantly in academic circles, over the question of a separate administrative law. At issue was whether, and how, the 'monarchical' practice of issuing orders, in effect since the eighteenth century or at least since the codification and creation of distinct ministerial responsibility at the end of the eighteenth century, had attempted to curb the state apparatus's seemingly insatiable appetite for pursuing the common good (to paraphrase Theodor Foerstemann).[23] Particular attention was focused on the police paragraph of the Prussian Legal Code (*Das Allgemeine Landrecht*) of 1794, which outlined the tasks of the police within the context of delimiting criminal and special police jurisdiction.

> The necessary institution for maintaining public quiet, safety and order, and for warding off danger to the public as a whole or individual members of it is the office of the police.[24]

Foerstemann's opponent, Hermann Rosin, appealed to the practice followed since the promulgation of the statutory code.[25] In his view, the Legal Code had not only not sought to restrict state activity to defence from dangers, but had also included the advancement of national well-being. Moreover, the Legal Code was to be considered alongside provincial laws which continued in force. Rosin referred to the fact that neither the manuals and commentaries nor legislative practice in the first half of the nineteenth century contained any contradiction between the police paragraph in the Legal Code (cited above) and the numerous and extensive determinations, general orders and instructions, decrees and rescripts. In particular, he based his argument on the Order of 26 December 1808, which provided for the 'improved institution of provincial, police, and financial authorities', and the Instruction for the District Governments of 23 October 1817.[26] These texts, which represented the first step in providing a legal basis for the administrative reform of the middle tier of government, expressly 'required' the newly formed police authorities, i.e. the former *Regierungen* now stripped of their judicial functions, to attend to the 'common good of our subjects'. A further paragraph in the 1808 Order makes this even more explicit: the 'activity of these authorities should not be confined merely to defence against dangers and disadvantages and the preservation of what already exists'; their tasks also included the 'preservation and advancement of the general welfare'.

Kurt Wolzendorff, an academic constitutional lawyer, offered the clearest assessment of the 'police controversy' in his 1905 study.[27] Wolzendorff showed that the Orders and Instructions decreed in 1815 and 1817 superseding the 1808 provision did not make explicit reference to this issue. Nevertheless, the broad range of activities assigned to the police authorities, from the 'quelling of riots' through medical and trade matters to the mint and 'public communication', made it quite apparent that the police were not to be restricted to the 'sphere of security' (see Appendix 2 below). In short, the dispute as to whether the persistence of the simultaneity in practice and unity in theory of security and welfare tasks was deliberate or an 'oversight' (of the police paragraph in the Prussian Legal Code) was superfluous. What was significant was the fact 'that the police paragraph, with its more restrictive emphasis, was simply no longer observed after 1808' – something, according to Wolzendorff, which could not be 'denied away'.

This approach finds support in two examples which reflect how consensus and theory were translated into practical hints for everyday administration. In the first volume of his manual on 'Police Administration', published in 1843, W. G. von der Heyde, onetime mayor of Calbe an der Saale and one of the most assiduous compilers of 'aid manuals' for police practitioners, noted: 'The entrustment of the highest authority in the state' permitted and required its 'bearers to concern themselves with the avoidance of future evils which could prove injurious to all in the state, i.e. to administer the police'[28] – an institution defined in the following terms: 'Police authority' is required and entitled 'via the power of police supervision to direct its attention towards the ascertainment of any dangers prejudicial to the safety and well-being of citizens'.

For von der Heyde, therefore, the warding off of dangers did not contradict concern for welfare – although he did not, in fact, cite the paragraph from the Prussian Legal Code which emphasised 'defence against dangers' in the context of 'welfare'.

In a 'Manual for *Landräte*, the magistracy and police officials', published in 1841 by C. A. Bielitz, a writer and jurist and the first commentator on the

Legal Code, the range of options open to those administering 'the police' was even wider. Bielitz's preface on how the administration served as the guarantee of the constitution began with a definition which laid great weight on the aspect of 'defence against dangers'. The police were 'indisputably the most important and beneficial institution within the state because through them disorder and danger are avoided, and crimes prevented or rendered harmless'.[29] The observation that the police were 'beneficial' carries with it the sense that the task of guaranteeing 'safety' did not exclude a broader interpretation. This aspect emerged a few lines later when Bielitz maintained that 'vigilant and strict policing makes up for some of the deficiencies in the constitution . . . [and] in the first instance the well-being of the citizens of the state depends upon it'. Despite the more restrictive wording, the paragraphs in the Legal Code were interpreted along these lines: the Code 'establishes the care incumbent on the police for general welfare'.

Although such arguments might be seen as vague, inconsistent, or even 'sloppy', such a judgement would do little to advance our study much beyond the narrow legalistic approach of the late nineteenth century. Certainly, it would throw precious little light on the significance of the equation of defending the state from danger and attending to its inhabitants' well-being. The practical conclusion of this equation is clear however: unlimited bureaucratic power of definition. At the same time, the most general purposes of the state could be appropriated to serve as direct guides in the day-to-day conduct of the administration.

Astonishingly, the first critical discussions did not begin until some fifty or sixty years after the formulation of these tasks. As far as practitioners were concerned, the enduring discrepancy between the practice of the administration and the sceptical questioning of the 'welfare' activities of the police within 'educated' circles since the late eighteenth century was evidently simply not an issue. And the failure of enlightenment or liberal-constitutional demands for controls on the bureaucracy was not a topic of interest even for academically remote observers – or, at any event, was not held to be a matter for particular concern.

Police II: The 'common good' and the bureaucratic power of definition

Within the administration, standard formulae were also evidently regarded as perfectly adequate *material* justifications. Of course, these were hardly fitted to refute academic criticisms. Their role was to express the internal consensus of the administration and confirm the basic agreement which prevailed within the 'corps of officials'. In the language of ministerial decrees, it was the officials' task, 'to attend to the best interests of the state and the common good of our loyal subjects'.[30]

This included the prevention and warding off of dangers; but it also embraced 'the greatest furtherance and increase in the common good of the citizenry'. All hindrances 'to the furtherance of the general well-being' were to be removed 'as soon as is possible within the law'. However, such a listing of the powers or 'objects' of the bureaucracy was not able to offer any more precise specification of the indeterminate and vague boundaries between the *possibilities* of intervention and the *obligation* to intervene (or the means legitimate in such circumstances).

'Common good' as understood by the Prussian administration did not imply some utilitarian notion of happiness, such as Bentham's 'greatest happiness of the greatest number' which, despite its diverse meanings, would have entailed some reference to the real lives of the social subjects.[31] Rather, the 'common good' combined general human, as it were supra-social, reason with practical vacuity and arbitrariness. It was broad enough to unite both enlightened-humanist or liberal critics of state omnipotence and arbitrariness with that strand of state metaphysics whose naive narrow-mindedness was little more than a caricature of Hegel's philosophy of right and which gave scant consideration to the possibility of a divergence between empirical reality (the Prussian state) and the Hegelian 'idea' of 'the' state.[32]

The 'common good' not only allowed but encouraged any perspective which saw the status quo as the best in the best of all possible worlds. One example can be seen in the case of a report by an otherwise unimportant official drafted in 1831. The author, Theodor Janke, noted in his brochure, published to mark 'Twenty-five years of state reform' that, 'Since 1807 the new social condition has been improved and ennobled in every aspect: social well-being as a whole has become more widespread and firmly established through institutions which embrace and efficiently advance the welfare of the generality.'[33] The individual elements of the 'common good', as perceived by the administration, and by the large majority of the ruling classes in general, can be seen in the list which he appended: 'Greater order, secure rights for persons and property, greater cultivation amongst the people and successful [economic] activity . . . and powerful external defence.'

The underside or obverse of the state claim embodied in the idea of the 'common good' had already been illuminated during the late-eighteenth-century debate over legal codification in Prussia by Johann Georg Schlosser. This enlightenment critic of Prussia trenchantly exposed this undiscriminating term: 'the common good cited so often in the Prussian legislation is a mixture of infinitely varying ingredients'.[34] In contrast,

> The state that is best established is one in which anyone may come to the lake and draw what they need, and what they may be able to endeavour to take. Consider how many thousand turns the state must make to maintain the plenitude of this lake? If you wish to simplify this machine then it must always turn on one side: only *one* on this side will draw, only *one* will mix the ingredients of the common good to his taste – all others will simply be there to turn and to fill the lake from which the *one* wishes to draw [emphasis in original].

We should merely add here that Schlosser's contemporaries already had to add the bureaucracy to the 'one', the monarch.

The injunction to pursue the common good, codified many times in the post-1807 state reforms, established a legitimacy for the (police-) administration which required no elaborate or fine legal constructions.[35] Ensuring that administrative conduct remained legal did not, accordingly, necessitate any specific legal norms or powers of judicial control. Certainly, there were conflicts over the boundaries between legal procedures and actions within the administration and especially between the judiciary and the civil bureaucracy; these concerned, to take but a few examples, questions of police and patrimonial jurisdiction, the eligibility of office holders to stand as witnesses, and the value of their evidence. Administrative activity was justified only from case to case 'through procedure' (Luhmann, *Zweckbegriff und Systemrationalität*), but was not guided by the permanently enforceable requirements of legality and its judicial procedure. If the aim of the state was established as a direct legal norm for the administration, it might even appear contrary to impose formal judicial constraints which could be invoked in individual instances.

The direct legitimation obtained from the goal of furthering the 'common good' had a number of interconnected and inseparable consequences. In the first place, highly divergent and antagonistic individual interpretations of the general norm for the bureaucracy were possible and legitimate: this created an internal competition over powers and their specific interpretation in individual instances. Legitimation by a 'general clause' could therefore lead to very disparate and contradictory behaviour by officials. This probably lay behind the particular displeasure of *Staatsrat* Friese in his 1808 report. The clause covered both constant intervention 'into society' and also persistent passivity *vis-à-vis* society. What was the 'general good' was, accordingly, entrusted to the judgement of the administration – and more specifically, its regional and local officials. The demands of the common 'best' bound together empty normative formulae with the delegated power of interpretation.

However, this construction established an additional ambiguity concerning not the direction of or preparedness for action but the *mode* of intervention or, where appropriate, passivity. In the first place the 'aims' could be interpreted as an obligation imposed on the bureaucracy by itself, and were indeed understood as such by its members. Careful consideration had to precede individual action. Equally, arrogance and ignorance could be justified and practised – both in the case of active intervention or passive waiting. For the apparatus this meant that its general powers could be employed either for blocking or loosening the hierarchical ties governing the lower and intermediate officials and levels of decision-making. For the public, the 'administered', such a form of alien bureaucratic–police control over its own interests and needs could considerably raise the 'costs' of domination.

This disequilibrium found its correspondence in the cordon placed around the judiciary. The possibilities for questioning administrative self-control through the judiciary, let alone limiting it, were few from the outset.[36] A general concession granted in 1807, which allowed judicial complaint to be made against police orders, excluded material compensation in the case of intervention by the state in the increasingly broad area of commercial privileges. Judicial practice soon produced an additional restriction: an administrative act could be nullified only if it injured express legal titles, not customary rights of usage such as pasturage 'in common' (in the wake of the 'division of the commons'). The bureaucracy therefore had considerable procedural protection from demands arising out of the 'mobile' society. The 'proprietorial classes' derived considerable benefits from this; and enjoyment of right to compensation was tailored entirely to their property titles.

The particularist interests and particular functions of the officials and bureaucracy themselves were systematically obscured in the legitimation they derived from the 'common good' argument: this also applied to those claimed for other social groups and for the establishment and safeguarding of the social modes of production and reproduction. Such a form of legitimation facilitated not only the articulation of the interests of the bureaucracy, but also its specifically bureaucratic form.

On the first aspect: the programmatic aims of 'state administration as the art of healing', as the Königsberg *Regierungsrat* Professor Hagen formulated the injunction to advance the common good in a textbook for future administrative officials, detached the bureaucracy from all social or environmental influences.[37] Marx's thesis in his critique of Hegel's philosophy of right on the 'imaginary generality of the particular interest' of the bureaucracy got to the nub of the issue. Where the explicit arguments and implicit mode of interpretation of the officials met, 'The bureaucracy takes itself to be the ultimate purpose of the state . . . state objectives are transformed into objectives of the department . . . and the department objectives into objectives of the state.'[38]

However, this designates only the most apparent aspect of the bureaucratic power of definition. For the parallelism between mode of interpretation and programmatic aims was also a basis for the formation of alliances, facilitating a case-by-case tying of administrative conduct to interpretations of the status quo or 'common good', which opened the door to particularist interests. In everyday practice this allowed the bureaucracy to link its own interests with the interests of those possessing more immediate power of disposition over labour-power and its product, ranging from the estate-owning Junker to the entrepreneurial class of the towns and western provinces.

Such a legitimation also easily allowed itself to become associated with a particular *form* of bureaucratic conduct – and this touches on the second aspect of how the bureaucracy perceived its interests. One of the characteristics cited by von der Heyde illustrates what lay at the heart of this form. Writing on the police's power to 'define the situation', he noted that the provisions under which the police obtained their powers were extremely flexible when compared with those for the judiciary. 'Any obstacle to safety or welfare within the state constitutes an object of their instruction.'[39] Police orders were amended 'with each new experience, are swiftly extended, swiftly restricted, swiftly abolished, and swiftly renewed once again'. The assertion that all bureaucratic conduct had to be directly accommodated to changed social realities fended off questions as to the particularist interests of those concerned, together with the rules which guided their perceptions and judgements. Of course, such a self-portrayal mirrored their claim to define the situation. Given the dominant mode of interpretation, the implications for bureaucratic conduct were that *prevention* would take centre stage, but prevention using *repressive methods*. Heyde wrote, 'obstacles and dangers must be pursued to their sources, and these sources must be capped'. The recommendation of prevention rested on the assumption that the vigorous use of violent methods was indispensable: 'Uncommanded, the police seek to prevent conflicts between citizens, to remove the occasion for such, to prevent outbreaks of quarrelsomeness and the taking of authority into an individual's own hands.'

The forms and means of 'prevention' had to be painful and palpable for the 'policed'; quite appropriately, they were termed 'means of coercion' (*Zwangsmittel*) in legal and administrative phraseology.[40] The emphasis placed on prevention did not, therefore, signify any reduction in the scope for the legitimate application of repression: in fact it was established more firmly and in some circumstances actually extended.[41]

Such theses were by no means confined to one section of officialdom. They can be found even amongst the small group of reforming officials responsible for the principal edicts drafted between 1807 and 1817. Johann Gottfried Frey, police director of Königsberg, and an administrator heavily involved in the preparation of the Municipal Reform Edict, provides a case in point. Frey was in favour of separating the police as an instrument of intervention from the administration of particular institutions, such as the poorhouses. He had called for a supra-local organisation in order to be able to exclude the 'merely local need' – something he was, however, unable to realise. In justifying the unique character of the police he cited the 'law of coercion' exercised by the police as something utterly unremarkable. This law was not only to 'render unlawful actions physically impossible' but also to 'remove everything which may obstruct, *if only remotely* the attainment of the state's objectives' (emphasis added).[42]

Crucially, Frey's remark isolated not a *goal* but a particular *mode of action* as the essential characteristic of the police. The identity of policing activity by the bureaucracy no longer consisted in safeguarding 'good order', warding off impending dangers or augmenting welfare but in the manner with which administration was carried out. And the confinement of 'the natural freedom of activity to those acts benefiting the generality and the coercion to realise it' could be observed both in 'welfare police' activity – such as the enforcement of compulsory schooling – and in the dispersal of riots.[43]

This justification of state violence by reference to an obligation to advance the 'common good' was very flexible. However, it rested on the assumption that welfare policing also involved safeguarding the prevailing patterns of judgement and interpretation of the ruling 'order'. At this level, any talk of the common good – a conversation, moreover, in which the bureaucracy addressed only itself – represented a compromise formula for cooperation and alliance, or at least a rhetorical agreement with the other socially influential classes and groups. Officials found themselves using arguments identical to those otherwise wielded by their most fundamental critics. If the 'foundations of civil order' were in jeopardy, differences as to the political organisation of this order paled into insignificance. 'The application of means of coercion is justified to secure' the foundations of 'civil order' against real or feared dangers.

Zachariae, the Göttingen professor and prominent liberal constitutionalist, used this formulation, for example, in 1842 to justify almost unlimited scope for police discretion[44] – in the context of a very uncompromising interest in the stability of 'civil' social conditions. Such a perspective allowed a constitutionally moderate 'rule of law' type of liberalism to find common ground with 'police' standards. The basis was the relinquishment of any doubts as to the social substance of the legitimating formulae and any attempts to examine the social consequences of the more precise surveillance of social processes which were called for. Such arguments allowed the freedom of the 'citizen' to be directly attended to by the violent character of the state. Or, in the formulation used by von Grävell, 'the means of coercion which the government needs in order to obtain obedience to its laws' are unobjectionable for 'freedom', 'inasmuch as they are themselves in accordance with the law. Given these prerequisites the means of coercion are merely protective measures for all-round freedom, and represent no danger to it'.[45] And, further, 'the government is obliged to keep in readiness at all times the means of coercion in order to dissuade any refractory subject from disobedience through the exercise of the superior power of the state'.[46]

This should, of course, be seen in the context of the sought-for constitution. Constitutional laws were not only unobjectionable but indispensable as far as the freedom of the citizen was concerned. Naturally, this did not necessarily answer the question as to whether justifying the aims of the state by such material arguments as 'the common good' meant that non-constitutional laws were a sufficient basis for the use of means of coercion. If a critic of the non-constitutional state makes an explicit call for means of coercion, what is the difference as far as practical administrators are concerned? Evidently, differing if not contradictory positions could agree on the need for the availability of unconstrained means of coercion.

That a complementary relationship existed between the bureaucratic administration of the common good, the exercise of police 'discretion' and the use of 'means of coercion' was simply assumed in the academic literature and guides for practitioners. Actual practice for officials and those directly affected needed no further description. And the reading public could inform itself by consulting a commentator on police affairs, such as Gustav Zimmermann – official propagandist in Hanover, trained jurist and holder of the office of 'secretary of the archives'. His perceptive articulation of administrative consciousness published in 1845 under the title *Die deutsche Polizei im 19. Jahrhundert* culminated in a formulation which, despite its pathos, accurately reflected the 'costs of police action':

The police should in certain respects cut through the confusion of modern life like flying cohorts: be everywhere and everywhere be active. Note, contain, correct and discover what strikes it as unlawful. On the spot and swiftly too, since the circumstances of the modern world do not suffer waiting, but like the chameleon, transform themselves under the hand or escape.[47]

3

'Common good', property and 'honour'. The mediation of general and particular interests

'Common good': the articulation of interests and social intercourse

The entrusting of the 'common good' to officialdom entailed a form of circular logic. Whilst obliging all levels of the administration to attend to the requirements of a specific concrete social condition, presumed to be beyond dispute, in practice it located the definition of this reality in the action, or inaction, of these same officials. It was, however, a very broad concept, capable of embracing not merely such administrative activity and inactivity but also of providing a focus around which dissatisfied or discontented elements could articulate their interests.

Naturally, those brought to the verge of starvation[1] during the bad harvests of 1816–17 and 1846–7, those reduced to poverty in the East Westphalian family linen industry in the 1830s and 1840s,[2] the masses of unemployed and hungry day-labourers and apprentices who poured into, and streamed out of, the large towns during the 1820s[3] were much less inclined to 'articulate' their critique of the prevailing order through verbal means. Their protests were not expressed in the 'concepts' familiar to the ruling or hegemonic classes: they rarely resorted to formal petitions, and certainly never to legal submissions. But they did not remain mute: their interests and ideas were expressed in tangible, but no less thought-out, actions in which the symbolism of the oppressor – the flag and marching column – was adopted and 'turned upside down'. Arguments around the construct of the 'common good' had little place. Rather, the 'common good' was a discourse specific to the literati, the academic and the 'cultivated' classes. In the broadest sense, it was a philosophically heavily loaded notion. Far from being merely casuistic and self-serving, it allied moral judgements with the apparent submergence – more properly concealment – of particular interests. Nevertheless, appeals to the 'common best' were more than a mere cover for private gain or meaningless propriety. As aware of their interests as those involved may have been, reducing every situation to a crude calculus of advantage and disadvantage was not considered acceptable: reputation and 'honour' could not be separated from the forms in which they were proclaimed.

Even within a class structure in which commercialisation and the advance of commodity production in the 'open countryside' as well as the towns were generating new social conflicts, the 'common good' effectively remained a matter of implicit understandings amongst the 'better orders' – moreover, a matter not in need of a great deal of discussion. It did not simply or even primarily represent a rational dialogue or the general weighing-up and balancing of interests. Rather, it concealed an elemental antagonism which the notion of the 'common good' allowed to be transcended, at least ideologically. Just as the use of dialogue in contemporary philosophical or political essays represented an art form in which open argument was more feigned than achieved, the 'common good' was not seen as a means for initiating a general debate between social classes and groups as to the reasonableness of their interests. Its role was to symbolise a dual concordance: on the one hand the affinity or identity between the ruling, profit-making and governing classes and groups and, on the other, the harmony between their ideologies and interests and certain class-specific forms of social intercourse – both in business and pleasure – the terms of which were set by cultivated discourse. The 'common good' embodied the political dimension of that unity of 'decency, order and morals' which had been the particular hallmark of feudal 'manners'.[4] As well as its external face – which as the 'representative public sphere' (*repräsentative Öffentlichkeit*)[5] was intended to exhibit the domination and elevated social status of the official, both on and off duty – we can also distinguish an internal facet where the 'public sphere' not only served to represent domination 'before the people', that is the 'dominated', but also facilitated intensive and efficient political communication in which verbal debates were one, but by no means the sole, element.

Central to these forms of political communication was the fact that an individual's own advantage could be directly coupled with the pleasures of 'private' life.[6] The rather formal gatherings of aristocrats, senior bureaucrats and bourgeois notables, and even more so their informal get-togethers and social events, excursions or hunts, exhibited an acute awareness by those involved of the concurrence of aesthetic and sensual enjoyments with the practical economy of time and money.

Naturally, securing one's interests in such a pleasurable manner had its price. And the seamy side would indeed occasionally explode into notoriety: 'scandal' – with all its embarassing, painful and often harmful 'ramifications' for those involved – exposed the tension woven into even the pleasurable pursuit of their particular way of life. And where not only spheres of interest but also the delicate boundaries of rank had been transgressed, or seemingly so, these conflicts could no longer be quietly, or at any event internally, resolved; two particular examples were the 1834 Trier casino affair, and, in the 1840s, the persistent frictions in Bielefeld between active officers – predominantly noble – and reserve officers made up of the local bourgeois.

The main function of socialising was to prove both to the individual and to others that harmony and unanimity ruled within one's circle. At the same time, it also afforded numerous opportunities for arriving at both an unforced and agreeable consensus as to what the 'common good' in fact represented. No special efforts had to be made to thrash out differences and arrive at common interests: official conferences or formalised debates were unnecessary and superfluous. The soirée, 'where twenty or so persons gathered together over a glass of wine and a pipe' proved much more effective and agreeable, as the newly appointed *Regierungspräsident* of Arnsberg, von Itzenplitz, noted after one such evening in Schwelm in 1845.[7] And the 'ease' of closed male society[8] found its counterpart in such 'feudal' pleasures as hunting with the county notables. Von Ernsthausen, later a *Regierungspräsident*, summed up the administrative rationale of participation in such 'excursions' in a reflection on his period of office as *Landrat* in Simmern and Moers (administrative districts on the left bank of the Rhine) during the 1850s:

> I have never seriously doubted that hunting and the occupation of any administrative official who is not actually chained to his desk are perfectly reconcilable . . . The hunt brings him into contact with a large number of quite influential people, most of whom belong to his district, closer acquaintanceship with whom must be a desirable thing for him. Acquaintanceship breeds mutual trust and the official can find out where the shoe is pinching.[9]

The 'mobilisation' of social resources: property and the interests of the propertied

The group of 'modernising bureaucrats' mainly responsible for the post-1807 reforms,[10] some of whom later held senior positions in the provincial administrations, regarded the growing commercialisation of exchange and the advance of capitalist relations of production in agriculture and industry as an ineluctable process. The Royal Domain itself had been subject to steady reform since 1763. And in agriculture[11] the trajectory of development had been set by the switch to wage-labour during the eighteenth century (very extensively so on the East Prussian estates) and the rationalisation of production through the consolidation of holdings and the apportionment of communal land. Even before the boom in grain exports in the 1790s, when the intensification of the demands on unfree labour reached its height, the commutation of services and reform on state farms had demonstrated the higher profits available to the owners, in this case the royal exchequer, from an economy based on wage-labour – at least in a period when grain prices were holding up over a number of years and revenue could be increased simply by raising output.

Economic factors were not the only spur to bureaucratic eagerness for reform. Rebellious peasant 'masses' in Silesia in 1792–3, and in several provinces in 1798 – openly based on the French precedent – had stirred fears of a revolutionary overthrow.[12] And after Prussia's defeat at the hands of Napoleon's army in 1806/7, the spectre of revolutionary France was compounded by a desperate and demoralising fiscal crisis. Senior officials and advisors saw the enforcement or acceleration of the commutation of services and the termination of feudal property rights on private estates as one means of escaping from the parlous state into which both the social order and state finances had fallen. And the only means available to them was for the administration itself to embark on a programme of reform in agriculture, flanked by similar steps in industry and the trades. No other option seemed capable of both diverting revolutionary energies whilst simultaneously mobilising society's financial resources to stave off impending state bankruptcy.[13]

Administrative stimulation of agrarian improvements and of industry also held out the prospect of setting the long-term course of social development,[14] a perspective by no means confined to the 'great' reform memoranda. Von Vincke, later *Oberpräsident* in Westphalia, formulated this outlook in an 1808 memorandum: 'The character of civil insititutions is determined not only by the character of the nation, as there is no reasonable ground why, conversely, the character of civil institutions cannot be shaped by the administration.'[15] In the 'completely new edifice' which was to be constructed, 'most people . . . would serve the common best interest because it calls for their own most precious interests'. Both self-interest and selfishness would be satisfied by the 'new institution' of the organisation of the state and the legal system.

It was therefore crucial that administrative activity to free the productive forces via the 'circulation of landed property' was matched by the 'encouragement of production and fabrication' – for Vincke with the aim of developing 'internal trade', that is a domestic market. Subsequently, the state would be able to confine itself simply to maintaining financial and monetary stability and could leave 'the translation of the awakened entrepreneurial spirits to private industry'.[16] Increased productive use of the land, industrial resources and labour-power presupposed the installation and permanent safeguarding of the private ownership of the corresponding properties. Appropriate forms of exchange and commerce also had to be made available to these – according to the doctrine – 'unhampered' economic subjects. This meant, primarily, developing the formal Roman legal elements within the idea of the 'rule of law' into the institution of unfettered private property.[17] No other form of legal, and simultaneously constitutional, change was capable of eliminating traditional privileges – either 'from above' or 'from below' – in a manner subsequently able to serve market-based circulation and accumulation. Juridical 'égalité' was therefore a prime symbol through which the principle of a 'self-regulating market system' (Polanyi) could be established – that necessary Utopia for the uneven advance of the capitalist mode of production.

There were two main fields of action. First, customary 'public' rights of control and usufruct had to be transformed into 'private' property. Secondly, this property's inviolability and alienability had to be established and demonstrated. On the first point: the 'mobility' of property, understood as unrestricted disposition and availability, could be cast in an appropriate juridical form only through the transformation of 'rights' into the Roman legal category of 'property'. Landed property, and in particular landed property with a feudal character, was the main target. The abolition of hereditary serfdom on Junker estates through the 1807 October Edict marked the clear intention of the ministerial bureaucracy to include the core elements of the social and economic order in the portentous transformation being pursued on the land. This was followed in 1811 by the Edict regulating peasant landownership, although its partial withdrawal in 1816 provided a swift demonstration of the limits of administrative intervention. Industrial production in the towns was subjected to administrative attention in the 1810 Trade Tax Edict and the 1811 Trade Police Edict, which implemented the abolition of guild restrictions already announced in 1808 (at least in provinces east of the Oder and in Brandenburg). The aim of these legislative measures[18] was to 'effect that beneficial change through which each individual is to receive the greatest possible freedom for the use of their capital, their mind and their physical powers'.[19]

How the political maxims informing these and other edicts were put into practice is not at issue here: suffice it to say that, far from being a uniform or consistent process, it was highly contradictory, and riddled with unclarity, not to mention incompetence.[20] More important was the fact that, as far as the state administration was concerned, 'property' could no longer be regarded as merely one juridical institution amongst several, one political catchword amongst many others. It was enthroned as *the* economic and social precondition for the 'common good', and hence the central point of reference for all administrative activity.

Naturally, this victory for the – in functional terms – bourgeois-capitalist notion of property cannot be considered in such 'pure' terms. Its progress ran parallel with another issue, raised in 1790 by one of the drafters of the Prussian General Legal Code (*Allgemeines Landrecht*), the *Landgerichtsrat* Ernst Ferdinand Klein, in the form of a question posed by a character in a fictitious dialogue on the subject of the French revolution. 'Must order begin by violating the sanctity of property?'[21]

This marked the second critical point in the establishment of property. Not only did it have to be advanced in opposition to those who appropriated the social surplus product solely as beneficiaries of traditional privileges and rights – a group already declining in numbers in the second half of the eighteenth century. The coincidence of intensive commercialisation and the first stages of capitalisation with the French revolution was also a very explosive mixture. Restructuring could be successful only if it could differentiate itself from this both threatening, and highly dynamic, process of political transformation. The elimination of the feudal character of the *ancien régime* in Prussia, primarily 'second serfdom' and 'inauthentic' peasant property relations in East Elbia, was seen as a thoroughly 'revolutionary' breach of the law by the former proprietors. This made it all the more crucial for the instigators of change to make it clear to the traditional ruling class, whose economic basis lay in privileged, state-protected landed property, that politically and administratively managed change in the legal and social order was not a revolution in the same mould as the French, and that furthermore only such a 'revolution from above'[22] offered some chance of effective resistance to the dreaded violent 'overthrow'. However, the argument that intervention into traditional rights and titles was justified on the grounds of the natural rights of the individual – that is a prior 'freedom' (prior even to the acquisition of property!) – was far from merely a deliberate ruse or false consciousness: rather it testified to the sense of mission and dynamism of the initiators of change. Any diminution of this freedom necessitated interference in the currently legal but, from the perspective of natural rights, now illegitimate and certainly uneconomic property structure – naturally for appropriate 'compensation'. Both political and legal arguments therefore spoke for the abolition of feudal servility. And by combining particular interests with the claim that everyone would benefit in the final analysis, this argument was able to legitimate, and possibly ease or even bring forward, intervention by the administration.

Klein's expression 'the violated sanctity of property' appeared to effect an easy union of both conceptions of proprietorial rights. His first thoughts were for the traditional doctrine of property, the property of special prerogatives and privileges. On the other hand, there was also a powerful case for transferring this 'sanctity' to property in its Roman juridical form. If the social order to be established was to rest on the supposed usefulness of this form of property, then support for such a transfer was at the least politically plausible, if not desirable: and in terms of legal principles it was an absolute imperative.

The significance accorded 'property' in the constitution is clear testimony of the state guarantee of its inviolability. However, the fact that special provisions remained in force which allowed property's internal affairs, so to speak, to remain a public matter constituted a breach of the principle of legal consistency and indicated the absence of an even pace to social development; for example, the confinement of estate ownership to the nobility, or the labour regulations for estates with their specific coercive relations for the servant – as exemplified in the specific section of the Legal Code and the Servants' Ordinance of 8 November 1810. In contrast, the 'full property', established in the subsequent codification of the *Landrecht*, and especially the post-1807 Edicts, represented both an unfettered and exclusively private power of disposition resting ultimately on the force of the state: 'The property owner is accountable to no one as to the use of his object.'[23] Conversely, the fact that even after 1807 the state continued to extend its guarantee to both old and new property had two consequences: not only could it render the legitimacy of the given state 'constitution' tangible to the owners of 'mobile' objects; at the same time, administrative activity became bound to the highly heterogeneous demands and difficulties of private proprietors, without any reciprocal possibility of using legal principles to subordinate the actual use of property to any continuing or comprehensive public assessment or critique. Disposition over property and the freedom of property owners correspondingly could become matters of public concern only on the second-order issues of complaints over injuries to (property-) rights.

Events in France must have elevated the importance of property to officials in at least two respects: firstly, as the foundation for the proposed expansion of production, i.e. as a title of disposition over resources and 'productive energies' and, secondly, as a symbol of legitimate authority. The functional requirements of economic mobilisation, first and foremost to raise tax revenue, and the necessity to mount a counter-revolutionary defence of the status quo thus mutually reinforced each other. The safeguarding of both 'old' and 'new' property consequently marked the boundaries at which illegitimate redistribution began and these boundaries could and had to be acknowledged and appreciated by officials, by their bourgeois beneficiaries and by Junker – and hence military – despisers of the civil 'state machine'.

This bifurcation of property within one all-embracing term was only the very imperfect reflection of a very complex social process. At the same time, it was indispensable if economic mobilisation was to be coupled with political stability. And this was beyond question, even for the most enthusiastic proponents of far-reaching 'liberalisation', such as Altenstein. 'The real task of the police is to safeguard the edifice of the constitution'; that is, the entire internal administration was, first and foremost, to be responsible for safeguarding the political order of the social relations of power and domination. And although the terms used refer to overlapping objectives, i.e. the safeguarding of property and the constitutional order, the 'basic constitution and the inner organisation of the state' were 'none the less something sacred'.[24]

The inviolability of property was to be secured in any form demanded by property owners. Redistribution – either by the state or unauthorised individual action, such as illegal use or consumption – had to be rendered impossible. At the same time, the calculated promotion and direction of productive and property interests (accumulation) could be legitimated by confining bureaucratic intervention to the changing of existing property *titles* whilst supporting *property relations*.[25]

Regardless of which path was pursued, it could only mark the first practical steps by officials in their furtherance of the 'common good'. Each in turn contained and created political areas of conflict which required officials to take up a position whenever they sought, used, or discarded information, and whenever they prepared, advanced, thwarted, or implemented decisions. Officials had to confront and come to arrangements with those who were much more immediately involved in the determination of the increase in and distribution of the social product and social wealth: with the owners of capital, of land and of factories, putters-out and merchants (*Kaufleute*). Not only did all these parties seek to maximise surplus-value within the sphere of production, but also to realise it in markets extending beyond their own immediate localities. And agreement on their essentially identical interest in the maximum utilisation of labour-power, and profitable and efficient production and distribution,[26] did not resolve the gap between these interests and those of the agrarian estate economy.[27]

The divergent economic bases behind these divergent interests can be seen in the demands and developments peculiar to individual groups and economic sectors; for example, the preference for free trade amongst the export-oriented agrarians in contrast to the demands for protection from those industries threatened by imports; the spread of extensive cultivation in the East; the overall need for a greater input of capital; the search for cheap labour-power in the estate economy and, after 1830, in the workshops and factories of the central and western provinces and in railway construction (less so in domestic industry with the 'self-exploitation' of its own labour-power).

For senior officials, the problem was not so much these differences of interest as the varying degrees of loyalty or 'appropriateness' with which they were articulated, either by Rhenish merchants or Junker agrarian critics.[28] Irrespective of conflicts between them, the administration had to remain alive to the *common* aims and interests of these groups. The defence of property – meaning not merely productive but also unproductive but none the less socially important property – marked out only one of these areas of common interest. Maintaining monarchical and bureaucratic 'order' and the 'constitution' of the state was its inseparable corollary. Although this did not yield any systematic general logic on which decisions could be based, it did generate a capacity for pragmatism, and suggests that these formulae were sufficiently flexible to allow for day-to-day compromises. We have to turn to concrete instances to discern the respective configurations of classes and forces, and hence the 'activity-limit' for both reforming and conserving actions. This limit was encroached on when the social pattern of appropriation and distribution of the surplus product, power and reputation was put at risk. Common interests were expressed as active distrust and intractability towards the non-propertied, at any event when their behaviour seemed to present an acute threat not only to individual aspects, but to the very fabric of social inequality – in the final analysis, the forms of social intercourse of the 'higher ranks'. Absolute unanimity prevailed on the need to outlaw both injury to property and any violations of public order. The ruling classes joined company with the governing classes to exercise the collective pursuit of both thieves and 'demagogues' – and in particular to suppress 'dangerous opinions' and any vociferous movement amongst the 'lower popular classes'.

But even this fine appreciation of the social and fiscal necessity for balancing interests was not of itself sufficient to ensure that those officials zealous for reform fulfilled the tasks set them in the same measure or at the same time. The mobilisation of productive resources, accelerated capitalisation and commercialisation – as indispensable as they must have seemed – implied not only legal intervention in the sphere of the 'First Estate',[29] but a possible acceleration in the economic demise of the estate-owning aristocracy.[30] Avoiding any fundamental or even short-term danger to the social order by destroying its social pillars – the very revolution which was supposed to be prevented – through bureaucratic hastiness (and possibly via provoking a rebellion on the part of the feudal estates against the reforms) meant accommodating the process of capitalisation to the central demands of the estate-owning class. It was therefore only a matter of consistency for the administration to succumb to pressure from the Junkers of Brandenburg and Pomerania to repeal, or extensively curtail, the 1811 law regulating the ownership of peasant property. Following the 'declaration' of 29 May 1816, the 'Main Statute' for settlement and regulation (Knapp, *Die Bauernbefreiung und der Ursprung der Landarbeiter*), only 'independent arable farmers', that is proprietors with a plough and team, were regulated.[31]

The enjoyment of ruling-class pleasures continued to be central to the behaviour of the 'feudal lords' during the transformation to capitalist agriculture and swamped any attempts to institute more rigorous and commercially minded management. The Junkers were not only concerned with their property as capital but also equally as much with safeguarding their former rights of sovereignty and usufruct, or at any event the privileges formerly attached to these rights. Junker resistance towards the planned changes in local government[32] in the 'older' provinces, which were intended to end patrimonial jurisdiction and control of the police, and their obstruction of stricter taxation, as envisaged in the plans for a uniform property tax,[33] all illustrate how interests found political translation under a regime of 'dual' property. That this defence of customary positions of power and interest was by and large successful, and ruled out any state intervention for a further fifty years, is not only testimony to the continuing social and political dominance of the aristocratic 'Estate', evident, for example, in the re-establishment of the Junker estate economy after 1815 by means of generous state aid[34] after its parlous state in the wake of the 1815–16 agrarian crisis and the war contributions: at the same time, the actual defence of the key seigneurial prerogatives in the fields of jurisdiction and police in the East – the *Gutsherrschaft* – also reveals the extent to which the interests and demeanour of lords 'of rank' found an echo amongst senior officials, irrespective of whether the latter were of aristocratic or bourgeois origin.

The political force of the aristocracy, whose economic foundation continued to be the estate economy, and its diverse but essentially stable alliance with the bureaucracy had its counterpart in the very limited political successes of the entrepreneurial bourgeoisie of the Rhineland, the Duchy of Berg (Düsseldorf, Elberfeld-Barmen) and the county of Mark (Iserlohn). This social group, although divided by numerous localistic and sectoral fissures, was unanimous on the need to transform its own, and other property, into competitive, profit-orientated capital (in particular in terms of access to and control over labour-power), visibly present in machines and factories – and increased tax revenue. Nevertheless, apart from its fiscal power, this group had only limited political opportunity to articulate its interests. And, although managing to register some achievements – securing the Rhenish, French-influenced, communal constitution giving equal recognition to town and country, with its property qualification or three-class franchise, Rhenish or French law with its juridical equality, that is the absence of 'exemption' on grounds of membership of particular estates, and trial by jury with open proceedings which became generally accepted and could be retained –[35] the merchants, 'factory master' and rentiers had no success against the bureaucrats' and Junkers' stubborn intransigence on the issue of the incidence of taxation. Their calls for a redistribution of the tax burden towards the eastern provinces and for greater access to the Provincial diets met with failure.

Property and poverty: on the conditions of 'national welfare'

As with the vague and elastic notion of the 'common good', the need to safeguard property could provide the bureaucracy with only the most general points of reference.[36] An undoubted and observable shift did take place in the weight traditionally given to those private rights in both persons and things which had given emphasis to individual usage. In their stead, property became linked with the power of disposition over means of production, and formed the precondition and means for an accelerating accumulation of capital whose wider dynamic would not, in turn, merely benefit the private interests of its owner.

Such an abstract and long-term perspective could not answer the pressing problems of everyday administration. The fundamental question which so worried Klein, the 'moderate' enlightenment jurist, also hung like a weight over the everyday uncertainties of the public official. Was not the notoriously unequal distribution of property a massive barrier to the freedom of the non-owners, the poor? The answer was determined more by political circumspection than logical consistency. Klein distinguished between 'general' freedom and the concrete – or, if one prefers – actual freedom of each individual: 'Thus if the state has otherwise observed its duty, and introduced a general freedom and powerfully protected it, it may not then attack the property of the rich in order to furnish the poor with a more comfortable or salubrious life.'[37]

This final phrase reveals a mixture of political caution with economic and moral judgements, which avoided having to deduce the necessity of 'freedom'. One of Klein's colleagues, the co-editor of the draft of the General Statutory Code (*Allgemeines Gesetzbuch*) and the Prussian Legal Code (*Allgemeines Landrecht*), Carl Gottlieb Svarez, did concede a formal and extensive right of intervention in private property – but, in contrast to Klein, gave no clear indication of under what circumstances this right might be exercised. Klein's reservations were therefore entirely compatible with Svarez's observation that, although 'each must be allowed free use of property', this was only to the extent 'that it was not prejudicial to others'.[38] This ascribed a fictitious clarity to the threshold of intervention, as in the commentary that state authority could impose 'certain limits' on the use of property only in the event of 'considerable disadvantage for the whole of civil society or at least a substantial part of it'.

Neither the provisions of the Prussian Legal Code[39] nor the catalogue of tasks set out in the provisions governing 'police' administration gave officials much assistance in the balance demanded of them between considerations of general utility on the one hand and the inevitable disadvantages for some if not for 'substantial sections' of society on the other. Little of concrete substance was provided by the twelve 'objects' allocated by the Order of 1817 to the Departments of the Interior in the District Governments which acted as regional authorities for the Ministry of the Interior and Police.[40] Although the first priority was assigned to 'sovereignty', including both 'constitutional matters' and 'matters of allegiance', this also embraced the 'granting of passes for travel outside the country'. In second place was the 'entire policing of public safety and order', which ranged from the 'prevention and quelling of riots' to the 'detection and apprehension of criminals' and the running of 'institutions for paupers, hospitals and poor relief' – the latter under the security police. Then followed 'police supervision of medicinal and health matters', fourth the 'agricultural police', then municipal government, education, religious minorities, and military matters. In tenth place came the 'censorship of all written material, inasmuch as this was not the responsibility of particular authorities', and finally any building works relevant to these 'objects'.

The list contained in a special order to the Director of Police in Aachen was considerably shorter, but no less to the point.[41] Officials were to attend to: 'In particular the policing of general security, roads, construction, food and health, markets, weights and measures, trade and industry, passes and aliens, fire regulations together with poor relief, lunatic asylums, censorship, and Jewish matters.'

However these instructions provided not even the slightest hint of whether and when 'concern' for property – both as defence and furtherance – was to be exercised, how it might or should conflict with concern for the life and subsistence of the 'administered', or how any conflicts arising should be resolved.

A careful reading of the 1817 Executive Instruction might, at best, yield some indirect indications which might slightly minimise these imponderables. But who could be expected to undertake such an intensive study? The sections which outline the 'obligation' of the district governments, 'to give due protection to the best interests of the state and the common good of our subjects', had appended to it a 'guiding principle': 'no one should be further restricted in the enjoyment of their property, their civil prerogatives and freedom than is necessary for the promotion of the general good'.[42] The enjoyment of property took precedence over other objectives or rights. Our aim here is not to provide a detailed analysis of administrative practice in the light of this instruction, or to set off one against the other but to assemble a number of pointers to indicate how this problem was perceived, dealt with, resolved, or ignored. To what extent, for whom and with what justification did officials regard themselves as motivated to investigate and pursue the interests of property?

For the police administration the issue of the benefits and necessity of property, or indeed of the proprietors, was posed particularly starkly in terms of the distinction between 'poor' and 'rich'. In France the revolution had brought about a redistribution decreed, or at least underwritten, by the state (its success or failure is not the issue here). Klein's remark, noted above, already demonstrated that such a strategy was inconceivable in Prussia. Property, even when it limited the freedom of the poor, was to be kept well away from any possible encroachment by the state on the assumption that the latter might seek to assert 'a general freedom'. This understanding also guided officials on the question of how to administer the Poor Laws – the 'poor police'. If state relief for the poor simply allowed the rich, or the owners of estates, manufactories and factories, or merchants to avoid paying the direct producers a higher remuneration for their labour-power or product, if poor-houses seemed to be inhibiting private demand, if the prospect of relief merely encouraged 'malingering', then obviously extreme scepticism towards administrative activity in this field seemed quite imperative. That this did not prevent officials from appreciating the scale of poverty is illustrated by the revelations of Leopold Krug, Prussia's first official statistician.

Krug's 'Observations on the national wealth of the Prussian state and the welfare of its citizens' (1805) contrasted this purported 'wealth' with the view that 'the surest sign of national poverty' was when the wages of its workers were 'just sufficient to stave off starvation as long as they remain in good health and in full possession of their powers', a finding not 'refuted or weakened by [the existence] of a few rich individuals'.[43] The main task was 'by and by to elevate the poor and indigent into the ranks of the prosperous, not steadily to impoverish the ranks of the well-to-do'. Like Adam Smith, Krug regarded the best means for this to be the creation of a free market for labour. In contrast, his attacks on 'artificial and contrived needs', and the luxurious manner in which they were satisfied, both of which were prejudicial to the 'well-being of the nation', hark back to the Physiocrats.

The drafts of the later reforming legislation also revealed a clear commitment to such a position; there would be no confiscatory steps against the rich or permanent subsidising of the poor. Altenstein's 1807 Riga Memorandum observed simply that 'impoverishment would be prevented by greater freedom of trade'.[44] Grävell, the suspended *Regierungsrat*, adopted an earlier and more robust tone. In 1820 he concluded that there were 'only three causes of all the moral evil' with which the police had to trouble themselves: 'coarseness, poverty, idleness'. The first was to be combated through 'proper upbringing' and 'strengthening of the will', whilst poverty, since it 'frequently and most commonly' was the product of idleness, was to be 'rigorously suppressed through the proscription and punishment of beggary'.[45] These were not, of course, new discoveries: Grävell simply played some variations on traditional themes and made them more readable and accessible. The corresponding good conscience, or intellectual justification, can be found in the position taken by Krug's successor at the office of statistics, J. G. Hoffmann. Hoffmann argued that in a phase of increased tension both within and between the classes, for example between peasants overburdened with debt and estate owners buying up their property, or between independent 'rich' and dependent 'poor' handicraft masters, the right of property was not there 'for the benefit of its owner . . . but for the benefit of the human race in general'.[46]

Hoffmann's justification for this both cynical and naively implausible claim entailed a rapid retreat into the great universals:

> Only through the right of property does that wonderful activity arise through which the human race attains abundance and diversity of material goods, whose infinitely growing ownership and enjoyment is one of the fundamental and indispensable conditions for an equally infinite development of its capacities.

This 'species history' perspective led Hoffmann towards an objective necessity which even the most impoverished and proletarianised members of society could not evade: 'In truth, he who has no place to call his own in which to lay down his weary head has no less need that property exists than the most powerful lord or richest rentier.' It was not merely that property as such was fundamental to the development of humanity – although not speaking of humane development, this is evidently what he meant – it was its unequal distribution which was crucial. 'Only through distribution into particular properties can *so* much be obtained from nature.' It was therefore entirely consistent for the role of the state to be wholly subsumed by the defence of property and the maintenance of its unequal distribution: 'The protection furnished by the growth of states is the condition for the secure and unconstrained ownership and use of property in the furthest corners of the globe and in untrammelled accumulation.' The ironic metaphysics of property advanced in Klein's fictitious dialogue is revealed in all seriousness here – backed by a theory more Ricardian than Smithian in nature. Finally, Hoffmann concluded, quite logically, that 'property is to be kept sacred' and 'faithfully defended with all the powers of body and mind'.

It would, of course, be wrong to regard Hoffmann's apotheosis of the principle of possessive individualism as typical – at least in this form – of higher officialdom. However, stripped of its bombastic simplicity, what is left is the clear primacy of the promotion and protection of private accumulation by the state and the law, as the optimal method for producing the 'common best'.[47] Hoffmann's proposals for the class taxation system of 1820 were fully in accord with these sentiments.

The mode of interpretation directly visible here was not only determined by implicit rules for disposition over material goods, rules simultaneously confirmed and constituted by the manner in which they were observed. In Hoffmann, in contrast to Altenstein and Grävell, property as the potential for increased accumulation clearly presupposed non-property. The exclusion of the non-entitled, the constant differentiation between these and those who were entitled, were the very conditions for the possibility of property rights at all, establishing them as a specific form of social relation – a relation between 'rich' and 'poor'. Poverty was neither individual failure nor a momentary blow of fate or 'distress'. Mass poverty was indispensable. In contrast to the Smithian optimism of the legislative efforts of thirty years previously, any real improvement in the condition of the poor was viewed not only as chimerical, but in fact as economically and politically destructive.

For officials, the perception of property was evidently inseparable from the way in which they understood poverty and impoverishment. The selectivity of their interpretation was especially evident in the partiality with which the 'old' property, that is the feudal structures of privileges, was connected with untrammelled private property. The owners of feudal rights were either guaranteed the continuation of these rights or were awarded lucrative commutation settlements. The, at least nominal, counterpart – protection by the owner and use of village commons was, at best, only occasionally registered.[48]

Officials did not consider that the annulment of such claims or common rights of usage merited any corresponding consideration or compensation.

The 'homeless' floating poverty of land-poor and landless 'direct producers' – that is the man- and maidservants in service as day-labourers or servants (*Gesinde*), the cotters, and lodgers, but also domestic industrial producers, urban day-labourers, supernumerary journeymen, or dependent masters, and factory labourers – was seen almost exclusively as an economic and demographic problem during the 1830s. It occupied centre stage in administrative, journalistic, and academic attention at a macro-social level, in numerous essays and tracts,[49] as the 'pauperism debate'. Officials were barely involved in such public debates between 'well-meaning citizens'.[50] Their positions, in which the practical translation of the property question is revealed, were obtained in internal reports.[51] As examples of these we consider two instances from the 1830s; although we cannot establish statistically that these were representative, they are nevertheless concerned with the central, and portentous problem areas of social development.

Poverty as an administrative problem: the crisis of domestic industry and the 'impudence' of the poor

The situation in Paderborn in the winter of 1835/6

Approximately one third of the families in southeast Westphalia were dependent on the proto-industrial linen trade, specifically the spinning of hemp,[52] for their meagre incomes. Their situation was repeatedly the subject of official reports (1820, 1822) which also dealt with the distress amongst the concentrations of domestic-industrial weavers and spinners in the Minden-Ravensberg district to the north of Paderborn. The reports represented a mixture of analytical uncertainty and practical helplessness in the face of the permanent 'indigence' of the land-poor and landless producers. For the vast majority of officials, glib moral indignation at the behaviour, in other words the survival strategies, of those afflicted offered an attractive way out, combining the maintenance of the social distance between subject and official – and hence confirming their status – with the bureaucracy's obsession with security.

In February 1836 the *Landrat* of Paderborn, von Wolff-Metternich,[53] in office two years at that time, submitted a detailed report in reply to the concern of a colleague, von Hiddessen,[54] over the 'increasing erosion of morals amongst the lower popular classes' in the Warburg district.[55] Although Wolff-Metternich felt that such observations were not overstated, he did not share Hiddessen's fears as far as Paderborn was concerned. The reason: 'poverty has not yet made the same advance'. But Hiddessen was quite right to cite poverty as the root cause: 'Poverty and the increasing undermining of morals march in step together.' 'Indigence' affected not only the 'lower popular classes' but the entire rural population of the region. This regional 'distress' had been the subject of years of 'discussion, argument, writing and negotiation as to the means of its amelioration'. Wolff-Metternich reiterated the causes and the discussion: replacement of the feudal relationship between peasants and lord by Napoleonic or Westphalian legislation and administration; 'nothing has appeared in its place to replace the previous patronage over the peasant'. He added the abolition of compulsory guild membership and the limits on the divisibility or alienability of peasant holdings. 'On the other hand, explanation has also been sought in the increased needs of the rural population, in increased tributes, burdens and taxes.' Many observers regarded the continued obligations or compensation payments due to the feudal lords as excessive in view of the increased taxes demanded by the state. 'And finally the indolence of the peasants has been cited': given failing grain prices 'in the current state of the market', 'arable farming as practised formerly has ceased to be profitable'; a 'fresh impetus' was required. The *Landrat* was evidently thinking of changed methods of cultivation and corresponding peasant initiatives which could be encouraged by the state. Which of these suppositions was correct is impossible to say: Wolff-Metternich inclined to the view that, 'all the circumstances touched on above have contributed towards bringing about the phenomenon of the current distress'. And which one, out of the overall set, was instrumental would depend on local circumstances. Nevertheless, 'peasant landowners' were to be helped, as proposed in suggestions for improving agriculture submitted by a Ministerial commissary.

However, for Wolff-Metternich it was not 'peasant farmers' who were at the heart of the misery but 'lodgers, *Heuerlinge* and day-labourers, etc.' – that is, not property owners but the landless producers who had replaced servant or family labour-power as tenants, leaseholders or wage-labourers (even on peasant plots of less than five hectares). They would not 'derive any direct benefit' from support for the peasantry – a view shared by Hiddessen, *Landrat* in the neighbouring county.

Wolff-Metternich's aim was to advance beyond merely noting the 'impudence' which he saw in the scorn of the peasantry and the 'so-called lesser folk' towards 'police authority'. Although both groups 'suffer indigence to much the same extent', the social differences between them were not to be overlooked. However, his analysis came to an end almost before it got started: by concentrating on 'morality' and emphasising his disgust at its supposed breakdown, Wolff-Metternich denied himself the opportunity of undertaking any serious social investigation.[56] The *Landrat* continued his report with a detailed description of the illegal and anti-police behaviour of these 'lesser folk' without any real attempt to understand the specific situation of lodgers (*Einlieger*) and the *Heuerlinge*.[57] Both lived under quite different circumstances[58] and the situation of *Heuerlinge* in the Delbrück area was different to the situation of those in other parts of the county or in Warburg. Whilst *Heuerlinge* had their own dwelling, and in many cases could lease a plot of land (in Delbrück for a period of one to four years), lodgers were much closer in status to wage-labourers. Such differences were, however, barely noted in official statistics. Moreover, whereas in Paderborn *Heuerlinge* worked mostly as agricultural labourers, in Delbrück and Minden-Ravensberg they tried to support themselves by domestic-industrial weaving and spinning. After 1830 both lodgers and *Heuerlinge* were squeezed by a combination of circumstances which inevitably worsened their already precarious existences: drastically falling earnings, because of the drop in the price of yarn, combined with steeply rising grain prices, together with fewer opportunities of employment for peasants as a consequence of the disastrous crop failures of 1829 and 1830. In the following years domestic-industrial producers enjoyed only brief respite. After the mid 1830s they were gripped once more in the pincer of persistent trade crisis and renewed increases in grain prices.

The fall-off in the market for domestic-industrial spinners marked the beginning of a structural crisis of proto-industry in this region. The simultaneous agricultural distress in the same region, aggravated by poor harvests, also closed off one possible avenue of relief. Official observation of this pressing situation was also generally lacking in acuity. None the less, at a conference of officials, factory owners, merchants and clergy with the *Oberpräsident* to discuss the 'distress of cotters and new peasants' following the 'year of distress', 1831, local officials[59] established that average annual earnings for a *Heuerling* covered only 70–80% of their cash requirements – in Paderborn around 60–70 Thalers. Actions for debt against them had doubled since 1816; in Lübbecke and Herford the increase had been threefold, and in Bielefeld as much as fourfold. There was an unmistakable process of 'advancing immiseration'. The conference participants agreed that, 'the enormous privation, in conjunction with the maximum possible efforts to cover the shortfall through overtime, has long since exceeded its natural limits'.[60] Vincke, the *Oberpräsident*, added in his own hand that, 'in contradiction to the theory, population had increased' not fallen, despite reduced 'means of purchase'.

Recognition of the intense 'self-exploitation' of *Heuerling* families engaged in spinning,[61] and the perplexity of even the most senior officials at the inadequacies of theory, did not, however, encourage them to pay any closer attention to the consequences of the contradiction between theory and the real world. The 'cold light of experience' was admissible only if it reflected the inevitability of a supposedly self-regulating market system. Administrative intervention in the form of encouraging emigration, 'state undertakings' (such as canal- or road-building) to create work, and, in this case, principally the granting of loans for several months to allow production to continue (with a loss for the exchequer)[62] was considered, but seemed incompatible with the 'central axioms of state economic policy'. Such measures would simply have been 'an expensive palliative which would merely drive the problem to its culmination all the more quickly'. However, around a dozen recommendations were accepted which, by improving the quality – and hence probably the profitability – of local products, offered the prospect of raising incomes in the long term rather than mitigating the immediate symptoms of distress.

A number of proposals were made, ranging from the establishment of model farms to suggestions that expeditions be sent to France and Russia to learn more advanced techniques for domestic industry. One proposed revision of the Poor Laws was that areas in which paupers originated should pay for their upkeep, in the hope that this would force them to exercise tighter control over the poor. Finally, the 'army of premature marriages' was to be contained by a lessening of the sanctions against extra-marital pregnancy. However, none of these proposals got very far with Ministers. Interior Minister von Schuckmann saw the situation as no more than a temporary phase of agricultural difficulty which could be dealt with by allocating larger plots: even increased schooling was considered unnecessary.[63]

Four years later the distress had abated somewhat. (The increase in the price of bread grains after the improvement in 1832/3 was evidently gradual.) The shock of the crisis was mere memory, and the scepticism over intervening to 'promote' trade remained intact and undiminished. To this extent, Metternich's perspective also reveals how officials perceived and made use of the experiences of their own officials and predecessors in office (in this case *Landrat* Freiherr von Spiegel). Metternich's report merely adopted the complaints of the propertied, elaborated them a little, and tacked on the specific problems encountered by state officials in implementing their instructions, or in fact getting any kind of hearing at all. The 'impudence' expressed in offences against the laws protecting property and persons was especially galling, and repeatedly brought to the attention of the District Government. Theft from fields, woods and gardens was a particular problem. The *Landrat*'s conclusion – 'One is quite properly asked, "Do we not have any laws which protect against such encroachments on property"?' Although Wolff-Metternich started by facing the complexity of the problems at hand, these were rapidly boiled down to one issue – endangered security. And the appropriate response to this was for the administration to set up its enforcement policing and maintain 'public safety'.

The perspective of the higher authorities: the reaction of the District Government in Minden

Two reports drawn up by *Regierungsräte* in the District Government in Minden in the spring of 1838 give some idea of how this problem was perceived and assessed by officials. The fact that these reports were written as part of an official examination by a candidate for office as *Landrat*, rather than for the ministries in Berlin or as instructions for *Landräte*, makes it probable that they contained everyday thinking on these matters with relatively little camouflage. The candidate was certainly not expected to write in the balanced style required of reports to be transmitted 'upwards' or of official directives.

The candidate, the 27-year-old Westphalian noble von Ditfurth, had been selected as the prime candidate for the vacancy from the County Assembly (*Kreistag*) in Bielefeld. His task was to complete three sets of work within a given time. The first asked for his comments on 'The reasons or lack of reasons behind the concerns which the spinning machines have aroused in Herford as far as the condition of the hand-spinners is conerned'. Winkelmann, the *Regierungsrat* entrusted with the job of assessing this paper, graded it as 'satisfactory' (on account of its brevity, not on any substantive matters) and passed it. He prefaced it with a presentation of his own views on national economy (something omitted by Ditfurth).[64] In fact, noted Winkelmann, 'handworkers had destroyed machines, and statesmen and philosophers had combated them with intellectual weapons'. But was this sanctionable or justifiable? The argument had to begin by considering the 'purpose of all machines'. This was, 'to make products cheaper and more perfectly'. Unquestionably, 'machines rendered human hands unnecessary'. But all the problems that this kindled were resolved for Winkelmann in the conclusion that 'this in fact represented a great step towards the improvement of the social condition'. He cited two reasons: one based on a general argument, but materially incorrect, and one more strictly economic – both, however, seen 'from above'. 'Through the machine we obtain new hands: children and the aged, unreasoning animals and even the elements can now work' (Winkelmann had evidently forgotten the labour of children and the old in domestic industry and in the family economy in general). The second point was taken more seriously however: 'it must be regarded as an increase in national wealth if we are enabled to obtain the same product for less cost as a consequence of machinery'. And for Winkelmann this indicated the general social benefit of the mechanisation of workshops by the proprietors. For, 'the greater cheapness permits greater consumption; one part of the population which was formerly excluded from purchasing the products of human hands is, with lower prices, also able to buy the goods, and their position is hence improved'. This simple economic mechanism was, therefore, sufficient to resolve all the frictions and conflicts arising out of the spread of mechanisation. 'The lower price effects the same result as an increase in well-being.' State interference in property or the free disposition of property owners over their property would therefore be both foolish and unnecessary. And there was a further undeniable gain: 'the other portion of the population which formerly could have commanded access to products by virtue of their greater wealth need only sacrifice a smaller counter-value to obtain the necessaries which have fallen in price'. What they 'save' can be invested or used for increased consumption; at any event, increased employment would be the consequence of the 'improvement in the machine system'. Moreover, state intervention or regulation would encounter a natural limit here, since the 'spirit of human invention will advance, new machines will be invented and old machines improved'.

The rest of the report is taken up with an assessment of Ditfurth's views. Winkelmann disagreed that the actual location of machinery was irrelevant. A factory owner based in Herford could save transport costs and put pressure on the wage-rates of the competing hand-spinners – although one machine was not in a position to make any major change in the market, that is, massively underbid the competing suppliers, the hand-spinners. Both authors had in mind here the 'lower rate' earned by the hand-spinner. Ditfurth and Winkelmann also looked at the possibility of hand-spinners diversifying into more specialist production, though in contrast to the 1832 conference, they regarded the widespread 'concern' raised by machine production as 'very exaggerated'. Although Winkelmann considered it 'advisable' for spinners to shift from coarse to fine yarns, a proposal raised some years previously, he did not support Ditfurth's suggestion that the problem could be dealt with by moving completely out of spinning into weaving. Here Winkelmann revealed his awareness of how the family economy functioned and its connections with agriculture, although his knowledge of the actual process of production was far from adequate. It was incorrect to suppose that weaving, in contrast to spinning, was not carried out by the entire family but only by a few adults. Winkelmann's observation that spinning was practised only as a 'secondary trade' also underestimated its significance for its practitioners' livelihoods.[65] Although he could see some of the factors militating against such a switch, he did not cite them (the lack of working capital for the purchase of a loom would have been a key obstacle, for example). As a consequence, his observations lacked authority and simply provided scarcely concealed evidence of his bafflement; in the eventuality of additional machines being introduced it would be 'good to ponder the introduction with all its difficulties, of other secondary trades'.

The extent to which general welfare was regarded as a product of the nation's wealth, the latter a direct result not of the activities of the direct producters but rather of factory owners, putters-out and merchants, can be seen in the comment which Winkelmann offered on the secondary question of the movement of interest rates. 'Where wages are high, this is often the effect of factories but never the cause of prosperity itself.' That the interests of rising production and growing 'national wealth' required a widening gulf between the lowest possible wages for workers and the increasing purchasing power of the 'proprietors' warranted no mention: 'policial economy' clearly implied the unconditional acceptance of the interests of the factory owners, and their incorporation into officials' own administrative practice.

The spectrum of positions held or considered worthy of discussion was rounded off by the assessment of Ditfurth's second paper, 'Complaints on the impoverishment of the common man' and its possible remedies. The examiner in this instance, *Regierungsrat* Krüger, found fault because – and this is very illuminating – the candidate had confined himself to the issue of the introduction of new machinery in his study of the 'new' poverty, the existence of which had been implicitly recognised in the very question asked of Ditfurth.[66] What Krüger wanted to hear was that the 'deterioration and demise of industry' was attributable to an 'excess of poor and irresponsible masters' together with the 'current inclination of all, including the lower ranks, to harbour pretensions above their station', the 'universal proclivity to luxury beyond the powers of their rank, the decline in morality'. Although Krüger confined himself to making allusions, it was evident that he regarded the introduction of freedom of trade as the root cause of the increase in the numbers of propertyless and their social and economic distress. He failed to see any link between structural changes and cyclical demographic and economic fluctuations which – given the administration's own basic principles – would be either completely beyond the grasp of legislation or administrative action, or only amenable to such within very narrow limits. Nevertheless his recommendation that tight control over the poor in 'pauper colonies' would enable control to be reasserted over the threatening 'developments in marriage, population and welfare' illustrates the extent to which he regarded institutional changes as the ultimate cause of social and economic change.

The conflation of property and security

Despite quite proper reservations about how representative such views may have been, or what influence they may have had over administrative practice, they do reveal how officials avoided differentiating between types of property – at any event, whenever property was felt to be in jeopardy. The division between 'productive' and 'unproductive' property became extremely blurred once 'danger' was sensed. As far as the Prussian bureaucracy was concerned, that 'stability in people and things' identified by the widely read French author Fregier[67] as the state's main contribution to production and 'civilisation' also embraced forms of property which evidently shielded particularist privileges against reform. Once the defence of property was seen as the product of police vigilance, then – given such an elastic interpretation of property – police activity became permissible on behalf of any property title. At the same time, the use of the state by property owners to underwrite their status encouraged an equation of proprietors with 'loyal citizens'. And conversely, official attention became wholly preoccupied with the suspicious and alien behaviour of the 'dangerous classes'. Evident mistrust of the motives and interests of the 'lower popular classes' soon swamped any analytical element in their descriptions of the latter's distress.

There was a clear absence of any perspective able to link the process of economic and social change – advancing capitalist relations of production and exchange – with the movement of population and the requirements of administration. The theses proposed to explain poverty were entirely predictable; complaints about legislative or administrative incompetence and negligence coupled with a moralising fatalism, inevitably confirmed by the 'evil' to be found everywhere in the shape of crimes against property. In comparison, accumulation appeared as an uncompromised and powerful aid, a steady and reliable 'invisible hand'. The support of this mechanism by various means directed against the maliciousness imputed to the propertyless was entirely logical: a demonstrative, emphatic and enforced 'improvement' in which the threat or use of violence inevitably went beyond the status of a mere instrument of discipline.

Taking the side of property in administrative practice, in particular in its form as a 'productive' resource, did not, however, meet with the unconditional approval of all members of 'civil society'. Open criticism was directed at the enforcement of the Poor Laws, which despite their very limited scope were seen as the product of an unnecessary, and possibly dangerous, 'philanthropy'. The main aim of gifts of food, bread or clothing was 'that there should be none in distress'.[68] For David Hansemann this represented the 'most powerful inducement to waste and idleness'. And both of the latter were 'the two vices which most rapidly fashion those subjects of the lower popular classes which endanger the security of society'. The examples considered above are ample proof of the extent of Hansemann's questionable generalisation of the very localised and limited support for the poor, most of which was in fact organised on a communal basis. However, our aim here is not to discuss the actual scale of social provisions for 'the poor'. The point is simply that self-perception of officials, evident or inferred in the instances referred to above, was not necessarily shared by their 'partners'. The logic of 'bourgeois' economics was not enough to establish a complete harmony of interests between the bureaucracy and 'civil society': and even the – in practice – extensive, renunciation of regulatory intervention[69] by the state was not enough to satisfy the representatives of the commercial and industrial bourgeoisie.

Administrative 'honour' and private gain

The distance and 'brusqueness' often criticised by third parties had another side: the 'honour' of the authorities, of their colleagues, their own office and the execution of their duties. And, although this 'honour' of the *Beamtenstand*[70] may have influenced the rigorous pursuit of 'productive', and also private interests, it could not actually oppose them except in instances of blatantly unproductive enrichment. Official pronouncements reflecting the self-image and justification of officials, with their focus on the promotion of the 'common good', were mostly for external consumption by the 'cultivated' amongst the 'administered'. Internally – almost exclusively so – official perceptions of both themselves and outside events were guided by 'honour'. It laid down the ground-rules for everyday conduct both in collegial bodies and in the officials' own chambers. 'Honour' drew its force from the rules of legitimate behaviour, whose unquestioning authority, in turn, was reinforced by their almost incidental and unconscious observance. The 'common good' was rooted in the rationality of market production and circulation, and these provided few reliable touchstones for how officials might conduct themselves on a day-to-day basis. The need to defend the political order and 'state as a whole' also provided meagre assistance in this respect. In contrast to these abstract formulations, 'honour' forged a link between the general objectives and the ordinary everyday life of the official. At the same time, it also expressed an arcanum of the bureaucracy, to which 'vile Mammon' and the principles of trade and commerce were to remain closed. None the less 'honour' was invariably linked with the designs of both individuals and the bureaucratic apparatus as a whole in securing and maintaining power. It was this many-sidedness which secured its instrumental utility as a symbol.

To illustrate how 'honour' worked in practice we consider two related, successive conflicts within a District Government. In contrast to the examples discussed above, these are not taken from the Western Provinces of Prussia but from Oppeln in southeastern Silesia.

A conflict in a District Government: I

In December 1840 a dispute broke out between the *Regierungspräsident* – the District Government President – of Oppeln, Count von Pückler, and the Director of the Department of the Interior, *Oberregierungsrat* Ewald. The affair began when Ewald claimed that Pückler had become entangled in a conflict of interests over a report he had submitted on the Upper Silesian Railway Company's plans for the proposed line of rail in the Breslau–Oppeln–Königshütte area.[71]

The course of events was as follows. In October 1840 the *Oberpräsident*, von Merckel, had instructed the District Government to prepare a report on the proposed railway, a responsibility allotted to them under the 1838 Railways Act. On 9 December, the report was delivered to the plenary session, not by one of the appropriate officials from the Department of the Interior, but by Pückler himself: the report was unanimously accepted and a week later was forwarded to the relevant official for co-signature. Three days later, on 19 December, Ewald submitted a dissenting report containing a number of reservations which had already been communicated orally to Pückler and other officials at the end of the plenary session at which the report had been accepted. The next day Pückler forbade Ewald to report his remarks.

Ewald's reproach was as follows. Despite his personal integrity, Pückler's status as a shareholder in the company concerned, in fact as a member of the management board, had 'restricted, even if unintentionally', his colleagues' 'freedom of decision' when he drafted the report himself: most importantly of all, he had 'without doubt raised suspicion' in the minds of the public. Although there was no suggestion of 'any substantial pecuniary interest', his personal involvement in the railway nevertheless meant that he would always have 'an interest in the issue'. Pückler's considerable engagement and in particular his personal tour of the proposed route and his passing over of *Regierungsrat* Heidfeld, who had been appointed as the competent official on the matter by Ewald, had violated a basic principle established for judicial officials, and which 'had always been observed' by officials in the administration even prior to the reforms, namely, 'in the event of any close or remote interest in a matter or even on account of having advised one party, [officials] should not only not participate in dealing with the matter, but should refrain from exercising a vote'. For Ewald, therefore, the issue turned on the fundamental principles of administration:

> The observation of this principle provides the country with a guarantee that the administration is free both from the substance of any personal influence and any not wholly impartial disinterested decision, and also from even the mere semblance of such.

The general interest of the 'administered' could be appropriately attended to only by a bureaucracy which had no immediate stake in specific, concrete issues. Mere distance alone towards social interests would rule out such problematic involvements. Only then could the 'all-round interests of the province' be properly understood and pursued – not via contact with 'particular' interests and possible individual gain. For Ewald, a long-serving official,[72] the bureaucracy, as the trustee of the 'general interest', had to remain disinterested.

As an experienced tactician, Ewald responded immediately to Pückler's instruction forbidding him to submit a separate report. On 23 December he reported the matter to the *Oberpräsident*, who had no other choice but to call on Pückler to produce a detailed report, thus exposing the issue. On 31 December Pückler drafted a very detailed response, consisting of sixteen double-sided folio pages,[73] additional evidence for the fact that Ewald's action had been seen in both official and personal terms as 'presumptive' and 'improper'.

Pückler made two initial comments: the first on the general procedure and the second on the specific course of events. In the first place, Ewald had appointed Heidfeld as principal official on the matter without the required consultation with Pückler himself, derived from his overall competence for the District Government. Of particular relevance was the fact that Heidfeld had also shown his 'reluctance' and had placed this on file. Pückler had not therefore wished to compromise Ewald by formally recalling the latter's instruction. Moreover, in order to spare Heidfeld he had undertaken the chore himself: Heidfeld's 'infirmity' and the urgency of the matter indicated by the *Oberpräsident* had prompted him to examine the proposed route 'on the spot' on horseback and speak with experts and other interested parties. Pückler's second point on these formalities was more substantial. His report had been unanimously accepted at the plenary meeting, which had included Ewald. Ewald did not seek to dispute or deny this fact. Ewald had only cast a vote against – the only vote against, in fact – on the question of whether he and not the principal official in the matter, Heidfeld, ought to draft the official report. This was the only issue over which Ewald had voiced reservations, and it was these reservations which were subsequently expanded into his 'minority report'. Pückler could quite legitimately claim that the appropriate place for objection, if any, was when the matter was deliberated, in fact when the request for the report on the railway was issued in October. If Ewald wanted to have his decision rescinded, he should have exerted himself then. Pückler could also point to the fact that, with the exception of Ewald's dissent, the vote at the District Government meeting had been unanimous. No member of the government who 'was involved in the railway' left the conference room or waived his vote.

However, as far as the matter in hand was concerned, the accusation of a massive conflict of interests together with an injury to the 'honour' of the entire government college created fresh contradictions. The first could have spoken more for rather than against Ewald's concern – over-eagerness, which was subsequently very difficult to conceal, could have led to Pückler's action. In contrast, Pückler's position was much stronger on the issue of the unanimous acceptance of the report. Whether and in what way the lack of support for Ewald may have derived from the dependency of the *Regierungsräte* on their *Präsident* – a dependency of which everyone was aware – is impossible to say: there may well have been some animus towards a somewhat individualistic departmental director, or indeed annoyance at a tactic which was difficult to understand, if indeed the *Präsident* had merited criticism.

As far as the main issue under dispute was concerned, Pückler had two arguments. In the first place, he neither had nor could he have had a 'particular' interest in the manner insinuated by Ewald, or as set out in the judicial regulations to which Ewald had referred. And, secondly, it could be argued that it was even necessary and desirable for the personal interest of officials in current issues to be sufficiently great for them to be motivated to make such a determined effort on behalf of the 'general' interest.

According to Pückler, he would have had a 'particular' interest only if, for example, the railway was to have been built across his own estates. However, such an unambiguous form of 'quite distinct individual interest' could neither be deduced from his involvement as a shareholder nor from his activity on the railways committee. Even a judge was not to be rejected on the grounds that he owned an estate or 'currently held title to capital'. 'Accordingly, the legislator has made a precise distinction between particular interests and general civic interests.' The ironic aspect of this appeal to legality can be seen in the observation subsequently inserted in the text that it was not until 1838 that a Cabinet Order confirmed that a holder of police jurisdiction, that is an estate owner, was also entitled to conduct proceedings, 'if there was a coincidence of the general with his personal interests'. Whether such evidence of strict adherence to legality in the case at hand is more an index of juridical finesse than proof of any absence of interest must remain questionable on even the more charitable interpretation.

However, the real cause of Pückler's objection and outrage at Ewald's attack was his conviction that the identity of his personal and the general interest was entirely in order. It could, 'not be seen as objectionable and damaging if the personal interests of members of the government very often and very closely are conjoined with the general interest of the country'. Were this so, the latter would be 'more actively and enthusiastically served'. This applied to the issue at hand,

> Since railways are an undisputed necessity of our age, of crucial import for the well-being of the provinces concerned, the companies undertaking their construction are serving the purposes of the government, and ought to expect not opposition but advice, support and alliance.

However, given the general and implicit agreement on this issue, Ewald's impertinent and emphatic conclusion that such a thesis logically implied *mutual* advantage could mean only one thing as far as Pückler was concerned: Ewald wished to harm him personally.

Pückler added a supporting consideration. Would not a generalisation of Ewald's position cripple the government and police administration in general? 'In the case of a police instruction, one would consider only one's own security, in the case of the building of a road one's own comfort in travelling, and in military matters the conscription of one's own sons.' In his 'usual civil circumstances' the official was constantly ultimately involved:

how could these interests be excluded? Pückler provided the answer himself by inverting his rhetorical question:

> No one in our administrative organisation has ever suggested the principle that officials represent a completely isolated caste: on the contrary, their closer association with the nation and the interests of its well-being is never deprecated.

Pückler's deliberation was certainly logical, especially for a 'core of officials' which regarded itself as the trustee of the general interest. If this interest seemed to be coupled with 'national income' such that the 'welfare' of all other 'subjects' and 'citizens' could be augmented only by the increased 'welfare' of the proprietors, especially of the means of production, then it was not merely cynicism or benevolent condescension on the part of Pückler if, as an estate and foundry owner,[74] he 'wished for an estate, or a house, or a share in a mine or a number of factory railway shares for every member of the District Government'. This would achieve two things: in the first place, the 'freshness of experience of life would be retained within the college', and officials would at least have some appreciation of the effects of their own activities. And, beyond this, it would avoid that 'in matters of industrial and intellectual advance, the populace might race ahead of the men who are called on to direct and promote [these advances]'.

Furthering the interests of the propertied in specific instances, at any event if they managed the productive assets gainfully and profitably, and at the same time integrating oneself not only in the social intercourse but also the personal economy of 'civil society' was the quintessence not only of Pückler's position as an individual, but also of his policies as *Präsident*, in company with the overwhelming majority of the college.[75] It seemed quite apparent that not only was there a harmony of interests, but also a compatibility between personal motives and individual, official, and social 'honour'. However, Ewald's critique was required to complete the hermetic circle constituted by this perception of 'general' interests: the policy pursued and defended by Pückler was discussed by Ewald solely in terms of personal and official 'honour'. The social costs of the pursuit of such a policy for a large, if not for the overwhelming, part of the 'administered' did not come into the debate, despite the fundamental character of Ewald's objections.

A conflict in a District Government: II

A fresh conflict between Pückler and Ewald some two and a half years later indicated how the precarious situation of the direct producers could find its way into bureaucratic discourse – at least as long as there was no immediate danger for the maintenance of security. The issue behind the conflict seems almost ridiculous, namely, whether Ewald had reduced and hence falsified the figures from a *Landrat* indicating the number of applications for permits by particular groups of factory workers to travel to Russian or Austrian Poland in the regular reports which in theory went directly to the King (an accusation which Ewald was quickly able to refute).[76] Pückler unleashed nine and a half pages of scornful and triumphant admonition,[77] his pen spurred on at the satisfaction of having caught his subordinate in a supposed act of impropriety. Sparing nothing in the way of verbiage, Pückler informed Ewald that injury to the 'sacred law' of the King and willingness to 'obscure, distort or colour the strictly established truth' was one of the 'most reprehensible acts'. Pückler's retort, although focusing on the violation of both duty and the 'honour' of the college, was clearly primarily intended to even the score between the two combatants. In view of the fact that the issue turned on merely one (!) out of dozens of figures in a report repeated every quarter, Pückler's dramatic tone was so evidently overdone that he subsequently sought to moderate it: he concluded with the sudden observation that he had wished only to give a 'serious but well-intentioned' warning. However, the hurtful effect of this magnanimous gesture was magnified by the fact that he also reported that he had taken steps to avoid more serious problems by interposing a special report of his own.

After rehearsing his gratification at Ewald's offence over a number of pages in which he contended that Ewald's breach of official duty and honour had verged on *lèse majesté*, Pückler finally arrived at the heart of the matter, at the issue which endowed the allegedly falsified figures with such major significance. The reason why Ewald had 'whittled at' the *Landrat*'s figures was evident:[78] the supposed rise in the number of applications for permission to leave the district from smiths, metalworkers and building workers did not fit in with Ewald's scheme of things: it was an index of the growing distress of these groups which was directly related to the contracting markets of the Upper Silesian iron foundries. In turn this crisis[79] was the direct product of the official policy of neglecting tight customs controls.[80] Ewald, who had 'already made up his mind', was a subscriber to this policy, a policy which in Pückler's view 'sacrificed domestic industry to the prevailing tariff system'. Pückler did not attempt to launch a frontal attack on the doctrine of free trade which was sanctioned by the political authorites; he did not for example enlist Friedrich List's arguments for a 'national system of political economy' expounded in 1841. In fact, in seeking to highlight the contrast between himself and Ewald – the disciple of a clearly ruthlessly inhuman 'merely' theoretical construction, namely free trade – he renounced any recourse to theory at all. However, someone had to 'state the price' which the victory of free trade 'would command'. And this price was nothing less 'than the prosperity of Upper Silesia and the state's other smelting districts'. The nub of Pückler's argument, therefore, was that it was not only the entrepreneurs 'or a usurping aristocracy who would have to pay the price', but that the 'people were also being crushed by the wheel of change'. This might be 'replete with blessings' for the 'state as a whole . . . for the customs union' – and he continued, with the undertone of a military commander who permits the advance of the army by sacrificing his own company, that he would not ultimately object to 'sacrificing the province entrusted to me' for a 'great cause'. However, one also had to 'consider the distress of thousands of hungry families' even if one refused them 'sympathy'. Ewald had seen these facts through a 'coloured prism'. In manipulating the figures he had sought to hide the real situation, the increase in distress and the failure or 'costs' of his opinions, not only from himself but also from his superiors.

Ewald naturally disputed this.[81] And he clearly had the advantage in the matter. Pückler's factual error was easily demonstrated – the *Landrat* had in the meantime conceded that the figures had remained unchanged for four years. At the least there was no provable increased pressure occasioned by greater distress to emigrate to Russian or Austrian Poland.[82] And Ewald did not seek to question the distress suffered by many families, in his view exacerbated by the state of the market.[83] However, he countered that 'artificial barriers to commerce' would not achieve anything. And it was also clear whom Ewald regarded as the main beneficiaries of a protected iron industry: the 'large landowners and a few big speculators who seek to tax the fatherland only for their benefit and enrich themselves yet further'.

Pückler sought to present himself as the sober empiricist who had no intention of becoming embroiled in a dispute with a theoretician lost in abstractions and fantasies, even when this theoretician went so far as to draw conclusions from sheer 'coincidences' and 'thin air'.[84] In a way, quite modestly, he was seeking only to assert the 'here and now': that is the distress and poverty of the victims as against global and long-term perspectives. As a consequence he had, for example, applied for monies for road construction to provide relief work. Of course, Pückler's engagement has to be set against the background of the railway conflict. Whereas in 1840 Ewald had pursued the question of illegitimate private interests, Pückler now saw his chance to reproach Ewald for the absence of any interest – despite his claims – for others and in particular for the poor. In contrast, Ewald had raised a dilemma which, for example, the 'assessments' of the Minden *Regierungsräte* had simply ignored.[85] Whereas they had made the cheapening of products solely dependent on increased production, Ewald posed the question – to use modern terminology – of market power. A heavily protected iron industry would be nothing more than an artificial 'forcing-house growth', able to flourish only at the expense of the 'consumers'.[86]

Discounting what was, for Ewald, the 'embittering tone' of Pückler's reprimand, the personal confrontation between these two officials – who must have had to encounter each other daily in the same building – represents a personification of the conditions of action which were evidently typical for the bureaucracy: the conflicting interests of the entrepreneurial, but at the same time very articulate proprietors, and their own administrative 'habitus'. This 'habitus' constituted the tangible expression and demonstrative self-confirmation of the commitment to a given 'order', and to the 'lawfulness' and 'legitimacy' of the official's own conduct.

The opportunities for the bureaucratic apparatus to decipher and deal with the 'cases' on its files as indices of social problems existed at a number of different and overlapping levels. More concretely, there were two possible interpretations of the social and human 'costs' of the spread of capitalist relations. On the one hand, the situation could be seen as an unavoidable, but limited, period of distress: eventually, if not quite soon, the developments at the root of the problem would yield an increase in welfare for all. Alternatively, distress and misery could be attributed to more specific causes and individual or group failures and weaknesses – although this argument, with its implication that there was always one or more 'guilty party', was appropriate only for specific and isolated situations. Pückler freely conceded that even if alternative policies were pursued – protectionism in this case – an unavoidable stagnation of trade could trigger a comparable level of distress.

Although such a perspective might permit the consideration of measures for the support of those who 'had to foot the bill' (to use Pückler's expression) in the form of extreme distress, such a policy was logical. Any conception which went beyond short-term temporary relief, donations of bread or potato seed, and at most the construction of roads or fortifications, represented a departure from the paths of traditional and strict patriarchal 'concern', especially in its arrogant Junker form.[87] Not only did such ideas have virtually no chance of being realised; they were also given a scant hearing.

In the autumn of 1843 the economic situation of the Silesian linen-weavers, who had been under massive pressure since 1838, deteriorated still further in the two other Government Districts in the province. *Oberpräsident* von Merckel, and the overwhelming majority of the *Regierungsräte*, ignored the distress until the early part of 1844. And officials continued to rule out any measures which might have encouraged the suspected 'idleness' and 'indolence' of those affected, even after the 'excesses' of June in which the better-off wool-weavers of Langenbielau and Peterswaldau had participated in episodes of machine-breaking. As far as the District Government in Breslau was concerned, profits earned by the capitalists would soon enable them to pay the weavers and spinners an appropriate wage. The changes in the class taxation system demanded by the latter, the adjustment of the trade tax (a reduction of the tax which was levied after the third loom), or the demand for the establishment of independent display offices came to nothing. Unperturbed, officials at both province and ministry level appealed to the principle of economic 'self-help'.

The attempt to induce merchants and producers in the Silesian linen-weaving districts to switch from the merchant-system (*Kaufsystem*) to putting-out (which offered the producers a little more security) was left to the initiative of a single official, von Minutoli. This was tolerated by the Ministry: however, by refusing to grant additional support, the Ministry effectively relegated him to the status of an outside observer of events, with Minutoli's colleagues following his activities with at best bemused astonishment or encouraging, but largely meaningless, exhortations.[88]

'The promotion of trade' found its counterpart in the 'Poor Law Police' (*Armenpolizei*). Both were envisaged as localised and immediate emergency measures. As long as both propertied and propertyless regarded economic success, that is sheer survival, as dependent on individual will, any relief measures were suspected of seducing those in distress into continuing indolence, rather than helping them. Administrative suspicion, well spiced with 'state economy' was, as indicated above, by no means directed solely at those lacking in means of employment. In the view of the administration, state support for the poor relieved the proprietors of the need to spend money on wages, with the cost being borne by the tax-paying citizenry.[89]

Such an interpretation therefore systematically obscured any question of 'tackling' the social conditions and consequences of pauperism and proletarianisation by means of what, in contemporary terms, would be termed 'social policy'.[90] In fact, no clear or consistent approach emerged in any way equal to the human problems created by the crisis of family production and domestic industry, and the uneven and gradual spread of wage-labour in both agriculture and industrial production.

Official 'honour': internal discipline – external distance

Both Ewald's criticisms in the railway affair and Pückler's accusation over the passport figures raised doubts as to the demarcation between the interests of officials. The issue around which these mutual recriminations turned was the injured 'honour' of those involved, of their profession and rank, and of officialdom in general. Of course, initially both opponents made good use of rhetoric. But the way in which such flourishes were used suggests that this malleable tool also simultaneously enabled them to express the special 'status' of officials – their unique mode of interpretation – in relation to their social situation.

In the railway affair, the 'point of honour' clearly allowed senior officials to pursue an evasive strategy: and, as the conflict developed, they sought to confine discussion solely to this aspect.

After stingingly rebuking Ewald for his lack of discretion, in late January 1841 *Oberpräsident* von Merckel passed the matter on to the Minister of the Interior, who lent every protection to Pückler and Merckel. The affair had no direct consequences for any of the parties involved and the route was eventually sanctioned on 24 March 1841.

'Honour' brought together 'private' and 'public' evaluation – and combined the commitment to 'service', both in the external sense (civil service law) and as internal compulsion, with the prestige of the institution. However, achieving a balance between compulsion and self-motivation which was tolerable to all the members of the institution necessitated a number of stabilising rules. The main purpose of such rules was to elicit demonstrative but unobtrusive respect in daily encounters between colleagues. The 'honour' of superiors required them to behave with 'decent restraint and consideration'. Subordinates in turn had to act 'in a seemly and modest manner'.[91] In the view of the ministers responsible for service discipline, each would then present to the other 'an example of proper self-control'.

'Honour' as an implicitly accepted code of behaviour served both to create social distance between officials and the outside world and to establish discipline within the service between superior and subordinates. In the railway dispute, 'honour' was primarily used as an internal regulative: and for

Pückler it was seen exclusively as such in the passport figures affair of 1843. During the clash over the railway route, senior officials regarded honour as being endangered not by any particular interests of Pückler in the matter, but rather by Ewald's attempt to bring his superior to book. But bolstering the hierarchy from within also meant protecting the hierarchy from external questioning, in this case by not undertaking any revision to Pückler's report. It was immaterial whether the *Oberpräsident* may have considered Pückler's activities to be a little dubious: the latter had not gone beyond the point at which the internal cohesion and prestige of the authorities would have been directly jeopardised by 'blatant' individual enrichment.[92]

Pückler's action in 1843 over the passport and tariffs issue demonstrates how 'honour' could be used to intimidate subordinates. However, in this instance collegial 'honour' had not been endangered by the supposed high-handedness of an official towards those in distress. Had this been so, the *Präsident* may have felt himself obliged to draw direct conclusions; for example, by requesting the Minister to issue an official caution and to warn the uncomprehending subordinate. What set the mechanism for the defence of 'honour' in motion was not any failure to appreciate the extent of the distress but a purely formal matter – an allegedly incorrect figure. Although this may have touched on questions of technical competence, or moral evaluation, it had no connection with the institutional and disciplinary 'honour' demanded by office.

Of course, 'honour' was not merely a synonym for discipline. It reflected a consciousness of the tasks required of the bureaucracy: the promotion of the 'common good', unremitting 'service' in the face of sceptical or stinging public and official commentary, and in the face of humiliation at the hands of one's superiors in a context of jealousies, rancour and intrigues by subordinates and between fellow members of the same collegial body.

The 'honour' expected, apportioned and divided within the core of the officials did not merely allow the 'internal face' of the hierarchy to be rendered more tolerable. In individual cases it also served as a decisive counterweight to the unreasonable demands of superiors – for example, as in the deep-rooted dispute between the *Präsident* and his deputy in the government of Arnsberg in the 1820s.

At any event, concern to maintain honour offered an unassailable form in which to establish some equivalence in a potentially highly conflictual relationship with one's superior. An official reprimand could provide such an occasion: for example, Pückler's reprimand of Ewald in July 1839. Ewald was called upon 'both amicably and urgently to turn his hand to achieving a more prompt and exact administration of affairs than previously'.[93] Pückler considered that Ewald often took on more than he could cope with and at the same time burdened the Chancellery with considerable amounts of copying work (such as complete volumes of general records or official gazettes for his personal use). Most of all, the delays which Ewald's behaviour caused had the embarrassing consequences that carelessness on the part of younger officials, for example of two young *Assessoren*, could not be reprimanded with sufficient force. Pückler considered that Ewald had accepted the admonition with 'openness and lack of prejudice'; at any event this is how he recorded his impression.

On the other hand, a subordinate's appeal to collegial 'honour', in this instance the admonished Ewald, offered a medium through which to articulate and defend the dignity and worth which these officials in turn claimed for themselves – if merely by rendering the aggrievement visible. In subsequent years the *Präsident* constantly found occasion to reprimand Ewald for his slovenly and careless organisation of work, his deliberate falsification of instructions, and unwarranted 'dogmatism'.[94] Ewald also strayed beyond the limits of accepted discipline when, in April 1844 without cause, he snapped at *Regierungsrat* Bauer, a member of his department, in front of his colleagues on the grounds that Bauer had allegedly bypassed his authority. The Ministries responsible for service discipline (the Interior Ministry and the Finance Ministry), to which both protagonists turned together with the *Präsident*, rewarded Ewald with a 'serious censure' on the ground that he had 'also caused annoyance to the college'.[95] Only the lower grade and less senior Bauer was transferred, although Pückler would have liked to have them both out of 'his' government.

'Honour' may well have been of particular significance to Ewald's sense of self-worth, given his circumstances. Aged 55 at the time of these conflicts, he had been in service as an official for 35 and a half years and regarded himself as a man 'who had grown grey, with honour, in the service of the state'. Beginning as an *Auskultator*, he had been in service in one District Government since 1805, with a brief interruption for voluntary military service between 1813 and 1815, and discharge as a captain in the *Landwehr* (Home Guard) in 1824. Although his career was above average, it was not extraordinarily so. In 1831, at the age of 46, he became one of three *Oberregierungsräte* and Director of a Department in Königsberg.[96] In this capacity he was transferred in 1838 to Oppeln, where Pückler, seven years his junior, had been *Präsident* for three years. However, this move did represent a promotion. He became leader of Department I (the Administrative Police) and obtained the salary appropriate to a director, for which he had been pressing for several years. Ewald belonged to that small group of well-thought-of and promoted officials – both as regards position and salary – but who none the less held only the lowest of the permitted decorations for his rank, awarded admittedly more swiftly than his predecessor in Oppeln; this was the Order of the Red Eagle, 4th class.[97] As far as his family circumstances were concerned, the personnel files state: 'married, father of four living children, of which none is maintained, without means'. The injury to his honour experienced by Ewald should not be overstated. He was still able to remonstrate with the *Präsident* on the latter's overhastiness over the passport and tariff question. Ewald became increasingly unwell during the 1840s, suffered from gout, and died aged 64 in 1849, in service, a few days before the 'March Events' in Berlin.

'Disinterested' officials: on the balance of 'property' and 'honour'

Oberregierungsrat Ewald was very much the embodiment, not least for his superior Pückler, of that type of official who was under attack from many sides, including the leading representatives of both the socially dominant and socially aspirant classes. Freiherr vom Stein's critique, based on a conservative, rural and rank-conscious perspective, conforms very substantially to the critique made by David Hansemann some 20 years previously (Hansemann being one of the leading members of the Rhenish upper bourgeoisie). In Stein's view, the officials were:

> salaried . . . bookish, living in a world of letters or the realm of their files, disinterested, since they have no connection with any of the classes constituting the state, they represent a caste for themselves, a caste of scriveners: propertyless, that is unmoved by any of the movements of property . . . taxes may rise or fall, traditional rights can be destroyed or perpetuated . . . the entire peasantry can be reduced to beggary . . . it does not disturb them: they draw their salary from the state and scribble, scribble, scribble in the calm behind the firmly shut doors of their offices, unknown, unnoticed, unhonoured, raising their children to be the same writing machines, and then die – unmourned.[98]

Such a damning judgement was wrong on one score, however. Lack of disposition over 'property', be this manorial or estate in nature, may have favoured cautious scepticism towards the special pleadings of the traditional landowning class. But it did not imply general passivity or apathy on the part of the bureaucracy. The reduction or abolition of constraints on trade and property seemed to have their origins in the actions of disinterested officials, and this made any concomitant 'costs' more acceptable to those agrarian or industrial proprietors whose interests were negatively affected by these changes.

Within the bureaucracy, the issue was not simply one of varying degrees of activity or inactivity, or of degrees of acuteness in their perception of events. The crux was the emergence of *alternative* principles of 'statecraft' for the promotion of productive resources and their subordination to commercial exchange. That such an alternative was not resolved in principle, or once and for all, but on a case-by-case basis is also evident from the consideration of the examples cited. The bureaucracy was not a single party: rather it existed as several, fluctuating parties. At the same time, it is clear that the articulation and resolution of this conflict amongst those who were active participants in the administrative formulation of the 'common good' remained highly constrained by an overriding common motivation – not to do anything to disrupt the delicate configuration of 'constitution', 'property', and honour'.

The examples clearly show that the options and actions of officials cannot be explained merely by reference to their individual ownership of wealth or property. The pursuit of interests, the pattern of perception and interpretation of senior officials was not formed in such a mechanical way.

'Property' had a central meaning for the entire social group of the 'bureaucracy' irrespective of their own individual ownership of property or holdings of wealth. The dutiful attendance to property in innumerable individual instances, and in particular the defence of property through very tangible police intervention gave an obvious outward signal of the maintenance of a functioning 'order' and effective legal norms under the 'rule of law'. At the same time, the protection and promotion of the 'profitability' of property seemed to offer the only chance for augmenting 'national wealth': and this allowed a link to be established with the notion that in the final analysis the processes of accumulation and mobilisation would automatically come to benefit the non-proprietors too.

The modes of perception and conduct of officials cannot therefore be reduced either solely to a desire to establish and expand the power and status of the bureaucracy, or to the direct consequences of economic imperatives. The first has to be complemented by the second, and in the process itself undergoes considerable qualification and constraint. In turn, if we consider the contradictory aspects which 'property' represented for some, if not many, officials, the second point also appears to be too generalised and hence not cogent. Once again, an appreciation of how interests were perceived and linked in concrete instances is central. And any investigation of such instances has to include some consideration of the 'inner lining' of social relations, even though these do not appear exclusively in the form of 'interests': that is the constant, everyday inculcation and impregnation of individual and collective experience, the 'colouring' of the perception of the world, and of both individual and collective honour.

The protection of property as the defence of order

For Prussian officialdom, the uneven emergence of a market-orientated economy stood under two watchwords: 'property' was to be defended, more particularly cultivated; and, at the same time, 'public quiet, security and order' had to be maintained. Each orientation in turn had two aspects. Whilst 'property' also included disposition over traditional privileges – that is, it had to attend to the interests of members of two models of social order – administrative concern for 'public security and order' combined the implementation of a quickening of economic activity (not only for the proprietors) with the defence of a 'regulated' inequality. Such a perspective envisaged the liberation and facilitation of individual powers of disposition with the unfolding of a 'civil' society in which matters would precede above all in a 'civilised' and 'morally appropriate' manner.

The functional utility of the central concept of 'order' was also displayed in another field: the long-term perspective that increased production at the instigation of the owners of the means of production was indispensable for the subsistence and possibly even for the long-term improvement of the position of the non-owners. But besieged by the quarrels and squabbles of everyday life, such an abstract prospect did not provide adequate motivation for the official's own activity. For deciding on the running issues of the day, the daily additions to the files, a readily available set of concrete and accessible rules of perception and behaviour as modes of interpretation proved an indispensable element in both personal and institutional stability. Not only was such an indisputable regulative mechanism necessary for the establishment of internal predictability within the bureaucracy, but also for the establishment of the claim to domination externally, that is, domination over the 'administered' – irrespective of the class to which they might belong. However, in the case of contacts outside the bureaucracy, appeal to 'public order' could also draw strength in the short-term from a directly obvious means of communication: its drumming in through the use of brute force.

However, more delicate means were required for internal discourse. In this sphere, the system of individual and 'official' honour relieved the tension which was the inevitable accompaniment of a simultaneous commitment to both the 'successful' promotion of welfare and property, and a concern with security. 'Honour' allowed a balance to be drawn between the interests of the apparatus, that is, in the first instance the interests of senior officials, and the distanced and not infrequently frosty collegial atmosphere of the everyday running of an office. An unstable equilibrium emerged between institutional exactions and the personal ambitions of the 'servants of the state'. As far as 'honour' was concerned, wealth – as an instrument of unrestrained enrichment – was unacceptable. The title to property had to symbolise economic activity, not only announcing a fundamental postulate for respect and security, but obliging its holder to daily self-exertion. If the behaviour of the proprietors could be brought into some form of consonance with this regulatory code (and its self-fulfilling prophecy), not only would relief, and from time to time direct subsidies, be justified to their establishments: such a step would also legitimate police and judicial intervention to secure the 'right' to disposition over property from violations.

The appropriateness of such a pattern of perception and practice was proved in the utility it possessed for both administrators, members of the entrepreneurial bourgeoisie and the Junker estate owners. Proprietors could sleep easy in the knowledge that state violence would in general rush to their aid when required without too many ifs and buts. And, for the administration, direct physical 'policing' offered an opportunity to render their claim to be in command of events plausible both to themselves and to the 'subjects'.

Christian Garve, the Breslau *Popularphilosoph* and perceptive social commentator, summed up this self-discipline imposed by the mystification of 'property', 'honour' and the 'common good' in an essay written in 1792. He noted that in bourgeois society, people were taught to 'regard all attacks on the life or property of the individual citizen as, in essence, attacks directly on the entire polity'.[99]

This process, through which customary feudal-aristocratic, traditional urban 'Burgher' and plebeian rights over property ownership and its 'just' use were undermined and dismantled by the fiscal and military apparatus of the *ancien régime* 'state', was often driven forward by the direct application of force. The civil and military 'servants of the state' who directed this process of accommodation and adjustment were not external to it, however: they were, and remained, subjected to it themselves and became cast in its mould.

4

The organs of coercion at work

The police dominion

Regulations and 'discretion'

The task of promoting the 'common good', which officials considered peculiarly their own, proved highly complex in practice. Administrative activity had two main focal points: the first was the establishment and advancement of unfettered power over 'property'; the second, the enforcement of 'public quiet, order and safety'. These two objectives, and official perceptions of them, frequently overlaid and obstructed each other 'in the real life of the state' (see Marx, 'Critique of Hegel's Philosophy of Law'). 'Property', in particular, remained an ambiguous and amorphous concept. In comparison, the pursuit of 'order' fostered a degree of unanimity: any differences or contradictions between ruling groups seemed trivial when set against the gulf which separated them from the bulk of the 'propertyless'.

State patronage of property encountered a number of obstacles. The classes and groups which owned and controlled capital and means of production did not always share the same interests; in fact, on occasions, their interests were mutually exclusive. Moreover, attempts by the bureaucracy to remove 'impediments to free movement' on behalf of the owners of the productive forces – for example, the freeing of land from its traditional obligations and its conversion into capital – inevitably involved human labour-power. And, despite the justification that distress was essential to stimulate economic activity and maintain social discipline, the Poor Laws nevertheless required that the 'deserving' poor at least should be offered relief.

The constant constraints on daily administrative routine were tightened still further by the memories of near, and only narrowly averted, state bankruptcy during the years of 'foreign rule' (1807–13) and the fiscal crisis which persisted into the 1840s. Many officials were caught between the contradictory demands of providing 'welfare' without expending scarce resources, and – most important of all – without unwittingly removing the disciplinary effect of an insecure existence. Their solution to this dilemma was not only to provide the most meagre level of relief, but to ensure that it was disbursed in the most selective and 'authoritarian' way possible.

Two further constraints on the promotion of free property were directly related to the character and particular features of the state apparatus. In the first place, the civilian bureaucracy was frequently obstructed by the universally visible and omnipresent military. However, the army was not simply a fortuitous presence, the product of political fancy. It symbolised the logic of the social and political edifice of the 'Old Prussia' of the eighteenth century, where it simultaneously served to absorb the surplus sons of the Junkers, drill its recruits into a prophylactic social discipline, directly discipline the 'subject' peasantry, and finally establish the position of the nation within the European 'concert of powers'. This external political role was given a boost by the wars of 1813–15. Although the social and economic bonds between the army – the officer corps – and the agrarian sector became looser in the wake of capitalist development, specifically the transformation of land into capital and the increased entry of bourgeois into the Junker class, the character of the state apparatus continued to be dominated by the habitus and pretensions of the 'feudal aristocracy'. The army itself also preserved these values, and in fact proved to be *the* crucial prop to Junker claims to power, especially via the medium of the state's policing activities. Urban property owners' freedom over their property was widely overridden, especially in the citadel towns. And the military intervened to direct the use of labour-power without any regional or local limitation.

However, any complete and unconditional alliance between the state administration and entrepreneurial interests would inevitably have collided with 'official honour'. Although the self-perception and demeanour of officials allowed them to intervene on behalf of commercial interests to avoid 'imminent damage' and remove 'impediments to the free movement' of property, a direct correlation between bourgeois-capitalist and official maxims and conduct remained taboo. Even the suspicion of any such 'convergence' had to be avoided.

Such a static depiction of the diverse interests and rules of perception and conduct cannot, of course, do justice to the conflicts and dynamics inherent in the position of public officials, some of which were revealed by the comments of individuals outside, and possibly opposed to, the administration. In the early 1830s, the Commanding General of the Corps of Guards, Duke Carl zu Mecklenburg – one of the sternest counter-revolutionaries in Prussia – observed with some satisfaction that, following the July revolution in France and the struggle for independence in Belgium, 'the revolutionary storm' had created a favourable climate within which social and political power could be reapportioned, and the aristocracy and army no longer marginalised, despised, or ignored.[1] The 'dramatic changes' had shaken both bourgeois and the state officials out of their 'indolent slumbers':

> The anarchist sirens in some parts of Germany, which had posed a threat to property, awoke an anxiety for their own possessions should similar circumstances ever come to pass [as had prevailed in France in 1830] . . . Admiration diminished, applause fell silent, and the mood of the country appeared propitious.[2]

Irrespective of the form in which the non-propertied raised their demands, the General regarded the use of direct, primarily military, force against such agitation as the tactic of first resort. Exhibiting considerable prophetic abilities he observed that, 'only material force will defeat theories which have become practical reality'. Such theories were 'like a predatory animal which having once tasted blood can never be tamed, only subdued'. Within the thoroughly materialistic perception of this deliberately reactionary military man, the defence of property offered a common objective around which the powerful and influential could come to a mutual arrangement, and which fully coincided with the preservation of the social order in general.

As far as the years after 1807 were concerned, the General undoubtedly overestimated the degree of discrepancy between bourgeois and administrative interests (and perspectives) on the one hand, and those of the Junker-military class on the other. The defence of title to property, and its material foundations, had already begun to function as the central operational principle of the state in 1789 as a reaction to the French revolution – leaving aside those qualitative changes in the concept of property raised in Chapter 3 above. The police-administration, which was entrusted with the task of establishing and maintaining state and local political rule 'prior to' or 'below the threshold' of an open revolutionary challenge, was also fully aware of the need for 'official attendance' to the 'everyday requirements of public safety and well-being'.[3] The advancement of the 'common good' through economic and social 'mobilisation' – the freeing of property – necessarily entailed both the safeguarding of property and the defence of particular forms of social intercourse. In short, 'order'. If officials 'on the spot' set out to guarantee, frequently to enforce, that 'stability in persons and things' which facilitated 'human industry' and 'civilisation',[4] not only could they count on the approval and encouragement of their superiors, but could also win the 'respect and trust . . . of the better part of the population', or the 'administered'.[5] The counterpart to the free movement of capital and commodities, as the motor force of social activity, was not some parallel unlimited free movement for labour but, first and foremost, strict discipline and unswerving obedience to any and all instructions issued by the authorities.

The breadth of policing was reflected in the extensive repertoire of 'legal means of enforcement and punishment' available.[6] Those 'servants of the state' entrusted with the task of policing were quite expressly granted a 'freer and less constrained procedure' than the judiciary.[7] Even local town and village constables were enjoined 'to act not simply by rote but to exercise independence and discretion'.[8] Such 'discretion' not only embraced the initiation of directly violent action against the population in the form of the 'restraining' repression of suspected or actual 'disorder', misdemeanours, or crimes. The 'enlightened' doctrine of police-administration also prescribed a policy of preventive obstruction.[9] Everyday police practice managed to combine these two elements into a procedure embracing both repressive and 'anticipatory' elements. That the line between the two was far from clear must have been a matter of indifference to those on the receiving end.[10] For the 'administered', the central concern was the way in which the distrustful vigilance of officers, physical violence, repression and preventive action reinforced each other. The prime targets for this 'official attendance' were the 'lower popular classes', the 'worst elements' in society' and the aim was to 'instil fear in them, and thereby detect and prevent a large number of crimes'.[11]

In comparison, the focus of the political or 'higher security' police – the control of 'public opinion' and, after 1819, the 'pursuit of demagogues' – was narrow in scope: its prime targets were mostly small rebellious groups and a few, generally well-known, academic bourgeois figures.[12] Although the 'secret police' could be severe and even brutal on occasions, their activities were never directed against an entire social class, against an 'estate'.

Local police officers were primarily concerned with one particular type of criminality. For Fregier, echoing a widely held and uncontroversial sentiment, the 'essence of crime' was 'always a forbidden action against the property of another', in comparison to which 'an attack on their person' was only an 'occasional' incident.[13]

Everyday police work consisted of two tasks: firstly, the identification of 'dangerous persons', and, secondly, their constant supervision and control. Those most suspected of not being entirely committed to the idea that the 'prime and pressing need of the entire population'[14] was the protection of property by the state were the propertyless – irrespective of any finer distinction within this group. Not only was the 'security police', in the strict sense, to serve as the 'good', or rather guilty, 'conscience outside of the individual'[15] for this majority of the population; this role was also to be fulfilled by the entire 'internal administration' (Lorenz Stein, *Handbuch der Verwaltungslehre*). What was threatening in such an atmosphere was less the prospect of continuous supervision and control than 'arbitrary violence',[16] the unpredictable combination of observation, surveillance and intervention in which those at the receiving end could only wait and hope that their treatment would be civil, rather than violent, in nature.

One dramatic, but not untypical, instance occurred in Cologne in the late summer of 1830.[17] According to local residents, on 31 August the local Inspector of Police, Schoening, 'quietly and calmly called on a large crowd of alley-lads and numerous onlookers to disperse', apparently successfully. However, both the inspector and his colleagues revealed a different face the next day. According to a *Bürgerwehr* patrol, 'the behaviour of the police was quite different to that of the day before, and stood in stark contrast to the mellowness' previously shown, or instructed, by *Polizeipräsident* von Struensee. 'There was no more talk of quiet, calm persuasion: the crowd was charged with fixed bayonets and rifle butts. Officers chased them with sabres drawn and the *Präsident* himself set about the populus with a staff.'

The local police and their field of action

The rules and maxims which guided police perceptions and conduct 'on the spot' can be fully understood only by considering the unique position of the local agents of the police.[18] The lowest rank of *Polizeidiener*, the constables,

1 Superintendent of Police, Berlin, *c.* 1830

(also termed 'sergeants' in those few towns in which the police were directly administered by the central state authority, such as Berlin or Cologne) were initially recruited from invalided soldiers. After 1834, the numerous complaints about their lack of physical fitness led to around half their number being drawn from the ranks of 'well-served' men with nine years' military service. However, the transition from military to civilian duties was not always a smooth one. In 1840, the District Government in Münster expressed concern that some non-commissioned officers, released from the military with a 'pension ticket', 'frequently neglected their morals' in the intervening period prior to their appointment with the civilian police. Three cases were investigated in 1839: one led to a loss of pension, and another to a year's confinement in a house of correction.[19] Permanent appointment by the *Landrat* or, in some of the larger towns, by the municipal executive (*Magistrat*) followed after a six-month probationary period. Costs were borne by the local parish or municipality.[20] Police officers who were awarded a permanent appointment then had the prospect of a permanent money income which, although modest, was insulated from the vagaries of the trade cycle.

The 40 Thalers a year earned by lower-grade police officers in Neuss in 1834, or the minimum of 70–100 Thalers set in Hamm as early as 1823 were barely enough to support a wife and children. Although higher than the incomes of domestic industrial producers, they were scarcely more than that of wage-labourers in reasonably steady work. Police officers could, however, expect some supplementary payments: 15 Thalers for their outfit, or 12 Thalers for supervising the local market (agreed in Schwelm in 1844), or bounties for the number of beggars apprehended (as in Berlin). Extra money could be earned by serving as a crier for private announcements, offering riding lessons (as in Iserlohn in 1850), or if the officer's wife ran a small shop. These lowest-ranking officers were often the only police presence.[21] In larger towns, such as Hagen, with *c.* 4,500 inhabitants in 1840, there were two officers, whilst industrial centres, such as Iserlohn, generally had three after the 1830s. In 1854, of the three officers in Iserlohn, the largest town in the Arnsberg Government District with a local economy based on proto-industrial small-scale iron manufacture, one was 63 years old (having first taken up his appointment at the age of 61!), one 41 and the youngest 34. Although the supervising *Landrat* regarded the latter as the only fully able-bodied officer, he was blessed none the less with 'weak mental powers'. The 41-year old was the sole officer fit for all duties, and had the additional virtue of 'always being sober'.[22] Although lower-grade officers had to demonstrate an ability to read and write, their skills in this field did not usually match the demand for official records and reports: as a consequence, the written element of their duties was kept to a minimum. It is the extent of this weakness rather than the fact itself which is surprising. Writing with amicable restraint in the 'Preliminary Report' to the first issue of the *Polizei-Archiv*, one of the first specialist police journals, the publisher noted:

> Some police officers, either through lack of appropriate education or practice, are utterly unprepared and therefore frequently unable to fully grasp quite clear instructions. Lacking any grounding in the concepts assumed by the educated drafters of laws and service regulations, they cannot discern their purpose.[23]

As long as the structure of local government remained unchanged – that is, as long as the financial burden on parishes and municipalities remained undiminished[24] – all attempts to achieve greater professionalisation through better pay, training, or the provision of more posts were condemned to failure. Despite some attempts by the District Governments responsible, nothing changed in the 'occasionally unfavourable circumstances of many police officers, who are expected to carry out their duties incidentally, without adequate time for them'.[25]

Not surprisingly, occasional proposals for a more stringent assessment of personnel in accordance with their performance – which would have implied retirement on grounds of invalidity or old-age for many of the more fragile officers – made little progress. Apart from the financial limitations, there were also worries that the reliability and loyalty of future appointees might be jeopardised by the prospect of an uncertain future.

The economic and social dependency of lower-grade officers on their superiors, mayors or bailiffs, and additionally on the compliance and 'interest in safety' of the 'better element' had its counterpart in typical complaints of negligence against the police.[26] The interests and attitudes of local ruling groups could also be seen in the spiteful treatment meted out to candidates for police posts. In one instance, in Iserlohn in 1838, the Town Assembly sought to frustrate the appointment of one officer. Although the candidate had 'conducted himself in a proper and orderly manner' during his six-month probationary period, local councillors were reluctant to appoint him because of his 'previous moral conduct' – a matter not specified in any more detail. The District Government in Arnsberg eventually threw out this apparently highly irregular and unprovable surmise and confirmed the appointment some two months after the original date.[27]

A typical day's duties convey some impression of life as a police *Offiziant* 'from the inside': 'attendance at the Mayor's parlour', constant readiness for duty, including supervising the transport of prisoners, delivering the occasional cuff to the 'administered', and dealing with complaints, for example from school pupils from 'good families' who had been arrested for throwing snowballs. Remarkably, many officers stayed in office for decades.

Iserlohn, for example, with 11,295 inhabitants in 1846, had three constables. In the 1820s the Mayor had pleaded that the two officers then in service 'were barely able to keep up with their duties at the Town Hall'[28] in what 'is acknowledged as a not unimportant factory town', their urgent priority being 'constant supervison' of the town's streets. The Mayor approached the local *Landrat*, Müllensiefen, and tried to convince him to release 24 Thalers to bring an officer out of retirement: after some vacillation, the *Landrat* gave his permission in 1824.

According to the 1843 'Standing Orders',[29] the three officers operating in the town after 1838 were to rotate duties on a daily basis: 'guard duty', 'watch', 'notification of official pronouncements by hand-bell', 'attendance' at the Town Hall, and 'attention to summonses, messages, and petitions with all their associated routine'. Each officer spent one day on watch, one as town-crier and deliverer of summonses, and the third attending the Mayor and delivering messages. If one was ill, the other two had to step in to ensure that the absentee's duties were performed. However, officers also developed some practices to ease the burden. Especially difficult or disagreeable tasks were postponed and ultimately forgotten about. Such methods did not really reduce the officers' dependency on instructions issued by the Mayor, their sole superior. For example, having decided that the duty-record was not being submitted for scrutiny with sufficient regularity and that the evening patrol of public houses was either too sloppy or not even carried out at all, the Mayor issued orders that public houses were to be inspected every evening between 8 and 9 o'clock, after which officers then had to report to him at home.[30] Duty was also required on Sundays. Officers 'were to report to the Mayor before Church and attend to his immediate instructions'.[31] One further example of the power enjoyed by the Mayor: feeling that officers were not exercising adequate control over street cleansing, he alloted each of them a specific area for inspection. Officers were enjoined to keep raw materials and waste — in fact the entire infrastructure of urban society – in 'order'. 'Streets and drains' were to be 'kept clean and thoroughfares were not to be defaced by the depositing of planks, woods, barrels, baskets, dung etc.': 'dung tips' were to be removed where possible, or 'fitted with the prescribed lid'.[32]

Police officers were subjected to other privations. In 1834 the Mayor of Trier issued an order forbidding more than one 'police agent' and one Gendarme from being present at the same time at theatrical performances.[33] Moreover, the priority of those officers in attendance was 'the regular clearance of the foyer of boys and other persons whose disagreeable racket not infrequently made it impossible to follow the music and performance in the theatre'. 'A large section of the public of all ranks attends these enjoyments and entrusts the protection of any members of their family remaining at home and of their property to the police.' The obverse of bourgeois peace of mind and civil tranquillity was therefore the incessant activity and vigilance of the lowest grade of police officers.

The Mayor of Minden extended his demands to cover times of the day or habits which might serve the ends of relaxation. 'Police officers may not patrol, i.e. walk, where there is nothing to observe or investigate.' Outings with the family or walks with friends or acquaintances also had to stop: police officers 'should go accompanied as seldom as possible, so that their eyes and ears can be fully devoted to their duties'. In general, it was left to the officer to devise a suitable way of 'combining duty, recreation and pleasure' which did not prejudice his official obligations. However, the inevitable isolation which followed from this had to be accepted as the condition imposed by the proper fulfilment of the officer's duties: 'such a man will eventually become a nuisance to others, but nevertheless will have time to pursue his duties'.[34]

One further disagreeable aspect had no connection with either the relationship with the 'public' or the officer's immediate superiors, colleagues or subordinates. It involved competition with other branches of the civil administration. The editor of *Polizei-Archiv* noted in his first issue: 'The lower and even middle ranks of administrative officials, finance officials, and judicial officials quickly get the better of the police officer . . . This discrimination is often discouraging and hampers the officer's effectiveness.'[35]

Some, at least rhetorical, recognition of the fact that such demands would impose a 'considerable burden in the period immediately following appointment' was provided by the Mayor of Minden; but he contented himself with the challenge — cynical in its laconic brevity – 'not to lose heart'.

Whether the outburst directed against the Mayor of Schwelm by one officer in April 1818 was exceptional or not is impossible to say. But given the large number of impositions to which officers were subject, their scale, and the sometimes highly objectionable venom with which they were accompanied, such scenes would have seemed entirely plausible elsewhere. The officer concerned, Mausen, had enacted a 'dreadful spectacle' at the Mayor's own front door by refusing – with 'great incivility' – to obey a mayoral instruction to take command of a prisoner in his own home at noon on Saturday and keep him under guard until collected by a Gendarme on the following Monday.[36] Despite his outburst, Mausen remained in service until

1842. Daily ill-treatment may not only have encouraged the 'customary inebriation' of police officers; it may also have clouded or given a one-sided edge to police perceptions. In Iserlohn in 1844, for example, a factory worker was beaten, arrested – apparently without reason – and his home preventively searched, only to be told on his release by the officer concerned that 'everything was in order'; and in 1845 the same officer unlawfully treated a Jewish 'businessman' as a hawker and searched his home.[37] Such incidents had no repercussions for the officers concerned. By avenging themselves on that part of the population towards which, according to the superior authorities, they were supposed to act as a 'good friend not a tormentor', they could make up for their ill-treatment at the hands of their superiors with little risk to themselves.[38]

As long as they were careful and knew the relevant provisions, decrees and instructions, but mostly with a liberal helping of cunning, police officers could also make the lowest in the local official hierarchy, the night watchmen, suffer for the indignities and adversities visited on their own heads. Police officers could assume the role of superior to night watchmen, or at least report on any violations of orders given by others, without any great fear of subsequent trouble from the victim – at the same time enhancing their own prospects. In December 1845, for example, two officers in Iserlohn, Knieper and Krüger, reported to the Mayor that, after having 'civilly' but unsuccessfully 'exhorted' the night watchman to obey the Mayor's instructions and sound a horn every hour around the town, they had no other option but to request that the dilatory individual concerned be summonsed and disciplined accordingly – which was carried out forthwith.[39]

The desire to seek some compensation for their daily travails was also clearly mixed with the awareness that their authority was only derived. In Hagen, for instance, constables adorned their dark-blue uniforms, contrary to regulations, with embossed buttons and a profusion of red piping[40] – a quite evident attempt to emulate the military, who had the advantage over police officers in that they could bear firearms.

Depending on local financial circumstances or pressure from the *Landrat*, 'night or tower watchmen, prison warders, market superintendents, field guards, and wood and path wardens' were also appointed for policing duties. For most of these officials, 'municipal service' represented an additional job; they could be dismissed without any formal procedure, and because they kept down the overall costs of policing, they were much more numerous than properly appointed constables or sergeants. In the Trier Government District, with a total civilian population of 440,000, there were in 1839 only 55 full-time police officers compared with 1,000 field guards.[41] In the Province of Westphalia, the first resort until 1819 was the Home Guard (*Landsturm*); that is, a body of 40–50 year-olds. In contrast, the *Bürgerwachtvereine* – citizens' vigilance associations – were required to 'return swiftly to the peace of their hearths'.[42] Occasional proposals for a 'citizens' militia' during the 1820s, the activation of such a body in non-garrisoned towns after the Aachen rising of 30 August 1830, and similar calls during the numerous hunger-riots in the spring of 1847 were not enough to overcome the great reservations, at least amongst officials at ministerial level, about taking these first steps towards arming the civilian population. However, the reality within those associations still permitted to exist, such as the Aachen *Wachtverein*, suggests, and would have demonstrated to contemporaries, that they were cultivating anything but a fighting spirit.[43]

The difference between those municipalities with their own police authorities administered on behalf of the state, and those administered directly by the state was minimal as far as the actual conduct of policing 'on the spot' was concerned, or the attitude to civilian reserves.[44] The ratio of police to population was no higher and nor did state administration offer any remedy for the lack of professionalisation: a six-month probationary period was required under both types of administration, although the municipal authorities had to be reminded about complying with this more often. The vehement complaints of 'prominent and upstanding citizens' in Cologne at the beginning of September 1830 (after disturbances at Aachen) were directed against the incapacity of one of the few state police authorities adequately to protect their 'peace' and property. In view of the prolonged absences of the garrison, these complaints led the citadel commander and *Polizeipräsident* to agree to the formation of a security association – a militia.[45] But, even in the face of increasingly frequent and 'tougher' rioting during the 1840s, the Government in Cologne remained deaf to the urgings of the *Prokurator* to grant an additional police-inspector's (*Kommissar*) post. Even the serious incidents which took place during the Feast of St Martin on 3 and 4 August 1846, in which the military frequently resorted to the use of firearms, and when both the *Regierungspräsident* and Director of Police were sharply rebuked for 'weakness' by the *Oberpräsident* of the province and Interior Ministry, did not lead the matter to be dealt with any more rapidly.[46] As early as February 1844, *Oberpräsident* von Schaper had drawn attention to the fact that the 'widespread incompetence' of all senior police officials in the Rhine Province – that is the state-appointed Presidents and Directors of Police – was well-known.[47]

The Gendarmes,[48] recruited from active non-commissioned officers (established in 1812, but reduced after 1820) and assigned to the *Landrat* or Mayor of towns serving as stopping points for prisoners in transit, and in special cases to other Mayors serving as head of the local police, were not only better paid than most local police officers, earning between 240 and 260 Thalers, but also rapidly showed themselves to constitute 'those organs of policing . . . which exercised a beneficial and emphatic effect on the security situation in the provinces'.[49] In the opinion of von Rochow, Minister of the Interior and Police, the 2–4 Gendarmes were, mainly for financial reasons, supposed merely to 'supervise' the local police in the counties (*Landkreis*) to which they were assigned, not substitute for them.[50] However, events in the middle-tier authorities contradicted him! In 1839 the *Regierungspräsident* in Düsseldorf, Freiherr von Spiegel, noted that the 'local lower classes respect the Gendarmerie even in the most agitated of situations', a view which recurred throughout the 1850s and 1860s. Spiegel added that this openly militarily organised and disciplined corps was more effective in controlling riots than even a troop of active soldiers. Von Bodelschwingh, *Oberpräsident* of the Rhine Province, had made it clear only a few weeks before that the Gendarmes often effectively had to replace the local police in rural areas, in doing so raising alarm in the Ministry and prompting von Rochow's observations that the tasks – in other words, the costs – of the Gendarmerie had to be curtailed. Von Bodelschwingh – incidentally, aged only 40 at the time – noted that

> it was widely complained that there were insufficient Gendarmes, and this does not seem unreasonable in view of the fact that, given the rapid increase in population, density had grown considerably and, as is generally acknowledged, the greater the proximity in which people live together, the greater the need for police supervision . . . The 2–4 Gendarmes in the large border counties, with a population of 30–40,000 souls each, represents the most obvious insufficiency when one considers that they are virtually fully occupied with the need to observe aliens and other border business, and that their effect on internal policing is virtually nil. There is almost no control of public houses, annual markets and other gatherings. However, the lack of restraint over the lower popular classes on such occasions encourages minor excesses which, if they were to become commonplace, could all too easily lead to greater excesses.[51]

The extent to which the higher civilian authorities regarded the Gendarmerie as a prototype professional police force – at least, on occasions – is revealed in a detail, minor in itself; namely, the proposal by the government in Arnsberg in 1853 that, instead of white straps, the Gendarmes should wear more black. Clearly, the highly visible strapping and waist belt had proved to be rather a hindrance in everyday police and investigation work. The Arnsberg officials justified their proposal to the Interior Ministry in the following terms: 'If the brass work on soldiers' helmets is blacked only in wartime, it should be remembered that the Gendarmes are *always* facing the enemy.'[52] Appropriate dress for the 'war of policing' was therefore indispensable. However, the suggestion did not meet with any recognisable success. But the key point was in the justification: in the military, warlike confrontation which officials chose as the main criterion for the use of civilian police – a war against 'enemies', a war whose aim could logically lie only in their annihilation.

The 'eternal circle': the undiscriminating hand of the law

The degree of police suspicion and the severity of their intervention, principally the level of violence to be employed, were determined by rules of perception and conduct rooted in social rank. The police did not simply perpetuate and reproduce inequality; by differentiating between groups according to the degree of dangerousness to the 'common good', they augmented existing lines of class and rank cleavage with an additional dimension. With a few exceptions, the 'higher', cultivated and educated classes were seen as those 'elements' which underpinned and supported the state; in contrast, the 'lower popular classes' constituted an unpredictable latent force whose menace could erupt on the streets, or in the taverns, at any moment – a ready refuge for anti-state 'machinations'. Although this dividing line appears simple and straightforward at first sight, in practice officers 'on the spot' often found it contradictory and confusing. Below we break it down into its individual components.

The breadth and diversity of police regulations – the summary of Heyde's *Handbuch* alone took forty-five pages – affected social classes and groups in very different ways. 'Safety' on the streets, rules for checking weights and measures, or penalties for exceeding set prices meant that the owners of domestic property, traders and small-scale industrialists had to make some financial outlay or accept limits to their profits. Yet the main beneficiaries of safe streets and fair trading were third parties, passers-by, travellers, and the settled population of towns and villages. In contrast, the non-propertied could gain from the strict supervision of weights and measures only by managing to become consumers: penalties for using hollow weights were of little benefit to those lacking the wherewithal to participate in the local market – that is, those obliged to seek subsistence from charity or by direct appropriation (theft, as far as 'good citizens' and the authorities were concerned).

The front line of police attention was occupied by the propertyless and the unemployed. But those in work, too, whether itinerant or settled, individuals or groups, could also expect to be the object of their vigilance. Officers were expected to keep a cautious and watchful eye on the 1.8 million men and women who had signed themselves into service as *Gesinde* (servants) – around a quarter of the economically active population. Such individuals were not permitted, 'to disport themselves in public houses without their master, or the supervision or permission of their master'.[53] Apprentices, journeymen, day-labourers and, in particular, 'vagabonds, beggars and the unemployed' also needed to be 'kept under observation'.[54]

These vague terms and the severe tone of the relevant regulations concealed a number of diverse social processes. Those provinces dominated by estate production, the *Gutswirtschaft*, were marked by 'structural over-population'[55] which had begun to make itself felt in the 1820s. The small peasant plots established on peasant land obtained through the commutation of services, together with *Instleute* plots on the estates themselves, not only met the increased demand for labour-power within the estate economy but, over the long term, generated an oversupply through the multiplication of new family units. Those *Instleute* and small peasants, together with their children, who were either structurally unemployed or who had taken up a secondary occupation in domestic industry, were joined by seasonally unemployed day-labourers. Regions with substantial domestic industry – Brandenburg, the Province of Saxony, and especially Westphalia and the Rhineland – were no strangers to trade crises, with their accompanying poverty and hunger. More serious was the fact that in the linen- and wool-producing regions, competition from both local and English factories had transformed what were once temporary problems into a situation of chronic distress (see pp. 45–51 above). In the urban centres, 'poverty' amongst the propertyless and mobile sections of the population, alleviated when at all only by irregular employment, had already been a feature of town life under the *ancien régime*. This highly heterogeneous group expanded very rapidly in the years after 1815 – in Berlin, for example, mainly via immigration from the surrounding areas: and, beginning in the 1830s, textile and metal-working factories also began to exert a considerable demand for 'free' wage-labourers. The dramatic increase in the number of the floating 'mobile' poor brought about by the generalised economic crisis of the early 1840s – the food crisis in both town and country in 1847–9 considerably worsening the distress – accentuated an old, but by no means unknown, problem.

The tenor of executive police conduct was very directly influenced by the increase in population and migratory movements, especially the massing of the propertyless in the towns, and, seasonally, also on the land. The relatively diffuse disciplinary tasks characteristic of policing under the *ancien régime* began to acquire a much more sharply defined social profile during the 1830s. General control of the subject population as a whole was supplanted by the targeted disciplining of those evidently 'dangerous classes' who lived, and had to live, from 'hand to mouth'.

Naturally, such a shift, or better intensification, of the focus of the interpretation of specific situations by the police could become a new source of vexation for officers: the considerable increase in the propertyless poor exposed the gap between the demands put on the police and their capacity to meet them.

The problem was compounded by the fact that this demand for control was a dual one. On the one hand, senior officers along with 'good citizens' and 'gentlemen' in the towns, administrative districts and villages expected their local police to maintain quiet and order in the locality. At the same time, peasants and agrarian capitalists, entrepreneurs, factory owners and, after the 1830s, the directors of railway companies were all dependent on the periodic availability of mobile, propertyless individuals as a source of labour-power. Police officers were often expected to accomplish tasks which, although appearing unproblematic from the remoteness of the administration, were virtually impossible on the ground: namely, the simultaneous husbanding and disciplining of the mobile propertyless.

The quantitative scale of the problem was evident. In 1846 Berlin had 389,308 civilian inhabitants.[56] On average there was one precinct superintendent (*Reviervorsteher*) and one sergeant for every 8–10,000 residents.[57] In many of the commercial and industrial centres, those classes regarded by the police as particularly suspicious amounted to, at the least, 45–50 per cent[58] of the population, and sometimes 70–90 per cent.

Long before the massive long-distance migratory movements of the late ninteenth century, and prior to the concentration of factory-based industry in the 1840s and its 'take off' after 1850, the traditional migrations of journeymen were paralleled by intensive short-distance migration by the propertyless – noticeable, for example, in the Berg-Mark district and the industrial areas of the Lower Rhine. There was also considerable regional migration from the eastern agricultural areas to the large towns of the central regions and eastern provinces, such as Berlin, Magdeburg and Halle, or – in the east – Königsberg, Danzig or Breslau.

In 1828, for example, 2,073 'boys and youths, men and widowers, girls and young women, women and widows' (the categories used in the official population statistics) migrated into the county (*Landkreis*) of Lennep, a locality characterised by domestic industrial metal-working and textile production. In the same year 1,816 individuals left the county. Given a total population of *c.* 55,000, this implied a 'movement' of possibly 4–5 per cent of the population. The only higher rates of immigration and emigration in the Düsseldorf Government District were in Elberfeld,[59] *the* industrial county in the District. The scale of movement into Berlin in the 1840s, most of which was regional in nature, can be seen in the following figures for 1851. With a total population of *c.* 420,000 there were 30,157 arrivals and 16,987 departures; of those drawn into the city, over 90 per cent – 28,491 – were 'non-independent', i.e. factory workers, journeymen and servants.[60]

Lower-grade police officers (*Offizianten*) had considerable difficulty in distinguishing between the floating, 'mobile' and resident propertyless elements in the population. Moreover, this distinction was itself very fluid and certainly always provisional in character. Determining who constituted 'the poor' also threw up similar problems: an official distinction was drawn between those in merely temporary straits, and those whose subsistence was permanently at risk. For the propertyless, the possibility of self-support not only depended on the price of bread or the level of seasonal demand for labour, but was also decided on a day-to-day basis by the demand for 'hands' – as porters or washerwomen – and also on the daily earnings, or lack of earnings, of married women, men and children.

The 1840s were a period of mounting everyday misery against a background of mass distress whose causes lay in the trade cycle. Figures for the poor and propertyless in Berlin for this period provide some indication of the sheer scale of the problem of control set for the police.

In 1846 the authorities counted *c.* 80,000 non-independent masters, journeymen, factory workers and day-labourers; in addition, in 1847, there were just under 23,000 domestic servants, most of whom were subject to the constant surveillance and authority of their 'masters'. Finally, in this case in 1849, more than 7,000 inhabitants were registered as 'paupers'. However, this latter figure is particularly misleading: legal restrictions excluded the vast bulk of the poor from the relative privilege of the few pennies and warm bowl of soup which those registered could claim each day. Only those with a residence permit of three years' standing issued by the Local Commissioner of Police (*Bezirkspolizeikommissar*) were eligible.

Some idea of the potential scale of this 'mobile' poverty can be gleaned from the number of those exempted from the class-tax due in small towns and rural areas. The percentage of the population not eligible to pay rose dramatically during the 1840s – from 3 to 6 per cent. For Berlin, this would have meant a minimum of 40,000 unregistered poor, plus at least 60,000 dependants. By 1830 more than 10,000 families in Berlin were already exempted from municipal taxes on grounds of 'indigence'.[61] This section of

2 Member of the Mounted Gendarmerie, *c.* 1825.

the poor increased by 480 per cent between 1815 and 1830, compared with an overall growth rate in the number of families of 25 per cent. By the late 1840s, Berlin would certainly have housed 210,000 to 270,000 potentially 'suspicious' individuals, between a half and two-thirds of the population. The problem was made more intractable by the fact that, unlike in other conurbations, Berlin's 'dangerous classes' were highly concentrated in a few districts. For *Polizeiassessor* Werner of Breslau, the second largest city in Prussia, such concentrations were not only conducive to the hazards of physical infection but also fostered the 'propagation and inheritance of crime'.[62] An 1828 report by the Mayor of Breslau summed up the problems of policing a large town: 'What does spell danger is the presence of so many indigent folk who, although kept under the watchful eye of the police, cannot be easily superintended in so large and populous a place as Breslau.'[63]

In the Eastern Provinces 'Polish Jews' were regarded as 'suspicious persons', or at least as vagabonds, as a matter of course; even when they were able to prove, to the annoyance of the authorities, that they actually maintained a household in Russian Poland, they were considered to have 'sneaked in' regardless.[64] In the Catholic parts of the country, pilgrims, participants in religious processions and all carnivals were objects of police suspicion.[65] Only processions which predated 'the unification with Prussia' were permitted. And masques were allowed only on payment of a fee to the local police authorities.

Depending on local circumstances, open police control was also extended to children and young people (chiefly from the families of the propertyless) – and not merely for such matters as the police ban on the throwing of snowballs. In 1822 the Mayor of the industrial centre of Elberfeld felt it necessary to issue an order prohibiting 'boys under 16' from 'smoking tobacco on the streets, in public places and thoroughfares and in all places subject to police supervision'.[66] Public houses and beerhalls were forbidden 'to allow youths access to their premises . . . for the purposes of drinking and gaming unless under the supervision of their parents'. The purpose of imposing and enforcing such a ban by the police (smoking incurred the severe fine of 3 Thalers, equivalent to two weeks' wages for an adult) was to control theft amongst youths. According to the local head of police, 'Not all parents exercise the required degree of care in the raising of their children . . . young people in particular become initiated into pleasures which some covet and which are beyond the means and incomes of their parents.' Intervention by the local administration and police was justified on the grounds that 'not only is a son being lost: the state also loses a citizen'.

However, the main objects of suspicion were unemployed 'factory workers'. And, after the events of 1830, weavers were held to be particularly inclined towards 'loitering, stealing, and begging instead of accepting the road-mending work offered them [by the state]'. Von Pestel, *Regierungspräsident* in Düsseldorf, did try to go a little further than outright moralising by explaining the weavers' behaviour in terms of their previous experiences in domestic industry as opposed to factory work. In his view, 'road mending is too unlike the employment to which they have been accustomed since their youth'.[67]

The definition of how 'suspicious' an individual was, was left entirely to the local police authorities – even after the 1850 Police Act. The 'degree of observation' was the product of local officials' interest in upholding structures of domination and state authority, their own standards of perception and conduct, and the concerns, experiences and legitimations in which these became crystallised – in short, local officialdom's 'habitus'. At the same time, the mobility of many members of those classes deemed 'prejudicial to public safety'[68] could not have made it easy even merely to identify 'wanted criminals, the work-shy and the indigent'.[69] The official response was to create a seamless web of registration (permits, residence permits, etc.) combined with the vigorous, but futile, injunction to the police authorities 'not to let travellers out of their sight'.[70]

The 'Service Instructions' issued by the Mayor of Minden in 1831 (see Appendix 3) illustrate how the authorities' sheer bafflement at how to get their lower-grade officers started on the work of detection inevitably became transformed into a massive demonstration of the latter's practical power of definition.[71] These officers, who were entrusted with the implementation of ruling norms and sanctions, were required to accomplish a 'reduction' in the 'complexity of everyday life' (cf. Luhmann, *Macht*, p. 9) using the lines of demarcation between social classes: 'families of the highest rank' on the one hand, and everyone else on the other. 'Stringent application' of police regulations in the former case could lead to 'a good deal of unpleasantness' and was anyhow completely unnecessary. By contrast, 'great stringency' was to be shown towards the remainder, especially those, 'who take in outsiders for gain and generally evade police supervision'. A number of relatively easily recognisable features were available to assist in keeping tabs 'on suspicious, unsuperintended strangers'. Particular attention had to be devoted to individuals, 'who go from house to house, who loiter aimlessly on the street and ask for directions'. Such people were quite evidently 'beggars and thieves calling for the greatest stringency'. Individuals who could not justify their presence with official documents or, 'failing all else, by the testimony of local residents', were considered 'suspicious' at the very least. 'Nationals not already liable for punishment for a specific offence are to be sent to the *Landrat* as vagrants for issue with a compulsory passport [i.e. despatch to their home district]'. Foreigners were to be kept in custody: 'they shall be detained until the authorities are convinced that no offence has been committed, and then they are to be expelled from the town'.

Not surprisingly, the instruction not to act against every resident, but once suspicious to mete out draconian treatment to 'suspected' persons, led police officers to conclude that what would best satisfy their superiors and provide for a measure of 'peace and order', both on the streets and in the police station, was a mixture of 'turning a blind eye' and sporadic brutality. Any rough handling of 'subjects' genuinely in search of assistance could always be subsequently justified as a product of their persistent intrusiveness. One incident in Iserlohn in October 1838 illustrates the point. A master tailor, Schule, had approached the constable on watch duty, Krüger, for help in restoring order at his home (no further details of the reason for the disorder were given). The request was refused and Krüger 'gruffly' instructed Schule to leave the office of the watch. Schule then 'pushed' Krüger away, both fell, and Krüger then struck Schule to the ground several times. The *Magistrat* ultimately decided in Krüger's favour on the grounds that Schule had refused to obey the instruction to leave the office.[72]

Administrative 'habitus' – the everyday linking of official modes of interpretation and demeanour (*Gestus*) – also regulated the exercise of 'discretion' in subsequent proceedings. Each situation called for fresh decision: would the aims of policing be better served by 'civility and earnest admonition' or was there 'no other way to restore quiet and public order except by the application of a strong hand'.[73] Officials confronted by that mixture of 'impudence' and 'indifference' which, in their eyes, was responsible for the fact that 'in all the branches of administration . . . the efficacy of the official is handicapped by the evident preference of petty folk for circumventing the law and avoiding its requirements' tended to favour the latter course.[74] The request for reinforcements of Gendarmes made by the *Landrat* of Paderborn was backed with precisely these arguments. Long-term distress amongst the propertyless and property-poor, combined with the growing structural crisis in the domestic linen-weaving industry, had particularly afflicted his county. 'Theft from fields and gardens is a daily occurrence.' His complaints were echoed by other officials, who also mirrored his preferred police practice. One report from the Police Commissary in Cleves, on the left bank of the Rhine, noted that 'nine-tenths of offences against police regulations consist of thefts from woods and fields'.[75]

Communal gathering places, that is the public houses, were deemed particularly 'suspicious'. The decision to enforce set closing times – the so-called 'Police Hour' – illustrates how the 'policing of public taverns' reflected the logic of the administrative distinction between 'harmless' and 'dangerous' classes.

An 1833 report on licensing hours prepared by the Ministry of the Interior sought guidance in a 1798 decree on the subject. This argued that

> people who frequent wine-taverns and places of refreshment serving *only* wine, and *no* schnapps or beer, belong to the more well-to-do and probably more cultured class. These are unlikely to create disturbances of the peace at night. Such establishments can properly be excluded from the requirement of a set closing time.[76]

This accorded with official observations made 'on the spot'. *Regierungsassessor* Diederichs, who visited the county of Lennep in 1835, found that the 'schnapps bars' were gathering places for the 'roughest folk' and the site of 'most of the numerous excesses which keep the police and criminal authorities permanently occupied'.[77]

Although Diederichs noted that the *regional* concentration of bars and public-houses was a matter of particular inconvenience to the police, he did not deal with this aspect in any further detail. The figures were later brought together by J. G. Hoffmann, Director of the Prussian Office of Statistics. 'Those parts of the [Rhine] Province with the greatest number of factories had, proportionally, the most public houses'.[78] The Government District of Düsseldorf, containing the intensive concentrations of domestic and factory industry in Lennep, had the highest ratio of public houses to population: 1 per 132 inhabitants. In Remscheid, an iron-making town, the ratio was as high as 1:85.[79] However, the density of industry and public houses did not always correlate so precisely. In Minden-Ravensburg, a textile locality, there were 446 residents to each tavern – far fewer than in Berlin or Breslau (253 and 266 respectively). This would suggest that it was the separation between agricultural and industrial production and reproduction, together with urbanisation, which created particularly favourable markets for the products of the public houses. Simple 'prosperity', cited by Hoffmann as the crucial factor in determining the density of public houses, was not in itself a sufficiently reliable indicator.

It was not those 'parts of the country in which prosperity, with all its beneficial consequences, had made little progress', but rather those with market-dependent industrial labour which had 'the greater number of public houses . . . with a relatively marked consumption of liquor' (Hoffmann, note 78). In such areas 'extravagant gluttony on market or feast days' alternated with 'utter privation on most working days'.

More concretely, Friedrich Engels remembered how 'in the late '20s cheap schnapps suddenly descended on the industrial district of the Lower

Rhine Mark'.[80] The potato distilleries belonging to the East Elbian Junkers – who had invested a portion of their commutation payments into the drink business – produced a poor, but very cheap schnapps, very high in fusel oil, which soon supplanted the customary corn schnapps. Engels described the consequences of this massive infusion, which allowed 'one to stay totally drunk for a week for 15 Silbergroschen':

> In Berg especially, and very especially in Elberfeld-Barmen, the mass of the working population fell victim to drink. 'Drunks' swayed arm in arm from alehouse to alehouse in great troupes, taking up the whole street, after 9 o'clock every evening. Eventually, accompanied by discordant yelling and singing, they would disappear home.

However, the volume of alcohol and the frequency and spread of drunkenness were not the only things which increased in the wake of this particular conjunction of circumstances. As the fusel oil took its toll, the quality of intoxication changed too:

> The effect of uncommonly large quantities of this drink on such an excitable and passionate people as the inhabitants of Berg was entirely as one might expect. The character of intoxication changed completely. Any entertainment which would once have ended with cheerful merriment and only rarely in excesses – admittedly not infrequently involving the use of a knife – began to culminate in depraved carousing, and never failed to conclude with a brawl in which knife wounds were rarely absent, and fatal stabbings ever more frequent. Priests blamed it on increasing godlessness; lawyers and other philistines on the dances held in taverns. The real cause was the sudden deluge of Prussian rot-gut which exercised its customary physiological effect and delivered hundreds of poor devils into imprisonment in the citadel.

Naturally, public officials saw in this phenomenon only disruption of the peace and danger to reliable citizens. Diederichs, for example, suggested that 'residents' should establish 'police watches', the main aim of which would be 'to supervise the numerous public houses and bars on Sundays and holidays, keep them to their proper closing times, and prevent, as much as possible, disturbances of the peace and excesses'. His proposal was nevertheless rejected by the District Government in Düsseldorf.[81]

The logic behind the constant renewal of regulations for the 'policing of public houses' emerges more clearly if we bear in mind the particular bureaucratic concern over 'excesses' and 'riotous assemblies'. The main sites for these minor, but by no means trivial, 'scenes' were the public houses. However, for officials, any massing of people, especially if they did not remain passive – that is, if they joined in a pub brawl – contained the seeds of a riot likely to 'endanger the existence of the state in its present form'. It followed from this that one central guideline of administrative readiness was 'the necessity to prevent riots by individuals discontented over some particular circumstance, as these can all too easily lead to the state as a whole being endangered'.[82]

Annual repeat performances of 'riots' could be expected at local popular festivals, ranging from carnivals, parish fairs, and shooting and harvest festivals. The outlook of senior officials can be seen in a report on the 'Management and order of parish fairs', prepared in 1847 by the Cologne Director of Police, Heister, and the Senior Mayor, Steinberger – a district particularly affected by the problem.[83]

The report took for granted that some customary, and in a certain sense trivial, 'disorders' would occur, including 'fighting and immoderate language'. These were 'general wherever people of the uncultured classes gather in numbers in the public houses, dance halls and on the streets'. Parish fairs presented the additional 'mischief of shooting and the throwing of fireworks'. Such festivals were, in fact, noted for the 'unbridled indulgence' in this activity. Although the District Government had banned the practice in 1836 and imposed a maximum fine of 5 Thalers, officials added – in what was evidently a non-controversial observation – that the ban, 'had had no more success in dispelling the mischief than any other penal law'. What was crucial was solely and simply whether the police were physically present and willing to intervene: 'In the meantime, supervision by police officers serves to keep the mischief within some limits.'

Seen from this aspect, the ban was 'not only expedient . . . it was necessary' – it could not be surpassed for simplicity. Moreover,

> any reduction in the penalty would appear to sanction the misdemeanour, and the powers entailed by increasing its severity would not only necessitate a higher level of authorisation, but under present circumstances would act as a goad to yet more offences.

Two things were therefore considered important: on the one hand, a straightforward legal rule, easy to apply 'on the spot', and on the other, and first and foremost, the alertness of the police. Under normal circumstances, 'that is, in the great majority of current parish fairs', 'prudent use of the usual means available sufficed to maintain order and prevent grosser excesses as much as is practicable'.

By 'the usual means', the police chiefs meant the 'presence of police superintendents, and patrols by sergeants and Gendarmes, equipped with suitable orders'.

Evidently, the Feast of St Martins occupied a special place amongst church festivals.[84] In 1846, during the festival preceding the report, a local resident had been shot dead by a member of the military. The feast required 'special measures': a joint proclamation by the state police and municipal executive (*Magistrat*) some days before the feast was to be issued to remind the population of the 'need to observe police instructions and regulations in the well-understood interest of all'. It was recommended that, 'the curious should be kept away'. 'Any gathering of masses of people and unnecessary loitering by those not entitled to do so in the Altenmarkt and nearby squares and streets' was to be prohibited. It was also felt 'expedient' for, 'directors of higher educational institutions and the school inspector for elementary education to issue a special warning to pupils in gymnasia and other schools concerning the dangers of idly roaming around in these localities'.

However, the officials did not rest content with such general appeals and admonitions. They also proposed

> to enjoin individual prominent citizens, and in particular members of the Town Council, to influence the good sense of the better part of the citizenry either by their presence, or, where necessary, by their words, and thus create a general feeling favourable to the maintenance of order and to the deterring of malefactors or those led astray.

However, experiences in Cologne itself (on 30 August and 1 September 1830), and in other places, had often shown that direct intervention or the visible presence of prominent citizens did not always restore 'quiet', although this symbolic underlining of everyday inequalities and opportunities for power did have a 'dampening effect' on many occasions. Such a display did not always involve the organisation of a full civilian militia (something permitted only in non-garrison towns and then not as a general principle). As far as officials were concerned, the mixture of a symbolic presence by the representatives of the local ruling class(es) together with the demonstration of their alliance over the issue of 'quiet and order' was sufficient. The District Government came to the same conclusion. Both parties were convinced – or at least the officials in Cologne 'hoped' – that 'keeping the military in readiness, but not actually using this ultimate and extreme means, would suffice'.

The control of both short-lived and permanent gathering and meeting places of the 'lower popular classes' meant that the main task of policing became the preventive 'control of strangers' and – supposedly identical – of 'suspicious individuals'. For didn't such persons exploit the poor level of communication between authorities and the lower level of policing in towns as compared with rural districts by the simple expedient of moving from place to place? Or, as the District Government in Potsdam expressed it,

> A number of cases have shown that dangerous individuals, who have committed crimes in Berlin, move to neighbouring small towns and find a place of refuge or residence since the slack administration of police protects them from detection. Instructions for pursuit issued from Berlin are of little value if the lack of a competent policing of aliens means that every trace of the crime disappears in the next town.[85]

The main victims of administrative hostility towards 'itinerants', exhibited in, for example, the 'Pass Police', regional searches for 'vagabonds',[86] house searches and the observation of taverns,[87] the introduction of travel and employment registration books and work tickets for railway navvies, were not 'criminals' or foreign, or revolutionary, 'emissaries', but those considered 'fully able to work, but lacking the willingness to do so'.[88] Some decrees issued by the Interior and Police Ministry even designated these groups as 'those subjects most dangerous to the state'. The irregularity of their lives was, of course, imposed on them by the cyclical fluctuations in the demand for labour against a background of oversupply.

Police officers' standards of perception and conduct imposed a very schematic view of the numerous differences and gradations within and between the diverse groups making up the propertyless and 'direct producers'. Important distinctions between agricultural producers, those in domestic industry, workers in manufacture and factory industry were ignored. And officers had little idea of the special features of the 'floating masses', who lacked not only material possessions but also had few opportunities to sell their labour-power, and were consequently forced to survive through 'non-legal' means.

Some idea of *whom* the police regarded as 'suspicious' can be gleaned from instructions specifying the level of vigilance required for particular groups. These do not, of course, indicate *how many* people were subjected to the attentions, and sanctions, of the police. Tables provided by the police themselves are of little value, providing neither the criteria used to distinguish between 'local beggars', 'vagabonds' and itinerant 'journeymen' (with invalid passes)[89] – as in the Rhine Province in 1831 – nor any method for identifying those subjected to repeated arrest. They also passed over the question as to who were resident and who travelling 'offenders'. To give one example: the Münster Gendarmerie compiled the following breakdown of the arrests of the approximately thirty-five Gendarmes in the district's 'Brigade':[90]

	1837	1838
Vagabonds	71	50
Thieves	81	76
Invalid pass	23	39
Begging	208	391
'Police misdemeanours'	298	271
Requisition from other authorities	31	51

The police figures also usually contained errors, some of which could have had serious consequences if undetected: and correction was likely only under exceptional circumstances. In one case, it was only when the local District Government became alarmed at the enormous increase in custodial sentences imposed by the police, as reported in the Coesfeld *Landrat*'s figures, that it was discovered that he had been entering hours in police custody as days.[91]

In another case, the District Government had evidently simply accepted the figures supplied by the Brigadier of the Gendarmerie for arrests made by his troops, although each of the five entries was identical to the previous year's submission.

A comparison between the figures for arrests by Gendarmes compiled for the Münster Government District, which had a number of solid areas of domestic industry in the north west but which was predominantly agrarian, and those of the Rhine Province[92] would suggest that the more marked development of domestic industry, manufacture and the first stages of factory industry, together with the greater urban density in the Rhineland, may have favoured patterns of behaviour more likely to attract the attention of both Gendarmerie and police. Although the 1838 Gendarmerie figures for Münster during a period of rising theft were still, proportionally, only half those of the District in the Rhine Province with the lowest figures (in 1831 the comparison was 0.12 per cent in Münster against 0.2 per cent in Düsseldorf), within the Rhine Province itself the situation was just the opposite: the more rural areas of Trier and Koblenz seemed to exhibit much higher figures than the urban-industrial centres of Cologne, Aachen and Düsseldorf:

Trier	0.4 %
Koblenz	0.65 %
Cologne	0.25 %
Aachen	0.3 %
Düsseldorf	0.2 %

However, the fact that the category of 'journeyman' featured so prominently in the figures for the Rhine Province does cast considerable doubt on the usefulness of these statistics for ascertaining which groups, and how many of their members, were the particular subject of police attention. In Koblenz, for instance, the Gendarmerie detained 111 'journeymen', compared with 13 in Trier, 10 in Düsseldorf, and 4 and 8 respectively in Cologne and Aachen.

The power of definition enjoyed by officials 'on the spot' thus constituted an element of statistical uncertainty. By the same token, it would explain the higher 'seizure rate' in some rural areas. The lower level of policing in the countryside, especially measured in terms of police manpower on the spot, could be offset by the pre-emptive application of more severe measures, including preventive arrests. Thus the figures above would reflect the scope for intervention available to the police – a power regulated solely, or primarily by the local lower-level police officers.

'The rule of law': arbitrariness and violence as the practical legitimation of police indiscrimination

The police had long possessed special powers for regulating the lives of the 'lesser' or 'lower popular classes', and in particular of servants (*Gesinde*), more than 80 per cent of whom worked 'in agriculture'.[93] Although maid-servants and farmhands entered into contracts that were nominally free, they were subject to the unique form of domination exercised through the Servants Ordinance, which remained in force until 1918.[94] The local police authorities – coterminous with the structures of patrimonial power on the land until 1872, and in practice until the abolition of the independent estate districts in 1927 – could, and in fact were, expected to offer 'provisional' assistance in the event of any complaints by Junkers about 'stubborn disobedience or refractoriness' on the part of servants (often their own). They also had to make notification of any grievances against the Junkers, on the rare occasions that such were reported; these primarily turned on the problems which cropped up in the everyday encounters between masters and servants: board or an allowance for keep, treatment by their superiors, or the issue of whether the servant could terminate their obligations before the due date – in short, a wide spectrum of actual or potential everyday conflicts. The involvement of the police authorities inevitably meant that what was in essence a matter of individual civil law was transformed into a public and disciplinary relation of labour and domination.

In the East Elbian provinces at least, general police conduct took on all the features of that specific relation of domination which formally applied only to servants. Seigneurial disciplinary rights, extensively retained in the Servants Ordinance, overshadowed the more limited rights possessed by the police, even when – theoretically 'free' – day-labourers were involved. And the practice by which Junkers delegated police powers to their 'commercial administrators, often clerks and bailiffs', who 'anticipate justice and customarily administer a sound *thrashing*' (emphasis in original), was by no means confined to Silesia.[95]

The change in patrimonial police powers in 1848, under which patrimonial authority was replaced by the 'order of the King'[96] as the basis of police authority, was entirely formal and had no effect on the practice of 'short shrift'.[97]

In the towns, the 'advanced guard' of law and order exercised under the auspices of the guild regulations was weakened with the dissolution of the guilds after 1808. Nevertheless, in workshops, manufactories and factories these corporate institutions of supervision and control were replaced by the regimentation of the 'owners' and 'masters'.[98] Corporal punishment, fines and dismissal were used in combination with practices intended to inflict social disgrace and stigmatisation – such as being recorded on a 'pillar of shame'. Any paucity of evidence for the infliction of physical punishment should not be taken as proof that such punishments were a rare or extreme step. On the contrary, they were so commonplace that contemporaries did not consider them worthy of particular mention. Dismissal, or the threat of it, was certainly often the simplest and most effective way of 'pacifying' unruly less-skilled workers. In contrast, it is impossible to say whether the expectation of an oversupply of labour would have led 'masters' to fire experienced workers for trivial offences. No official regulations existed which matched those imposed on servants in rural areas; but, in practice, the common view was that any lack of 'refinement' or civil 'manners' was to be made up for by the exercise of strict police discipline, or, as an official in the Berlin Police *Präsidium* noted in a memo to the Interior Ministry in 1812,

> although, in my opinion, it can never be the aim of the state to turn factories into places of correction, giving factory masters more authority over workers in their employ than a master has over his servant, it should not be forgotten that the bulk of these workers are the children of poor parents and persons of very low education. Even when their work is precisely assigned, they ought – in the best interests of the whole – reasonably be expected to lend a hand even to tasks not specifically allotted to them. In short, and with some limitations, the same relation-

ship should prevail here as exists between master [*Dienstherr*] and servant [*Gesinde*].[99]

The nature of the labour process itself, with its functional demands for punctuality and the careful handling of tools and raw materials, meant that the act of expending labour-power itself subjected the direct producers to constant drilling in every detail of everyday life. The central virtues to be instilled were 'cleanliness' and 'love of order' – meaning, in the latter case, an all-embracing commitment to the prevailing order and its inviolability.

The police themselves lacked the 'time and inclination' to correct the wayward conduct of the urban sub-proletariat and sub-peasantry.[100] Rather, 'subjects held to be suspicious' were not investigated by the police, for whom 'ascertaining the reason behind the offence of "loitering" was considered unnecessary'; 'they simply arrested the first people they could lay hands on', as the 'radical' author Ernst Dronke noted sardonically.[101] For some individuals, this was the start of a never-ending circle. Permanently on police files, repeatedly clapped into jail or the workhouse, they constantly appeared to be poised on the verge of further 'contraventions'.

Civil officials appreciated only partly that the domination exercised by the police-administration and the judiciary reinforced the continuous process of social devaluation and stigmatisation. Although they acknowledged that the life-cycles of those who came to the attention of the police or courts were not determined by individual characteristics, but reflected a blend of social and regional factors, official descriptions none the less concentrated on individual, and by implication avoidable, weaknesses and failures.

And, although officials were capable of drafting dispassionate accounts of social and economic conditions, they never accepted that the 'deviant' or forbidden conduct which they described may have been provoked, or at the least, occasioned by the activities of the state. Police officers might act to repress lapses before they took place, but were more likely merely to note and – if possible – correct them. However, it would have contradicted every principle of official conduct and organisation were 'subjects neglected in every respect since their youth' to have evaded 'repeated punishment for theft' or 'criminal investigation for crimes against the security of property' simply because of some social or economic distress or the lack of 'breadwinning employment'.[102]

Official correspondence – that is, permitted opinions – reveal that the only conceivable motivations for the conduct of individuals and groups 'from the propertyless and indigent classes' were seen as religious or mystical impulses, political 'conspiracy', genetics and instinctive reactions. The stereotypes of 'itinerant Jewish merchants' or the propertyless on the very margin of subsistence reveal this particularly clearly.

To cite merely one of numerous examples, a report drafted by the *Landrat* of Neuss in 1834 devoted particular attention to both actual and potential 'dangerous elements'.[103] The *Landrat*, von Bolschwingh, was especially concerned about 'Jews and journeymen'. The former 'roamed through every province and country haggling', an alien and strange international society of thieves consisting of 'fellow believers', seemingly beyond police control. More important, however, was the 'number of journeymen wandering aimlessly', 'refusing work out of idleness even when it is offered them'. Their 'door-to-door beggary' could not be stopped even by the police. By concluding his report here, this senior official in a district very directly affected by the 'costs' of a sectoral boom in effect ended where he should have begun: his observations registered little advance beyond ignorance, prejudice and the 'common-sense' parroting of these obvious symptoms. Although the mainly peasant agriculture of the area had not suffered a bad harvest or price collapse in 1833/4, those living in the western part of the county lost out in the boom experienced in the domestic silk industry in Krefeld in the years after 1832. The only beneficiaries were the merchants and putters-out, who found they could get higher prices for the finished articles. It was the owners of capital who gained, not the 'direct producers', who also often owned the means of production under these systems.[104]

In contrast to this 'official view', a report on the situation in Cleves, a border district on the north west bank of the Rhine, drafted by a Düsseldorf *Regierungsrat*, typified one alternative perspective, combining a degree of awareness of social and economic factors with the assertion of an ineluctable 'criminal' life-cycle. Writing in July 1839, the author, Fasbender, noted that the main result of the 'lack of factory industry' was that the children of the propertyless could not find work:[105]

> The fact that a cow is led to graze in a roadside ditch by a small boy or half-grown girl is a pernicious form of employment indicating poor husbandry. However, this abuse is actually cited as an excuse for non-attendance at school.

For Fasbender, the key issue was the inescapable aftermath of such childhood experiences:

> Such isolated cowherds, or those from parishes with communal rights in the forests, provide the raw material for subsequent field thieves and poachers, and these in turn become smugglers – a pack of mischievous good-for-nothings.

Such individuals not only endangered 'property' and civil morals, discipline and good order. The relative attractiveness of a career in crime – indirectly confirmed here – also reduced the supply of 'fit servants' for peasant farms, 'the propertyless class being over-accustomed to obtaining an easy and blatantly immoral living on the border'.

One solution would have been the rapid abolition of communal woodland rights. In Fasbender's view, such a step would have been 'economically beneficial as well as of undoubted moral utility' both to the administration and 'well-disposed residents'.

The police mind flattened and eliminated any of the real material differences, and differences in outlook, between paupers and proletarians, subjecting both to hostile suspicion and severity 'from above' – including physical force where this was deemed appropriate. For senior administrators, their 'official attendance' to the requirements of order was in no sense seen as incompatible with the administration of beatings to underpin patrimonial, patriarchal, or capitalist authority. Even with the 'best institution, the common man still needs a physical compulsion'.[106]

Naturally, the bureaucracy's claim to operate under the 'rule of law' could not be left entirely out of account. None the less, although official's used the idea of the 'rule of law' to reinforce their claim to legitimacy, this did not create any untransgressable boundaries in terms of their conduct. Respect for the 'rule of law' could be demonstrated to the public in two ways, without any abandonment – or at least only minor limitation – on the status and role of violence within the overall system.

The first: the definition of a sphere of justifiable exemptions from the 'strict formalities' in the case of allegedly minor offences gave scope for the exercise of considerable powers of discretion. 'Moderate corporal punishment', up to 20 strokes, could be imposed in 'summary' police proceedings. In 1833 the Interior Minister, von Brenn, banned the beating of 'persons of the female sex over the age of ten'. Three years, later, his successor, von Rochow, had already suggested a possible way of evading this proscription. There was, 'no rule against those who contravene the law subsequently being punished by their parents in the presence of a police officer'.[107]

The second: the exploitation of the potential dual standard inherent in the implementation of the 'letter', or almost so, of the 'rule of law'. This is best illustrated in a concrete example: in the late summer of 1844, the *Landrat* in the mostly Polish-speaking county of Neustadt in the Government District of Oppeln, von Wittenburg, had had three men arrested in the town of Zülz. They were subsequently subjected to a brutal beating in order to extract information about their suspected involvement in a theft and the activities of a gang which had been disrupting the area. One of the men had been given forty (!) lashes and lost consciousness several times. His mother, a 'cottager widow' took the issue up in the Regional Court of Appeal, the *Oberlandesgericht*, in Ratibor. This, in itself, was highly unusual: the prevailing feeling was summed up by the Düsseldorf *Assessor* Diederichs:

> It is barely possible for a complaint to be made over an individual instance of partisan treatment or violence. Hundreds shy from treading this path, preferring to suffer a small injustice in silence rather than attract further disagreeable consequences.[108]

The court instituted 'fiscal investigation' against the officials – a shortened procedure intended merely for 'minor misdemeanours' not punishable by more than a fine or imprisonment up to six months.[109] The charge read that Wittenburg had 'grossly ill-treated' the three men.

The information forwarded to the District Government by the judicial authorities in December 1844 produced an immediate reaction.[110] On 6 January 1845, the District Government applied to the Minister of the Interior for a resolution of this 'conflict of jurisdiction': that is, to suspend proceedings until a special court (only established in 1844) could clarify whether the case fell within the competence of an internal administrative – disciplinary –

investigation or was a judicial matter. The District Government, specifically its deputy *Justitiar*, the *Assessor* Count Eulenburg, and *Abteilungsdirigent* Ewald (see pp. 53ff), together with the entire department and full college, felt that, although the incident had involved an 'overstepping of a number of limits', it was a case of an administrative misdemeanour, not assault – a criminal offence. Their argument was an attempt to balance the deed against the office. The *Landrat* was 'legally entitled to dispense corporal punishment and deprive individuals of their liberty, within certain limits'. The 'degeneration' of legally permissible 'discipline into assault' would, therefore 'merely represent an instance of exceeding the prescribed degree, and should not be torn out of context'. In the *Landrat*'s case, the justifying context was that he

> had been engaged in investigations into a large gang of thieves who had been pursuing their mischief in his county. He had achieved some positive results. And, although the difficulty of his task should not have led him to exceed his powers, it is evident that such an investigation could not be pursued with too much gentleness'.

And beyond the point at which the *Landrat*'s excessive zeal was possibly not justified by his existing police powers, the District Government introduced a supplementary, formal argument:

> . . . if his severity gave grounds for complaint, then it is our responsibility, his superior authority, to determine whether this severity was excessive and whether or not it may have been excusable, or necessary, in the given instance.

The conflict, or dissent, between the administrative and judicial authorities was not confined to this particular case. The District Government was quite explicit in its view that this was simply one more instance of a persistent bone of contention between itself and the courts. There were 'regrettably all too many cases . . . in which – on precisely these grounds – inquiries were instituted against estate owners, as the holders of police jurisdiction, without any notification to us from the courts'. However, as *Polizeiherren*, and holders of local police powers, the Junkers were subject to the control and supervision of the state authorities, and as far as their powers were concerned, were to be treated as officials of the state. Insistence on this procedure by the courts would inevitably impinge on the activities of those concerned:

> Under such circumstances, it seems harsh not to put them under the same protection enjoyed by state officials in the exercise of their duties. A good part of the energy, without which they could not possibly satisfactorily fulfil their obligations, must inevitably be wasted if they are constantly haunted by the fear of investigation and punishment.

Legal norms therefore had to take second place to the material demands of 'security', which was to be achieved through police discretion and the exercise of force. Where there was doubt, the freedom to take decisions – a freedom appropriated by the police themselves – had precedence over 'general legal norms', even though these would 'only' have involved the Prussian Legal

3 Police officer in Berlin, *c.* 1830
'So it's you again, vagabond. What are you up to?'
'Oh, officer, in summer I'm footman at the church gate when wedding carriages come, and . . .'
'. . . Yes.' And in winter?'
'In winter, I improve myself at the Halle Gate [the site of the reformatory for morally wayward children].'

Code, a system established by the ruling classes themselves and certainly inimicable to any hint of egalitarianism.

The Interior Minister's reply took four months to arrive, not because the authorities in Berlin regarded the issue as trivial, but because of the amount of time involved in corresponding with the Ministry of Justice, and obtaining and evaluating court records. In fact, the Ministry of the Interior was in full agreement with the District Government on the issue of Police Courts: the fact that it offered no more than a general corroboration of the District Government's position was due to the fact that the entire issue had been submitted to the Ministry of State for legal consultation and resolution – a process not completed until 1848. On the case itself: although the Minister of Justice may have agreed that the case was one of official misconduct, consideration of the files did give cause, in the Interior Ministry's view, to reflect on whether the seriousness of the incident might not warrant a criminal investigation – or to put it more bluntly – would the standing of the authorities and the 'honour' of the members of the District Government not be better served by an open and direct approach rather than an internal whitewash?

The inquiries pursued by the Government in Oppeln took a further three months. On 9 July, *Assessor* Eulenburg was at last ready to present the case to the Ministry for a final decision on the need for a criminal investigation. He began by presenting the statements of the victims. The first of the three men, Michael Zimolka, maintained that he had been tied to a chair and uninterruptedly beaten by two men for half an hour until he lost consciousness; the two then poured water on him, and set about him again until he made a confession. However, Eulenburg added that subsequent examination by a 'notary', 'County Physician', and 'County Surgeon' had found 'no external signs of ill-treatment' and 'no trace of injury'.

The second man, Gottlieb Hoose, alleged that he had been given five lashes on the back. Although he had made an immediate confession, 'he was given a couple of hundred blows' on the next day for 'denial' of his involvement in other thefts, and was also kicked in the side by the *Landrat*. The examining officials did indeed find that Hoose's back was 'swollen, green and blue' four days after the incident. However, the physicians added that 'no prejudice to health had arisen as a result of the correction'.

The third, Joseph Gutsfeld, also maintained that he had been beaten several times: on one occasion, the *Landrat* himself was alleged to have set about him with a leather whip. As with Zimolka, 'none of the physicians could detect even the slightest trace of ill-treatment'.

This was claimed to be 'everything' which the records held on the subject of the 'correction' meted out to the three men. Eulenburg also noted that four further accused, by the names of Theuer, Wistuba, Gonschior and Kawathelke, had also received 'their due'.

All in all, the *Landrat*'s records contained, according to Eulenburg, 'numerous' entries of 'corrections', which there was no reason to suppose were inaccurate or incomplete. The files noted that, on 15 August, Zimolka had received lashes for 'several weeks' casual vagrancy'. On 23 September, Hoose was treated to fifteen moderate lashes 'on the back' (as he had a 'slight rupture') for 'vagrancy' and 'denial'. Two days later he was beaten again for 'lying'. According to the testimony of the files, Gutsfeld had been given three lashes on 12 August, once for 'lying and vagrancy', the second time because he had 'grievously assaulted a shepherd boy the previous year', and finally again 'for lying'.

The statements made by subordinate officers – who, apart from the *Landrat* in the incident mentioned above, were the only parties to have actually inflicted a beating – did nevertheless fill in the omissions in the *Landrat*'s reports as to the quantity and intensity of force used. Prisch, the prison warder, and Tschope, the *Executor*, admitted that Zimolka had not 'received more than forty blows at any one time' – that is, had quite evidently been given several beatings. He had been unconscious 'twice', which explained why one of the two had 'poured a glass of water on his face'. In contrast, Hoose had 'never been unconscious'.

It was apparent from the outset that, during the course of the police investigation, one incidentally carried out contrary to regulations since there had been no consultation with the court authorities, the *Landrat* had ignored the regulations set out in the Criminal Code, according to which no examining magistrate should 'venture' 'to coerce any accused person by means of threats, violence, blows, punches or the infliction of physical suffering to obtain the truth.'[111]

Beatings were also forbidden for 'lying'. Wittenburg's excuse relied on the loophole, firstly, that police and judicial rules were very vague, especially as regards the degree of permitted punishment, and, secondly, that the common law provided for different punishments for different social groups – and favoured corporal punishment for the 'lower', 'uncultivated' classes.[112] Both could serve as justification for the casual and repeated beatings meted out. Quite simply, beating was regarded as permissible, if not actually called for, as 'correction'. Since it appeared that the accused were evidently guilty of a police misdemeanour ('vagrancy'), corporal punishment was – within bounds – permissible as punishment: and, as the lowest level of permanent police authority, the *Landrat* was entitled to order and administer it. The *Landrat*'s position was further bolstered by the fact that physical correction for 'lying' was not outlawed until 24 December 1844, after these incidents had taken place. In Eulenburg's view, Wittenburg was fully 'empowered to dispense punishment'.

Eulenburg concluded that, although Wittenburg's conduct had been 'irregular and impermissible', the offence none the less did not go beyond official misconduct, and ought to be dealt with via internal disciplinary procedures. There was no suggestion that any official had committed 'a common crime . . . or misdemeanour', which, in the normal course of events, would have implied a court trial and possible dismissal.

The object of reproach was not the deed itself, but the fact that the 'degree of correction had exceeded what was allowed'. Administering correction 'three times in one day', or 'until the onset of unconsciousness' was not allowed. 'A serious warning' would have been entirely adequate. What was crucial was the establishment of the correct balance between ends and means: in this instance, the preservation of public safety had taken precedence over the exercise of too many niceties – especially in view of the 'sly and deceitful ways of thieves'.

Whatever the motives and interests of the accused, as far as the police were concerned any attempts by the 'administered' to defend themselves or their interests against unpredictable and brutal physical intervention by the authorities, and their strategies and tactics of 'reappropriation' for a 'just distribution' of earthly riches, represented a 'wilful and deliberate' offence against the indisputable right of property and security. As far as the *Justitiar* was concerned, the 'result' obtained by the *Landrat* was sufficient vindication: in the final analysis, his 'zealousness' had rid the entire district of a pestilential gang of robbers. Eulenburg concluded, somewhat sardonically, that 'the courts would have been hard put to it to obtain such a result'. A few days later, the District Government concurred. *Oberregierungsrat* Ewald appended the appropriate memo to the Ministry: 'Wittenburg's good service in the interest of public safety is gratefully acknowledged even by the Royal Court of Appeal.'

During the following weeks, however, the Ministry decided that there was still a possibility that an official *offence* had been committed. The incident appeared to be one of an 'instance of private rage', the imposition of a punishment without proper sentence: a criminal investigation was unavoidable. As the matter was proceeding within the Ministry, Wittenburg – unaware of these developments – had asked the *Regierungspräsident*, Count von Pückler, to support him in obtaining a release from his office, or a 'reduction' in duties. Neither party made explicit mention of the underlying reason. Wittenburg cited the general 'increase in duties', which he had undertaken anyway only from a 'sense of honour'. Although Pückler acknowledged that the office of *Landrat* represented a 'focal point at which all the threads of administration – from above or below – intersect', he did not accept that the burden on Wittenburg was particularly great.

The verdict finally arrived more than a year later, on 20 October 1846 (more than two years after the incident). Wittenburg was sentenced to a fine of 100 Thalers (*c.* 10 per cent of his annual money income from the office) for 'assault committed in office', which was, however, 'without deleterious consequences for the parties offended against'. In doing so, the court kept to the lower range of punishments available to it: the offence was punishable by fines of from 80 to 200 Thalers or by between two and six months' citadel 'detention' or imprisonment, the latter to be decided by the court depending on the social position or 'rank' of the accused. The verdict was immediately accepted on the instruction of von Bodelschwingh (previously encountered as the *Oberpräsident* of the Rhine Province and now Interior Minister).

However, what was significant was that, after this public gratification for the victims, von Bodelschwingh issued the following assurance to the District Government in Oppeln on 16 November 1846:

> The imposition of a punishment for overstepping official powers, if this is motivated by an excess of zeal, does not in any way [appear] to impinge on honour, and, given his otherwise good conduct in office and the total blamelessness of his character, I can only wish that he withdraw his application for release from office . . . and I would regret it were he to insist on leaving his position.

The District Government was instructed to inform the *Landrat* of the Minister's view.

Wittenburg 'accommodated' his superior's wish. Although obliged to accept a public defeat – that is, one under the full gaze of the rival branch of state power – his superiors at all levels had put on record that they did not regard the event as jeopardising individual or collegial honour. In fact, the principle of excess which he had put into practice was entirely compatible with the administrative policing incumbent on all officials.

The extension of preventive repression: the 'dangerous dream of the working people'

With the expansion of industry, particularly factory industry, and, from the late 1830s,[113] of railway construction, one group within the overall category of 'suspicious persons' became the particular target of police interest: the producers – both in factory and domestic industry, and within the latter both those in manufacture and the handicraft trades. Of these, 'those periodically brought together from diverse areas for the purposes of railway construction' were held to require special vigilance.[114] The main concern was that these groups could become a burden on communal relief unless, as in the case of 'vagrants', they could be consigned to the workhouse (for up to three years), or, better, expelled from the country altogether. In addition, these concentrations of 'beggardly and hopeless proletarians' seemed to offer ready material for a 'general assailment of private property together with a simultaneous attack on the state'.[115]

The authorities in Berlin were especially worried that railway navvies, individuals devoid of any form of property, 'might become estranged from their homelands and detached from their accustomed employment, their homes and local churches, and could in many instances abandon themselves to disorderly and immoral conduct'.

However, investigations carried out by a number of *Landräte* early in 1843 revealed a more complex picture. Whereas officials in Silesia and Westphalia were very concerned to employ – and control – the working 'masses', many of whom were far from their own homes, the authorities in the Rhine Provinces seemed less troubled. Von Schaper, the Province's *Oberpräsident*, summed up the position. Ministerial worries had

> been borne out only to a slight extent. There was no lack of the necessary competition between workers in these densely populated areas, and most work had been carried out by people from the vicinity.

The railway managements could also take their pick of the available workforce, and had done so with considerable 'stringency'. The authorities had also proved cooperative: 'Judicious application of the rules against non-sanctioned persons and other official measures for surveillance and control made no small contribution.'

Such preventive measures provided an effective – occasionally draconian – obstacle to individual acts of resistance, not to mention mobs and riots. The *Oberpräsident* concluded laconically,

> More cannot be justly expected. It will be difficult to find a means able to act on the inner life of the people: at least, none of the authorities I have consulted has yet succeeded in supplying such a means.

Railway construction work was also inherently short-lived, rarely lasting more than a few months in any one locality. For Schaper, the greatest challenge to the police in the maintenance of long-term public safety would come from the more enduring changes in the industrial structure — principally, the establishment of factories.

A report by the Berlin police *Präsidium* in response to plans to establish a factory gives some indication of how the police and administrative mind saw events – although, in this case, their objections were overruled by the Ministry of the Interior:

> Circumstances in the capital do not make it desirable for large factories to be established employing a large number of people at low, and, because of industrial fluctuations, varying, wages. The uncertainty of income, and in most cases their inadequacy for local circumstances, will lead to the creation of a large mass of proletarians: these would not be desirable anywhere, but least of all here in the royal capital. Recently there have been disturbing signs of dangerous coalitions. The police *Präsidium* would have to declare its unambiguous opposition to any steps which might favour these questionable industrial institutions.[116]

The 'popular movements' of 1848–9 reinforced police mistrust of those dependent on wages and outwork in the industrial centres. The request for a police superintendent specifically for Iserlohn from the *Regierungspräsident* in Arnsberg in 1850 was typical. In 1849,

> the ease with which the entire factory population of the town, circa 80 per cent of the overall population including their families, could be led into disaffection from the law, how this volcano spreads its fissures in all directions, was made frighteningly clear.

Regierungspräsident Naumann outlined a counter-strategy based on a division of labour: 'The prevention of such outbreaks requires that a stronger power must stand in readiness on the spot.' At the same time, 'the sources [of the outbreak] should be ascertained and thwarted in good time. This is the task of the police-administration.' Some weeks later a second report from Naumann clarified what he had meant by the term 'stronger power': a military garrison. In short, his strategy was one of suppression by the military and prevention by the police. For 'a deep embitterment is creeping in the silence' – worse, 'the dream of a general levelling between the rich and poor has taken firm hold amongst the working people'.[117] This 'dream' and its political consequences – trade unions and workers' parties, not least strikes – subsequently became one of the main driving forces behind police activities.

Steps to tighten up the organisation of the police were particularly in evidence. And these were not confined to the 'higher' or 'security police', as was the case with the Berlin police under von Hinckeldey in the 1850s.[118] After 1849, the police in administrative centres such as Koblenz and Trier, and industrial conurbations, such as Krefeld, Elberfeld and Barmen, were temporarily detached from the municipal authorities and put under the command of specific police departments. At the same time, the constabulary (*Schutzmannschaft*), which after 1848 was organised in Berlin on military lines analogous to the Gendarmerie, clearly registered some successes, at least in the eyes of its superiors.[119] During the 1860s the state resumed its practice of trying to offload the costs of policing. A number of the police departments established by the state were dissolved and put back under municipal control. In 1862 the Minister of the Interior proposed to the District Governments that the Gendarmes might be turned into police sergeants in the large towns. This would have eliminated the obvious and persistent frictions between the Gendarmes and police officers, conflicts in which their respective civil and military chiefs also became embroiled. It would also have implied the professionalisation of the constabulary. Officials at regional level were against the plan. The *Regierungspräsident* in Arnsberg stressed that the boundary between town and country was very fluid, and that in his own area industrial producers were found mostly on the land. The *Landrat*, to whom the Gendarmes, but not police sergeants, were directly subordinate, therefore required 'strong means of execution'.[120] After the experiences of 1849 with the 'easily ignited and no less potentially violently explosive, industrial workforce' (in Iserlohn, Hagen, and Elberfeld in the neighbouring Government District of Düsseldorf), it seemed imperative that the supervision of the local 'armed force' should be in the hands of the *Landräte*, who were not 'too close' to the population, and the Gendarmes, with their tried and tested military organisation and character. In fact, the 1863 Gendarme Manual expressly stated that 'Gendarmes are fellow soldiers not fellow workers'.

However, efforts to raise the number of police per inhabitant, and adjust this figure to the degree of danger supposedly represented by the populus were delayed until after the expiry of the Socialist Act in 1890. A ratio of one executive officer to 2,000 residents was supposed to be the minimum – with an aim of 1 to 1,200 in the industrial towns.

One parallel development to this was the increase in the dependency of the local communally organised police on the higher supervisory authorities. *Landräte* and District Governments, in part, assumed the right to issue regulations and sought to eliminate any local 'weaknesses' by demanding reports and exercising extensive powers of control.[121] In addition, in the 1890s state police forces were established in industrial towns without regard to cost. Six district police superintendents were appointed to oversee the regional coordination of the political, 'higher', police in the administrative 'open field' of the Ruhr area, with its patchwork of factory villages but few real towns.

However, the reorganisation or expansion of the police was merely a means or consequence. As far as the senior officers and officials were concerned, what was crucial was that every policeman on duty was utterly convinced of the 'danger threatening both the state and the existing order of things in general' (a formulation used by the Ministry of the Interior in 1851 to ward off a request for more specific instructions).[122] The 'social question' – the obverse of the 'dream' of social equality outlined by Naumann – was correspondingly only ever perceived in the form of 'suspicious or potentially disaffected outside factory hands', and 'unemployed or workshy individuals' who, according to a decree issued by the Interior Ministry of the 1850s, 'were to be rigorously expelled wherever they multiplied danger to public order', unless they were 'locals, either by birth or three years' residence'.

Restrictions on the right of assembly and association, the denial of freedom of combination until 1869, and its subsequent erosion once conceded, together with other draconian measures imposed 'from above' – all elements in the 'minor state of siege', especially the power to remove unwanted persons – had become well-established and accepted forms of policing prior to the introduction of the Socialist Acts in 1878. Such practices were not, moreover, confined to the traditional public sphere. The overriding maxim that the existing order should be preserved frequently allowed the dividing line between private interests and public authority to be breached. For example, in 1877 a number of collieries and large factories in the Arnsberg district applied for 'special police protection' at their own expense: no problems were encountered in deputising a number of officers to this task. The only aspect which troubled the higher authorities was that the 'official standing' of these officers might be 'compromised by their use for private purposes, such as the delivery of messages'.[123] If the bearers of sovereignty could so easily become fellow workers, then care had to be exercised in linking the rationality of domination at factory level with the apparatus of state authority.

Despite the 'tightening up' and reorganisation of the police in the 1850s and 1860s, the Ministry of the Interior – which bore ultimate responsibility – did not grant the police powers commensurate with their organisation until after the miners' strike of 1889, which had been suppressed with considerable bloodshed by the military. The administrative authorities then decided that the police had to be capable of 'effectively countering public disorder at the outset' and in particular the activities of 'the working masses who were inclined to such disorders' which had to be 'strangled at birth'.[124]

And, as much as the military commanders wanted to retain control and ultimate decision over any possible intervention, they were also eager to reduce the less 'satisfying' work of ordinary policing as much as possible. Police deterrence against such dangers therefore had to perform the feat 'of being both vigorous and cautious':[125] in other words, of acting both militarily and as a civil power at one and the same time. And should officers find themselves compelled 'to intervene with arms, they must make immediate and effective use of their weapons', including firearms. 'So-called warning shots are to be strictly avoided'.

Police jurisdiction and corporal punishment

Although the exercise of penal authority was merely one amongst a number of police tasks, this 'police jurisdiction' was customarily dealt with separately in police manuals. Any consideration of this distinct sphere will inevitably entail some overlap with the material discussed in the previous sections of this chapter. But whereas these dealt with the standards and practices of officials, this section is concerned with their procedures. We have already noted that the actual practice of police observation and intervention was not exhaustively defined in advance: they could take a variety of 'hues'. Nevertheless, one constant element of police conduct was the imposition of punishment 'on the spot'. It is therefore unlikely that those very same officers – or their colleagues

– would want to be able to differentiate between investigation and prevention, on the one hand, and the exercise of police jurisdiction on the other. Constant pressure to act from the 'public' and from their superiors, combined with their entanglement in highly complex situations on the ground, meant that police officers were rarely able to make such distinctions.

The 'natural border' between police and court jurisdiction – aspects of an 'open border'

Von der Heyde's manual on police penal powers (*Polizei-Strafgewalt*) defined a 'police misdeameanour' as a breach of the law which did not 'undermine the main purpose of the state': examples included, 'culpable recklessness, dangerous carelessness, vexatious immorality'.[126] A 'summary' process seemed both quite adequate and entirely unobjectionable in such instances – a view shared by Ministers and members of the Council of State.[127] The 'entire efficacy' of police jurisdiction 'depended principally' on the 'swiftness with which the individual conducting the investigation intervened'.[128] Not only would this facilitate establishing the facts, but 'any delay in the investigation will also entail delay in sentencing'. And this could jeopardise the entire logic of giving the police the authority to impose punishment: 'Delay in administering the less serious punishments which are normally reserved for lesser police contraventions largely negates their deterrent effect.'

The objective was therefore an abbreviated summary procedure, in which the 'strict formal requirements of juridical proof' would not apply. Rather, officers were to 'proceed initially in accordance with their conscientious convictions'.[129] Inevitably, such attempts to mark out a distinct sphere of police jurisdiction, with its own procedures, encouraged rather than deterred unequal treatment, discrimination, arbitrariness and excessive severity.

The initial problem was to establish a clear dividing line between the penal powers of the police and those of the courts, and moreover one which could be easily applied on an everyday basis. Merely differentiating the two spheres according to the severity of punishment would not suffice, and in fact presupposed that such a difference already existed. (According to the Prussian Legal Code, the police could not impose a punishment exceeding fourteen days imprisonment, twenty lashes or a fine of 5 Thalers.)

A passage from a lecture by Svarez reveals the extent to which even enlightened and reforming codifiers remained oblivious to the practical problems of demarcation. In his 1791/2 Crown Prince Lectures, Svarez cited an example to illustrate the difference between the two sorts of jurisdiction. Police punishment could be inflicted on those, 'who, in violation of police regulations, place flower pots in their windows'. In contrast, those who, 'even though only out of careless and gross oversight, throw something out of a window and inflict bodily harm on a passer-by' would be subject to the punishment of the courts.[130]

The crux was, of course, that the second case could easily arise out of the first: in practice both spheres were closely interlinked. In addition, the police were also obliged to make the 'first intervention', that is initial and preliminary investigations, even in criminal cases.[131] Given the undisputed powers of the police to be the sole arbiter in those cases impinging exclusively on 'public quiet, safety and order', such a linking of circumstances during a 'first intervention' could, despite formal prohibition, be used to overlook the fact that the actual offence involved a 'mixture' of police misdemeanour and 'deliberate or indictable offence', and hence justify dispensing punishment on the spot.

Three pertinent cases were cited during the discussion on police jurisdiction in the Council of State in 1826.[132] The fact that each took place under the umbrella of patrimonial police authority had no particular bearing on their general relevance for the totality of police jurisdiction east of the Rhine. West of the Rhine, together with the former Duchy of Berg, where French law still applied, judicial police courts remained untouched. Courts of first instance were presided over by justices of the peace (*Friedensrichter*), with appeal to the *Zuchtpolizeigerichte*, courts for the trial of misdemeanours.

In the first of the three cases, a certain von Bülow-Cummerow, an estate owner from Mark-Brandenburg – and an implacable opponent of any moves towards either bureaucracy or legal codification – had sentenced a schnapps distiller to three days' imprisonment on his estate. The reason,

> because he had abandoned himself to drink, had then sworn and cursed, placing the village at risk of fire through his disobedience and negligence, had called on other servants to disobey orders, had refused to disclose who had been in his tavern and, with a torrent of abuse and insults, had resisted the confiscation of a suitcase.

As in the other two cases, the issue here involved a disturbance of the peace; but this was compounded by affront and insubordination, 'offences which do not number amongst police contraventions', as the Council of State stressed. In the second case an estate owner had imposed twelve lashes and one day in jail for ill-treatment of a servant; and, in the third, a different estate owner had sentenced a weaver to three days' imprisonment for refusing to accept his secretary's instructions during a banquet which the Junker had held for the village. The Council of State summed up its disquiet on the implied abstract issue in the following terms: 'Where would it lead if an estate owner were able to punish abuse allegedly directed at himself?'

One aspect of the problem could be disposed of at the outset: in each case, the custodial sentence was below that legally prescribed for 'offensive language' (*Injurien*). Even 'mild affront' could have incurred two to four weeks' imprisonment or hard labour.[133] Given that estate owners would not have wished to be deprived of their workforce without very good cause, such punishments would certainly have represented an unattractive alternative. And in that respect these cases were typical. This aspect is also reflected in the varying reactions of the authorities in each case. Whilst Bülow got off with a reprimand from the District Government, the other estate owners received court sentences of a fine of 30 Thalers in one case and eight months' (provisionally) citadel detention in the other – a form of confinement which impinged little on the honour or even comfort of the detainee.

The 'natural border' between the jurisdiction of the police and that of the courts noted by Heyde was not only hard to pin down in practice in individual cases. Out in the 'open country' it remained of merely academic interest, an empty expression shifting position depending on local social and economic interests and power relations – one link in an unbroken chain of domination. None the less, it was also the site of a growing conflict between the administrative and judicial bureaucracies.

The competition between these apparatuses was not only a matter which engaged ministerial officials or remained confined to the patrimonial structures of East Elbia. The entire internal and police administration, including those communal authorities which exercised police powers on the state's behalf, made use of police jurisdiction. And, despite a recommendation from Klein during the codification debate, following the 1808 administrative reforms 'police jurisdiction [could] be exercised by all police authorities, urban and rural, including those municipal executives entrusted with the administration of the police'.[134]

Some sceptical officials in the Council of State wanted to leave 'open . . . whether this rule, through which so many small local authorities have acquired such extensive police jurisdiction and are removed from the competition of the courts, is necessary and useful'.

Klein, for instance, had expressed reservations some thirty years previously: 'It is, in general, desirable that any police punishment, be it large or small, should be imposed only by a proper justice.' It was 'always a matter of regret when the state has to entrust such inquiries to persons lacking in the appropriate mode of thinking, experience and knowledge'.[135]

At the same time, despite these reservations, some members of the Council of State did concede that there was 'much truth' in the view that the police authorities ought not be to 'compromised by the contrary decision of a judge or inhibited in their useful activities by a long wait for such a decision'.

The widespread practice of police punishment, especially on the East Elbian estates, inevitably touched on the judiciary's claims to exercise jurisdiction – that is, a claim raised by a competing apparatus of domination. On the face of it, patrimonial police authority exercised, as a rule, by lay persons in wide tracts of the 'open countryside' represented an attack on the 'honour' of judicial officials, judges, prosecutors and procurators. For such officials, the 'rule of law' in a state whose constitutional practice had been codified at the turn of the nineteenth century was *their* domain. Senior officials of the judiciary and their local representatives claimed the right to exercise all juridical powers, even in spheres where the Junker ruled local affairs. However, their attempt to assert this claim came to nothing.[136]

It was mostly the defenders, rather than the critics, of the status quo who used arguments rooted exclusively in terms of legal or administrative necessity. The arguments advanced by the advocates of the prevailing position in the Council of State – that police jurisdiction was exercised without legal training – was irrefutable:

> In the domains, [it is exercised] by domain officials and intendants, and in

the towns in part by Directors and Presidents of Police, and in part by the municipal executives, none of whom have judicial qualification or formal examination, and in the absence of consultation with a member of the judiciary'.[132]

This argument was initially intended to head off the claim that jurisdiction in the municipalities was exercised by [illegible] officials, and that, unlike estate owners, these offered more of a guarantee of conformity with the rule of law. However, the [illegible] premise of the argument lacked any empirical foundation whatsoever: that it was quite sufficient simply to keep a watchful lookout for signs of abuse, in which case District Governments could provide redress if necessary, depriving Junkers of their police authority.

Apart from the fact that this argument utterly ignored, and possibly encouraged, the intimidation of the dominated through the initial trust granted to the estate owners – regardless of subsequent [illegible] – officials [illegible] or the [illegible] on the estates by subsequent interference. Only extreme lapses were to be handled outside the discrete procedures of an internal hearing. More exposure would merely undermine authority. [illegible] Dronke depicted the course of such an internal hearing following a complaint in a fictitious, but certainly quite realistic, case. A journeyman shoemaker complained to a Director of Police about the conduct of a superintendent; the superintendent was asked [illegible] and naturally gave only his version of events, [illegible] was that the journeyman's brother, [illegible] improperly expelled from the town, and [illegible] entirely probable that one's patience will eventually run out with such people who, despite their evident and partly admitted guilt [illegible] continue to use the most imbecilic lies, tricks and impudence.' A few days later the shoemaker was summoned and rebuked for his impudence in making a complaint after his unlawful conduct. As the shoemaker tried to answer, he was promptly thrown out. A second attempt at complaint over this subsequent treatment by the police was rejected. Dronke summed up: 'this is not an uncommon course for such complaints. On the first occasion the higher authority will take subordinate officials under their wing inasmuch as they are closer to them than to the complainant; in the second, they are involved as a party.' We should add that this scene was staged in a town, theoretically less shut off from public scrutiny than the 'open country'.

There were also technical administrative problems in rural areas as far as the 'right of complaint' and supervision of abuses were concerned. Full-time administrative institutions were thin on the ground; they were also closely involved with the authorities they were supposed to be controlling. The *Landrate*, for example, had to be drawn from the local landowning class, and at a personal level usually continued to socialise very intensively with it. Under such circumstances it was unlikely that information about possible abuses would ever arrive regularly or promptly at the doors of the District

Governments, even when local officials and the few mobile Gendarmes kept a watchful eye.

During the 1826 debate on police powers in the Council of State, the minority who favoured restricting patrimonial powers made no attempt to conceal the implications of social transformation, more specifically the consequences of the capitalist transformation of agriculture. Whereas estate owners might once have plausibly possessed the 'capacity to exercise any kind of jurisdiction', this was 'now' much more unlikely, 'since the ownership of a manorial estate and its associated patrimonial jurisdiction is no longer confined solely to the higher ranks, but can fall into the hands of the lower'.[140] This threw a particular light on the argument employed by the majority of the Council of State who favoured using 'education and previous life history' as a kind of ersatz qualification for Junkerdom, with less emphasis on formal academic training and more on the subject's overall way of life, 'honour' and military career. Naturally, the implication was not mentioned: state officials would grant the Junkers an acceptable level of police powers, and hence in a sense guarantee the essence of Junkerdom, whilst carefully controlling access to these powers by selecting out only 'suitable' bourgeois estate owners – some of whom would be members of their own caste.

However, the sceptics did not have their way. In 1827 a unanimous ministerial report (admittedly with the exception of the Justice Minister) and majority report from the Council of State confirmed that estate owners should judge all 'minor' police offences (with a possible punishment of up to fourteen days' imprisonment, a 5 Thaler fine, or moderate 'correction' of up to twenty strokes) without recourse to specialist judicial officials or justiciaries (*Gerichtshalter*).[141]

Estate owners were thus expressly empowered to continue their previous practice as they thought fit, something which varied considerably from region to region. In the Province of Saxony, for example, the authorities reported that estate owners not only extensively assumed *responsibility* for the whole of police jurisdiction, but also actually *administered* it themselves. The estate owners could easily vary the practice by which jurisdiction was exercised, and those subject to estate authority had to steel themselves for a change each time their estate changed hands. In the District of Potsdam the practice was very diverse, with some jurisdiction in the hands of the individual estate owners and in other areas in the same District under the administration of justiciaries. The District Government in Potsdam also made it clear that it was more than tolerant on the matter of the failure to appoint a justiciary: the Government never interfered if those estate owners exercising local jurisdiction 'were qualified to undertake proper inquiry'.[142] Formal qualification took second place to administrative judgement and discretion; under such circumstances, ruling interests, and the social and personal affinity between officials and Junkers, inevitably overtook legal niceties.

The substance of police jurisdiction extended over the entire sphere of 'public quiet, safety and order' in the broad sense of 'welfare and security policing' established in the Orders of 1808 and 1817.[143] What was not clear, however, was whether local police authorities could punish only offences against the respective local police regulations or whether they also had jurisdiction over violations of the general regulations in a county (*Kreis*) as decreed by Provincial and District Governments.[144] There was also one fundamental ambiguity. Should the level of punishment imposed under police jurisdiction be restricted to the limits with which the holders of police authority on the estates had to be content when they exercised police authority personally instead of delegating it to a 'justiciary'? Could they merely impose punishments of up to fourteen days in jail, 5 Thaler fines or 'moderate correction'? This limit was also significant in another respect. The Criminal Code (*Kriminalordnung*) of 1805 had established that, where summary sentences within this limit were imposed convicted persons had no other recourse than complaint to the superior administrative authorities; formal appeal through the courts was granted only for more severe sentences (which, according to the Code, could also be imposed by the police).

On 8 March 1830, at the instigation of the Minister of the Interior, the King issued a Cabinet Order – against the wishes of the Minister of Justice – confirming a procedure which the Interior Minister had portrayed as the current practice.[145] The authorities on the spot – and in particular the patrimonial police authorities – were given licence to punish *all* police misdemeanours 'where the misdemeanour contravenes local police regulations', almost always the case, according to the Minister. Moreover, the contravention should not have been associated with the committing of a crime, as the judiciary would then assume responsibility. However, with the exception of that jurisdiction exercised personally by estate owners, 'this power of the local police authorities may be applied without limitation up to a certain level of the legally threatened punishment'.

In the case of any complaint or appeal (*Rekurs*) against a police sentence, the limits already cited remained in force. The accused could proceed to the courts only when these limits were exceeded. This was another failure for the Minister of Justice's attempts to extend the powers of the judiciary. He had called for any misdemeanour which exceeded these limits for 'minor offences' to be brought before a court in the first instance (see p. 107 above).

Fictitious 'equality before the law' and the 'mixing' of powers

During the 1826 Council of State debate on patrimonial police authority, the (unnamed) sceptics raised the point that establishing a viable system of police jurisdiction would entail more than mere organisation and training:

> It involves more than knowledge of police laws and proficiency in administration. First and foremost it demands impartiality and tranquillity of mind: these alone enable the investigator and judge to distinguish truth from falsehood, premeditation from thoughtlessness and carelessness.[146]

There is even some evidence of understanding for those at the receiving end of these administrative powers and practices. In some cases, 'which

4 An arrest

Beisele:	Arrested!? Why?
Gendarme:	I've been following you for three streets and against all convention you've neither smashed a street lamp nor shrieked. You are therefore suspected of involvement in a clandestine conspiracy whose aim is to make a fool of public authority.
Beisele:	And if we had smashed a street lamp and shrieked?
Gendarme:	In that case I would have arrested you only for disturbing the public peace.

include the most trivial of contraventions . . . the explanation will be wearisome and the decision difficult'.

In plain language, what this obscure formulation meant was that the plethora of police tasks and regulations not only had a widely varying impact on the 'administered' but could also make it difficult for officers 'on the spot' to behave 'appropriately' when confronted with the maze of rules and norms combined with direct pressure exerted by local power groups.

As far as the authorities were concerned, in theory at least, police control and punishment was to serve 'general concerns' and 'protect the whole', not merely further individual interests. Police administration was, therefore, aimed at 'prevention' and the deterrent effect of rapid retribution. As reports and recommendations from officials in Berlin constantly reiterated,

> The petty sins are the most common; they occur more frequently and must be swiftly dealt with. Punishment, if there is to be one, must follow

> immediately on the deed . . . The situation is different with more serious matters. These are more infrequent, they must be dealt with more formally, and the care to be taken in ensuring that the accused is not exposed to arbitrariness or ill-treatment may become the overwhelming concern.[147]

This lofty perspective obscured the fact that, as far the dominated classes were concerned, those 'petty' ends were precisely those which played the greatest role in securing their everyday subsistence. The mere risk of incurring a police punishment whilst engaged in 'normal' everyday life inevitably exposed them to constant arbitrariness and ill-treatment.

Such policing inevitably became preoccupied with controlling that sphere of communal life which, for the propertyless, must have represented virtually the only social space within which they could pursue their social interests and material needs. Although travellers from 'better circles' also fell prey to the pettiness and harassment of the 'Passport and Aliens Police', those most vulnerable were itinerant journeymen, the diverse and numerous floating poor, forced to move from town to town, and direct producers released by their employers: the greatest suspicion was attached to those falling into the police categories of 'vagrant', 'beggar' or 'Jew'. Provisions intended to prevent 'riots and tumult' also, in practice, became targeted upon very specific groups. Although heads of households and the owners of workshops, manufactories and factories could incur penalties for neglecting to keep their 'pupils' and workers under lock and key, the main aim of these provisions was to prevent non-approved 'spontaneous' gatherings in public places.[148] Parties, demonstrations, marches or masques held by the propertyless, who naturally lacked access to private houses or gardens, inevitably fell victim. The breadth of this form of domination, which also had recourse to a particular notion of morality, was also evident in the numerous regulations governing drinking places – and not merely in the form of controls on the drinking hours. The threat of punishment for landlords who failed to take adequate steps to prevent 'excesses' or report travellers to the police, as required by regulations,[149] reflected their ambivalent status as far as the authorities were concerned – small landlords whose social role involved more than simply selling their wares. Landlords evidently often played the role of link between 'polite' society and the underworld. Apart from their own pecuniary interest and gain from their trade, they also had to be accommodating to their customers, even when these were the 'toughest folk'. Police punishment in this field rested on a kind of collective preventive measure.

Here, as with 'misdemeanours incurred in the keeping of the so-called Feast of St Monday',[150] Hevde recommended, somewhat laconically, 'severe police punishment', in doing so merely drawing the conclusion from a number of individual ministerial decrees and the absence of any specific statutory punishment. Although the Prussian Legal Code forbade gatherings of journeymen 'amongst themselves', it did not prescribe a penalty. The fact that 'severe penalties' might involve exceeding what was allowed under police powers owing to ambiguities in the law rather than sheer police ill-will is illustrated in the example of police conduct towards 'wilful youths'.

Heyde's commentary prescribed 'severe police punishment' both for the 'instigators' of a riot and for 'wilful youths', 'who cause unrest on the streets and in public places, commit gross immorality, or indulge in screaming and whistling liable to give rise to a mob'.[151] The Prussian Legal Code devoted a paragraph to each type of malefactor; and, although each was apparently assigned a different degree of punishment, both were in fact subject to the same overall limits[152] of six weeks' imprisonment, 50 Thaler fine or corporal punishment.[153] 'Instigators' were to receive up to six weeks in jail or 'a corresponding fine or corporal punishment'. 'Wilful youths' were to be punished with 'an appropriate custodial sentence, corporal punishment, or detention in a house of correction'. This was intended as a 'discretionary punishment'. Heyde was therefore quite correct to equate the two. In contrast, his use of the term 'severe punishment' overlooked the fact that not all police authorities had the same powers to exhaust the full scope of the permitted penalty. Patrimonial holders of police jurisdiction could act only if the case was expected to involve a 'minor misdemeanour' (up to fourteen days' imprisonment, etc.). Otherwise, the matter was to be referred to a legally trained justiciary. Heyde's formula, however, enabled the barely legally-literate Junkers to assume, in perfectly good faith even, more extensive legal powers much more easily than before. The only alternative was to make an implicit prejudgement of the case. A legal procedure could be followed on the estates – that is, excluding any 'mixing' with criminal acts and with due regard for the different powers of estate owners with jurisdictional powers on the one hand and proper justiciaries on the other – only by prejudging the severity of the offence before the trial, that is, via an illegal procedure.[154]

As far as those at the receiving end were concerned, what was paramount was naturally whether these arrangements increased or diminished their punishment. Whereas punishment by the police invariably meant, or at least included, corporal punishment, the courts could be relied on to impose a term in prison. For owners of the means of production the main consideration – not only on the land – was continued access to the labour power of the convicted person, together with low rates of occupancy, and hence lower running costs, for the local jail. The only individuals likely to be in a position to pay a fine of 2–3 Thalers were itinerants such as travelling merchants; such a sum would have swallowed up at least a half, if not all, the monthly cash income of a servant or day-labourer. Estate owners, in particular, who were able to combine in one individual the roles of proprietor and police authority imposed or urged the administration of draconian – but short – corporal punishments and paid scant attention to the doubts expressed by senior officials that such punishments represented insufficient deterrence or retribution.

Such doubts were less evident amongst the prospective and actual victims. A long period of imprisonment could have almost incalculably serious consequences for survival, even where the family could act as a safety net. On the one hand, public flogging bit not only into the flesh but also the self-esteem and 'honour' of those undergoing it. In the absence of concrete evidence, we can reconstruct the complexity of their situation only in the most general terms. Even 'well-meaning' observers could not have access to this inner aspect of external punishment (cf. pp. 119ff below).

The tendency of those entrusted with police powers to use the general police clause to assume powers and 'intervene' with draconian and excessive punishments against particularly susceptible or visible social groups is illustrated in the following case from Pomerania.

On 5 February 1829 the Minister of Justice approached the Minister of the Interior with a request to induce a Pomerian Junker – through the agency of the District Government – to amend an excessive and, formally, unlawful Police Order regulating the fees payable by market-stall holders on his property.[155] The Order not only entitled the Junker in question, von Bonin-Lupow, to levy a substantial fine (1 Thaler) from those who had not paid the fee but, and more disquietingly for the Minister, also provided that

> those who did not accept the stall assigned to them but insisted on their own could expect to be arrested for disturbing the peace and fined 5 Thalers or be given a corresponding term of imprisonment.

It was not merely the patent fact that the individual holding police authority, Bonin, had sought to 'supplement' the revenues of the landowner – Bonin himself – as the Ministry of the Interior had observed. He had also instituted a list of penalties 'without higher authority' and thus improperly extended the right to the personal *exercise* of policing and police jurisdiction to embrace the right to *decree* what police regulations should exist. What was remarkable, however, was that, following the first complaint from the Ministry of the Interior, the District Government in Köslin had ruled that Bonin had acted entirely properly.

Nevertheless, the information which trickled back to the centre about the Bonin affair was probably untypical: its disclosure had been entirely fortuitous. In an evident attempt to raise the official standing of his action, Bonin had had the entire matter published in the Köslin District Government's 'official gazette' with no resistance whatsoever from the local officials, who were subsequently entrusted with the investigation into the issue.

Patrimonial police jurisdiction: the legal equation of private and 'general' interests

Bonin's case illustrates one widespread and controversial aspect of how the police courts functioned on East Elbian estates: not merely the possibility but the inevitability of a collision – or perhaps collusion – between particular private interests and the 'general' interests of policing. The estate owner was a private proprietor; at the same time he was entrusted with the stewardship of the 'common good' on his land. The Prussian Legal Code's ban on 'self-help'[156] evidently stood in competition to the extensive, but diffuse, powers exercisable under the authority possessed by the police. The central authorities first set about a more precise definition and demarcation of the problem in

November 1830. Cases in which estate owners were 'dealing in their own concerns' and where they could 'be regarded as a party to the case' were to be entrusted to a third party, either a justiciary or the local *Landrat*.

Something of the character of what customarily passed for justice on the estates is revealed by the response of the Junkers to these proposals: most regarded them as an unwarranted attempt to intrude into their time-honoured powers and sphere of influence. Their formal objections were submitted in 1834.

In the same year, von Bülow-Cummerow (see p. 104 above) submitted a case involving an estate owner and factory master for decision 'at the highest level'.[157] The estate owner, in company with his son-in-law, had detained a member of the fire-watch, who lived on the estate, in the servants' quarters for leaving his post (although nothing had gone amiss as a result). He was then sentenced to two days in jail in the nearest town and given no opportunity to appeal to the District Government. In fact the convicted person went directly to the courts. In turn, his case against the estate owner and his son-in-law was accepted by the Minister of the Interior, as Police Minister, on the grounds of wrongful imprisonment and duress: furthermore, the Minister did not apply to have the proceedings quashed at that stage. Astonishingly, the application for this came from the Minister of Justice with the approval of the King. Setting aside this 'political word from on high' in favour of a Junker, the legal point at issue was left unresolved – namely, 'To what extent is the authority to undertake a personal inquiry and punish an offence constrained by any self-interest arising out of a police misdemeanour?'[158]

For the Ministry of State there was no perceptible threat of a perversion of the law through the existence of such an interest. In fact, 'in a certain sense every individual has an interest' wherever the police were required to intervene since 'the police always act in accordance with general concerns and for the protection of the whole'.[159] Police officials and those exercising police authority 'generally' found themselves in a situation 'in which they would pursue their own interests to a greater or lesser degree at the same time'. The Council of State adopted a similar line. 'If the personal interest of an individual, and this can always be the person who has to execute police measures, were necessarily to be excluded from such execution, the inevitable outcome would be a complete lack of the means required for policing to be carried out at all.'

By implication, this principle applied not only to the policing of estates, but also to the local police in the towns, to judges, bailiffs and mayors in Westphalia and the Rhineland, and the *Woyts*, the District Mayors in Posen.

Such an apparently logical solution left no room for differences in power or conflicts of interest. Real inequalities of power and interest seemed of little or no consequence. Nevertheless, the solution was not entirely legally watertight: there still remained the question as to whether the police authorities, in addition to their own tasks of policing, had not also acquired the power to intervene in 'legal actions proper' outside the sphere of 'public safety and order'. This was mainly an issue in conflicts between master and servant east of the Elbe where the police authorities represented not only the court of first and often final instance but also the employer and police rolled into one. According to the position taken by ministerial officials, such conflicts ought to have gone before a justiciary or *Landrat*. Admittedly, this remained a fairly bureaucratic and academic recommendation, if not an act of downright deliberate self-deception. For, aside from the personal dependency of the justiciary and the affinity and common interests between Junker neighbours, even when one was the *Landrat*, estate owners could easily inflict police punishments on servants 'according to the degree of their culpability' for failing to 'perform their duties with due industry and attentiveness'.[160] This legal option, which Heyde had extracted from an article in the Servants Ordinance, enabled estate owners to act in their own case without further ado.

Police regulations did not differentiate between servants and day-labourers as far as these provisions were concerned. Servants could also be punished under Article 77 of the Servants Ordinance: 'no legal redress is available where a servant enrages his master through unseemly conduct and as a result is rebuked or mildly assailed'.

Abuse and assault were regarded as 'moderate punishment' which masters were entitled to inflict outside of any police or judicial penal structure: under such circumstances it is difficult to see when and how any man- or maidservant could ever subsequently bring a complaint to the *Landrat*.

Legal disputes with servants or temporary wage-labourers over issues of wages or dismissal could still be brought before the courts, but this would only have involved demands for recompense from masters who had already enjoyed the service – the labour-power – of the direct producer. An Order issued in 1838 granted the exercise of personal authority by estate owners for 'minor misdemeanours' (subject to fourteen days' imprisonment, etc.) even where 'their personal interest coincided with the general interest'.[161]

Responsibility for drawing the line between personal jurisdiction and the jurisdiction of a justiciary or the *Landrat* was devolved upon the local holders of power, especially under the estate economy. Their interests, and their moods, took precedence. The Junker, or 'that person deemed suitable to represent him by virtue of their reliability and training', that is the 'tenant, supervisor or bookkeeper'[162] not only had a practical headstart when it came to defining the situation, but could also rely on legal backing. The immediate imposition of a punishment, in the form of confinement or 'correction', enabled them to impose their power directly and immediately on the convicted person, not merely for that one, undoubtedly painful, moment but also through its recollection as a bitter and unforgettable warning for the future. This applied even where masters were subsequently called on to pay fines and, in extreme cases, actually did so.

The case of a village mayor from the Government District of Danzig, gives a vivid illustration of the support lent to the autonomy of police courts by the administration. The case involved a collision between the property interests of an estate owner, whom the mayor had to represent, and boundaries of departmental activity. However, a number of massive and openly illegal excesses were left completely unpunished.[163]

In 1828 the mayor involved, Reinhardt, had inflicted 'corporal punishment and a summary procedure' upon two self-confessed pig thieves. When questioned about the incident by the judiciary, the Ministry of the Interior justified the mayor's conduct – which represented an invasion into what was clearly within the ambit of the courts – with the argument that he 'had clearly intended only to shorten the penal procedure'. Although such a wish was 'contrary to the law', it was 'entirely excusable'. 'Consideration must be given to the extent to which the property of people on the land was endangered by the growing number of thefts.'

This was not, therefore, a case of a 'private concern' peculiar to the mayor, or of any 'desire for retribution'. Although it had entailed a breach of service conduct, it was in no way criminal, as the judiciary alleged. In the latter's view, Reinhardt had arrogated a 'sovereign right' of the judicial authorities, under which all proceedings against theft belonged to the criminal courts. The Ministry of Justice added: 'that Mayor Reinhardt is also accused of inflicting twenty lashes on a suspect in the case of the theft of a cow, although these suspicions were not subsequently corroborated'.

The specific question mark over the mayor was clearly not the major issue for the justice department. Rather, its representative sought to undermine the case of the internal administration, which held that swift punishment was essential if thieves were to be effectively deterred:

> If the growing frequency of theft on the land is to be effectively prevented then the full penalty of the law must be applied. If a mayor theft is only punished by the police with a quite inadequate penalty, this will, of necessity, militate against *this* objective. Furthermore, such police punishments for a criminal offence are beside the point since they cannot obviate the initiation of full criminal proceedings.

The judiciary therefore inverted the criticism usually employed by officials of the administration. The full severity of the law required a proper penal procedure, possibly culminating in two years' hard labour in a house of correction and under some circumstances 3–4 years, possibly with corporal punishment.[164] The intervention of the police would merely obstruct the imposition of really stiff sentences, and the desire to inflict swift punishment would merely negate the desired deterrent effect. Officials such as Reinhardt had to be dealt with 'without respite'.

However, the Justice Minister did not prove successful in his efforts. Von Schuckmann, the Minister of the Interior, angrily rejected the criticism that this issue turned on prejudice to a sovereign right.[165] Rather, the judiciary should look to their own house – and he cited the case of a court in Breslau which had been reprimanded by the Ministry of Justice for exceeding its powers.

However, Schuckmann avoided the substantive argument. Evidently, he either regarded the question as to what constituted an appropriate deterrent as so delicate that it was more expedient to let the matter rest, or he saw the judiciary's arguments as merely tactical moves in a departmental conflict – not worthy of direct reply. There are some grounds to suppose that the former was the case. The draconian sentences which the courts could impose for theft would have meant considerable economic losses for estate owners: they would either have had to manage without the services of a trained worker for a considerable spell, or take on unskilled day-labourers as replacements and train them.

The private interests of the estate owners were therefore quite compatible with the current practice under which corporal punishments and fines, but not long jail terms, could be imposed. In fact, any stepping up of the activity of the courts would have led to considerable losses which would soon have outweighed the benefits of a more powerful deterrent.

Schuckmann brusquely concluded his letter with the caustic observation that the Justice Minister merely wanted to introduce the French departmental system – and that he would not be 'taken in' by such manoeuvring. The Ministry of Justice subsequently returned all the files to the court of appeal in Marienwerder, where the case had originated, but not without appending the rebuff from the Ministry of the Interior.[166]

The administration's power of definition through police jurisdiction

The power of definition exercisable within the practice of the police courts proved itself as effective for the – contradictory – constellation of ruling and governing classes. And, inasmuch as police jurisdiction lifted some of the burden off the authorities and courts, even the judiciary could benefit from it. *Landräte* and District Government *Präsidien* were then able to confine themselves to the, in all likelihood, small number of 'appeals' (*Rekurse*) – we do not know the exact number. And, according to statements from officials, the courts had to concern themselves only with the small number of major police cases, at the most as court of appeal.

More important must have been the fact that the essential casuistry underlying police powers permitted and facilitated the equation of administrative 'discretion', political arbitrariness and social discrimination. As the legal form of this domination, 'jurisdiction' therefore possessed both a legitimating and a threatening element.

In addition, the availability of such formal legal components as 'appeal' allowed professional jurists to feel comfortable with the existing allotment of powers and procedures. Although denied a role in the sphere of police jurisdiction, they could nevertheless cultivate the impression that all the activities of the state were suffused with the principles of the 'rule of law'.

However, police jurisdiction was at its most useful in administering and dominating the propertyless, and property-poor, producers. Having disciplined estate subjects was as much in the interest of estate owners, intent on profit and status, as of the higher echelons of the administrative and judicial bureaucracies. In the final analysis estate owners were merely seeking to establish 'public peace' and maintain the penal authority of the state with what were essentially complementary methods. The vague, and frequently ignored, 'natural border' between the authorities only rarely and exceptionally endangered the acceptance of police rule, even by those subordinated to it.

One of the rare figures to make objection was the liberal jurist Heinrich

Simon, who emerged as a critic of the 1844 judicial disciplinary legislation, over which he resigned as *Stadtgerichtsrat* in Breslau. He was also active academically, and co-authored with Ludwig von Rönne the comprehensive constitutional work *Die Verfassung und Verwaltung des Preußischen Staates*. Simon was certainly untypical of his class, for whom violence and arbitrariness were a normal part of everyday life. His protest against his treatment at the hands of the Breslau police, *Aktenstücke zur neuesten Geschichte der Preußischen Polizei*, published in Leipzig in 1847, created possibly even more of a sensation amongst the reading public than Ernst Dronke's *Polizei-Geschichten*. After all, Dronke had 'only' exposed the less spectacular discrimination against 'the lesser folk'.

At any event, the stable but unequal equilibrium between the demands of the rulers on the one hand and the passivity of the ruled on the other was not markedly undermined by such isolated objections. The mass social movements which broke out as hunger riots in 1847, more strongly in early 1848 and again in 1849 were not caused by mass anger at the police or police jurisdiction.[167] Their origins lay rather in a fateful conjunction of structural and demographic changes in agriculture – relative overpopulation and unemployment, bad harvests, lack of food – 'overmanning' in the handicrafts sector and persistent crises in domestic industry. The growth and spread of the preparedness to resist and even revolt evidently took place both 'below' as well as 'above' the level of everyday domination. The 'extendable field of police jurisdiction'[168] continued as the chosen instrument for the day-to-day maintenance of social inequality.

That such procedures were executed not by lower ranking officers on the ground but by their superiors proved to be no handicap. In the first place, they usually became involved after a patrolling 'constable' or one called upon to make an 'initial intervention' initiated a charge. And on the other hand – and this was no less important – even the Council of State had to recognise that 'any knowledge of the law . . . is not demanded from any police authority within the entire kingdom'.[169]

The claim to the rule of law: its limits on arbitrary power

The practice of domination on the ground turned on the, legally clad, capacity of the holders of police authority to keep on top of the local situation and assert their own power, status and economic interests in the face of resistance and other, just legal, forms of insubordination, such as passivity or collective inattention. On the East Elbian estates, the general power and domination of the state was given a special edge by the massive social and economic weight and power monopoly of the local structures of domination, the *Gutsherrschaft*.

In contrast, legal norms had a much more 'multi-layered' relevance. For the broad mass of the dominated, such norms – if perceived at all – could only have conveyed a sense of a greater semblance of constitutionality (meaning limits on unequal and arbitrary treatment). A welter of individual, but communicable, experiences of police 'short shrift' constantly reinforced distance and suspicion. Nor did the regional and ministerial heights of the state apparatus, or bourgeois entrepreneurial and Junker proprietors – the beneficiaries and guarantors of this system of power and domination – harbour any illusions. The efforts to justify the Order of 31 March 1838 (which allowed action to be taken against disturbances to peace and order, even when the police authority's own individual interests were at stake) within the restricted circles of the Council of State indirectly indicated the bureaucracy's expectation that such a regulation would bolster the widespread practice of 'short shrift' employed in instances of self-redress by Junkers. The open, yet formally correct, assertion that this coincidence of interests between private proprietors and general policing was both unproblematic and entirely legal called for both magisterial arrogance and bureaucratic hairsplitting on the part of the administration. And the administration was able to supply both.

This permanent, even if sometimes only sporadic, consonance between the interests and modes of perception of the state administration and the holders of local power created almost unlimited room for manoeuvre for the 'masters of the local situation', whose practice was only rarely and incidentally exposed to scrutiny or control. Ironically, this fact also prevented the actual exercise of arbitrariness from being isolated from the patchwork of legal concepts and ambiguities – for example, over the level of punishment allowed – as well as outright illegality enshrined in law. The attempt by Silesian Junkers to assert their group interests on the matter of the defence of property and punishment of theft provides a case in point.

Although theft was a criminal offence, not a police misdemeanour, there is considerable evidence that it was punished via 'short-shrift' procedures, especially on the estates (as in the case of Mayor Reinhardt, pp. 114–16 above). However, Silesian Junkers failed in their efforts to release estate owners, in practice the local police authorities, from the obligation to call in a justiciary for common theft where the loss did not exceed 5 Thalers. The right to impose punishments was to be transferred from the (patrimonial) courts to the police authority – and hence directly to the estate owners. The Junkers' petition (submitted on 24 February 1828) argued that the alternative to police jurisdiction in such cases – in practice, their own jurisdiction – would be a slow and costly formal court hearing.[76] 'A judge, they contended, had a different outlook to officials: 'he usually has a great deal of work elsewhere which he will be ill-disposed to interrupt for petty concerns as long as his attention remains confined to more weighty legal matters'. Von Merckel, the *Oberpräsident* of the province, confirmed the current situation in his own report.[77] 'It was not uncommon for the penalty for petty theft not be imposed until after a delay of six or seven months', by which time the convicted person could no longer be 'tracked down'. And the plaintiff's costs where the convicted person was unable to pay often ran to twenty or thirty times more than the original loss. In general, there was a 'disinclination and apprehension' about 'bringing a thief to a court hearing'. The consequence was that 'crime remained unpunished'.

However, Merckel did not agree with the Junkers' proposal to remedy the situation, a by-product of which was a bolstering of the 'authority' of the police. For, he argued, 'it is essential that police authorities have proper judicial qualification'. The severity of the possible sentences also required, at least in the case of repeated theft, that, as the Junkers themselves argued, the case be brought before a judge. Even on a first offence, the punishment for theft could exceed fourteen days' imprisonment, a 5 Thaler fine or 'moderate' correction. Imposition of such a penalty would entitle the convicted person to appeal to the courts – with no overall saving of time. What was required, in Merckel's view, was an even more extensive revision of the relevant provisions, although whether the better solution was to shorten court procedures in line with police requirements or, conversely, to give police authorities greater competence for judgements with 'full judicial effect' was left open. This proposal by the *Oberpräsident*, who acted as the Commissary for the Ministry at provincial level, discharged the Minister from any obligation to act. The matter could be referred to a law reform commission.[172] There was no change in the provisions already existing in the Prussian Legal Code or the tougher regulations of 1799.

However, Merckel's report barely touched on one other consideration which influenced ministerial officials in their decision to reject any extension of police powers. That such a consideration existed can be seen in a report drafted by the Ministery of the Interior: 'As much as it is desirable for proceedings to be shortened in matters of petty theft, it is almost of greater importance that no one who is innocent should be punished or that excessive punishments should be inflicted.'[173] Even if such an observation was written merely for the files, one does occasionally glimpse that the 'educated' elements amongst higher officialdom did feel uncomfortable about the mode of domination perpetuated through 'short-shrift' procedures.

'A note on beating': correction 'for improvement'

Ordinary police officers and their local superiors had, as even the editor of the entirely loyal *Polizei-Archiv* noted, a marked 'enthusiasm for beating'.[174] Beatings were not merely an immediate response; they also preferred 'physical correction' as a formal police punishment. And as officials themselves reported, the prime victims of those 'zealous' floggings of up to twenty blows were primarily 'beggars, servants, so-called street urchins and other persons of the lowest rank'.[175]

This practice was also fully in accord with the higher police authorities' attempt to measure punishment in accordance with the individual's 'degree of cultivation'. In 1831 the Interior Ministry recommended that servants 'with a higher level of cultivation' should not be subjected to corporal punishment unless absolutely prescribed.[176] Certainly, soldiers on leave and members of the *Landwehr* were to be spared such treatment – one palpable advantage, at least, of military service.[177] Whether and to what extent such a restriction was actually adhered to must remain unanswered. Since the provision applied to members of the *Landwehr* until their fortieth birthday, it would have exempted a large portion of the male working population, including estate

5 'Mechanical progress'
For the Munich Journal *Fliegende Blätter* this was evidently something imaginable only in Tsarist Russia. It noted: 'A newly invented beating machine by Teodor Prügeloff [a pun on the German word for beating] in Petersburg'.

farm hands and agricultural day-labourers, from physical punishment. Enforcement also required particular vigilance from the police and made it difficult, at least in theory, to treat all suspects equally.

The basic approach of all grades of officials was characteristically set out in 1795 in a statement from a judicial, that is pre-reform, *Regierung*. 'The abolition of the right to beat does not appear to be entirely appropriate as regards the lesser civilised class of humans, whose behaviour still depends in large measure, it seems, on brute impressions.'[178] And, although this report was concerned with servants (*Gesinde*), it certainly corresponded with administrative perceptions of direct producers as a class and the broad spectrum of urban and rural propertyless over subsequent decades. It was for this reason, rather than any limited capacity to exert control over the practice, that District Governments and Ministries merely confined themselves to checking the worst excesses and abuses. Not surprisingly, this neither substantially reduced nor suppressed the practice of corporal punishment. In fact the *Polizei-Archiv* was moved to observe that this inclination to brutal violence, 'has no wish to depart from the middle ranks of the police', despite the 'protection of the constitution for citizens against officials'.[179]

With the exception of the fairly effective reduction in the number of permissible blows, the sporadic and often contradictory instructions and orders calling for less corporal punishment achieved only limited success. In the view of the victims, most of these orders were a cynical sham; at best, they expressed concern but were ineffective. The 'Village Handbook' of a subaltern officer, designed as a 'popular emergency and help manual for village parish councils, mayors and estate owners' is illustrative in this respect: 'In determining the measure and method of corporal correction, one should be mindful of the sex, age and physical constitution of the condemned person and where necessary obtain the testimony of a physician.'[180] The case of the *Landrat* Wittenburg, described pp. 93ff above, gives some idea of the value of such medical testimony. One attempt to reduce the amount of corporal punishment was von Benn's efforts, as Minister of the Interior, to introduce an age limit of ten years for girls. However, his efforts were swiftly undermined by his successor, von Rochow.[181] A number of the traditional instruments of chastisement were also banned. A 1796 decree required the rod, widely used in the eastern provinces, to be replaced by the 'customary leather strap', with the blows to be 'imparted to the back on top of clothing' in 'moderate quantity'.[182] An 1832 order banned public pillorying or putting in the stocks. Most other of the diverse forms of physical punishment were also forbidden; these included the 'Spanish coat' (a variant of the 'Iron Maiden') and the 'fiddle' (a heavy piece of wood hung from the neck and hands of a person in the pillory).[183]

Nevertheless, such individual proscriptions, whose effect – it must be repeated – was by no means assured, may have had the effect of making domination more secure, as Hoffmann, editor of *Polizei-Archiv*, cynically observed. It was believed,

> that in some districts where there was a great deficiency of enlightenment, the officer, who is better dressed and more cultivated than the victim, still has to have the right to beat or have beaten the individuals concerned. And these in turn rejoice in our present happier times. Whereas their grandfathers may have had fifty to a hundred beatings, they receive only twenty to twenty-five – a difference of 75–80 per cent. And who could complain about such a trifling thing as that?[184]

That such apparent relief by the victims may have served more to cloak the injury to the damaged or 'lost honour' simply did not occur to Hoffmann. His report lacked the insight of Garve's observations on the subject:

> Every human being, no matter how coarse, has a keen sense of what is right and wrong. And, although the blows may not hurt the peasant, they embitter him; and even if they do not do this, they humiliate him and make him servile.[185]

What the advocates of corporal punishment had left out of account was that amongst 'servants', the combination of 'servitude and poverty' would soon lead to 'deceit, secrecy and theft'. Deceit would constitute the expression, if hidden, of their sense of justice and their striving for recognition and 'honour'.

Despite the reduction in the number of permitted blows and the ban on particularly tormenting instruments, a wide range of forms of corporal punishment, and their associated diverse forms of suffering, remained. Hoffmann, for example, identified the following phases in the life of the East Elbian peasant: 'beatings on the hand, beatings in school, beatings in service and in the office'. In the case of beatings on the hand there was a further distinction between those administered by the father and those administered by the mother; and further,

> the guild master who knocks in craftsmanship with the belt, or the teacher knowledge with the ruler, so that finally the now thoroughly chastised subject is ready to enter public life and continue to experience this rich dish of beatings behind the façade of public affairs.

And irrespective of any formal bars, 'the instruments of beating have spawned their various degenerate offspring – sticks, belts, staffs, straps and clogs'.[186]

Although the reduction in the overall incidence of corporal punishment may have rendered this picture less typical, it certainly continued to be entirely conceivable. Aside from any ethical aspects, such a life-cycle inevitably raised the question of the 'consequences of beating for the victim, apart from pain and dishonour'. For Garve, the answer was clear: neither deterrent nor improvement, nor compensation for loss. Moreover, 'the brief pain of one day had little effect on the hardened body of the habitual criminal'. Again although Garve would certainly have observed, or had reports, of this 'pain and dishonour', this experience at second hand could not convey precisely how being beaten altered the self-image of the victim or the view of the 'better orders', the authorities and officials.

As far as the administration and 'cultivated' public were concerned, there was only one essential justification for beating. It established an incontrovertible distinction, or more precisely made a peculiarly rigorous travesty of the differences, between the beaters and non-beaten on the one hand and those to be beaten on the other. And by being a function of individual guilt and frailty, rather than of differing life situations, beating transformed this extremely palpable boundary into an issue of morality. The beaten were merely being given their due desserts for their deficient – but in theory attainable – individual 'cultivation'.

This justification also implied limits on the practice of corporal punishment. Not every 'administered subject' required such energetic assistance to attain 'cultivation', a distinction which could foster the illusion amongst those who were no longer beaten that they would never be beaten that they were much less exposed to ruling [illegible] than the beaten. Beating was really, therefore, an act of charity: 'The main aim was improvement and the prevention of future offences.' In contrast the main aim of punishment was 'retribution'. The latter could, and had to be, more brutal and severe.[187] The actual relevance and yet brutal consequences of this distinction are illustrated by the beating machine invented by Meyer, a police officer in Langenbielau.[188] In 1848 the residents of the town presented a petition bitterly complaining about this instrument of torture. And although Meyer's machine was characterised as 'hard and severe' by the *Landrat*, he considered it entirely legal.

Although a division of labour existed in the exercise of corporal punishment at a local level, there was no marked dissent or argument. The *Polizei-*

Archiv noted for example, 'the head of the office will prefer to let his subordinate have his way than blunt his pen with the required notices and warnings to the criminal; this also saves somewhat on fixed costs for writing materials'.[189]

In the early part of 1848 a critical but moderate journal, *Epigonen*, published a report on the experiences of a political detainee, whose description of the prevailing division of labour and administration of 'short shrift' seems mild in comparison with the practices noted above.[190] What impressed itself upon the author was not merely the brevity of the treatment, but the apparent acknowledgement by the authorities of the victims' way of life compared with the urge to 'improve' observable elsewhere. Again, there was no personal experience of physical pain and public humiliation. The episode he described took place in Westphalia:

> My informant once observed how friend Bunte [a warder] appeared in the yard, where a bunch of gypsies was assembled, carrying a heavy stick. And while the senior official, Herr Möller, looked on from the window, Bunte tore into each individual specimen of humanity, ripping through their bags and anywhere where he found eggs, ham or bacon, brandishing his stick and demanding at each blow, 'Where did that come from? Where did you get that?' such that the person under investigation could not answer. Having worked his way through the entire row, these children of the Orient were then thrown into jail, to be released the next day.

On the continuity of police jurisdiction after 1850

After 1849–50 the jurisdictional powers of the local police authorities were made provisional. At the same time, physical 'correction', which was banned in 1848, was removed and the maximum imposable prison term reduced to three days.[191] In practice, however, the local power structure retained its ability to impose violent penalties. In contrast to those districts where French law still prevailed, the residents of the 'older' provinces continued to be deprived of independent courts for the hearing of misdemeanour trials, although special justices were provided in 1849 (1846 in Berlin) to decide on cases where the punishment might extend to a fine of 50 Thalers or six weeks' imprisonment. In 1856 these justices were also granted jurisdiction in such offences as 'vagrancy, begging and malingering'. This shift in jurisdiction did provide some relief from corporal punishment for the urban sub-proletariat. Nevertheless, it was not enough to bring about any real mitigation of arbitrary police 'displeasure' and 'administrative bias'.[192] The police authorities and officers were able to compensate for the restrictions of their penal powers by imposing more and longer periods of detention.

Any gains from the reforms of 1849–50 were also jeopardised by the fact that by 1852 provisional penal powers for misdemeanours had been returned to the local police authorities in the provinces east of the Rhine. And one leading Berlin police official encouraged his colleagues to make good use of their restored powers, 'to raise the diminished authority of the state'.[193]

Interim conclusion: the link between the form of authority and the form of law

Police *intervention* encompassed the interlinked phenomena of 'observation' and the use of 'the strong hand' – each was the mutual condition for the other. And police *jurisdiction* allowed this link very wide and flexible scope. It fulfilled a variety of functions: it could be employed within bureaucratic discourse, but could also be used to obstruct criticism from the 'cultivated classes' or even suppress it completely. Police jurisdiction therefore both maintained and legitimated the domination of the state and administration, at the same time allowing those entrusted with police authority to equate their own private interests with the 'general', 'security' interests of the state. By alloting penal and corrective powers to the police-administration rather than the courts, police jurisdiction also contributed to the undiscriminating practice of police officers and other agents of police jurisdiction, especially within the estate economy, which lumped together as 'dangerous' the entire class of the propertyless.

The disciplining and punishment of the dominated, that is the repressive regulation of any scope for the propertyless 'masses' to articulate their interests, could rely not only on formal legal powers, but also on a more substantive justification: the claim that these practices were all directed at the social, and in particular the individual, improvement of the 'administered'. Reference to the actual deterrent effect and, at times, to the 'improvement' of those subjected to police punishment was central to the rhetoric of police 'discretion'.[194] In police eyes, prevention of breaches of the law meant prevention of moral lapses and defects. Police powers therefore constituted a self-enclosed and self-legitimating system of observation, intervention, punishment or correction – always under the threat or use of force.

Police supervision and police detention

The interlocking character of violent domination, calculated – yet naive – self-justification of officials and the constant drilling of the dominated is well illustrated in the phenomena of 'police supervision' and 'police detention'.

These forms of police suspicion and intervention were closely related. Each represented a point at which the control of the 'administered' by the penal law and control by the administration intersected. In the provinces to the west of the Rhine, together with the former Duchy of Berg (Düsseldorf), a form of police supervision requiring a decision of the courts was introduced in the 1808 *code pénale*.[195] In contrast, in those provinces subject to the Prussian Legal Code the institution of 'indeterminate sentencing' continued.[196] Under this system the court not only placed the convicted person under police observation after their term of imprisonment was concluded, but also imposed an additional period of 'custody' or 'detention'. Matters then rested in the hands of the police. The courts in the non-French legal areas were not granted the power fully to determine the length of detention until 1850 when the provision of the *code pénale* was adopted. Police supervision could follow on from a custodial sentence, and like the latter could be contested in court. Nevertheless, the police were not excluded as the courts then passed the matter on to the local police authorities for enforcement within a prescribed period of time.

Up until 1850 police officers in those provinces covered by the Prussian Legal Code had extensive powers of 'detention'. This had two implications. On the one hand officials could detain people on their own initiative with the objective of administering 'correction'. On the other, the enforcement of an 'indeterminate sentence' imposed by a court was left to police discretion. Lower-ranking police officers could, or had to, extend or shorten the detention of delinquents after a custodial sentence – normally imposed for crimes against property – according to their own judgement. The relevant criterion for the decision to impose detention in a house of correction or workhouse was supposed to be 'improvement' – in concrete terms, meaning that the person concerned would be released once the police were satisfied that the detainee had secured a source of income; as a result, this practice became known as *Erwerbsdetention*, detention pending gainful employment. However, cyclical and structural unemployment meant that this condition could often not be met. Consequently, after 1821 it was regarded as sufficient if the administration of the institution concerned considered that the 'powers or skills' and the 'will of the convicted person' for 'honest employment' were adequate. In addition, where the court prescribed 'real improvement', the institution also had to consult a teacher of religion to assess the 'moral condition' of the convicted person. Houses of correction evidently tried to make maximum use of their permitted discretion to save expense and cut down their work-load. As a consequence, in 1839 the *Landräte* were brought into the procedure. These were to issue a recommendation as to whether any planned release was 'advisable on police grounds'. And, in general they appeared to veer on the side of caution, seeking at all costs to avoid any recurrence of criminal activity or any additional costs which would be incurred in any further observation or detention.

As well as being empowered to do so by the courts, police officials could also detain entire groups from the broader spectrum of 'suspected persons' on their own independent discretion.[197] For example, the power of the police to detain beggars, vagabonds and tramps was expressly confirmed by the college of Ministers, the Ministry of State in 1830 for those areas covered by the Prussian Legal Code. Moreover, the authorities were not bound to a particular length of detention. Ministers argued, for example, that it was 'unnecessary for the police authorities to fix the period of detention for an apprehended beggar as a penal sentence' for the new penitentiary in Magdeburg. The sole aim had to be that anyone held in detention should 'have the will and opportunity to seek their living without further burdening the public'. For the police, the association between insubordination and immorality amongst 'troublemakers' – who only 'simulated' distress – placed their extensive discretion beyond question. Of course this self-justification had to be brought into accord with the sovereign claim that the 'administered' were handled 'under the law'. Some provision had to be made to protect the procedure from possible appeals through the courts. The formula expounded by the internal administration shows very pointedly how the police power of definition functioned. Accusations that an unlawful denial of freedom had taken place could be averted through the expedient of instructing the authorities supervising the police to exercise due attention to prevent any possible abuses'.

Prescribed periods of detention were not only sensible from the point of view of any subsequent examination by the courts or – less probably – by the 'cultivated public'; they also made the actual work of administration easier. Von Schuckmann, the Minister for the Police and the Interior, and von Danckelmann, the Minister of Justice, were both obliged to concede this to some degree. Danckelmann, for example, had initially argued that a prescribed detention of several months for a first offender was 'too hard'. In March 1830 officials from the Ministry of State agreed to a minimum of six weeks for Magdeburg, to be increased to three months for the second offence, six months for the third, and a year for the fourth.

Within the bureaucracy, or at any event within the Ministry of Finance and Police (which re-acquired its autonomy in 1831), further consideration was given to allowing the police to impose somewhat longer periods of detention, that is retaining the widely applied practice of imposing at least six months' detention. This was specifically intended for rural areas where the likelihood and the costs of re-arrest were much higher, and begging on grounds of 'indolence' and 'idleness' was 'morally' less justifiable than in the towns with their mass poverty.

This not only reflected a particular distrust of the massive concentrations of the poor in the urban centres but also the fact that the police authorities in the 'older', estate-economy-dominated provinces were faced with a rapid increase in the number of landless and land-poor subjects in the 1820s and 1830s. Given the limited availability of state agencies – that is, the very sparse network of Gendarmes – a long period of detention could bring some respite, and possibly even act as a deterrent. For were not unemployed day-labourers or the unoccupied children of servants or *Instleute* less the victims of economic fluctuations or population growth than merely 'workshy'? And shouldn't they therefore be treated as dangerous and 'objectionable elements'? Officials in the Ministries of Police and Finance, together with their Ministers, pressed for a detention period of six months for the first offence, and up to two years in the case of a repetition, with a review every six months. The model was to be the powers used under the provincial poorhouse regulations, and in particular those applied in the 'district work- and poorhouse' in Benningshausen, Westphalia. Here there were no fixed sentences, merely six-monthly reviews. In April 1831 the new Finance Minister, Maaßen – in agreement with the new Minister of Police, von Brenn – explained the logic behind as long a period of detention as possible.

> It is well known that apart from strictly prescribed, appropriate, and uninterrupted employment in the poorhouse – that is aside from the changed circumstances of their lives – the moral effect of detention, isolation from civil society, and allocation to a class whose way of life is

6. 'Zealous enforcement of the ban on smoking in public places', *c.* 1847.

> the subject of public scorn has a powerful effect on the reform of the inmate. It is therefore very important that the first term of detention should effect a change in the views of the beggar, for if a second were to prove necessary the feeling of shame might well be blunted and the efficacy of the moral imperative already cited would no longer apply. Moreover, we should not ignore the opportunity to observe the inmate, become acquainted with his ingrained evil ways, seek to eradicate them, and finally, through employment, make work itself a need and a pleasure.

Evidently Maaßen was not disturbed by the utterly untenable argument at the heart of this thesis: the probability of renewed imprisonment was evidently so great, and the chances of 'improvement' so meagre, that only lifelong 'detention' would meet the Ministers' criteria. Accordingly, the two Ministers called for a minimum of six months on the first instance of detention – as was practised in Mark Brandenburg. In the event of a recurrence, the person was to be detained for two years with a review every six months. However, von Mühler, Dankelmann's successor in the Ministry of Justice, drew up an opposing report about a year and a half later which noted that the institution at Benningshausen, selected as a model by Brenn and Mühler, was not a 'real poorhouse'. The 'real distress' was not to be found there; there were no 'cripples', 'old men', or 'enfeebled persons with no one to care for them'. The institution was populated with beggars who had been caught for the third or more time: it was not a poorhouse but 'a workhouse'. Typically, however, such distinctions fell upon deaf ears in the police-administration. Such legalistic hair-splitting seemed utterly irrelevant. For officials in the Police Ministry any attempts to highlight the distinction between judicial detention and police 'corrective detention' missed the point. They were not interested in striking the proper balance between severity and mildness towards those who were detained. Irrespective of any proven hardship, all were subject to suspicion and reproach for a way of life which was held to be both morally objectionable and inimicable to the requirements of police order. And drastic steps were entirely justified wherever the bureaucracy's control seemed at risk.

The decision of the new Minister of Justice prescribed an initial period of up to a maximum of six weeks. Increases in sentences were as follows: three months, six months, and in the event of a third repetition of the offence, one year. The Ministry of State was quite happy to allow the varying practices and regulations in different provinces, or between town and country, to continue. A uniform legal provision began to appear necessary only when the numbers of propertyless began to multiply in the towns after the 1830s, with a parallel increase in misdemeanours and crimes against property. The law 'for the punishment of vagrants, beggars and malingerers' was passed on 6 January 1843, and was fully in accord with the police perspectives outlined above. The progression was: jail, followed by detention of up to three years depending on the decision of the police (articles 1 to 8) with almost unlimited discretion given to the local or at least regional police to impose a further period of custody in a 'house of correction' (in the absence of 'adequate employment', article 9). A Cabinet Order issued on 17 March established that six months' imprisonment for begging was to count as a police penalty. Aside from the areas covered by French law, this left the matter entirely to the police authorities. And the Ministry of Justice noted that in the event of longer punishments for 'vagrants and malingerers' the regional police authorities (that is the District Governments) could detain the convicted person after completion of their jail sentence for a further three years. In addition, *Erwerbsdetention* (see p. 125) could be added to this. But these broad police powers were not merely confined to the post-imprisonment period; prior to the decision of the court, the Ministers of the Interior and Justice expressly empowered the police to 'detain' the accused even 'if the court conducting the proceedings has reservations about continued detention'.

For those at the receiving end, a penalty imposed by a court or corrective detention imposed by police did not signify the end of administrative observation but rather its recommencement. And this also applied to the areas on the left bank of the Rhine. The Minister of the Interior himself was forced to concede that police supervision in these parts of the country, even for those freed on a pardon, 'can be seen as a real punishment' – which, according to the letter of the law, was a matter reserved for the courts. Notwithstanding, he did not order any change in the prevailing practice, which 'in most instances is very useful', unless the pardon expressly ruled out police supervision.[198]

The first regulations on 'normal' police supervision were issued in 1797.

The different regulations were subsequently brought together in a ministerial circular of 12 September 1815.[199] The circular required that those discharged from prison, those 'provisionally found not guilty', and especially 'and as a matter of course all those who, either on account of their previous life or through a voluntary or enforced lack of an adequate wage are dangerous to public or private safety, should be placed under police supervision'. This embraced not only those released from jail or houses of correction but also 'unemployed nationals or aliens and all journeymen not in work'.

Security was not the only factor to be taken into account. The District Government in Potsdam, for example, cited economic benefit and its duty to set proper standards. If local authorities, 'treat discharged convicts as their special charges, help them in seeking an honest existence, and devote special care to their duty of surveillance over them, they will be working for the noblest aims of the institution of the police'.[200]

Evidently furthering the individual welfare of those who were to receive 'correction' was inseparable from exercising rigorous control over them. Such furtherance without regimentation seemed quite impossible, and regimentation without this aim seemed less legitimate. Certainly, the regulations were concerned solely with the exercise of control. One much consulted police manual expressed this idea in the following terms:

> The individual placed under police supervision should not be allowed to live by town gates or in such places where observation is rendered more difficult or impossible. Persons with whom the individual under observation is in contact, and with the same reputation, must be ascertained. His neighbours should be asked how he obtains his subsistence. Public houses must be asked how much he consumes there and how often and how high he gambles.[201]

Naturally, insufficient numbers and frequent unavailability for duty placed limits on how extensive such permanent regimentation could be. Nevertheless, a ministerial report of 1829 does show that the lower authorities made strenuous efforts in this direction. In fact the Ministry had to order a cutback: 'Constant presence at a particular place should not depend on the decision of the police authorities in the absence of a court decision'. More than 'personal appearance from time to time' was not to be expected.

Local officers did, nevertheless, occasionally express their weariness. Would not deportation offer a better way of permanently freeing themselves of 'criminals, vagabonds and able but indigent malingerers', as practised in England for example? However, a question to this effect from the Mayor of Halle, received a negative answer. Such a practice 'could not be implemented at the moment': it would require the – unattainable – collaboration of a 'foreign state'. There was therefore no alternative to 'strict police supervision'.[202]

One incident in the industrial centre of Iserlohn gives some indication of practice on the ground.[203] During the early part of 1836 an individual raised a complaint about the local police authority, that is the Mayor and his senior, the *Landrat*. These had decided to place him in the workhouse in Bönningshausen, some forty kilometres distant (see p. 126 above). The District Government in

Arnsberg called for a report from the *Landrat*. The *Landrat* noted that the complainant was strongly suspected of theft, but was forced to concede that, despite being kept in custody, this suspicion could not be confirmed; the suspect had been released in the autumn of 1835 because of lack of evidence. However, as far as the *Landrat* was concerned this man was unquestionably a 'danger to public safety'; rigorous police supervision and ultimately detention in a workhouse were the only possible solutions. The impact of such stigmatisation on the person concerned can be seen in a few comments made in the report. Evidently the suspect had not succeeded in renting a place to live. He therefore voluntarily sought accommodation in the town jail. Moreover he was unable to find any work other than road building for the municipality. This was particularly dubious for the *Landrat* since the town had previously bought him a spinning wheel (or more likely made one available to him against an advance) – as the *Landrat*, with some praise for the initiative of the local authority, added. Ultimately, however, detention had remained the only solution.

This clearly represented a massive collision between the desire of the administration to allow the person under observation a 'reasonable use of their personal freedom' and their unbridled mistrust and consequent ruthless control. Certainly, the implementation of any order via the customary instruments of police practice ruled out any of the prescribed 'moral improvement' from the outset.

Available figures give little idea of the precise contours of this everyday practice, and in particular the element of violence entailed in police observation. The sources do not distinguish between observation and control orders imposed by the courts and those imposed directly and independently by the administration. If credence can be given to a report prepared by the Berlin police *Präsidium*, the number of instances of observation in Berlin increased both rapidly and steadily: from 7,816 in 1838 to 13,246 in 1847.[204] It is notable, however, that cases of reported theft grew at a much lower rate over the same period, around 20 per cent whilst the population grew by around 50 per cent to *c.* 390,000. Assuming that police suspicion was concentrated on the 170–210,000 'working people' and 'poor', 5 to 7 per cent of these (including 40–60,000 dependants) would have been under constant police supervision in 1846, with some 'mobile' observation for those who moved.

Comparable figures for the province of Posen for 1839 cite 2,453 cases in the Government District of Posen and 1,025 in the District of Bromberg, equal to 0.3 per cent of the population. This much lower share of the population compared with Berlin does not however mean that the 'lower popular classes' were seen as proportionally less 'dangerous'. Rather there were simply fewer police and Gendarmerie per inhabitant in the 'open country'. Including officers, each of the 84 Gendarmes was responsible for 250 square kilometres, or more than 13,000 people. The number of cases of supervision may also have been a reflection of conditions within the self-regulating unit of authority, the independent estate district (*Gutsbezirk*), which possibly offered refuge for any 'stray sheep' able and willing to work.

The first steps towards a constitutional regime, codified in the 1848/50 constitutions, did not prevent the 'continuation of administrative police supervision',[205] that is, the desire to maintain permanent control over subordinate social groups in both town and country. The practice of supervision and detention marked them out, and branded them with the status of a potential counter-power, a permanent threat to the prevailing order. And the practice also went far beyond merely tagging individuals. In the provinces east of the Rhine around 50 per cent of those accused of theft in 1832 were actually convicted (the figure was 47 per cent in 1833). Police supervision was obligatory on completion of sentence. For 1832 this meant a total of some 23,500 cases under supervision. In the mid 1860s the executive authorities' obsession with maintaining strict control via supervision earned a rebuke from the Minister of the Interior. The 1866 provision, which divided those under supervision into two classes depending on their capacity for improvement, was clearly given only token adherence. The Minister's intention to make promotion into the first category serve as a form of 'goal of betterment' was simply ignored by local officials who continued to confine themselves to strict segregation.

The possibility of improvement was built into the logic of this practice, both for individuals and as a collective destiny. Supervision inevitably gave way to intervention and sanction – if they had not already preceded it. Snooping and informing under the formal label of police supervision did not replace, but rather came to symbolise the more directly violent forms of police activity – intervention, 'correction' and punishment. Far from being alternatives, they complemented each other in the everyday practice of domination.

The evident link between treatment at the hands of the police and social rank meant that the exercise of 'discretion' was only apparently 'arbitrary'. For those individuals defined as 'dangerous', police officers on the ground were always willing, with the encouragement of their superiors, to place security first and enhance or replace the activities of supervision with brute force. But this did not mean the end of supervision; it merely restarted the cycle. For large sections of the class of 'direct producers', and first and foremost for the floating destitute population, 'police supervision' ultimately became a synonym for that standard of individual 'cultivation' deemed appropriate for them by the authorities.

The military dominion

The military watch

In 1840 more than 50 per cent of the 3.8 million civilian town dwellers in Prussia lived in the garrison towns, each housing at least a company or a unit of comparable strength (80 to 120 men).[206] The burden of providing constant billets for garrison troops or occasional accommodation for units in transit fell largely upon this urban population. The state's chronic financial crisis meant that the billeting of troops on civilians only very gradually gave way to the construction of new barracks or the rebuilding of old. The presence of military watches also meant that the civilian population experienced a variety of other impositions. Military guards, usually consisting of one or two sentries but with access to a dozen or more reinforcements where necessary, were not only expected to guard military facilities, but also mounted constant sentry duty and patrols around prisons, banks and other civilian buildings. In the twenty-six citadel towns they were most in evidence controlling the movement of persons through the town gates, sealing off ramparts and circular walls, and generally maintaining 'quiet' in the town.[207].

These duties were by no means merely symbolic or of purely internal military importance. Some idea of the functions officially allocated to them can be gleaned from the instructions issued by both military and political Ministries. It should be borne in mind, though, that any policing carried out by the watches took place under military regulations: the 1788 infantry regulation (slightly amended in 1817)[208] continued in force until replaced by a special instruction issued in 1844, an indication of the lack of impact made by the administrative reforms introduced between 1808 and 1817. The provisions of this original regulation were so vague that they required a constant exercise of discretion either by the guard on duty or their immediate superior, the officer of the watch, often themselves only a private or non-commissioned officer; it was at this level that decisions were made to intervene or deal with any incident with varying degrees of vigilant inactivity. Watches were to function as 'aids to the police', and had to be 'situated at the centre point of the town'.[209] 'Where only one watch is present, its prime purpose shall be that of policing.' The regulation went on to consider the procedures to be followed when the watches were called upon by the civilian police; for example, they should arrest only those 'notified' to them by the police. Their duties also comprised exhibiting a military presence on their own initiative, which included taking action where necessary. Watches were to 'fall in with rifles in the event of riots, funerals, fires, etc. in order to establish immediate order'. The precise manner in which this should occur was left to military custom and practice, depending on local or regional circumstances. Commanders were also expected to assess the balance between the usefulness of their intervention and any possible prejudice to the 'honour' of the armed forces.

One regulation 'for the arrest of civilian persons', decreed in 1802 but confined to Berlin,[210] gives a somewhat clearer idea of the expectations of superiors in such instances. The watches were to accede to all requests or 'requisitions' made by police officers. In addition they were also expected to respond, without delay, to calls 'from private households . . . in the event of attempts to detain and apprehend a thief or any other felon or disturber of the peace'. And where 'brawling and the usual commotions associated with it' were observed watches were also to intervene on their own initiative, both on the streets and in private dwellings. The operational instructions for such eventualities gave an effective *carte blanche* for any form of intervention – a 'sufficient number of men shall be sent to restore order'. The power of definition, the moods, whims and general discretion of the watches were further bolstered by the provision that anyone 'failing to show due respect' was to be immediately arrested. More detailed specification of what such subordination might involve was confined to such vague formulations as 'verbal insults', 'physical assault', and 'other insubordination'. However, aside from these more dramatic but probably infrequent occurrences, a third regulation placed the entire breadth of urban life, and in particular that of the plebeian and proletarian classes, under the supervision of the 'watches, patrols, detachments, or individual sentries'. These were empowered to take immediate action whenever, 'in their view', contraventions took place of police prohibitions on 'the smoking of tobacco on the streets, the fast driving of carriages and horses, the deliberate damaging of lanterns, riding, driving, and carting on the pavements, and other similar violations'. These provisions also offered some protection in instances where soldiers of the watch had made mistakes which could not be ignored or covered over. No resistance was to be offered to the watch 'on the pretext' that soldiers had exceeded their powers. Where this happened, the 'injured party' was to be given 'appropriate redress'. What was considered crucial – and made plainly evident to both soldiers and civilians – was that 'public quiet and safety could not be maintained without unconditional obedience to the watch'.

The distribution of watches throughout the garrisons would certainly have given the impression that 'the entirety of public life to some extent proceeded under the eyes of the law-in-arms'.[211] In many cases soldiers of the watch were more numerous, and certainly more visible, than the civilian police or Gendarmes. For example in Trier (not a citadel, but a large garrison town in the 1820s and 1830s) ten sentry posts were under permanent military occupation except during autumn manoeuvres. Five of these were in the barracks, powder magazine and artillery depot.[212] Military security was maintained even when the garrison was absent, a task not entrusted to voluntary or hired civilian watches. It embraced the house of correction, the main government treasury, and at other times the town jail, military hospital, district poorhouse and 'the main watch'. During the eleven months when the garrison was in the town there was one member of the watch to each 1,300 civilian residents, and during manoeuvres one to 1,850; this was higher than the ratio of civilian police to residents, which stood at one to 2,000.

The extent to which guards on watch duty availed themselves of the extensive powers appropriated by the military authorities cannot simply be attributed to the inclinations of the 20 to 22-year-old sentries on watch, and their longer serving NCOs and young subalterns. In the long term what was involved was a form of social exchange: the reaction of civilians threatened or imposed on by the military could always turn into direct action, either immediately or at the next best opportunity – a 'provocation' which the soldiery, for their part, had to parry. Although the law and the interests of the ruling institutions entrusted the definition of the situation to the soldiers 'on the spot', how this power of definition was translated into actual practice – that is, the real pattern of enforcement, assertion and refusal – depended on the specific situation and balance of forces in the conflict involved. The treatment meted out by each side in these conflicts could prove a spur to extend or refine their tactics – and humiliation 'today' always left open the prospect of success 'next time'.

Offence to the watch

The limits of the military power of definition were reflected in complaints by superiors about resistance and offence shown to guards. One typical such complaint can be seen in the anger of the military headquarters in Danzig at the behaviour of the courts – which were regarded as the civil authorities – in 1824. The commander complained that insults and misdemeanours so often directed against military personnel, patrols and watches were being insufficiently punished, given the circumstances known to prevail here. Those apprehended were either given an interim pardon on grounds of lack of evidence, or merely a minor punishment . . . after a delay of several years'. It was not surprising, 'that such misdemeanours are regarded almost as permissible by the local refractory mob, and are then repeated on an ever-growing scale'. For the commander, such an anti-military posture worked to the 'disadvantage of the morale and reliability of the garrison'. Some form of remedy was therefore urgently required.

The commander also pointed out the close involvement between military and civilian security interests. The actions of the higher regional court were not only detrimental to the military but also failed to promote 'public peace and safety'. Soldiers felt

> that even a minor violation against law and order committed by themselves would be quickly and severely dealt with; in contrast, those committed by a civilian, and offence or injury meted out to guards engaged in strenuous duties, were either not punished at all, or punished only slightly or after a considerable lapse of time.

The upshot was that guards 'were either timid in executing their duty or might resort to taking matters into their own hands'. The General cited two examples. One watch consisting of four soldiers had been 'intimidated' by a 14-year-old lad to such an extent that he had had time to call up a 'rabble' which had then 'assaulted' the watch. And in one instance of 'self-help' by soldiers of the watch, a corporal replied to an instance of abuse from the public 'with two sharp sabre blows to his opponent's head'.

The deployment of overpowering physical force – that is firearms and edged weapons – either as a deterrent or as the result of lessons learnt in a previous humiliation was not solely, or primarily, the product of any lack of precision in military regulations but resulted from the actual course of events, and the ensuing confrontations, when the watch intervened.

Central in the minds of the military commanders was that the 'authority' of their watches should be maintained. Concern for public quiet and safety simply served as an occasional back-up in their arguments and conflicts with the judiciary. The outlook of leading members of the military was typified in a complaint by the Governor General of Silesia, Lieutenant General Grawert, in 1807. Insult or injury to the watches had always been treated as *lèse*

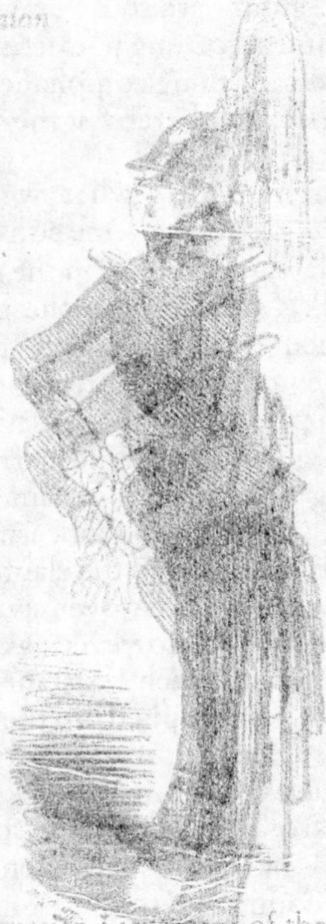

7 How the Royal Prussian Lieutenant of the Guard, Baron von Stierwitz, selects gloves of an inferior quality as he fears that he may have to touch the rabble whilst eliminating them.

majesté.[214] More recently the presumptional arrogance of the "other" estates has evidently triumphed.' The implicit conclusion is not difficult to discern: if the military no longer represented the sovereign directly and for all subjects, then the 'honour' of the army, and with it the 'foundation' for the security and existence of the state as a whole, had to be defended with even greater resolve.[215]

Although identifying the security of society as a whole with the absence of offence to even one soldier of the watch may have seemed somewhat exaggerated to some military commanders, there was nevertheless an important and valid military reason for their preoccupations with this issue. This sense of military thinking can be seen clearly in a complaint made by the commander in Danzig that the 'morale' of the troops might be placed in jeopardy.[216] This must have referred to two things. On the one hand lack of respect regardless of the form it took detracted from the ceremonial dignity with which the military presented itself and from the general claim of the state and the monarchy to exercise domination, expressed in the form of the watch. This implacable form of domination, or more specifically domination in *Prussia*, ritualised in the watches was highlighted in a Cabinet Order issued in

1845: 'irrespective of whether the garrison is large or small, the changing of the guard and the appropriate honours are to be executed with the greatest seriousness and in their entirety and according to existing regulations'.[216] For, 'this is the most certain means of establishing compliance with the law without the application of excessive severity and thereby at the same time securing the respect of the subjects'.

At any event the watches embodied what was special about their institution: they were military *par excellence*. One consequence was that they always had to appear in immaculate uniform, or in the disrespectful words of 'gawpers', 'thoroughly titivated'. Confusion on the part of soldiers of the watch might also have impinged on the military rule of unconditional obedience to command. Failure to punish offences against the, publicly stated, inviolability of military personnel to the same degree as offences against military hierarchy and regulations behind barrack walls would have been regarded as compromising the military's claim to represent a 'total institution'. This was undoubtedly a matter for concern, as any lack of respect towards the watch simultaneously endangered the claim of the state as a whole to exercise universal domination, in particular over civil 'subjects', which the watch was supposed to demonstrate. However, as long as the civilian authorities could rely on the army, any such resistance was not regarded as especially threatening. And this even applied in the case of much larger movements amongst the 'popular masses': if necessary, the military would put them down 'without overmuch ceremony'.

If every act of disrespect towards the watches, irrespective of how trifling, could – and for the officers must – have had such extensive consequences for the functioning of the military, commanders were only acting consistently when they sought to bind all civil authorities to this position – accompanied by demands for appropriate retribution and punishment. And the military did indeed regularly complain to the judiciary: in 1821 the military command in Magdeburg and the military command in Danzig; in 1827, 1829 and 1834 the Governor of Berlin, von Tippelskirch; and in 1835 even the Head of the Council of State and Commanding General of the Berlin Corps of Guard, Duke Carl zu Mecklenburg.[217]

In addition to their attempts to exercise direct influence over the courts through complaints to Ministers, leading military figures also tried to tighten up the watches' operational regulations and, at the same time, provide a legal basis for the somewhat exposed position of the watches before the courts. In 1821 the military and the Minister for War made an application for punishments to be made more severe and for the 'probative force of the watches' to be strengthened.[218] The argument was that, in contrast to the provisions of the Prussian Legal Code, soldiers of the watch ought not to be regarded as prejudiced from the outset in the absence of witnesses if they themselves were the subject of proceedings, unless their conduct in general undermined their credibility.

This provision for 'probative force' was given particular emphasis by Duke Carl. At the same time he reduced the entire problem to the complaint –

already old hat by 1835 – that military authority was disintegrating amongst the civilian 'public':

> Formerly the mere appearance of armed force was customarily sufficient to terminate any disturbance to the peace. Now the tumultuous mob enjoys clashing with the military. In large part this is attributable to the diminished respect for and reduced fear of the watches and sentry posts.

One cause was held to be the insufficient training of soldiers 'during their prolonged youth and short period of service' (two years in 1835). The other reason was considered to be the treatment of such cases by the courts. 'Soldiers are deterred from making use of the real power at their disposal as officers of the watch.' The reason was that, 'if their commands are not issued with the requisite degree of politeness, proceedings are instituted against them'. And this unsatisfactory legal position was not confined to verbal conflicts, for

> they must eventually likewise meet disobedience, gross insubordination, derision, and not infrequently acts [i.e. acts of violence] with acts of violence. They often come off worse as the weaker party, including before the courts, and as a consequence frequently permit what they ought not to have permitted.

The burden of proof in court lay with the watchguards. There was no obligation on civilians to produce counter-evidence and neither was there any easing of the requirements for oral evidence. What was urgently required was 'shorter trials and harsher sentences'.

Although leading military commanders and Ministers of War repeatedly complained to the Ministries of Justice and the Interior (in 1821, 1829, and during the course of the debate after 1835), they finally conceded that there was no pressing need for a corresponding statutory regulation.[219] For the representatives of the civil administration the problem was not merely one of any possible inconsistencies in the common law, but also the possibility of unequal treatment between those areas covered by the Prussian Legal Code and those covered by the Rhenish Code. Moreover, the military could not really argue that either the absolute number of pertinent cases or the trend could be regarded as disturbing. And this must have applied both to the crimes of 'abuse and insubordination' and how these offences were treated before the courts. The civil administration and the judiciary were little impressed by the claim that many incidents went unreported because the military authorities feared that any legal proceedings would go against them.

An estimated total of 235 persons was brought before the courts in Berlin between 1791 and 1801 for 'brawling with soldiers' (i.e. evidently with the watches), that is 21 to 22 per year on average. Of these 59 were acquitted immediately and 9 after subsequent appeal; 140 received prison sentences and 27 were sent for hard labour.[220]

Between the spring of 1827 and October 1829 the courts gave judgement on 103 such cases, that is, approximately 40 per year.[221] And in the four years between 1835 and 1838 this number rose to 220, with a jump from 33 in 1835 to 50, 74 and 63 in succeeding years.[222] However, as the criminal department at the Berlin city court added, this growth after 1836 corresponded to an increase in all other categories of crime. In response to complaints from the city Military Commander, von Tippelskirch, about a steady increase in these crimes, the local superior court had also put on record the need to identify the cases and the parties involved much more accurately.[223]

The judges coolly observed that 'the number of punished excesses against military personnel on watch duty reported does not appear to have significantly increased', taking into consideration the growth in population, and in particular the social character of those who disobeyed the watches. 'For the most part it involves persons of the lowest popular class.' Their sporadic aggression was, accordingly, perceived as being entirely to be expected, and for the judges no occasion for particular anxiety. As far as the officers of the court were concerned, such 'excesses' against the watch were no more disturbing than the 'Dutch courage' of these members of the 'meanest estate'; they were both constants in the social hierarchy, and could be held in check with the granting of fewer acquittals. As they added somewhat complacently, the practice of granting pardons had diminished 'respect for the law and the fear of punishment amongst the subject population'.

During the course of a renewed attempt to achieve legal regulation of the rules of evidence – together with more severe penalties – prompted by a riot in Berlin on 3 and 4 August 1835, and inspired by Duke Carl's memorandum, this cool but entirely ruling-class perspective acquired a weighty representative within the military itself. In 1839 the Governor of Berlin and the successor to Duke Carl in the chairmanship of the Council of State, General Müffling, added his support to Mühler, the Minister of Justice, whose report dismissed the need for any statutory regulation providing specific penalties and less stringent rules of evidence for the watches.[224] For Müffling the main consideration was that, although 'insubordination by civilians against the military was very frequent', it was not 'rooted in any tension between the two groups or in any inclination to disobey the law itself'. The driving force between such disruptive incidents was neither anti-military sentiment nor revolutionary potential. He also cited 'drunkenness'. In his opinion, this constant element in plebeian and proletarian behaviour was the crucial, and in this respect not particularly disturbing, cause both in Berlin and in other provinces. Müffling's position ran contrary to that of his own Ministry, where the head of the 'General Department of War', General von Schöler, had justified the demand for more severe penalties and relaxed rules of evidence for military witnesses with the argument that preventive deterrence would offer those affected more consideration and forbearance;[225] and, moreover, that there was a coincidence of aims between the 'military interest' (the enforcement of immediate peace and order through direct threat, with no unnecessary involvement in civil disturbances) and the police objective of 'inducing the lower popular classes without resort to duress'. This would, of itself, prevent 'excesses' and render the 'immediate use of armed force dispensable'.

Müffling's report halted further attempts to obtain special penalties. What remained was the question of rules of evidence. Parallel to this – and dating back to 1825 – the military had made several proposals which were considered by the Ministry of State for overcoming the uncertainty of the watches by issuing a general instruction (Berlin excepted, because it was already covered by the regulation of 1802). Uncertainty as to the powers of the watch could lead, in individual instances, either to 'weakness' or excessive zeal. Either could culminate in court proceedings, in which the military felt themselves to be at a disadvantage from the outset.

The military's fear of revolution: a general watch instruction as a remedy for the 'mania for change'?

One political event above all brought together all the military's complaints about their ambiguous powers and the steps needed to clarify the situation: the revolutionary movements of the autumn of 1830 – even though in Prussia these mostly took the form of localised riots and revolts, notably the uprising of the Aachen cloth weavers on 30 August 1830. A few months later the Minister of War, von Hake, sent a comprehensive memorandum to the Minister for the Police, von Brenn.[226] In Hake's view the entire complex of 'rights and obligations' of the military watches required immediate resolution. This not only included the question of the burden of proof and harsher sentences for insubordination; the powers of military personnel on watch duty with the right to arrest civilians 'on their own authority' also required regulation. There was a pressing need to clarify the question of jurisdiction during disturbances, together with the 'obligation upon civilians to obey instructions of officers of the watch and other military commanders'. Little help could be expected from the provision of an appropriate regulation through the major legal reform hoped for in the *Gesetzesrevision*. Specific legislation was required. And, in Hake's view, this should be undertaken immediately by a Commission without time-wasting correspondence. Hake concentrated his attention on the central political issue. The matter 'had acquired a particular importance because of the portentous circumstances of the time'. And his colleague, the Interior Minister, would naturally 'share the view from the perspective of the police interest that a statutory determination of these questions would be particularly desirable at this time'.

Nevertheless, the War Minister's interest went beyond the somewhat crude aim of merely cutting through red tape and organising a demonstration of the state's military power. He also wanted some acknowledgement of the fact that such a comprehensive law 'might be seen as evidence of mistrust in the loyalty of the subject'. Given the prevailing circumstances, it was important to avoid such a misunderstanding. Care therefore had to be taken in the drafting of the text. At the same time, Hake evidently regarded the danger of revolutionary eruptions as so pressing that his desire to prevent an uprising outweighed any possible hurt to a subject's pride. At any event, he wanted the instruments of intervention to be completed as swiftly as possible. For,

> one could not conceal the likelihood that the accursed spirit of the mania

for change and resistance to the lawful order which has broken out in so many countries of Europe, even in Germany, might also gain ground in one or the other of the provinces of our Fatherland.

Hake's appeal was not immediately successful. No new steps were taken to consolidate the various proposals, including draft legislation, on the military's use of weapons, nor were any existing initiatives brought forward. The law on the use of weapons was eventually prompted by the memorandum submitted by Duke Carl, Commander General of the Corps of Guards, in 1835 and came into force in 1837. The 1835 August riots in Berlin also led to a regulation on the use of the military during disorders, a field of action in which the watches were also engaged, which marked the first occasion on which the scope of military intervention was made known to the 'public'. One problem remained unresolved until 1844 – a problem almost more important for the civilians affected than these provisions for more extreme incidents. In January 1844 an Instruction was issued regulating 'arrest and formal detention' by watches.[227]

The watch as 'auxiliary police'. Unclarity and executive power 'on the spot'

The regulation of the respective interests of the civil and military apparatuses was considerably delayed by the central problem encountered in all their mutual dealings: what were their powers, and how could they be clearly defined and observed in practice? The question had two aspects. One could be described as a conflict over the function and operations of the military. Were they auxiliary police or organs of the police themselves acting on their own powers? The second concerned the difficulty of resolving or deciding this problem so that the 'executive power' of soldiers, especially those soldiers of the watch, was neither 'too great' nor 'too small'.

The military were permanently obsessed with trying to reduce their commitment to the watch, both in scale and intensity. The reason can be read from a Cabinet Order of 1810: 'internal and police watch do not properly belong to the character of the soldier'.[228] For military commanders, the issue was not merely one of reducing the physical burden, avoiding the exertions or unpleasantness involved in contact with civilians, or ensuring that adequate military drill and training could take place within the barracks or on the parade ground. Neither was the desire to save on soldiers' pay and allow extended leave of prime importance – although the Cabinet Order to reduce the scale of the watch (6 August 1820) did indeed cite this as a factor.[229] More fundamental was the military's fear that police activity – either temporary or permanent – could lead soldiers to acquire non-military, or even anti-military attitudes, perceptions and behaviour. The main aim of those taking this view was to put a stop to any attempts to establish hard and fast regulations for the watch, arguing that any formalised – even though restricted – auxiliary role would embroil the military in a logic which could compromise their direct link to the sovereign. And from a practical point of view such a provision might also cripple the very military readiness on which the civil power so evidently relied. This incompatibility was stressed during the 1837 discussion in the Council of State on the law and the use of weapons. All other representatives of state authority entitled to use firearms, 'border, customs, forestry, hunting and even Gendarme officials' were 'instructed in the particular characteristics of their duties . . . over a long period through careful instruction on the maintenance of order with the exercise of forbearance towards those who seek to disturb it'. Their training also rested 'on their experience' and 'the example of their superiors and more senior comrades'. This endowed them 'with all the circumspection reconcilable with their individual natures'. Otherwise they could face dismissal. But, above all, these civilian executive officers could rely on the fact that the military would intervene 'to enforce wherever they failed'.[230]

In contrast, the 'character which must be developed within every warrior is of a quite different type'. The army's role was 'to resist external aggression at any cost'. Everything else 'flowed from this objective'. However, 'such a capacity for defence rests on the most unshakeable resolution within every warrior not to spare the enemy until they are completely vanquished and utterly defenceless'. Any soldier who might 'spare' the enemy or 'otherwise be answerable for every small excess' would be virtually unemployable for his primary purpose. At any event, 'any enjoining to such utterly unwarriorlike caution' could dangerously jeopardise the military spirit.

However, the logical corollary to this argument – namely the complete withdrawal of troops from service as auxiliary police – was out of the question. Aside from problems as to who should exercise the final say over the 'civil', that is the non-military sphere of social relations, fiscal and practical considerations also played a role. The available finance, which was subject to political constraints, did not allow for an appropriate reinforcement of state and local police forces; nor could a military presence be withdrawn from civilian areas – sentries, at the least, would be needed to guard military facilities and could not avoid coming into contact with the local population.

Advocates of the military's special status and its unrestricted power of decision were therefore obliged to win broad scope for manoeuvre in the event of any lapses on the part of their 'young men' on the watch or in the event of deployment during riots. And this they were able to achieve without too much effort. The statutory provisions on the use of weapons simply stated that it was the military who should determine their use; and the military would be deemed to have 'acted within the limits of their powers until the contrary is proven'.[231]

Such a provision would scarcely favour, let alone enforce, any 'unwarriorlike circumspection'. However, consultations over an Instruction regulating other areas, primarily powers of arrest, ground to a halt on the problem of finding an expression which could be easily formulated but was sufficiently precise. Two points were of particular importance. One was put forward by the Military Regulation Commission under the chair of the Prince of Prussia, Prince Wilhelm, as the, 'important question which had to be resolved in practice every day; should watches proceed independently against those who transgress police regulations or must they await requisition'.[232]

The reply from the Ministry of War repeated the position already worked out four years previously with the Interior and Justice Ministries:[233] 'the maintenance of police instructions is initially the task of police officers, and military watches should generally await their requisition'. Watches were to 'intervene on their own initiative to maintain public safety, peace and order' only in cases of 'imminent danger'. Furthermore, any 'general obligation on soldiers of the watch to maintain specific police regulations is incompatible with their function and duties'.

The small number of soldiers available meant that the 'extent of such an obligation' could not be fully covered. The diversity of local circumstances would also have necessitated many amendments and specific regulations. As far as the Ministry was concerned, the only conclusion was to 'provide a general indication of the circumstances' under which independent intervention was permitted. The officers and civil officials in the Ministries also learnt the lesson from their experience with the revised and extended version of the 1802 regulation and an instruction on powers of arrest dating from 1828 (also confined to Berlin).[234] This document retained the legal division between 'criminal offences' and 'police misdemeanours', 'all disturbers of public quiet and order' and finally 'those who appear to be highly suspicious either of having committed or being about to commit an offence'. Even the examples cited ('robber', 'incendiarist' or, for police misdemeanours, 'vagrants' and 'participants in brawls') were scarcely sufficient to clarify to the common soldier when he was required to intervene. Moreover, this assigned the entire sphere of police surveillance to the watches – an instance where those advocating military restraint or restriction failed to assert themselves in 1843/4. Although the final version of the Instruction in 1844 omitted the blanket requirement to arrest all those 'discovered committing a misdemeanour', the restriction to those 'contravening generally acknowledged local police regulations' still called for a considerable degree of general policing by the watches.

This provision certainly gave both senior officers and civilian authorities fewer opportunities to call on the military than was still possible under the 1828 Berlin Regulation. However, civilians could derive only small comfort from the removal of the legal basis of the military's obligation to intervene in civilian matters: it was precisely these 'generally acknowledged' proscriptions which affected those forms of everyday behaviour, such as singing on the street and public smoking, which were regarded either as particularly improper and therefore of considerable symbolic importance for the 'lower popular classes', or which at least served to make everyday life easier, such as driving carts over the pavements.

This did not exhaust the scope for ambiguity and confusion for both military superiors and subordinates. The Commission which drew up the regulation was also concerned about the question as to how private individuals who called on the support of the watch could demonstrate their seriousness. Even the Ministry of War could not give a clear answer. The section requiring that those calling for such assistance had to give 'due' account of themselves was the only means by which the diversity of individual situations could be taken into account; but this left a great deal of decision to guards 'on the spot': 'The means of obtaining such subjective conviction are so diverse that they cannot be specifically denoted here.'[235]

Attempts by military commanders to provide a cover-all regulation therefore broke down over the concrete form in which their soldiers, as watches, came into contact with the behaviour and conflicts of 'the civil estate'. A no less important distinction created further practical difficulties: how could military personnel be clearly distinguished from civilians? As the Interior Minister sympathetically observed, failure to do so could lead to embarrassing complications for officers: for example, were the watch to arrest a person in civilian dress and subsequently discover that he was an officer[236] – officers could be arrested only in the act of committing a crime, not a police misdemeanour (such confusion was not possible in the case of non-commissioned officers or 'privates' as these ranks did not have the right to wear civilian clothes). The final version of the Instruction apparently resolved the dilemma only in favour of the soldier on watch duty; officers in civilian clothes were to be treated 'virtually' as civilians, that is, could not fully claim the protection which applied to officers in uniform. But they were not to be given completely the same status as civilians. Uniformed officers could be arrested only for committing a crime, not a police misdemeanour; in contrast, officers in civilian dress could be arrested for disobeying an express instruction from the watch, but not for contravening police regulations. Watches therefore had to differentiate between civilians, who could or had to be arrested immediately for committing a police misdemeanour, and a second species of person dressed as a civilian who could be lawfully arrested only after non-compliance with an explicit instruction (for example, to stop smoking).

In general the 1844 Instruction did not provide a solution. It merely reformulated the crucial question for the watches. How were they to behave so as not to arouse offence to superiors or dignitaries, but on the other hand so as not to conjure up massive 'popular rage'? Any legal formulation of watches' *power* of definition on the spot could have proved to be an *obligation* to employ this power. As a consequence, the military favoured brief instructions suitable for daily use.

In a widely distributed instruction book for non-commissioned officers, Regimental Commander of the Guard, Count von Waldersee, noted laconically that 'the proper aim of the watch' consisted in 'the safety of the objects under guard and the maintenance of public order'.[237] There was no mention of the watches' auxiliary police function cited by the Minister: the police as the manifestation of the 'official attendance' to the daily needs of the 'administered' were unreservedly and simply subordinated to the watch. The position was summed up in a 'popular soldiers' catechism in a few verses of doggerel:[238]

The man who stands at the sentry gate
Look – who then decides his fate

As a general rule of conduct, the author proposed:

> Keep your pitch nice and neat
> Drive out mischief from your beat

And in the event of insubordination from the public:

> Strike that sentry with a blow
> And the feel of his bayonet you soon will know
>
> If your're on guard at the colonel's house
> Don't let beggars in and out

A few lines later:

> Uproar, parade, it doesn't matter
> whatever happens give a shout

and finally:

> Don't let wagons run amok
> Stop that driver's impudent look!

The military 'auxiliary police' as permanent police

Far from providing mere 'policing assistance', military watches were called on constantly. The 1837 Council of State debate on the law regulating the use of weapons provides some evidence of how much the watches were used to establish civil quiet and order. Leaving aside the differing views as to the degree of statutory regulation required, all council members – military officers and civil officials – were unanimous that

> the military is very often called on to perform arrests in the garrison towns even in cases of minor disturbances. The first and most common means of assistance in the event of an argument or fight on the street or in a public house, in apprehending a thief or the like, is to call the nearest watch when no executive officer of the police is available (a common occurrence in the nature of things). Frequently, in fact customarily, this involves drunks who have got agitated in the course of an argument. Thereupon, not surprisingly, acts of resistance to the watch easily occur.[239]

Such confrontations,[240] or more precisely this stage in the proceedings on the street, in a bar or in a private house, inevitably exposed the differences between the behaviour of the police and that of the military. The members of the Council of State agreed that soldiers could often not succeed without resort to their weapons. Watch details were not only greater in number than the police (2–4, or possibly 8–10 men as against 1–2 police officers), but, most importantly, each carried a rifle with fixed bayonet. However, in general this could not be employed as a firearm. Soldiers on police missions 'did not carry live ammunition'[241] outside the watch-posts proper. None the less, even without bullets the rifle represented a very powerful club and edged weapon, and was certainly more awesome in appearance than the truncheon or bayonet used as a hand weapon usually carried by police officers. Only the Gendarmerie, few in number, carried firearms: border and customs officials had weapons only at border posts. Even if the more conciliatory majority on the Council of State was right in thinking that bayonets were 'not as dangerous' as firearms, in contrast to the police the watches nevertheless combined both greater numbers and the ability to deploy 'cut-and-thrust' weapons, the unwieldiness of which was usually more than outweighed by the much more massive blow they could inflict.

Although such general observations can provide no more than an outline of typical watch behaviour, they do reveal the existence of a distinctively *military* method for dealing with non-military persons: less 'circumspection' and more 'short shrift', together with the use of larger numbers and the threat, and active use, of edged weapons – not perhaps dangerous to the lives but certainly to the limbs of those arrested or felt to be guilty of an offence.

In the garrisons, the military watches were usually far more the visible representatives of state power and domination than the civilian police. However, their presence as police was by no means regular and constant. For the *Bürger* and other residents – and even more so for municipal officials and other local dignitaries – the disturbing propensity to violence inherent in the military power of definition was expressed in the unpredictability of watch guards and their commanding subalterns.

Two examples. In the summer of 1836, the District Government in Koblenz complained to the Ministry of the Interior about the laxity of the main watch at this important centre of military and civilian power. During the course of a disturbance and 'uproar', 'it had taken some time before the military authorities from the watch deemed it necessary to despatch some troops'. But, once called on to disperse, the 'onlookers' had responded immediately.[242] In contrast, in March 1846 the citadel authorities issued a complaint about slackness on the part of the civilian police. Only two police 'sergeants' and one Gendarme had been visible as representatives of the civil police during a scuffle between soldiers and civilians in front of the main watch; and they had reported the incident only after a request from the officer. It was 'evident' that no more senior officer had been on the spot, although the Mayor lived nearby. The citadel Governor noted that he could 'intervene militarily only' if requested to do so by a civilian police officer, unless the watch itself was under direct attack. However, he added a clear warning: 'being able to wait until called on by the police presupposes that the police themselves take action in good time'. The Governor also demanded the presence of, at the least, the local police superintendent.[243]

But, whereas the civilian authorities could do no more than to complain about the military, the military commander had a real alternative available if, in his view, civil measures or precautions were inadequate during incidents of disorder: he could intervene on his own initiative if he regarded the situation as one of 'imminent danger'.

Conflicts of powers – agreements of interest – protracted decision-making

The procedure which ultimately produced the order on the watch guards' power of evidence was drawn out in the extreme: twenty-six years elapsed between the first steps in 1821 and the final outcome. And, even after legal consultations were finished in 1843, a further four years were required before a regulation came into force – and even then it had virtually no effect. Nevertheless, the length of time involved and the persistent disagreements as to how the regulation was to be formulated should not be viewed as an indicator of any fundamental conflict of interest between the civilian authorities and the military. Neither party disputed the emphasis which had to be placed on 'security', nor the basic need for the military to retain a presence in everyday civil life. What were controversial were the *forms* of state control and discipline. The same applied for the wearisome process of decision-making which led to the directives and authorisations to be applied in the event of arrests prior to the 1844 Instruction. The 1837 law on the use of weapons enjoyed the fastest legislative passage. For the military, the crucial interest was securing short yet open regulations, which would enable them to make decisions 'on the spot', but not oblige them to maintain a continuous presence. In contrast, as far as the municipal, regional and administrative authorities were concerned, only the constant presence of military watches could guarantee safety and order in the towns.

In fact, local authorities often tried to have permanent garrisons established in their areas.[244] And, in those towns that were already garrisoned, any military manoeuvre involving a few weeks' absence of the troops seemed to provoke a collapse of 'civil order'. At the least, such manoeuvres imposed a further burden on municipal finances, which had to provide substitute watches or remunerate civilians who took on security tasks, as in the Rhine provinces in the years after 1829.[245] In the 'older' provinces, the citizenry was obliged to undertake security tasks even when the garrison was present if it could be shown that the number of full-time troops was not sufficient and that soldiers were having to take on watch duty more than once a week, or after 1820 more than twice.[246] Repeated references to the actual limited amount of security provided cut little ice; as did the argument offered by the Ministry of War according to which a soldier of the watch could 'offer protection only from overt violence', 'but a cashier who slept in the ante-room was more use than ten sentries'.[247] The Cabinet Order to reduce watch duty, decreed in 1820, provoked very active resistance from those judicial and administrative authorities directly affected. Local financial interests and the need to maintain symbolic authority clearly pulled in the same direction. Even judicial officials, such as von Gärtner, President of the District Court in Naumburg, who normally greeted military demands and practices with great scepticism, joined in: he expressed regret at the withdrawal of the watch from a number of police departments and jails which – in his view – had to be under military guard:[248] 'For in truth one cannot envisage a nobler or more useful service for the residents of the city than for the military in peacetime to protect the life, property, and security of citizens against the attacks of dangerous criminals.'

The representatives of civilian state power wanted military force available to deter actual or supposed 'disrupters', both symbolically and in practice. Moreover, they were quite prepared to sanction a legal form which endowed the military with a final power of decision over such situations, and hence over their own conduct.

'Conscious collaboration' of all the organs of domination: the new legitimation for the military's rights

The reluctance of civilian ministerial officials to ratify the, in practice, indispensable presence of the military in all local public police matters abated after the middle 1840s with the looming prospect of a 'more excitable' population. The riots and increase in the crime figures in the late 1830s, and then again after the middle 1840s, clearly raised considerable fears about the 'safety' of both society and the state.[249] In 1846 the specialist within the Council of State concerned with the question of probative force, Privy Counsellor Ulrich – a judicial official – expressed the thinking at the heart of this turnaround.[250] The need for a special regulation for the watches could no longer be assessed simply by figures for actual convictions or lesser sentences: 'these figures alone are not the decisive issue'. Rather, the 'uniqueness' of the position and circumstances of those 'military persons engaged in public service' was justification enough for the planned regulation. Ulrich then outlined the elements of this unique position, its elementary function and significance for the entire social status quo:

> The soldier on duty or in command has a public vocation: he represents the power which protects civil order and private safety and he has the duty, even at personal risk to himself, to resist those who would seek to damage it and to ensure that the guilty do not evade legal punishment. His office therefore makes him the opponent of those who would seek to disturb public order. Such attempts are seldom committed in broad daylight and in the presence of many unconcerned persons but usually at a time and in places which facilitate the execution of the crime – that is during the evening and night or in isolated places. The soldier who finds himself on duty under such circumstances will therefore, as the sole barrier to the intended violation of safety or public order, become the object of attack of such malefactors, especially if he is obliged either to resist their undertaking physically or to arrest them.

In Ulrich's view the prevailing legal position and court practice could have fatal consequences:

> The principle that the statement of a military person engaged in office lacks the quality of credible evidence because of personal involvement is an endangerment to public order. It removes from these persons the protection of the laws which they are obliged to administer at personal sacrifice and risk from the attacks which they may suffer as a result of fulfilling their duty. It encourages the disturbers of public order by

> ensuring that they will remain free from punishment. It weakens the standing of the public authority, and consequently multiplies the incentive to insubordination. Indeed, it creates a very evident motive for destroying the testimony of members of the military engaged in their duty through attacks on their person.

This situation was seen not only as a threat to those immediately affected or to the army. The ramifications were also felt to be disturbing as it became evident that the military was to be regarded as the permanent reserve power for the civilian central authorities. And the system of the military watch had become an indispensable buttress for ruling institutions: 'The moral consequences of these circumstances are of greater importance than they might appear at first glance. More than any other age, ours demands the conscious collaboration between all those organs called upon to maintain civil order.'

The burden placed on the military eased only with the progressive professionalisation and militarisation of the local police, and the introduction of the constabulary in Berlin in 1848 and outside Berlin after the 1860s. Watches were reduced, but did not disappear completely. Soldiers acting as police remained visible both as a symbol and a real presence in many towns up until the First World War.

Permanent states of emergency: the citadels

Collaboration between the military and the police went much further in the twenty-six citadels than in other garrison towns.[251] Although police powers were nominally in the hands of the civilian authorities, the regulation which provided for the issuing of police orders 'as they concerned citadels and garrisons' revealed the extensive powers possessed by the military. In case of disagreement during 'imminent danger' the Commander or Governor (the latter in Berlin, Magdeburg and Koblenz) acquired the sole power of command.[252]

For the Prussian army these 'surplus' powers were not merely a reflection of the unique logic of the institution of the citadel. Their power of decision within citadels – more precisely the power of the respective commander – was both a symbolic and a real quantity. It harked back to the 'besmirched' honour of the corps, and the imperilment of the state itself. In 1806, most citadels had capitulated to Napoleon's troops without a fight – a shameful failure, especially in the eyes of reforming officers such as Scharnhorst and Gneisenau.

During the summer of 1808, still in the aftermath of this massive blow to the code of military honour of his fellow senior officers, Gneisenau – who had acquitted himself brilliantly in the defence of Kolberg – drafted a memorandum which took particular issue with the office and characteristics of the citadel commander.[253] Writing as an officer who had personally succeeded in this post, he noted caustically that the 'accommodation' of commanders in 1806 who 'had allowed their political views to impinge on their duty . . . merited death'. Although it should have been self-evident, it was nevertheless vital to make citadel commanders realise that their task was 'to drive out force with force . . . not to listen to blandishments'. Only a direct order from the supreme commander, the King, could release them from this duty. Commanding officers also had to be properly trained. The 'rigours of siege' called for a 'robust constitution'. The commander was often needed at night and the 'unity of military, police and judicial power in his person did not permit him the necessary rest during the day'. And, although Gneisenau fully appreciated that 'a Prussian officer and soldier does not like to be confined in a citadel', this did not mean that preparations for the worst were to be treated as an incidental matter and left to semi-invalids and men in their dotage.[254] A draft instruction which he prepared some months later echoed these sentiments. One passage in particular illustrates the link between the ongoing and prospective role of the military in the citadels and this activity of permanent preparation. It was not enough 'merely to think of the narrow defence of a citadel and the means necessary for it'.[255] Rather the commander had 'to accumulate as much of them as he can'.

Constant preventive measures and the orientation of all military activity to the ultimate 'day of enclosure' and its associated 'state of siege' inevitably embraced civilians – and in particular the civilian residents of the citadel towns more than elsewhere.[256] Civilian life was dominated not only by the material needs of the garrison, but also by the strict requirement for internal tranquillity in order to conserve and develop troop morale. An 1809 provision on the relationship between military and civil authorities elaborated what this meant for life in the citadels: 'Prior to enclosure, all those persons whose conduct could be prejudicial to the defence or who cannot be adequately provided for during the siege are to be removed from the citadel.'[257] Such a provision, uniting military, psychological and political precaution, gave the citadel commander enormously wide powers, including constant surveillance of the population as well as more material planning.

This provision did not have any immediate effects. It was the partial mobilisation of 1830–1 which brought home to regional and citadel commanders the need for instant readiness. The issue was brought to the attention of the civilian administration via a report prepared by the Commander General of the Rhine, von Borstell, in February 1831.[258] The report, aimed at all Provincial Governments, set out on the assumption that approximately one quarter of the residents of the citadel towns consisted of persons 'utterly lacking in means', unable to provide themselves with sufficient food. Nevertheless the General did not argue that all of this group should be evacuated; the prior establishment of food storage depots could provide some help. Only those who were 'badly disposed and unreliable should be removed from the citadel'. For the General the expulsion of these 'people' who, as far as the military were concerned, were a potential hazard to good order, was a task which could not be delayed or avoided. Food resources might be stretched out; smaller rations or the slaughtering of horses offered some possibility of flexibility. But the maintenance of the fighting spirit of the troops allowed no room for manoeuvre. Preventive intervention, that is forced expulsion, appeared to be the only appropriate solution. Over the following months District Governments were required to ascertain the number of those who would have to be expelled from fortified places in their districts, to establish the procedures to be used and in particular the places to which those evacuated would be moved. Civilian officials raised many objections. They could not establish precise figures (as in Cologne, for example) and in Aachen the Government estimated that around 50 per cent of the 2,800 residents of Jülich would fall into this category; nor could they find appropriate places to send them. One particular problem was that many of those involved were 'women, children, the old and the sick who are unable to earn their own living'. The outlying parishes would therefore resist any evacuation and central state funds would not be in a position to help.

In Koblenz a conference between the District Government and the *Landräte* was relatively quick to establish how the military demand for the expulsion of 3,500 persons could be achieved.[259] The objections of the officials proved fruitless: officials in the District Government and the *Landräte* tried to comfort themselves with the fact that each of the parishes within up to 50 kilometres radius would have to take only one family each, of four to six individuals. In contrast, the District Government in Cologne soon drew attention to the fact that any preparations for such an evacuation would be 'disturbing in character' and that extreme care had to be exercised, even in the process of establishing the figures.

This was, of course, essentially a tactical argument, cleverly exploiting military concern about unrest and turning it against its originators. If even the preliminary steps towards prevention were disruptive would it not therefore be more advisable to abandon these preparations and act only when there was an immediate and palpable threat of invasion?

Nevertheless a provisional agreement was reached in Jülich about how many places would be required for those expelled: despite this, an inquiry from the local commander as to what would be done in an emergency with the 1,300 persons who could not be provided for within the citadel went unanswered in the summer of 1832.[260] For both officials and officers the diminishing likelihood of an imminent invasion coincided with the emergence of a new debate within the administration as to whether the civilian authorities should remain in their posts or retreat to the interior – a question which was not resolved until 1840 when the possibility of a massive invasion resolved the issue in favour of large-scale retreat by the District Governments. In 1830 the only agreement was that the local treasuries would have to be swiftly moved.

In December 1832, that is more than eighteen months after the first initiative, the District Government in Cologne reported that its estimate of those to be removed from the city was 'at least 12–15,000', that is 20–25 per cent of non-military residents.[261] At the same time, the commander in Wesel reported only 1,070 'heads', 10 per cent of the non-military population.[262] These reports were initially forwarded to the provincial authorities, the *Oberpräsident*, and the provincial military command. The District Government in Cologne added that 'according to agreement' negotiations were also proceeding between the provincial military command and the local commanders on this issue, but that nothing had been officially declared.

The District Government in Cologne took the opportunity to raise the possible consequences and ramifications once again. Great care had to be exercised as far as those at the receiving end were concerned: there 'was already talk', and 'excitement amongst the lower popular classes' was to be feared. Matters should be resolved amongst themselves, face to face. Although the main concern in the early 1830s remained the 'often protracted' calculation of the number of civilian and military dependants to be removed from the citadels, the pattern of 'military order and civilian execution' reasserted itself in this field – although perhaps not unambiguously and mechanically implemented.

Little changed in this pattern over the next years and decades. The military need for citadels went unchallenged until the First World War. In the period under consideration here the basic provision was merely reaffirmed in 1840. However, the issue was taken up again by both military and civilian authorities in March 1848, although 'internal' pressures – that is, the revolutionary movements of the same year[263] – put a stop to any revision of the figures. The powers held by commanders continued in force for the rest of the century, but were never directly used in preparation for an evacuation.

In 1831/2 the decisive criterion for the military in determining who was to be removed was political or social unreliability. This yardstick not only shaped the perceptions and judgements of commanding officers during dramatic incidents or for long-term planning: suspicious vigilance was also to guide everyday conduct – at least, this was the advice given by the more battle-hardened officers. And although 'undertakings'[264] by residents would not have such dire consequences in peacetime as during a siege, the citadel nevertheless had to be protected against spies – that is, unauthorised entry to the fortifications and noting down of its layout. The watch therefore had both to demonstrate and exercise an element of warlike reality every day (and every night).[265] One author of a manual advocating that the main watch should assume responsibility 'for military police surveillance in both town and citadel' considered that the main issue was 'surveillance of the residents', an argument backed up by warnings of the awful consequences of diminished vigilance, and references to shameful capitulations in the past – Ostend in 1706, Mannheim in 1795, and Tortosa in 1811.[266]

Suspicion towards the population was at its height in the western provinces, both from the military and civilian authorities. Their geographical location made it necessary 'to keep an especially watchful eye on the inhabitants of the citadels', as Police Minister von Wittgenstein instructed all District Governments in the west shortly after taking control of the region in May 1816.[267] Immigration permits for foreigners could be issued only on the recommendation of the respective District Government, and after approval direct from the Ministry via the citadel commander.

However, everyday police matters could not be decided by ministerial orders. In Cologne, the local agencies of the state also acted on their own initiative. In the early part of 1830 (that is, prior to the disorders later in that year) the citadel commander and police headquarters agreed that 'military patrols would be put at the disposal of police inspectors at night, on Sundays and holidays, and especially during fairs'[268] – a regulation welcomed by the corps headquarters staff. The fact that by not giving command on the spot to the military this regulation ignored the proper division of authority in the event of military intervention into civil policing matters was not considered a relevant objection. The 'institution established appears appropriate to local conditions'. Why this surprisingly simple agreement was concluded becomes evident a few lines later:

> It is undeniable that the prevalence of all types of excesses and crimes in the towns of this province is due mainly to the fact that they house a mass of homeless people and vagrants, not only from this region but also from abroad.

This not only placed great burdens on the system of poor relief, but also 'disturbed police order and security'. The presence, conduct, and appearance of the obviously growing number of propertyless in the towns conveyed a picture of a growing threat to the military's interest in safety and security.[269] Some concessions on matters of protocol or precedence could, therefore, be tolerated if they held out the prospect of reinforcing the striking power of the state.

For the residents of citadel towns and their surrounding villages, the military presence was all-embracing.[270] Daily civilian life was also affected by less formal burdens, such as soldiers' off-duty 'pranks'[271] and the intensive control of residents: for example, inward and outward movement through the gates; the locking of the gates at night; the ban on building within the field of fire around the citadel, that is, a radius of 975 metres measured from the top of the fortifications; application of the hunting laws in this area;[272] and restricted access or prohibitions on visiting the city walls. Citadels also had more watches than other garrison towns, and in some citadels a large proportion of the troops were billeted on civilians (Cologne, Magdeburg).[273]

The wider deployment and greater number of watches must have created considerable scope for conflict. And, since citadels had to remain operative at any cost, the military's reaction would, in all probability, have been much more massive and drastic than elsewhere. To cite one example from Cologne, of the few available to us: on the evening of 5 November 1838 – a few days after the 'commotions' outside a Canon's residence on 26 October – an individual 'citizen' who had been asked to remove his pipe from his mouth in front of a powder magazine had answered the guard in a 'crude and insubordinate manner'. The sentry immediately resorted to violence and struck the pipe from the man's mouth. This action was to have considerable consequences for the sentry. Under cover of darkness several other men bombarded him with stones, with the clear aim of establishing whether he had a loaded weapon on him. Having established that his gun was not loaded and that he had no ammunition they attacked him and 'assaulted him with stones, sabre blows and kicks until he became unconscious'.[274]

The behaviour of the guard was criticised not only by the local military headquarters but also by the provincial military command in Koblenz, who noted that such independent action would inevitably cause 'excitement'. During the tense situation which followed the forced transfer of the Archbishop of Cologne in 1837, senior officials considered it vital that the military representatives of the state, in particular, should avoid any provocation. In contrast, it would have accorded with the military code of conduct and been entirely 'worthy' had the guard 'made use of his weapon'. Specifically, this would have involved 'threatening with the bayonet and, in an emergency, using it; and if necessary, for one's own safety, using firearms'.

Thus, even in the case of a relatively minor incident – a dispute with one individual – moreover an incident which in no way resembled or could have resembled a riot or even a disturbance, soldiers were instructed to insist on short shrift, but by 'official' means and according to the model of military combat. Soldiers were – literally – not to get their hands dirty, but to confine themselves to the means of coercion at their disposal and wield this potential for violence without delay.

Not surprisingly, the military's ambitions were most apparent and least inhibited in the smaller citadel towns. The general implications of this can be seen in the sarcastic comments by the *Generalprokurator* Ruppenthal in September 1832 (later *Regierungspräsident* in Cologne, and after 1839 leader of the Rhenish section of the Ministry of Justice). Writing to the Minister of Justice, von Kamptz, on the subject of a citadel order issued by the commander of the citadel in Saarlouis about the 'unseemly behaviour of citizens to the watch' (a command which the commander admitted was not adequately confirmed in court decisions), he noted that the order, 'gave every soldier on duty the right, in fact the obligation, to investigate any action by a citizen in order to ascertain whether it was an insult or not, and in the case of the former to punish this wrongdoing with flint and sabre'.[275]

Although this questionable command was amended, the omnipresence of military policing was more difficult to remove, as the 1838 Police Code for Saarlouis shows. This envisaged the exclusive presence of a military guard outside 'dancing entertainments', a provision found to be 'appropriate' by the Ministry of Justice in 1837. And this also was in accord with the ministerial approval of the arrest of a citizen in a public house by the military guard in 1836.[276]

An 1844 citadel order for Minden, Westphalia, with around 10,000 civil inhabitants and 1,500 soldiers in 1840, shows that policing by the military was not confined to individual events or minor matters.[277] Sixteen pages were devoted to instructions about instances in which soldiers could, as watches, 'carry out arrests by virtue of their office for contraventions of citadel police regulations'. And, as the legal official in the District Government established, this included a number of areas in which the 'personal freedom of residents would be considerably threatened' were the watches to make an immediate arrest. Nevertheless, a subsequent instruction not to intervene immediately for such offences as 'looking at the fortifications' or 'walking dogs on the promenade', but merely to issue a warning and make an arrest only if a reminder was needed or if the order was not obeyed, seemed to him to invite insubordination. The municipal executive's subsequent view also combined a realistic acquiescence in the face of what could not be changed with resignation based on experience that 'the sharp edges of an order are soon blunted'.[278]

However, the opportunity was not lost to draw attention to a particularly two-edged provision:

> It is worthy of gratitude that the watches are instructed to look out for wanton women. But it might be better if completely inexperienced recruits should be spared this task. Moreover, how should one decide that any particular woman numbers among that category which has to be removed?

Developments in Jülich show the extent to which the military control could take hold of such a small citadel town. In one report on the situation in Jülich prepared in 1841, the *Oberpräsident*, von Bodelschwingh, noted that the increasing poverty which had been observed there over a number of years was very closely connected with this all-embracing military presence.[279] Since 1830 travellers had been deterred by the 'almost constant strict control of the gates'. The city gates were also too low for many wagons and Jülich had almost completely ceased to serve as a resting place on the journey from Cologne to Aachen. Bodelschwingh's observations had little impact, however, despite the fact that he was far from hostile to the military. Jülich retained its citadel status until 1867.

5

Emergencies and the requisitioning of the military

Riot control and the 'protection of the state as whole'

A taxonomy of riots and forms of state intervention

Irrespective of whether their purpose was pleasure or protest, official manuals ranked public gatherings of the 'administered' solely in terms of their relationship to 'public order': 'disturbances', 'tumults' and more seriously 'rout', 'riot' and 'revolt'.[1] In official eyes, all were the work of the 'lower popular classes', 'a chaotic mob'. From the 1830s onwards, attention was directed increasingly at the 'labouring masses', and in particular at railway construction workers.[2] Notwithstanding any finer distinctions between mere 'incidents' and 'excesses', as far as those in positions of responsibility on the spot were concerned, such happenings – especially after 1848/9 – represented localised violations of that general 'public quiet, safety and order' which the law required the police to maintain (Prussian Legal Code, Part II, Section 10, Article 17, 'The Duties of the Police').

For officers on the ground, these incidents were not markedly different from the everyday clamour and boisterousness which they encountered, in particular 'the nightly thronging of the less cultivated popular classes in the beer halls and schnapps houses'. And the demands they made on officers also broadly matched those experienced when their attempts to serve summonses for the payment of fines or taxes, or execute tasks 'on requisition' on behalf of other branches of government, met with resistance. All required careful observation and judgement of the behaviour, gestures and remarks of others, combined with the appropriate face-to-face response. Although, in the final analysis, such situations were defined to the advantage of officials, they were none the less fraught with uncertainty.

The threatening character of riots and tumults evidently lay first and foremost in the 'congregation' of large 'masses' of people. Even when they remained fairly passive – which was frequently the case – they demonstrated an unfamiliar potential counterforce:[3]

> The first duty of the general security police is the protection of the state as a whole . . . From this emerges the need to prevent or suppress any riotous

assemblies of individuals discontented over a particular circumstance, as these most easily lead on to a prejudicing of these interests.[4]

The sheer visibility of such instances of insubordination gave a foretaste of the possible limits of the authority and legitimacy of the state 'to protect the existing order against the enemies of public safety, life, freedom and property'. Seen in this light, any 'excess' directly jeopardised the 'noble purpose and great calling of the officers of the police'.[5]

Prior to the 'great spurt' (Kuznets, *Modern Economic Growth*) of factory industrialisation in the 1850s, public protests in the first half of the nineteenth century had a variety of causes, ranging from the endemic, and often cyclically aggravated, threats to employment and subsistence presaged by rising food prices relative to wages, to conflicts over localised political or economic power and their symbolic, usually religious, expression (1837–9).[6] Although protests were local in character, they were far from being merely 'reactive',[7] aimed simply at 'restoring' a traditional way of life, whatever this might have been. Rioting domestic-industrial producers or the unemployed were not engaged in 'blind' protest against the increasingly insecure prospects for their markets and livelihoods. In the textile trades in particular, the family-economy mode of production constituted a foundation for autonomous resistance which, through invoking long-enjoyed 'rights', contained elements of an alternative conception of social organisation.[8]

Despite this diversity of causes and forms, the response of the authorities to protest varied little from incident to incident. Police practice in town and country was broadly similar, and the precise form of police administration also had little bearing. What was important was whether a garrison was on hand – with the twenty-six citadel towns representing an even more special case.

The usual practice in rural areas and non-garrison towns was to rush two to four Gendarmes to the scene. These were assigned to the *Landrat* for 'efficiency' and were recruited and organised along military lines. Normally, however, Gendarmes had to be requested by the local 'Director of Police': this could be the Mayor, or in the 'old' provinces, or those east of the Rhine, a member of the municipal executive, a bailiff or an estate owner (and in Posen after 1836, the District Commissary). Simultaneous notification to the *Landrat* also allowed him to get to the trouble spot, although – as a number of severe reproofs from District Governments and Ministries reveal[9] – this was not always done. Where 'persuasion' or the threat of military intervention failed, or was met with kicks, as in Steinfurt (Westphalia) in October 1833,[10] the *Landrat* or his representative would go on to requisition additional Gendarmes (at most two or three). In the most extreme circumstances help would be sought from the nearest garrison while local officials tried to 'reason' with the crowd – unless, that is, the garrison itself had prompted the trouble.

In non-garrison towns the procedure for 'subduing' excesses and tumults differed only from the rural practice in the fact that two or three executive police officers would have been supposed to be on hand or on patrol.

However, 'even the slightest difficulty' in 'subduing' a 'riot' – that is, if 'indicating' to the mob that they should disperse was of no avail – left no other option but to call up the nearest military for assistance.[11]

Following the Aachen 'revolt' of 30 August 1830, such requests became the rule, either immediately following the onset of trouble or even beforehand as a preventive measure. The 'propertied'[12] and civil officials were plagued by fear of revolution – a fear fanned rather than allayed by official publications.[13] None the less, although much more rapid and, after 1830, less questioned, resort to the military may have overshadowed the immediate and demonstrative use of judicial authority, it did not replace it. The police authorities, who were required to make the 'initial provisional investigation', sought to unburden themselves as rapidly as possible by calling in the state prosecutors or, in the older Prussian provinces, 'Examining Magistrates' (*Inquisitionsrichter*). At the same time, the judiciary could complement the more direct intervention of the police by adopting a broader and less situation-bound perspective, which in turn conferred greater legitimacy on the judicial process.

The appearance of the military within a few hours if cavalry were involved – or the next day – and the associated display of, usually, light weaponry were almost always sufficient to quell any disturbance.

The control of tumults amongst railway constructions workers

Unrest involving concentrations of 500–2,500 railway construction workers – sometimes even 15,000 – was a different matter, and severely tested the authorities' ability to maintain social discipline in the period 1832–47.[14] The response of the authorities to these novel, organised and offensive tactics by waged workers was increasingly harsh. And threats to react with the use of weapons were made good in 1845 at Schildesche, near Bielefeld, when workers were confronted by a bayonet charge.

The need to forestall the numerous instances of such unrest in the 1840s forced the provincial and central authorities to maintain permanent surveillance. However, the Ministries of the Interior and of Finance rejected applications from the District Government in Arnsberg and the Westphalian *Oberpräsidium* for a more modest military presence, the provision of state police officers at the railway companies' expense, and the establishment of commissions of arbitration to include not only the local police authorities but also workers, on the grounds that such measures were either inappropriate, or, in the case of the commissions, would interfere in private legal matters and existing judicial procedure. Proposals for 'religious disciplining' also failed to find ministerial favour.[15] Only 'more stringent police control' was seen as appropriate for dealing with the 'general dissatisfaction with the level of wages and efforts to impose higher wages through incitement'. And, since any necessary military intervention was 'in the public interest', the Ministries felt that the costs could not be charged to the private requisitioners, the railway companies. A number of individual proposals from *Landräte* in Silesia for the suppression of the 'brute violence of the worker masses' by confronting it with the 'greater force of the state', and in particular the 'prevention of outbreaks through the moral impression imparted by proximity to the latter' – that is, the wider dispersal of military units to 'maintain police order' with costs borne by the companies – were deemed impracticable.[16]

Those few attempts by members of the higher bureaucracy to treat and understand railway workers' protests as harbingers of a new type of collective action were mostly in vain. The momentous realisation that 'police supervision alone' was not sufficient to prevent this new form for the articulation of interests was swept aside in a short internal exchange of memoranda between the regional authorities and the Ministries.[17] The bureaucratic mind could simply not accommodate the fact that a link might exist between the resistance of these mobile workers and the spread of capitalist social relations. The upper echelons of the apparatus merely called for renewed vigour in the implementation of its schematic approach to pacification in a policy not open to discussion and certainly not to change.

The provisional character and failure of non-military repression

Every police manual for 'practitioners' cited the 1798 provision, according to which military assistance was not to be shunned in the event of 'riot' or 'tumult'. Although this principle was not immediately reapplied following military demobilisation in 1815, it was progressively rehabilitated in subsequent years. Up until the early 1830s, for example, the stentorian and 'vigorous' appearance of the *Landrat* or 'individual detachments of Gendarmes' represented measures prior to,[18] and occasionally instead of, 'a military detachment of superior force'.[19] Where the *Landrat* had access to a 'civil militia' as well as armed forest rangers, as in an outbreak of machine breaking in Eupen in 1821,[20] or could assemble 'civilians with lances', as in a recruitment riot in Ahrweiler in 1831,[21] such alternatives were not chosen because of any conscious reservations about the 'grim, severe and violent military spirit';[22] rather such short-lived, direct mobilisations of threatened or endangered burghers and their subordinate client class were simply used as a substitute for military intervention. Parallel to this, however, after 1815 the older municipal 'citizens' guards' (*Bürgergarden*) were either progressively relegated to the status of mere appendages of the military and confined to watch duty or, as in Berlin in 1825, disbanded entirely.[23] Many citizens preferred to pay for the thirty Gendarmes required in Berlin rather than entrust the task to their fellows – or themselves. Protection from actual or imagined dangers was evidently seen as being more reliably exercised by institutions specifically established for the purpose. The price – less say in the administration of the police and stricter police supervision of everyday life – was readily accepted, especially as the prime sufferers were the 'lower classes'. The bureaucracy could also reconcile itself to this development since it alleviated one of its most persistent worries – issuing weapons into civilian hands. After the Aachen revolts of 30 August 1830, the civilian 'Defence Associations' (*Schutzvereine*) were allowed to exist only in non-garrison towns, or when the garrison was absent. As with other means of coercion, the

8 'The restricted freedom of association'
In the name of the law!! According to your notification to the appropriate authorities you were supposed to gather here together at 3 o'clock sharp. As ten minutes have now elapsed, I therefore declare this to be an unlawful union. You must separate immediately.

Landräte were responsible for their supervision.[24] District Governments, *Oberpräsidenten*, and even more so the Ministry of the Interior, basically mistrusted any armed attempt at pacification which was not directly organised by the state, even where 'good citizens' were involved. A spontaneous revival of the '1830 Association' in Geilenkirchen in 1838 was strictly forbidden by the Ministry of the Interior.[25]

The hunger riots of early 1847 prompted more calls for a 'civil' or 'security' guard. A memo advocating extreme caution drafted by the Director of the police department in the Ministry of the Interior, Mathis, generated even greater scepticism from the *Oberpräsident* of the Rhine, von Eichmann:

> the [possible] intervention [of a civil guard: AL] will lead to the exercise of military authority by the citizenry. There will also be calls to exercise such authority in garrison towns since such self-help will no longer be regarded merely as a duty but as a civil right. We would then have a national guard which could easily enter into some very trying conflicts with the military.

Eichmann added that the Commanding General of the Rhine Army Corps was 'in full agreement' with his view.

The two issues raised by Eichmann, encroachment into the military sphere of competence (even where this relieved the troops) together with a drive to much more portentous social 'movements' and political revolution, aroused concern not only amongst military officers – civil officials were also perturbed.

The transition to the March Ministry in 1848 had no effect on this outlook and the corresponding administrative actions. Permission for the newly allowed militia, who were assigned military rights in the event of tumults by an order of 19 April 1848, to make an intervention *before* regular troops was confined to an internal memorandum.[26] And passive opposition to the establishment of the militia in rural areas and most medium-sized and small towns effectively blocked the implementation of the October 1848 legislation. By the time the law was formally rescinded in the autumn of 1849, it had effectively become a dead letter.[27]

Military intervention

The method of requisition and the course of intervention

Watches, with their one to two, and at most forty to sixty, men were frequently involved in policing. However, they did not suffice for anything more than 'casual unlawful assemblies' of a few individuals. And travelling time meant that they could respond to requests for assistance only from villages in the immediate vicinity of garrison towns.

The calling up of a full military unit to the scene of a riot required either that the alarm should be raised by the watch or formal requisitioning by the civil authorities. In the latter case, the prescribed procedure ran via the *Landrat* to the *Regierungspräsident* or *Oberpräsident*, each of whom could apply to the Commanding General.[28] In practice, the authorities on the ground almost always went directly to the nearest regiment or battalion commander, or commander of the – quite often – autonomous garrison companies. This, the shortest path from local police authority to the nearest military commander, was chosen so often, in fact, that in 1830 the local police were instructed to include the *Landrat* at the least in the procedure, with a subsequent immediate report 'upwards'.[29] The bureaucratic hierarchy therefore underwent a formal inversion, at least in part, during 'crisis situations'.[30]

Military principles required that, whenever possible, intervention should take place with 'concentrated force'. For this a compact detachment was indispensable. As a rule, companies (or squadrons in the case of cavalry) of at least eighty to a hundred men, or more rarely columns of around thirty men, were deployed. Detachments in battalion strength – that is 600 or more – were regarded as the normal or minimum level only in large towns or where the requisition was made under particularly alarming circumstances – as at

Schildesche in 1845, where a battalion was despatched to deal with riots by railway construction workers.

Sidearms or light firearms were rarely loaded at the outset, although the Cologne watch did do so in November 1838 following some minor riots against the watch which had taken place in the wake of larger religious conflicts; the same happened during the 'potato revolution' in Berlin in April 1847. The loading of weapons in public was regarded as part of the ritual employed to intimidate and suppress disturbances, as in Schildesche. But there were also technical objections to carrying loaded weapons. Until the introduction of the percussion rifle after 1839, any unintended shaking could trigger the weapon. During the tumults in Berlin on 16–17 September 1830 even the Commander of the Guard, Duke Carl zu Mecklenburg, stated, 'loading should be delayed for as long as possible'.[31]

According to the 1798 Instruction, which was confirmed in 1835, loading was to culminate in the 'Commanding officer or sergeant of the detachment sent to pacify the tumult calling on the assembled crowd to be peaceful and disperse'.

This was to be repeated twice. If the 'mob' was too large then 'drum beats or trumpets' were to replace shouting. Anyone who did not 'immediately' obey these signals, 'was at risk of being accused of having punishable intent'. 'Due obedience' was then to be enforced through the use of weapons.[32]

However, as a reminder from the Commanding General of the VII Army Corps in Münster to the Commander of Minden showed (31 October 1832), the actual procedure often deviated from this. During the riots in Aachen in 1830 officers had omitted the call to disperse and gone into action immediately. As a consequence the ultimate verdicts against the participants were less severe!

The 1798 Instruction was also used in areas in which French law prevailed. It was not until the autumn of 1832 that thought was given to the question of whether the provisions of the relevant act of the 28 Germinal VI did not require a civil official to deliver the order to disperse in the event of, as yet, 'unregulated' non-revolutionary tumults – with the implication that this official would be directly involved in the military action.

The issue was decided by the Police Minister, von Brenn, following a proposal from von Pestel, the *Oberpräsident* who had raised the problem. In the first place there was no point in publishing the 1798 Instruction in the Rhenish provinces, even as 'supplementary provisions'. But, in order to avoid possible criticism from the courts, in future the civil official present was to give the order three times. However, it was up to the commanding military officer to indicate 'the final sign for dispersal' – 'drum beat or trumpet sound'. After that, weapons were to be used. The Minister of Justice for the Rhine Province, von Kamptz, gave this procedure legal sanction.[33]

In November 1846 the Minister of the Interior, von Bodelschwingh, issued a confidential instruction to the *Oberpräsident*, for the eyes of the *Präsident* and the 'highest administrative officials of the large towns' only, confirming that close cooperation was vital but that the military was to have the final say. 'In public riots or tumults' the civil and military authorities were to work 'in cooperation' as far as was possible.

However, in emergencies military officers retained the power of decision: in any event, the military were exclusively responsible for 'all measures of suppression'.

Use of weapons, tactics and control

The appearance of the military, 'the display of (as a rule) light weapons' and 'blows and jabs' (with the flat blade of a sabre, bayonet or butt) usually represented the culmination of military physical force. The use of firearms was rare (1817 in Breslau, 1831 in Inowrocław – as a military 'punitive expedition', 1844 in Langenbielau, 1846 in Cologne, 15–16 March 1848 in Berlin, and many times after 18 March 1848). However, massive and brutal use was made of riding into the crowd and hacking with the flat and often the sharp edge of the blade – the latter a speciality of the Berlin Gendarme (for example, 1833, 1835 and 1847 in Berlin, 1830 in Cologne, 1837 in Münster, 1844 in Düsseldorf, and 1845 in Schildesche – where bayonets were also used on three occasions). With the exception of 1848/9, cannon were brought up only twice and then were not fired: in August 1817 in Breslau (during a tumult involving the Home Guard) and in August 1831 in Königsberg (a plebeian mass protest against the lack of proper ceremony in the burial of cholera victims).

Cannon were also requested by *Oberpräsident* von Vincke during a protest by brass workers in Iserlohn which had been prompted by attempts to use women and children to undercut wages: Corps Headquarters held them in readiness but did not despatch them.[34] These instances illustrated that the principle of suppression 'at any price', accepted by civil officials in Breslau in 1817, was not necessarily taken to its logical conclusion.

The use of weapons was first brought under statutory control in March 1837. However, compared with the 1820 Gendarmerie regulations it merely offered the highly flexible principle that means were to be 'proportional' to the circumstances. There was no requirement that weapons other than firearms should be used first; nor was there any injunction to exercise 'the greatest restraint', either with firearms or edged weapons. It was presumed that, unless there was proof to the contrary, the military 'would act within the limits of its powers when employing weapons'.[35]

No specific provision was made for one particular tactic: the rather exiguous rules governing house-to-house fighting were simply carried over. New editions of the relevant manuals first contained sections on 'street fighting' in 1849: their main recommendation was 'merciless severity'.[36] Or, to use the words of a reviewer of two books on the street fighting in Berlin and Dresden in 1848 and 1849, 'the more rigorously the evil is opposed, the more impotently the darting tongue of unrest will lick at the iron heel of the soldier bearing down on it – and the more certain the banishment of any desire to repeat the attempt'.[37]

The use of cavalry units to attack crowds 'from above' proved particularly effective against tumults. Mobile columns of infantry also showed their worth in rural Posen between 1830 and 1832. This form of intervention was employed in early 1839 in the Neuß–Krefeld–Cleves area, in Silesia and Posen in the 1840s, and on a large scale in every province in 1848/9 (sometimes under the nominal control of a civil commissary).[38]

The fact that the military power of definition of 'quiet and order' was not always fully legally regulated had little impact on the practice of junior officers weary of routine. Commanders, that is staff officers and generals, tended to be more circumspect – or less decisive. But this did not apply where the army itself or military installations were under actual or feared attack, as in August 1817 in Breslau, or February 1839 in Neuß during a temporary mobilisation of the *Landwehr*. Military operations were on an even more massive scale in Posen, which many military personnel regarded as a colonial situation under permanent threat of disruption from the Polish population. Commanders considered themselves to be in a permanent, if undeclared, state of war. A letter from von Roeder, the Commander General, dated 1 December 1830, conveys some sense of the military view of the local situation. He hoped that a 'raging [i.e. Polish] noble' would give him 'a pretext' to 'exercise a freer hand and instruct the civil authorities as to what to do': it was 'incredible how incompetent and obstructive these authorities were in any instances which diverge from the normal bureaucratic routine'.[39]

Unlike the Commander of the citadel in Cologne following Martinmas in 1846, the Commanding Officer in Posen received no reprimand. Lund, the Lieutenant Colonel in Cologne, had allegedly allowed 'an appearance of uncertainty' to manifest itself:[40] 'Having introduced an armed force, he should have opposed the civil authorities', which the Ministry regarded as too passive.

'Troop reliability': the recruitment and stationing of military units

The lack of vigour perceived by senior commanders and ministerial officials in Cologne was not simply the result of individual weakness or the 'increasing discontent' produced by decades of 'routine' and snail's pace promotion.[41] There was also a clash of interests which could, on occasion, induce caution. The requirements of civil order in situations in which the police had lost control had to be set against the interests of the officer corps,[42] in which Junkers monopolised positions of command, in not 'unsettling' their troops – especially in the service of the ill-regarded and generally ungrateful entrepreneurs and burghers of the Rhine province. Each incident necessitated a judgement as to whether the prestige of the army, which had been painfully restored during the 'wars of liberation' between 1813 and 1815, ought to be exposed to the disagreeable hazards entailed in safeguarding bourgeois property.

Events in Posen, where there were numerous desertions in the autumn of 1830, and in Cologne exposed the extent to which 'reliability' depended on the proper choice of recruit. Cologne was the base for the 28th Infantry Regiment, and up until the 1840s for the 16th as well. The 28th Regiment was recruited from the Lower Rhine area, including Cologne itself; the 16th drew its recruits from Siegerland, Elberfeld and Iserlohn, was protestant, and accustomed to both a different political tradition and socio-cultural 'habitus' to the mostly Catholic population of Cologne and especially its lower urban classes. The 16th's brutal manner against riots earned them the dubious nickname of the *Hacketauer* – the 'Let-Them-Have-Its'. On the the other hand, the case of Trier illustrates that socio-cultural 'closeness' between troops and rioters was not the sole factor influencing troop conduct: the 30th Infantry Regiment, which was based in Trier and which recruited from the town and its environs after 1830, proved 'imperturbable' when used locally in 1848.[43]

Such 'imperturbability' is testimony to the breaking-in accomplished via the coercive instrument of 'the military', with its 'specific internal relation of authority', its own jurisdiction, the extensive disciplinary powers wielded by superiors, 'constant' supervision and corporal punishments for soldiers of the second rank (those previously punished and deprived of rights).[44] Attempts to harness any existing emotional bonds of solidarity, and possibly forge new bonds, also certainly played a role. In addition to stressing the monarch's role as 'father of the people', great emphasis was placed on 'regimental and soldierly honour'. Evidence of how much everyday incidents could test such symbolism can be found in an event recorded in one of the older regimental histories, written before the later successes of 1864–70/1. The author described how in 1821, the Commander of the 24th Infantry Regiment, stationed in Neuruppin (Brandenburg), publicly rebuked a soldier in front of the assembled regiment and threatened him with a severe punishment were he to repeat his offence of fetching 'wood from the forest with a handcart'. It was considered 'contrary to the honour of a man of the ranks to lower himself to the standards of the town paupers'.[45]

The numerous institutional safeguards and more explicit measures to 'bolster' discipline could not disguise the fact, however, that the 'exactions' imposed on those 'members of the less cultivated classes' liable for military service were frequently much greater when they had to confront 'their own kind', either on watch-duty or if deployed against riots. Nevertheless, in contrast to watch duties, military commanders and civil officials were not overly troubled by any major repercussions amongst soldiers carrying out riot control. In 1844 the Commander General of the 8th Rhenish Corps, von Thile II, noted 'no perceptible diminution in the determination of the regiments against riots and excesses',[46] an observation which held good for active soldiers over the following years.[47] And no real change had taken place when one year later Thile himself suggested that the 'inclination to domesticity' amongst officers could be combated by more regular and thorough rotation of garrisons.[48] Although such a rotation was ordered in late 1846, it was suspended in 1847 at the insistence of the Minister of Finance: more 'mixing' of German and Polish recruits was to occur only in the 2nd (Pomeranian) and 5th (Posen) Corps.[49]

Leaving aside the Corps of Guards, which had the pick of recruits from every province, preventive restationing of troops was a relatively rare event after 1830. Some of the Polish-speaking detachments were transferred from Posen to Thuringia and the Rhineland and replaced by battalions recruited from neighbouring Middle and Lower Silesia. Rotating the garrison as an automatic prophylactic procedure was not considered until the 1846 decree noted above. Although battalions, squadrons and batteries on garrison duty changed towns every two to three years, they always remained within half a regimental district and after 1820 did not go outside the limits of the army corps (which in general was confined to one province). Of the nine army corps a small number did, nevertheless, cross provincial boundaries: the 5th into Lower Silesia, the 2nd to Posen, the 7th (the Westphalian) into the Rhine province (that is, Aachen, Cologne and Düsseldorf).

The pattern of dispersal and recruitment was not only intended to shorten the military's lines of administration. Nor were strategic considerations alone decisive (the possibility of having to fight on fronts in the east, west and south). The main consideration was the ability of local areas, especially the towns, to absorb the troops. The state's parlous finances imposed tight constraints on barrack building. However, civilian billets were not unlimited, and were often unacceptable to the military authorities. This was certainly one reason behind the fact that, aside from manoeuvres, troops had been mobilised and concentrated on a large scale only twice prior to March 1848.[50] The first time, in the Rhine province in the autumn of 1830, was prompted by considerations of both internal and external security, and involved the transfer of the 4th Army Corps from the Province of Saxony in late 1831, and the putting on readiness of the 1st, 2nd, 5th and 6th Corps. The task of the 4th Corps was 'to protect the citadels, populous towns and factory districts of the Rhine province against the spirit of internal unrest and disorder'.[51] The second instance, between December 1832 and March 1833, took place on the Belgian border and involved mainly the transfer of those sections of the 7th Corps stationed further east. In 1846 smaller detachments of troops were sent to the Silesian border to guard against Polish rebels – the first time that soldiers were transported by rail.

The abandonment of prevention: vigorous 'treatment' in emergencies

The higher military command shunned both involvement in, and especially responsibility for, measures aimed at preventing or pacifying civil unrest, particularly in 'factory districts'. As far as they were concerned, the time-consuming procedure of 'requisition' by the civil power was quite sufficient to protect the 'state as a whole'. Any shortcomings in the procedure were more than outweighed by the disadvantages entailed by the alternative: a wider dispersal of troops, hampering that training of detachments within the battalion which commanders saw as of vital tactical importance.[52] The sparse deployment of troops in the Government District of Arnsberg provides evidence of this; despite the urgings of the *Regierungspräsident* following the Iserlohn riot of 1849, the military refused to change its mind.[53]

The military also resisted all efforts to give entire provinces a 'military finish' by supplementing the *Landwehr* and deploying it more widely, with two companies assigned to each county (*Landkreis*).[54]

However, the passivity of the prophylactic approach changed swiftly once any real disturbances or 'movements' occurred. Having decided upon intervention, either on their own initiative or at the urgings of civil officials, military commanders immediately brought to bear every and any means which seemed required to ensure an effective and 'honourable' deployment: this could involve the despatch of large numbers of troops (with the more long-term stationing of soldiers, as in Neuß in 1839), the demonstrative threat of the use of weapons, and, on many occasions, at the minimum the exhibition of the force, speed and power of their weaponry, including the deployment of cavalry. Once in action officers closed their ears to any civilian objections or criticism. If the citizenry or civil officials had already demonstrated their lack of any 'sense of order', or had not acted with sufficient vigour to implement it, the decision as to the required 'serious and vigorous treatment of any public disturbance' could safely be left to the officer on the spot or, where necessary, his superior.[55]

Case study: the 'tumults' and repression of the Krefeld silk-weavers, October–November 1828

On 20 October 1828 police officers in Krefeld found an anonymous 'threatening letter'[56] demanding that putters-out and manufacturers in the silk-cloth industry[57] should refrain from cutting the prices paid to weavers for finished cloth. The matter was reported to the local Police Superintendent, Walther, who in turn notified the *Landrat* in Krefeld after the discovery of a second note on the 25th. For the authorities there was little time to lose: a meeting of weavers had been called for the same evening in the town's main square. The *Landrat*, Cappe, who had been in office since 1817, instructed the Mayor, Jungblut, to adopt a cautious and placatory approach in the event of the meeting taking place: he was to 'direct the people to return to their homes' and, if possible, avoid the direct use of force.

Cappe was evidently under the impression that the threatened 'riotous assembly' of domestic industrial weavers, together with the working members of their households, might attract over half the *c.* 16,000 inhabitants of the town. His instruction to exercise caution was, therefore, in no way an expression of understanding for the plight of the weavers, let alone sympathy – a rumour which subsequently moved Cappe to issue a stinging rebuttal to the District Government. Cappe was only too well aware of the quantitative and qualitative shortcomings of the civil authorities in what was a non-garrison town. Apart from the one Gendarme (out of three) who could be considered 'hale', the authorities had only three fit police officers at their disposal. Although a further four were on the payroll, the *Landrat* regarded three of them as 'weaklings' and the fourth had been suspended from office for eight months 'for fraud and embezzlement'.[58] In fact this was not exceptionally few compared with other towns (see pp. 70–7). The number of police officers per resident at 1:2,660 (excluding the suspended officer) was also about average.

The anticipated numerical superiority of the protestors was not the only subject of official concern. Even the expected disruption to local routine would not have been particularly exceptional: the meeting would have been preceded by three public holidays. Between 1 and 3 November there was All Souls Day, a Sunday, and a Monday at which All Souls Masses would be read – the Protestants or 'Calvinists' had also already started celebrating the 'Feast of St Monday'. At any event, von Pestel, the *Regierungspräsident*, noted in a report sent to the Ministry of the Interior after the disturbances that no work was done on these days, 'rather the workers frequented the public houses'.[59]

However, the large numbers involved inevitably accentuated the 'normal' level of administrative vigilance: that is, the absolute and omnipresent imperative to 'prevent or suppress riotous assemblies of individuals disaffected by some particular circumstance'.[60] This obligation mirrored the notorious anxiety of both higher and 'executive' officials of being taken by surprise by resistance or an opposing force. Any, and in particular any vociferous, violation of public quiet not only signified an offence to several of the numerous police regulations and criminal laws: it also represented a direct threat to such an 'elemental pillar' of the state as officialdom. More precisely: any 'casual mob' contained the seeds of potentially much more serious ramifications, at any event for senior officials and the drafters of police manuals. 'Disquieting resistance' could easily flare up, a mass acting in unison could then form up, culminating in a 'rout' or even 'full-scale riot'.[61] But what seemed simple and straightforward in theory, the 'appropriately vigorous intervention' prescribed in the manuals,[62] could prove much more ambiguous under the complex pressures of a specific incident. Certainly in Krefeld the representatives of the local administration, and in particular the Mayor, did not see any link between the feared 'commotions' and the security and stability of the state as whole, their own future career prospects in the state administration, or even feel it necessary to place their forces on alert.

As the individual responsible for welfare and public safety in the town, however, the Mayor could not entirely avoid taking action. And in this respect – in contrast to the Superintendent of Police – the *Landrat*'s instruction had properly observed the division of responsibilities. Admittedly, the power of command delegated to the Mayor was immediately re-assumed by the *Landrat*, who not only ordered 'maximum conciliation' but simultaneously called for the names of 'those who draw up and write posters' and all 'mischief makers' to be ascertained 'with all secrecy and discretion'. The Mayor passed this order immediately to the Superintendent of Police. Matters evidently remained quiet on the 25th, at least to judge from the subsequent actions of the higher authorities.

On 25 October, in addition to initiating various police measures, the *Landrat* also reported to the District Government in Düsseldorf, which in turn passed the information to the judiciary (the Düsseldorf office of the investigating authorities). 'Mere exhortation to commit offences' was deemed 'punishable conduct'. The Senior State Prosecutor (*Oberprokurator*) was called on to unearth the 'prime mover in this ominous outrage' and 'bring him to a well-deserved punishment'. At the same time, the District Government instructed the *Landrat* to allow the town's police officers 'in their capacity as auxiliary officers of the courts' to initiate 'full proceedings on all the events which have taken place'.[63]

One week later, on 5 November, and before the police or judicial investigation had produced any tangible, or at least officially noted, results, the Mayor was 'urgently' obliged to prevail on the *Landrat* to bring the District Government in directly: 'Peace has not yet been restored and yesterday evening was threatened yet again by even greater misconduct.'[64] On the evening of the previous day, at around 10 o'clock, protesting silk-weavers first broke the roof and windows and some of the furniture of a factory manager's house, and the windows of sixteen other 'manufacturer's homes'. Rumours about a cut in rates had spread throughout the town on the previous day. On Tuesday, 4 November, one week after the weekly 'delivery day' for finished cloth, thirteen or fourteen putters-out had displayed new wage and piece rates, some of which were 15 per cent lower than those previously paid.[65] The authorities' view of these events was as follows:[66]

> On this day, towards evening, a number of mobs gathered and proceeded, at first singing then more rowdily, through the streets, refusing to obey the police: finally, they set about the windows of a number of factory owners' houses and destroyed furniture in the lower rooms, where violent resistance was offered to the police. They could only be removed with the active assistance of well-disposed citizens and the application of force and strength.

This was, of course, merely a summary report of events. The competent officials at District Government level did not report in detail until after quiet had been restored. This detailed description of events was forwarded to the Minister of the Interior some two months later.[67] The report distinguished two phases: initially 'a number of factory workers gathered in several public houses around midday, appeared in small groups on the streets around 9 o'clock and marched through the town to the accompaniment of a drum and led by a flag in considerable number, yelling and singing'.

This 'mass' was confronted by the few police officers available. Given the darkness, barely penetrated by the small number of street lanterns, and the singing, drumming and yelling of the crowd, it was hardly surprising that they were 'unsuccessful' in their efforts at 'dispersing and clearing' the procession.

The protesting weavers 'unexpectedly' broke the windows of the businesses and homes of several – seventeen altogether – 'factory proprietors'. Meanwhile, the Police Superintendent had not remained idle. Gathering 'approximately twenty to thirty citizens' who had assembled in a nearby tavern and 'armed' themselves (the precise weaponry was not specified, though it is very unlikely to have been firearms), and bolstered by these reinforcements, Walther 'called on the tumultuous mass, which must have totalled 2,000 persons, to disperse quietly in the name of the law'. This initially met with success: 'Although accompanied by gross abuse and threats to the manufacturers, the mob withdrew.' However, the protesters returned without warning and now directed their attention to one of the homes of a manufacturer's clerk, where they not only smashed windows but also destroyed part of the roof and – as noted in the initial report – got into the interior of the house and wrecked the furniture on the ground floor:

> In the same moment as this outrage was being committed, Police Superintendent Walther, who together with the police officers and citizens who had come to his aid was chasing the mob, reached the front of the Mayor's house. Once more he called upon the crowd to disperse, failing which force would be met with force. However, the rioters paid no heed, and every request made to them was met by stone throwing from the crowd, as a result of which the Superintendent of Police sustained a not insignificant wound to the head. He now ordered that the disturbers of the peace be engaged, and together with his helpers advanced into the mob with sabre drawn; alarmed by a few sabre blows, the mob then flew in all directions and, still issuing renewed threats and curses, dispersed. All remained peaceful on the nights of the 4th and 5th.

Despite the evident, and demoralising, disparity in numbers, the police had stood their ground. And, following the initial fiasco, their leader had refused to bow before circumstances and assembled a demonstrative front of those burghers who stood to gain from the intervention of the police. Using this expanded formation, he had been able to register an initial success: the mob had retreated and only symbolic damage had been done. At any event, the behaviour of the police had not directly provoked any repetition or escalation of the action – such as the destruction of the Mayor's house, the property of one of the linchpin 'middlemen' for the owners of capital. Faced with the prospect of such a massive violation of property or, more to the point for the officers concerned, of disobedience and renewed confrontation, they had turned to their last resort – their edged weapons. The morale and implacability of the officers may well have been boosted by anger at the attack on a superior and thus, by implication, on their own ranks.

In his first formal report to the *Landrat* on 10 November (submitted only after a direct instruction from the District Government), the Mayor conceded that sheer physical presence and determination could not make up for the inadequate number of civil agencies of authority and their inadequate tactical and organisational preparations. Although police officers had been on their guard for any budding commotions during the day, no one had believed that 'the threats would be realised, as happened on that night'.[68] This was also intended to defend the Mayor's own personal inactivity and excuse his anxious avoidance of the scene. For their part, the Superintendent and his subordinates had remained 'on the spot', despite the brusque judgement of one 20-year-old citizen that 'the police were absolutely useless'.[69] According to the Mayor's own report, he had been left 'defenceless' until the morning of 5 November: allegedly, he had discovered 'what had happened from a friend', 'inquiring from the police' only the next morning. As 'commotions' flared up again on the morning of the 5th, the Mayor responded in his own way – he instructed one of the constables to ring out a warning proclamation prohibiting all 'riotous assemblies', requiring public houses to close at 10 o'clock in the evening, banning gatherings of more than four men on the street at the same time, and, 'in particular', forbidding yelling and screaming on the streets: 'every citizen is instructed to comport himself peacefully'.[70]

A more detailed version of this order was countersigned by the *Landrat* in the afternoon and intended for publication in the *Intelligenzblatt*. However, it did not appear in the next day's edition but in the subsequent one, a week later! This longer version also included a prohibition on 'boisterous conduct' in beer and schnapps houses; parents and guardians were made responsible for 'any misconduct on the part of their children or those in their care'.

Compared with the much more precise provisions of the 1798 Instruction 'On the prevention of tumults', which was also tacitly applied west of the Rhine,[71] the *Landrat*'s order was very much a product of the heat of the moment. 'Factory entrepreneurs' and 'manufacturers, and especially those with spinning-mills' were enjoined to enact measures to keep workers, day-labourers, journeymen and apprentices in their dwellings.

On the morning after 5 November, that is immediately after the first 'excess', the *Landrat* informed von Pestel, the *Regierungspräsident* in Düsseldorf (some 20 km distant), in person and asked for military assistance. Pestel then went to his opposite number in the military, the commander of the 4th Division in Düsseldorf, with a request for the 'despatch of a troop of cavalry'.

The highest level of regional government thus 'requisitioned' the military to restore 'quiet and order'. Although this was not formally legally correct, it did correspond to the substance of the law, as established in a Cabinet Order to the Minster of War on 17 October 1820 (but never officially decreed to the civil administration) under which the civil or police authorities possessed sole competence to suppress 'a brawl, unlawful assembly, or any other commotion prejudicial to public quiet . . . at the outset and maintain quiet'.[72]

At the same time the civil authorities were entrusted with the responsibility not to confine themselves to their own resources 'for any longer than they can in probability expect to achieve their purpose with the forces at their disposal. Once the danger threatens that these are no longer adequate, they are required to call on the intervention of the military.' This, of course, implied that 'leadership and command' would pass to the commanding officer. (At this stage we are not concerned with the general tenor of this order, which expressly conferred and confirmed the 'superarbitrium' of the military for matters involving both the political judgement of a situation and the decision to intervene: we return to this in the following section.)

The 1798 Instruction (*Zirkular-Verordnung*) contained similar provisions, and continued unchanged as a guide to the civil power. The order provided that 'those police officers in the vicinity are to proceed swiftly and without delay to the scene, detain any disturbers of the peace and earnestly indicate to the assembled mass that they should peacefully disperse immediately'.[73] As with the 1820 Cabinet Order, the next stage envisaged the inclusion of the military, without making any explicit reference as to which agency should exercise jurisdiction. The 1798 Instruction stated: 'If this is not heeded they must seek

9 'Berlin in the 1850s. A voter visits his Deputy. On arrival in Berlin he is taken between two constables and most cordially escorted to his hotel. After the most thorough establishment of his identity, he is granted permisssion to go about his business.'

assistance from the nearest watch and at the same time ensure that the Governor, or other military commander in the town, and the Director of Police are promptly informed of the incident.' Given the 'military condominium in all police matters' (M. Lehmann, *Scharnhorst*) which characterised everyday reality at local level under the fiscal-military 'state machine' of the eighteenth century, it was considered only natural for the military to take the reins – this was the usual practice on the many occasions on which direct force was used by the military under the *ancien régime*.

Whether the officials who resorted to action on 5 November 1828 were ultimately motivated by a validating juridical construction or historical reminiscence is impossible to say. The course of events would certainly suggest that ingrained standards of perception and behaviour played a greater role than deliberate reflection. Recruitment or cooptation into the official 'corps' and professional socialisation into the 'honour' of the calling and status of an administrator established the preconditions for the realisation of a common interest above hierarchy, personal animosity and intrigue, an interest capable of commanding obedience and – if perhaps grudging – respect for any measures taken wherever the authority of the police or the administration was, or seemed to be, in danger.[74] Irrespective of any 'deeper' interests and unexpressed desires for power, domination, status and reputation, the insistence on gestures of submission from subjects became the central point of reference and unity for officials, at least in situations of acute danger.

Given the complexity of pressures coming to bear in any given situation, the initiative as to who was to define the situation and determine the further course of events inevitably devolved upon those agencies directly involved. The constant refinement of new Orders and Decrees at ministerial level as to which agencies were to take precedence in defining the situation was largely immaterial. Any relevance such schemas did possess was, at most, as subsequent admonition 'from above' and justification 'from below'.

The latent anxieties of the administration when confronted with immediate danger were reflected in the fact that the normally circuitous official route for requesting military assistance could be shortened in emergencies. In 1815, in the wake of the administrative reforms, it was decreed that the regulation of relations between the civil and military power and the 'requisitioning' of troops fell within the jurisdiction of the senior authorities at province level (the *Oberpräsidium*). However, these authorities were, quite literally, remote from the local scene – *Oberpräsident* von Ingersleben and the Commanding General von Borstell were both based in Koblenz, some 140 km from Krefeld. In the absence of any effective technical means of communication some 'short circuiting' was vital. An entire day's delay at the very minimum – occasioned by the return journey of a courier – could have had incalculable ramifications for the town at the heart of the trouble.[75] And, when the *Regierungspräsident* directly approached the local divisional command headquarters, he found 'great willingness to accommodate'. Accordingly, at around 5 o'clock in the evening of 5 November the detachment sent by the division, a half squadron of hussars with fifty horses under the command of a first lieutenant, arrived in Krefeld. On the following day, according to the subsequent report of the District Government in Düsseldorf, the troops had 'terrified the malefactors' without any need to make 'serious use of their weapons'. The hussars had advanced against the 'great mass of people' which had 'gathered on the streets and begun to stone windows', either at a walking pace or at a trot; in a second manoeuvre, after darkness had fallen, they dispersed the crowd on a boggy field, almost certainly threatening with the flat of the blade and also very probably striking out at anyone within arm's or horse's length.

On Thursday, 6 November, the day after the arrival of the military, the court officials – who had been initially notified after the discovery of the 'threatening letters' – set about their task. Thirteen detainees were transported to Düsseldorf, and by 11 November this number had risen to forty-six.[76] At the same time, the local powers also seized on the initiative of the town's burghers: on 7 November a sitting of the Municipal Council drew up a plan to establish a voluntary 'Security Corps'. A triumvirate commission was established on the same day to implement the proposal.[77] Although it was not uncommon for 'good citizens' – that is, the propertied and educated – to put on a show of force and participate in the re-establishment of public order, such an institutionalisation of an 'armed corps', rather than a mere night-watch association, was unusual. This matter took up a good deal of the *Landrat*'s and District Government's time over the coming weeks. *Regierungspräsident* von Pestel pushed for the force to be established as swiftly as possible. In his view, however, a merely voluntary set-up was not sufficient. The force required a proper police regulation to establish its rights and duties, and specify where responsibility lay.[78]

Any unrestrained and uncontrolled interventions by a civilian militia would not only have been unacceptable to the Ministry of the Interior but would also have departed from the standards of administrative discipline so fundamental to the *Regierungsräte* in the District Governments. Their desire to formalise matters was motivated less by any fear that 'lay citizens' might become the victims of a brutal attack, than that officialdom might lose control over an institution entrusted with police functions. The District Government approved the plan, but restricted the corps' life to three months.

An Instruction was eventually issued by the Mayor on 26 November (after amendment at the instigation of the District Government), and both *Landrat* and the District Government pressed for the corps to be set up without delay. However, its extensive responsibilities meant that the 'greatest vigilance' had to be exercised in the selection of its members. Only those deemed 'best disposed to the maintenance and establishment of peace and civil order in accordance with their circumstances' were to be eligible.[79]

The day on which the municipality resolved to establish the corps, 7 November, was also the date on which the *Landrat* initially reported on the factors lying behind the cuts in wages and piece rates.[80] One reason cited to him was the marked increase in competition from Swiss silk-manufacturers, 'who have access to day rates which simply cannot be compared with those prevailing locally'. This new situation had 'led local manufacturers to come to an accord' to cut wages – a procedure which, as with the arguments adduced by the putters-out, were recorded without comment. This did not satisfy the District Government. On 9 November it instructed the *Landrat* to provide a more detailed explanation of the motives and actions of the 'factory owners' by 1 o'clock the next day – a command which the *Landrat* passed on to the Mayor.[81] The fact that the District Government felt moved to send a reminder on 10 November is some illustration of how seriously they saw the situation. Their main concern was whether the 'reduction in rates could be termed unjust and excessive in any respect', as this would have constituted a contravention of Article 414 of the *code pénal*.[82]

The arrival of the military on the scene marked the final victory of 'severity' over the 'conciliation' adopted at the outset. And the increasing number of arrests also showed that court proceedings against silk-weavers were likely to continue. On the ground, the key figure remained the *Landrat* and his immediate staff. This amounted to his *Kreissekretär*, who could deputise for him only with the express permission of the District Government, and one 'fit' Gendarme, out of the three theoretically available. On 7 November, two days after the arrival of the military and the day after the courts had set about their task, Cappe sent a confidential letter to Pestel,[83] with the objective of protecting his own position in the matter. His hard-luck letter sought to correct any impressions or rumours that 'he had advised that no greater pain should be added to the poor and oppressed folk, who are being forced to starve to death'. He then tried to excuse his 'evident hurry and cursoriness' in the preparation of his first report. Not only was he suffering from a 'very heavy cold', which had caused him 'almost to lose his voice', but he also had a 'terrible headache'. And this was not all. 'The examining court officials also demanded information on local conditions.' Cappe was not only burdened by the need to police the town and cooperate with the courts; he also felt obliged to maintain some direct contact with the ruled: 'I had to give advice to the parents, wives and daughters of those arrested.' The subject population also presented itself in another connection: 'Most intolerable of all, prominent gentlemen constantly approach with absurd proposals.' All in all, he was 'out of his senses'.

We can disregard the required blend of self-pity and self-importance – a tone which registered the distance between himself and a higher authority which, although severe, was ultimately dependent on its subordinates. In general, the situation remained fairly 'open'. Both general prescriptions and daily routines provided latitude for, and legitimated, a wide range of approaches, embracing both 'conciliation' and 'severity'. However, the official directly responsible for taking action had to be either on the spot or sufficiently close for immediate reports and notices to be issued by him or pass through him.

The scope of the power of definition enjoyed by the senior official on the spot depended on the 'influence' which he could exercise over his superiors and the other authorities which relied on his collaboration. The framework within which citizens could be issued arms and formed into a 'Security Corps' had been defined by the District Government; the *Landrat* was merely an intermediary and executor of Instructions issued from above. Nevertheless, there was no disagreement between state officials and the authorities on the spot over the central question involved – that, aside from physical fitness, the paramount consideration in determining who could join such corps was *political reliability*. Of greater immediate urgency was the issue of the military presence, where there was little consensus between those involved. The Divisional Command, and especially the superior, and remote, Corps Headquarters Staff, repeatedly pressed for the troops to be withdrawn as quickly as possible. Central to their case was the shortage of troops for such long-term operations once winter leave began.[84] In contrast, the *Landrat* had already applied for the troops to stay indefinitely on 7 November.[85] And, since the military was seen as reinforcing the police and not simply as quelling the immediate trouble, he quite logically sought to have the cavalry replaced by infantry. The District Government conceded this on 8 November, and immediately forwarded their assent to the Division: the request was met, but the number was reduced from fifty to thirty men (plus one officer, four NCOs and a bandsman). The exchange took place on 11 November.

A few days later, on 14 November, Cappe submitted a more fundamental argument: 'It seems to me', he noted, 'that our significant military force should not exist merely for external enemies, but ought to be used no less appropriately to resolve disorders within the state.'[86] Whether Cappe's application on its own was sufficient to induce the District Government to provide military support, and to obtain the agreement of the Divisional Command, must remain an open question – the direct intervention of *Regierungspräsident* von Pestel on 16 November would suggest that it was not. Corps Headquarters had ordered the infantry detachment to march back to Düsseldorf on that day. Pestel visited the town in the morning to see the situation for himself: the officer in charge, the *Landrat* and the Mayor, together with other residents, all urged that the military should remain. Pestel then applied both to Divisional and Corps Headquarters for the detachment to remain 'until he applied for their withdrawal'.[87] A countermanding order was to be sent in the event that the detachment had already left the town. In fact, the officer in command in Krefeld, a first lieutenant, had already warned the Division, and this in turn had suspended the order to march.

On 17 November, Corps Headquarters reported in detail to *Oberpräsident* von Ingersleben. General von Borstell began by testily listing all the inconveniences involved in the operation and the arguments against it:[88] the reduced strength of the garrison, the inconvenient toing and froing (he thought that the detachment had in fact left Krefeld) which would make a 'bad impression'. Finally, and principally, the reasons advanced by the *Landrat* and *Regierungspräsident* were unconvincing: 'quiet had been restored'. Further disturbances were only possibilities, not firm certainties. And, should this happen, 'rapid assistance' was available given the short distance between Krefeld and Düsseldorf. For Borstell, the situation involved the use of troops for illegitimate purposes – bolstering the civilian police under circumstances unfavourable to the military (there was no garrison in Krefeld, and, with no normal training or watch-duty, the stay in Krefeld meant weakening the forces available in Düsseldorf). Von Borstell then changed the thrust of his argument: if the civil authorities considered that a military detachment was indispensable, he would agree to this. But the responsibility for any deployment which might incur the displeasure of Berlin would then lie exclusively with the civilians.

Ingersleben replied the same day. He felt it 'advisable for the military detachment to remain in Krefeld', on the assumption that it had not already left (in which case a return was not recommended).[89] Referring to the 'circumstances noted' by the *Landrat* and *Regierungspräsident*, he observed that he could 'escape further responsibility' only by agreeing to the application made by those informed – and subordinate – officials on the spot. Borstell transmitted his agreement the next day,[90] and Ingersleben informed Pestel that it was up to him to agree a date for withdrawal with Divisional Headquarters in Düsseldorf. The question of charges to be levied – which Borstell had mentioned – was to be 'quietly passed over'.[91]

Two weeks later the *Landrat*, Mayor and *Regierungspräsident* felt that troops could safely be withdrawn. On 30 November von Pestel sent a letter of thanks to the lieutenant in command in Krefeld, and on 1 December informed the Provincial Government that the detachment would leave on 4 December. In the meantime, the Provincial Government arranged to reinforce the Gendarmerie in Krefeld by the temporary provision of an NCO and three Gendarmes.[92]

During the period in which the military remained in Krefeld, the District Government had also set about securing more information as to why the weavers' rates were being cut. On 15 November Pestel reported informally to Berlin that it had been 'by no means proven that the reduction implied an *excessively* low wage, still less ill-treatment'.[93] The District Government's annual report to the Ministry of the Interior, forwarded on 24 December, contained more detail: the author was *Regierungsrat* Sybel.[94]

After setting out the market situation facing the silk industry in Krefeld, and the difficulties of obtaining reliable information and documentation on the position of the direct producers, Sybel concluded that his investigations had revealed great disparities between the figures supplied by the owners and those of the workers – he did not state where the workers' figures originated; manufacturers and putters-out had successfully obstructed the formal questioning of the workers by the District Government. The truth therefore lay 'somewhere in between: with appropriate diligence and by confining himself to essentials, the factory worker will be able to continue to find a living in Krefeld'. (By way of comparison, Sybel had also considered conditions in Elberfeld and Mühlheim am Rhein, just north of Cologne.) The proprietors were certainly not guilty of culpable conduct. Sybel not only dispensed with any direct inquiry amongst those affected; he did not venture from his office to observe what the proposed changes would mean in practice. Irrespective of the outcome of the study, 'there was no obligation on the manufacturers to increase wages' – even if these dropped below the minimum required for subsistence. For Sybel this was an assertion of the exigencies of the market: 'The manufacture of an article which would have to be carried out for a high wage, but which could not be carried out, would cease.'

Pestel's report of 15 December argued more politically and tactically when he noted that the 'intervention of the state authorities' in the 'internal commerce' of 'market relations' was impossible. Such relations were 'inviolable'. In contrast, Sybel concentrated on the, for him, irrefutable economic rationality at issue: providing welfare would contradict its own aims if it interfered with the position of economic subjects in the market.

The ensuing silence from Berlin would suggest that this was also the view taken in the Ministry. At any event, there was no administrative investigation, let alone any actual measures. Instead, the policing exercised on the spot was singled out for praise. The Ministry declared its 'satisfaction with the vision and energy of the authorities involved and the officials concerned'.[95] This ministerial praise led to tangible advantages for the local Superintendent of Police, Walther; he was rewarded with the considerable bonus of 100 Thalers. In contrast, the 5 Thalers which the local council agreed to pay the lower level police officers in return for having 'to frequent the town, and sometimes the public houses, to ascertain what the unruly populous might decide to do' seems very modest indeed, even considering that it was intended more to defray their expenses than recognise their efforts.[96]

The conclusion of the affair naturally looked very different to those directly affected by the 'lengthy presence of an impressive authority' (that is, Cappe, the *Landrat*), namely the arrested weavers. Of the forty-six who were taken to Düsseldorf, thirty-one could not subsequently be criminally prosecuted. It can only be supposed that they were punished by the police (as 'malicious youths'). Criminal charges were brought against fifteen weavers, who were brought before a Court of Assizes (a jury court) in

10 'Long live hospitality'
The picture of Berlin shows a terrace consisting (from left to right) of the Passport or 'Deportation' Office, the Town Jail, and the Workhouse.

Düsseldorf. On 2 November 1829, one year after the incident, the court reached its judgement.[97] Difficulty in proving the charges was evident: most of the accused were acquitted. However, three were found guilty and given draconian punishments; two were sentenced to four years' imprisonment for facilitating the 'assault on Superintendent Walther through punishable riotous assembly and incitement', and the third was convicted of 'wilfully destroying, with other persons, windows and shop windows of several factory owners in Krefeld' and sentenced to five years' detention in a house of correction, a fine of thirty Thalers (or an additional month's imprisonment) and lifelong police supervision.[98]

The pressure to act: violent intervention as the only alternative?

For the organs of state power, direct confrontations with unruly subjects meant asserting control over a situation whose outcome was usually unpredictable and which could often be physically threatening. The tactical options prescribed in manuals and orders provided no guarantee against an 'executive officer' on the spot making the 'wrong' decision. In fact, this applied both to general policy objectives as much as to specific instructions. Each was little more than an assemblage of abstract formulae, whose application in practice essentially served to legitimate the techniques of police power actually wielded on the ground. At best, they offered an umbrella clause tying together the enforcement of the disparate prescriptions and proscriptions (some oral, some directly physical), encouragements and demands towards the 'administered' which constituted the daily routine.

One order issued by the Police Minister to the Mayor of Wetzlar in 1816 reveals how the uncertainty experienced on the ground was simply mirrored in the directives handed down 'from above': in this case the direct application of the general police formula as guidance in a specific incident – redress for a citizen complaining of excessively harsh treatment at the hands of the police. The aim of the police, in the Minister's view, was quite simply 'the safety of persons and property . . . and the welfare, comfort and enjoyment of life of the same'.[99] Such a paraphrase of the 'common good' provided no directly usable rules for police conduct. At the same time, superiors could resort to it to lend weight to any criticisms of the lower ranks.

The need to interpret and translate general police objectives, literally on every street corner, responsibility for which fell on the lowest-ranking police officers, was therefore a constant one. Moreover, it was a need which had to be met under great pressure of time and often in dire emergencies. Merely providing more specific instructions would not have fundamentally resolved the problem. Situations in which inequality had to be both proclaimed and asserted could not be mastered through the overwhelming power of the police alone, despite the great disparity between the protagonists. Resistance could never be entirely ruled out, even with the most massive use of force. On the other hand, it could not be planned for in the police's tactical calculations. The habitus of officers on the ground was therefore marked by the active suspicion and mistrust that the worst might happen, that insubordination might erupt into a movement of revolution.

Once an assault or riot was under way, officers were relieved of this constant necessity to interpret and translate general aims into particular situations. Compared to the general objectives placed before the Mayor in Wetzlar in 1816, an instruction to police officers in Münster (4 April 1827) seems quite specific:

[Officers] must attend to quiet, order and safety during gatherings in public places, markets and on public holidays, in hotels and public houses: they shall proceed from the point of view that the police are needed only to prevent disturbances to a social and pleasurable life by others, and that, as a consequence, they may not hinder those who wish to pursue their innocent and permitted pleasures as long as they do not disturb the peace of others, break the law or commit crimes.

However, once a riot has begun they must proceed swiftly to investigate the cause of the commotion, and seek to disperse the crowd by their earnest entreaty; if this does not immediately succeed, they are to call their superiors and proceed according to Article 3.

Article 3 stated:

if their forces alone are insufficient to induce obedience, they shall call on their nearest neighbours, who are obliged to assist them, or fetch the Gendarmes or officers of the watch.'[100]

Exactly how police officers were meant to combine this inconspicuous yet demonstrative, beneficent yet brutal, but most of all effective presence received little clarification in the widely used manuals, such as Heyde's *Polizeiverwaltung*: 'At public meetings and large gatherings be a vigilant but not uncongenial spectator.'[101]

More formally, but no less ambiguously, after the 'unruly movements' of 1830, the Ministry of the Interior called upon officials to 'combine, in appropriate measure, prudent, circumspect but above all humane, modest and unpretentious conduct with firmness and determination the instant these are required'.[102]

This dilemma also afflicted the District Governments. Von Nordenflycht, the 63-year-old, long-serving *Regierungspräsident* in Marienwerder (he had been in office since 1830) figuratively speaking merely shrugged his shoulders when asked by a *Landrat* about what action should be taken over rumours of Polish activity during 1848. Not only those officials immediately concerned but every official seemed placed in the position of Buridan's ass:

It would be equally inconvenient in the case that the rumours were unfounded to resort to measures which might arouse attention, just as, in the opposite case, the administration would be responsible if it sought to neglect any steps needed to protect public quiet.[103]

The sheer abstractness of the objectives which were to guide the civil representatives of state power and sovereignty in critical situations merely induced the authorities to offer clearer regulations or alternatives for the more exceptional instances. The interests and experiences of officials obstructed any more specific 'if–then' regulations, in particular at the lower levels of the hierarchy. Why this is so will be discussed in the concluding chapter.

Requisition of the military: the restoration of the military's power of final say, 1820

Only one example of a forceful application for a more precise specification of responsibilities and procedures could be found during the period dealt with here. The events of early 1820 are important because they not only marked the beginning but also the abrupt end of attempts to limit, and possibly remove, the military's power of final decision via the 'royal path' of administration – that is, the administrative prescription of powers and procedures. On 5 April 1820, in the wake of a *Landwehr* mustering riot which had been 'quelled' by Gendarmes with the 'meagre personal participation' of the *Landrat*, von Pestel, the *Regierungspräsident* in Düsseldorf turned to the *Oberpräsident* in Cologne, Solms-Laubach:

> I am not one of those officials who so gladly see the gloomy side of things, suspect disorder and public insubordination and believe that its roots are spread everywhere.

Nevertheless, Pestel believed that disorder could arise, as the riot had shown. What would be desirable would be an

> instruction indicating the principles on which the senior administrative officials in a province, together with the [*Regierungs-*] *Präsident*, should and may act until the *Oberpräsident* can intervene . . . My own principles dictate that it is the first duty of those officials who initially intervene in a situation of public disorder to conduct themselves quietly and with restraint, but also with all earnestness once this means has proved unable to restore order, and I am convinced that, once the call to obey the law proves ineffective, force must immediately be met by force. This is the most certain way to avoid even greater evil. Without an instruction, and because matters often take on a different appearance once events are under way, it is easy to be found wanting in such moments of danger, and it therefore would seem to be appropriate, and fair, for the officials, on whom the entire responsibility rests, to establish firm principles against which they can measure their conduct.

On 31 May, comparatively swiftly in these matters, Chancellor Prince Hardenberg turned down the application from the two Rhenish *Oberpräsidenten* (a unified Provincial Government was not established until 1822). Hardenberg argued that the provision of such an Instruction would convey the impression that the administration was unnerved; moreover, given the difficult distinction between incidents, such an Instruction was barely feasible. Principally, however, it was 'not necessary for a judicious police officer'; it could 'very easily constrain his actions and render him uncertain' – and, on top of that, no other *Regierungspräsident* had come forward with such an application.[104]

A solution was provided none the less by the Cabinet Order issued on 17 October 1820. This assigned responsibility for implementing state authority 'on the spot' exclusively to the perceptions and interests of the military (cf. pp. 170–1 above and Appendix 5):[105]

> If, on observing the disorder, the military commander considers, in all duty and conscience, that the civil authorities have delayed overly in requisitioning military assistance, he is authorised and required to intervene without requisition from the civil authorities and to assume command to which the civil authorities will then be subject.

This is not the appropriate place to explore all the processes which led to this portentous Cabinet Order – moreover, one which remained in force into the twentieth century. We merely note here that, in 1810, officials had observed that the issue of jurisdiction during civil disorder had not been resolved in the wake of the post-1808 administrative reforms.[106] On the immediate background: by 1819/20 the 'final stabilisation of the politics of restoration' (Büssem, *Die Karlsbader Beschlüsse*) had been accomplished within the German Confederation. At the same time, both the civil and military powers had been confronted by a series of 'commotions' after 1817. The hunger riots were a direct reflection of the poor harvests of 1816–17.[107] Riots occasioned by the mustering of the *Landwehr* expressed the changed political form and level of demand made by the state on individual and social resources.[108] In contrast, the anti-Semitic 'Hep! Hep!' movements of 1819 – specifically plebeian and peasant responses to the 1816/17 crises – were confined to a few areas on the left bank of the Rhine.[109]

The 1820 Cabinet Order retained the 'first intervention' powers of the police. However, the local military authorities, who – according to an 1819 provision – had to be informed by way of a warning in any event, were to 'observe the course of the incident and undertake any necessary preparations'.[110]

What was crucial was that the anticipated field of action – which was to be completely cleared of police – and in particular the definition of what this field encompassed, was left entirely to the military 'superarbitrium': if the commander, in 'duty and conscience', considered that the civil authority had delayed, he could intervene without requisition.

Although not formally secret, the Order was never officially announced to the civil administration or the public. None the less, it brought to a close a brief period of administrative uncertainty over relations between the civil power and the military on this issue. And it restored the standard for the exercise of policing by the state which had characterised the eighteenth century – a standard which had been open to change, at least during the short period of administrative reform.

6

Citadel practice – the pathology of bureaucratic experience in Prussia

The guarantee of 'public quiet, safety and order' in everyday life

Memories of the traditions of the *ancien régime* meant that the military's legal power of definition over civil, and hence administrative, everyday life was not considered unusual. Although the post-1807 Reform Era appeared to widen and give legal confirmation to the autonomy of the bureaucracy, in fact this proved to be a short-lived episode. Against a background of a recently surmounted food crisis and rising concern over revolutionary 'machinations',[1] the legal backing given to the final say exercised by local commanders in 1820 simply set a formal seal on a practice which had, in reality, continued virtually unchanged (see pp. 178–9 above) and provided explicit legitimation for the attempt,[2] generally successful up to that point, to perpetuate the traditional Prussian practice of 'military condominium in all police matters' (M. Lehmann, *Scharnhorst*).

However, this new demarcation of powers, which simultaneously confirmed traditional areas of jurisdiction and influence, did not constitute a 'zero sum game'. The consolidation of the military's power of final say did not lead to an equivalent loss of influence for the civil administration. In contrast to the *ancien régime*, the renewal and increased formalisation of the military's powers freed civil officials from many of their anxieties about insubordinate, rebellious and even revolutionary movements: all would be well taken care of by the now militarily 'strengthened hand' of the state. This not only influenced how the administration went about the daily routine of 'attending' to social hierarchies, and the forms of social intercourse which this demanded: as the social guarantor of power, the army could also open up new territories for the bureaucracy.

Officials claimed to promote and advance the 'common good'. This involved periodic demonstrations of deeds deemed to further the 'cultivation' of individuals and the 'well-being of society.[3] The military's underwriting of the power of the administration, combined with its forceful intervention when required, also proved both useful and functional in this field. The civil bureaucracy and the military shared a number of interests, not merely from a 'defensive', in essence, counter-revolutionary, standpoint, but also in terms of 'conservative modernisation' (Barrington Moore jnr, *Social Origins of Dictatorship and Democracy*) and its associated 'revolution from above'.

Nevertheless, there were continuing differences between the military and the civil administration over everyday matters. Although civil officials were only too glad to see the military become involved in the 'production of security', the unproductive consumption of scarce resources by troops which this implied aroused concern at the upper levels of the bureaucracy. Since 'national welfare' could be augmented only by cultivating a class of well-capitalised proprietors and maintaining control over a class of industrious direct producers, 'security' (for property) and 'order' (for the workers) were always a means of activating society in the desired direction – never an end in themselves. Moreover, honour for officials and honour for the military were not entirely the same thing. Whereas honour for the bureaucracy was rooted in the certainty that they alone quietly sacrificed themselves for the 'general good', honour for the uniformed members of the East Elbian estate-owning aristocracy lay in slavish adherence to an all-embracing code of conduct. The stolid reserve exhibited by civil officials often clashed with the affectations of the honour-obsessed, and showy, Junker. The latter's arrogance at court and in provincial society seemed, to officials, to correspond with that impertinent intrusiveness which they so often demonstrated in their official conduct.

However, these potential conflicts and contradictions were outweighed by other factors. Within the bureaucracy itself, the suspicious defence of their unique brand of honour served as cushion to soften and smooth out the many conflicts and unpleasant episodes which they experienced with Junker officers. At the same time, primarily in fact, any realisation of 'freedom' and 'equality' which officials (or at least many officials) sought to achieve[4] was subordinated to the requirements of order and security in their own bureaucracy, for which the revolutionising of society had been, or still was, an ever-present threat. Officials' obsession with 'security' meant that any local insubordination was immediately perceived as a threat both to themselves and to society at large. Such a structure of interests and experiences offered no foundation on which to build an alternative to military forms of state authority. In fact, the opposite was true: every movement within the emerging bourgeois society further cemented the desperate symbiosis between the institutions and standards of domination characteristic of the military and those of civil officials.

Naturally, for the dominated the manner and behaviour of those officials 'on the spot' was of much more direct relevance than the conduct of officials in the Ministries and Regional Governments.

The standards of lower-ranking police officers, in many cases isolated and often semi-invalid communal and state 'servants' with a military 'past', overshadowed – if not rendered utterly irrelevant – in East Elbia by the methods employed by the Junkers, marked the meeting point of general 'system' interests, the predilections of the bureaucracy and the needs of the 'administered'. It was at this level that the distinctive dynamic continuity of a particular administrative practice for securing 'quiet and order' was developed. What was decisive was that the behaviour of the executive organs 'on the spot', and, shortly after that, of senior officials trained in the interpretation and formulation of legal norms all conformed to a stereotypical pattern: whenever these officials found themselves confronted by a 'riotous assembly', they would, almost without exception, come to one conclusion – that only violent 'short shrift' at the hands of the military could establish and guarantee the 'quiet and order' which officials demanded both for the public sphere, and for society in general.

'Citadel practice': the routinised violence of the bureaucracy

The re-establishment of the military's ultimate power of command in 1820 (see Appendix 5) merely multiplied the pressures on civil officials confronted with civil disorder. If they were too 'weak', the officer present simply, and publicly, could take control of the situation. And if the military remained inactive, they, in turn, could expect a swift reprimand or even punishment from their own superiors. This combination of extensive scope for action and the 'unlimited superarbitrium of the military authorities'[5] inevitably magnified the immediate pressures on the civil administration. Hardly surprising, therefore, that this constant yet unpredictable and unquantifiable pressure could suddenly explode into outright brutality as one, always available, option for resolving the problem at hand.

Occasional reservations on the part of District Government officials trained in the finer points of law were not voiced outside their inner circle. Faced with assaults on their own safety, and confronted by the unpredictability of any such situation, the small number of lower-ranking police officers on the spot had little else to fall back on except the patterns of behaviour in which they had been inculcated. The injunction to adopt a 'commanding tone',[6] as with other rules of perception and behaviour, stemmed almost exclusively from the military sphere, or, in the case of some *Landräte*, more directly from the Junker or bourgeois-patriarchal *ganzes Haus*.

Internal bureaucratic regulations which demanded that officials should appear united and 'tightly' disciplined reinforced their obsession with the visible or 'public' facet of conflicts. Successful policing was evidenced by external discipline and visible gestures of subordination and obedience. And the numerous successes made possible by direct military means encouraged officials to pursue the same course on each new occasion. A 'keen eye', 'courage and vigour' were not merely empty phrases but described what was deemed appropriate and necessary in police conduct.[7] Locally acquired 'long experience and practice' which might have prompted more sensitive behaviour – less conspicuous but more effective for long-term 'pacification' – stood little chance in comparison.[8]

A concept of policing emerged – or, more accurately, became consolidated – within which the original wider understanding of police objectives became severely narrowed down. The 'first and most sacred duty'[9] of officials became the 'maintenance of public quiet'. And the most effective means of achieving it was evidently 'impressing the mob militarily'. Based on the premiss that the state was a citadel under siege, officials developed a corresponding 'citadel practice', characterised by a dogged yet brutal and violent style of defence which dispensed 'short shrift' to their innumerable 'foes'. This type of behaviour primarily mirrored the interests and dispositions of the lower ranks of the police, shaped and hardened by local conflicts and interventions. In fact, the use of violence – that is, requisitioning the military – against the 'lower popular classes' was not expressly prescribed 'from above'; but failure to do so was reprimanded in 1830, and then again subsequently in 1840 and 1846.

Whilst the habits of perception characteristic of 'citadel practice' did not primarily originate within the upper echelons of the bureaucracy, they began to shape this group's outlook during and after the 1830s. The following argument advanced by Count von Arnim, *Regierungspräsident* in Aachen in 1836, typifies both their application, and the 'qualitative leap' after 1830:

> The incidents in August 1830 and several more recent events [riots one year before] suggest that it is inadvisable to allow towns which are filled to the brim with the rougher classes of factory and manual workers to be left without military occupation for any length of time.[10]

Scepticism and caution towards the military and military procedure were the exception rather than the rule. The attempt by Freiherr Spiegel, *Regierungspräsident* in Düsseldorf, to obtain some limitations on billeting and the deployment of mobile columns in the Neuß-Krefeld-Kleve area in early 1839 was not only ineffective but also demonstrated a failure to appreciate the realities of the situation. In Spiegel's view 'military force' was a vital, but essentially second, resort in peacetime, and its application was only to be 'permitted once all other legal means have been exhausted'.[11] However, this 'liberal' argument, which called for an administrative separation of powers, merely confirmed the actual, and legally quite proper, substitution of the 'first' by the 'second' instance. The crucial point was who was to decide when non-military means had been exhausted, and which criteria for this decision were customary and regarded as legitimate.

A report drafted at the same time by the permanent ministerial commissary in the Rhine province, *Oberpräsident* von Bodelschwingh, illustrates the marginality of views such as Spiegel's. In late April 1839 Bodelschwingh responded to Spiegel's report of 'great agitation of Catholics against Protestants'[12] in some of the counties west of the Rhine. Bodelschwingh's first step was to try to clarify the background. The religious conflict which had been simmering for many years was also an expression of social antagonisms. In particular, the 'rich manufacturers' in the textile industry in Gladbach and Grevenbroich were Protestant: these were 'concerned as to the real danger to their lives and property'. In fact, their 'not always sufficiently well-concealed fearfulness' had contributed to 'sharpening the scorn of the Catholic population'. There were also 'influences' from Belgium, but no more details were forthcoming. Local 'revolutionaries' took conditions abroad as their model. The 'lower popular classes' were also 'corrupted by the lively smuggling trade'.

Although this senior official was fully aware of the underlying conflicts of interest and socio-cultural differences and did not believe that 'agitators' had disrupted an otherwise harmonious scene, he did not see any immediate danger. The 'events' were of 'little import', not much more than 'abuse and threats'. In the most extreme cases they were 'directed at the Prussians' in general: officials had been dubbed 'Gueux' – as Bodelschwingh very didactically explained, a 'nickname originating in the old wars of religion'. The economic situation in both industry and agriculture was regarded as healthy. There was 'sufficient employment in the factories' and agriculture had been 'worthwhile' in the preceding few years, at least for those peasants who possessed land.

Bodelschwingh's résumé of the security situation was as follows:

> It is my view that these areas are currently no more endangered than any other parts of the province. There is a wide gulf between individual threats and real agitation; moreover, there is not the slightest indication that any disruption is planned.

This assessment indicates a distanced and cool observation of events which did not try to generalise from isolated incidents (the unrest in Cleves and Neuß). This makes the measures which Bodelschwingh recommended all the more remarkable. The aim was 'in part to improve the mood in the most endangered parts of the province, and in part to combat vigorously any impending danger'.

Bodelschwingh proposed five measures. Two were concerned with relations between the state and church and involved the appointment of priests; two aimed at improvements in the quality of local police and administrative personnel and an increase in the number of Gendarmes in the province as a whole by about fifty, a rise of 25 per cent. The fifth, and most detailed, proposal concerned the 'circumstances of our present military occupation', where, for Bodelschwingh, the main issue was to bolster military support for the administration. There were two separate aspects to this. On the one hand, Bodelschwingh wanted the pattern of deployment to be changed: regiments were to be removed from their recruitment districts so that 'soldiers who, in the vicinity of their families, were barely distinguishable from citizens' should have 'fewer opportunities for contact' and be less susceptible to 'sedition'. At the same time there was a pressing need to bring in detachments from the older provinces into the Rhine province as important and 'populous towns' such as Elberfeld, Barmen and Krefeld were, in military terms, completely 'exposed'. Although it was no longer possible to shift entire regiments 'without arousing concern and suspicion in the province', there was one possibility: the seven reserve regiments in the province could be brought up to combat strength. Such a relatively inconspicuous move would effectively increase the number of troops in the province by 6–7,000, and represent a reinforcement of the 7th and 8th Army Corps of the order of 35 per cent.

This was *Oberpräsident* as military strategist: but Bodelschwingh did not let matters rest with the simple expedient of increasing troop numbers. He also tacked on a proposal for their deployment and for the establishment of garrisons. With one eye on those counties 'whose maleficent mood has occasioned this report', he proposed that a garrison be installed at Wickrath, a moated castle some 5 km south of Rheydt. This had served as military quarters during the 1830 mobilisation, but had been abandoned because of the danger of fever. It was subsequently established that the problem could be solved by a programme of draining. Bodelschwingh regarded such a garrison as 'highly desirable', as he added to his report, since 'it was so situated that any minor excesses could be swiftly subdued and this would prevent any greater misfortune'.

The proposal got no further, however. What was crucial was the military's uncompromising insistence that they alone should be responsible for such decisions and for the establishment of criteria for deployments. But persistent financial problems also played a role. Between them they managed to prevent both the covert increase in troop numbers and the establishment of a garrison next to the Rheydt-Gladbach textile district in the topographical gap between the garrisons in Düsseldorf (about 25 km to the north east) and Jülich (about 25 km to the south).

The failure of the *Oberpräsident*'s initiative is not the central issue for us. More significant was his general outlook and the detailed consideration which he gave to ways of implementing his proposals. As far as the administrators of this particularly 'excitable' province were concerned, the military was by no means a competitor or irritant – a dangerous instrument of violence only to be summoned in the direst of emergencies. On the contrary, Bodelschwingh regarded the military presence as indispensable. Troops were both a helpful and credible support in his efforts at repressive prevention, and in an emergency could be rapidly transformed into preventive repression.

Conflicts and tensions in the other 'flank' province, Posen, some six months later exhibited a similar pattern. A report by the local Director of Police, von Minutoli, noted that 'street commotions' had been expected following the forced transfer of Archbishop Sunin from Posen to Kolberg, Pomerania. Attacks, threatening letters and assaults on Protestants and 'Prussians' were also noted by the police.[13] The Minister of the Interior considered military intervention, but both the Director of Police and the *Oberpräsident*, von Flottwell, advised against it. The 'apparent equanimity' of the authorities was much better fitted to maintain order than any 'obvious concern and a large security apparatus'. In this, their view accorded with that of Bodelschwingh in the Rhine province. However, their advice did not draw out the real differences between the two provinces. In Posen the 'strong hand' of the military was already well established on the ground, unlike Bodelschwing's province, which still lacked such a presence. *Vis-à-vis* the Minister of the Interior, Minutoli and Flottwell opted for the retention of the wide range of methods for maintaining control available to them against the background of a military presence; their immediate 'equanimity' was merely tactical. Thus, even when the civil authorities behaved with circumspection, as in Posen, there was nothing to indicate that they were committed to any organisational, institutional – let alone practical – alternative to 'citadel practice'.

Although citadel practice embraced a range of actions exercised by civil officials and the civilian police, as a substitute for a military presence which had perhaps not arrived or was not even expected, it was none the less governed by the military's logic. Even situations which civil officials held to be an acute threat to 'quiet and order' made the military no more ready to involve themselves in anything more than a very short-term application of force or demonstration of their weaponry. They refused to be drawn into longer-term active deterrence, lasting possibly several days or even weeks, and certainly did not wish to become involved in preventive planning. Such steps would have been seen as compromising the military's powers to define and determine 'quiet and order'. These reservations were by no means the product of caution on the part of civil officials that military intervention could be an extremely potent, possibly too potent, 'medicine'.[14]

In fact, as the ultimate guarantor of 'system maintenance', military logic spoke against the unpredictable wear-and-tear which might result from more frequent full-blooded deployment (that is, over and above the watch). Commanders feared that intervention by a popular, conscript, army into internal, social concerns – questions of property rights and control over labour-power – might 'unsettle' their troops. There were also constitutional constraints. The more effective tapping of existing sources of revenue, or the creation of new sources, required the participation of the Estates. The limits on spending forced the military to concentrate their resources on securing strategic points: there was simply not enough money to pay for large-scale operations anywhere in the country. Financial constraints also made it impossible for the military to take up all the personnel resources theoretically at its disposal. Induction rates fell to below half of those actually fit for service during and after the 1830s. Most of all, these financial and political problems limited the prospects for a civil alternative, that is the development of an entirely civilian institution of coercion.

Proposals for an alternative police 'power of execution', more flexible in operation than the military, were overruled by complaints from officials about the insufficient number of Gendarmes.[15] And following the riots in Aachen in 1830, any revival or encouragement of the traditional Citizens Safety Associations was confined to towns lacking a garrison. Fears about arming the citizenry prevented such associations from developing into an alternative to state violence. The *Bürgerwehr* militia, founded in 1848 and abolished in 1849, also failed to provide a satisfactory substitute for the army. For some officials it simply represented an unnecessary complication in the usual procedure which, despite its drawbacks, was relatively straightforward precisely because it was dominated by the military.[16]

Spiegel's arguments against the immediate intervention of the military (see p. 185) are primarily evidence that the homology between military and bureaucratic patterns of behaviour did not necessarily guarantee effective collaboration between the civil and military authorities: the recorded complaints from the ministries about shortcomings in communication provide a good indicator of these problems.[17] The unresolved issue of which party held primacy in the fields of politics and domination respectively was fought out in disputes over jurisdiction and etiquette. These were either 'provisionally' resolved by a process of negotiation between competing authorities and commanders, or settled by a swift intervention. None the less, such conflicts strengthened rather than weakened the symbiosis[18] between the civil bureaucracy and the military apparatus.

Not surprisingly, this was a somewhat unbalanced relationship. The civil authorities could assert their sovereignty only by circumventing military requirements or military jurisdiction, either in the form of a civilian regulation on riots and tumults or via the covert infringement of rules for the compulsory registration of those liable for service in the *Landwehr*. In contrast, the military could present their *faits accomplis* at an entirely different level by direct intervention in civilian administrative areas of competence and civilian resources: examples included determining the criteria for conscription in the army or *Landwehr*, billeting, and the building of fortifications. And, as desirable and legal as the military pacification of tumults may have been, it still demanded sacrifices on the part of the 'administered'. Although their sufferings for the 'general good' were regarded as legitimate, this was more assumed than proven.

Given this forced underlying symbiotic relationship, frictions between the civilian and military apparatuses did not prevent civil officials from accepting military criteria for 'quiet and order'. And they certainly did not reduce the administration's readiness to accept, and even to demand, the military's power of definition. Standards of conduct and perception were shaped – or, more accurately, confirmed – in the interaction between the immediate interests of local officials and the broader requirements of bureaucratic organisation. Their maxims were not simply a reflection of the bureaucracy's desire to extend its powers; and nor were they solely the embodiment of the pursuit of offical 'honour'. The administration's understanding of 'the common good', which managed to encompass so many particularistic interests, shows how well the 'aims' of the bureaucracy provided for the core elements of the social structure as a whole: the consolidation and security of 'free property', bureaucratic domination and its legitimation through the crown. Although these core elements may have required more discursive elaboration and explanation in individual instances, such as conflicts between different classes of 'proprietor', they were unquestioned in the establishment of 'system limits'. Whilst the defence of these limits must have coincided with the elementary self-interest of officials, it also designated their 'objective' social function.

The fact that the bureaucracy's 'aims' required constant interpretation mirrored the context within which the internal administration acted. Administrative 'citadel practice' was the militarised extreme of official conduct emerging from the combination of communal and local experience with a distinctive administrative mode of perception of 'system limits'.

No great significance should be attributed to instances where the military did not intervene or were not called on. Such instances did not initiate any steps towards the development of other means for achieving the desired public quiet: and they certainly did not prompt any public debate. A report of a hunger riot in May 1847 by the Senior Mayor and Director of Police in Koblenz, Bachem, reveals the degree of administrative fixation on military methods of achieving 'quiet':

> Yesterday I delayed as long as possible in obtaining military assistance in order to show that the police prefer the path of conciliation, and in the conviction that too rapid a resort to the military would expose us to the criticism of excessive haste and unnecessary severity. Today I will show that such consideration must have a limit, and that armed force must intervene where good words are not heeded.[19]

For those at the receiving end, such 'good words' were delivered with an undertone – that 'other tones could be struck' at any time. The 'conciliatory' approach of police officers was meant to accompany, not replace or render superfluous, political authority in its military guise.

The impact of citadel practice on the subject population was the 'certainty that where necessary, the strong hand would soon hasten to aid the law'.[20] Even sceptics such as Spiegel could not deny that the restoration of quiet prior to the arrival of troops was frequently possible only because 'the fear of such may have been aroused', with the prospect of the swift and massive use of force. For the dominated, only the revolutionary movements of 1848–9 provided a short-lived and localised liberation from this fear.

The censorship of public discourse[21] and the flexibility of the 'rule of law' (discussed on pp. 89 ff, 93 ff above) were not necessary prerequisites for this practice of domination, but in terms of prevention they certainly helped. Acts of violence committed by the state were insulated from any public outcry from 'the policed'.

'Citadel practice' as the 'militarisation' of the police and internal administration

'Citadel practice' may be described as the adoption of military patterns of behaviour into civilian police administration. It therefore represents a variation on the general theme of the military character, or militarisation, of police-administration in Prussia, and the Prussian bureaucracy in general, from the eighteenth century onward.

Our characterisation of the administration of policing as 'citadel practice' is not, however, merely an *ex post facto* judgement. Contemporaries, such as the democrat Karl Heinzen, also condemned the fact that the 'military state' and the 'bureaucratic state do not merely coexist but are fused together'.[22] Heinzen's main criticism was directed at the schematic thinking, harshness and spread of military manners which were the consequences of processing increasing numbers through the 'military machine'. The outcome: 'the spirit of the military system is not exhausted in military service and routines but is carried over into the civil bureaucracy where it begins to dominate. The bureaucratic machine is a version of the military machine'.

This equation of the bureaucratic and military state is only one of various contemporary critiques. There was some dispute within the 'cultivated public' as to which, the military or the police-administration, would win out in the longer term. The following article, unpublished at the time, by Theodor Fontane, later author of one of the most acute fictional portrayals of the social texture and divisions within the Prussian ruling class, illustrates the argument. In the late autumn of 1849 he delivered a stinging rebuttal to the widespread view that the 'military state' represented one stage further on from the 'police economy' in terms of 'severity, arbitrariness and loathesomeness'.[23] The young 'Old Prussian', who had followed the 1848 March events in Berlin and whose admiration for all things Prussian had remained intact, saw such a position as a complete inversion of both current trends and historical development. Unlike the modern police state, the military state of the *ancien régime* had never excluded the 'rule of law'. But in Prussia, at least since late 1848, 'naked and inexcusable effrontery by an inglorious and disobliging police' had become an everyday occurrence. Moreover, the categorisation of such 'petty' police practices under the honourable title of the military state by observers lent them an undeserved 'veneer of grandeur'.

Seen in the context of the 'performance' of the organs of the state, their uniqueness and the efficacy of their norms and orientations, the perceptions of *both* Heinzen and Fontane reveal real elements of the practice of domination. Of course, there was no 'fusion' in the sense meant by Heinzen. And any closer scrutiny of the framework within which the military and the police acted also reveals that his claim that these agencies were genuine partners was also false. Heinzen was correct on one score: the adoption and implementation of military-style conduct by the police would rapidly have been experienced by the subject populace as the simultaneous infliction of every variety of means of domination – supervision by the police *and* surveillance by the army, police truncheons *and* the butts and bayonets of the army. If we leave aside Fontane's apologia for the old Frederickian military state and 'rule of law', we are left with his reference to the daily, yet unpredictable, combination of mistrust and arbitrary conduct by the agencies of the state: he missed the point, however. The police did not dominate the military apparatus or military logic; rather, the police had simply adopted military standards.

The fact that the police-administration possessed only a *semblance* of autonomy was strikingly illustrated in the justification offered by the Commissary *Regierungspräsident* in Düsseldorf, von Möller, in 1849. The state of siege executed by the military, during which all 'executive authority' passed to local or regional commanders, was, 'merely an extreme local police measure'.[24] Such a seemingly small matter as applying to the regional commander for permission to terminate this 'condition', did not require any higher authority.

According to the constitutional order introduced in 1848–50, the 'state of siege' adapted not only the military power of definition but also the civil administration's 'citadel practice' to the requirements of the, by then, semi-absolutist system.

The uneven, but unmistakable, permeation of military standards and professionalisation into the civil apparatus of coercion, the 'sword of internal order', in the following decades gradually rendered direct military intervention largely superfluous; but this did not imply any parallel reduction in the violent nature of the state or the exercise of 'citadel practice'. The security police, the conventional police, and large sections of the internal administration saw themselves more than ever as engaged in their 'unceasing war' against the 'enemies' within.[25] And the models of policing were those already developed in the patrolling of the 'lower classes', the propertyless and the unemployed. The implementation of the 1851 statute regulating the state of siege was typical. Prior to 1914 the imposition of a state of siege was an infrequent necessity for the military or civil authorities with, at most, half a dozen instances; but it was always the *civil* authorities who called for the suspension of their own powers (such as occurred in 1871 in Königshütte, Upper Silesia, or in 1885 during a strike wave in Bielefeld).[26] And in 1909 it was the civilian District Government in Merseburg which requested the despatch of troops from Magdeburg and Halle to the mining district of Mansfeld, where machine-gun detachments and patrols were sent on to the streets 'to quieten the population' with fixed bayonets and live ammunition.[27] This form of demonstrative military prophylaxis was a central element in the structure of the *Kaiserreich*, although its actual implementation was the exception. Both the civil and military powers agreed that the police should take precedence in combating unrest, with the military being held back as 'the last card' for as long as possible.[28]

There was only one exception – the 'Zabern incident'. On 28 November 1913, the Colonel of the infantry regiment stationed at the small garrison town of Zabern in Alsace ordered fully equipped troops, with live munitions, on to the streets to restore order. The Colonel's anger had been aroused by civilian complaints about the military's offensive manner to Alsatians, some of whom had even gone as far as mocking an officer and troops of the guard. Thirty passers-by were arrested by the military and detained overnight. In the subsequent court martial the military jury ruled that no offence had been committed as local officers had simply been acting on the powers conferred by the Cabinet Order of 1820. The Ministry of Justice opposed the army on the grounds the Order was no longer valid: under the 1850 Constitution enforceable orders had to have been officially published. However, the Ministry's ruling remained confidential and its distribution was confined to the Ministries. Nevertheless, it was the symbolic dimensions of the case which immediately turned it into a major political issue. 'Zabern' was fiercely debated not only in the German press and in the Reichstag but throughout Europe. The military's prerogative to assess and decide on civil concerns – to execute a superarbitrium – remained essentially untouched. What this revealed to contemporaries was the peculiarity of the 'real' constitution of Prussia, that is, the extra-legality of the military, which claimed to be responsible only to the Monarch. In return, the Emperor was able to exercise 'absolute Kommandogewalt', absolute power of command.[29]

Aspects of international comparison: the Prusso-German *Sonderweg*

The claim that this characteristically violent form of domination is attributable to the 'peculiarities'[30] of modern Prussian-German history evidently calls for international comparison. In turn, such a comparison requires a clear understanding of the framework within which state violence, its forms and functions are observed. Elaborating such a framework helps us avoid being misled by superficial features – or, at the least, enables us to locate them within a more rigorous methodology: similarities and differences first emerge through the comparison of institutional structures, standards and behaviour.

We propose to tackle this problem along two fronts. Firstly, what were the differing speeds and forms taken by the intensification of *commodity production* and supra-local *market-relations* – that is, the forms and mechanisms of indirect, impersonal power and appropriation? And secondly, which institutional, socio-cultural and procedural arrangements favoured the *use of force* as means of asserting the aspirations to power and domination of particular social classes and groups?

England represents the industrial-capitalist 'pioneer',[31] where chronically weak bureaucratic institutions for supra-local rule combined with the sporadic, but massive, use of force.[32]

Although France enjoyed an earlier economic take-off than Prussia, its subsequent development proved slower.[33] The term 'absolute monarchy' undoubtedly fails to capture fully the mutual accommodation, interpenetration and competition which prevailed between the traditional local powers of the Estates and the various branches of the central fiscal, police and military administrations.[34] However, the exercise of domination in France after the *ancien régime* was marked by a centrally controlled and highly bureaucratised armoury of powers, ranging from judicial authority to the direct use of violence.

England

In England there was a strict institutional separation between the regular standing army and the police. This was as true of the local constabulary of the eighteenth and early nineteenth centuries as of the modern, highly professionalised London police, which was brought under state control in 1829 and which served as the model for the police system introduced throughout the country after 1856.[35]

Up until the 1760s, local protests did not specifically undermine or endanger the continuation of 'paternalist' forms of domination, which, although successful in shifting the social and economic costs of domination on to the 'lower orders', also gave scope for the development of a specifically 'plebeian, popular culture' for the propertyless and direct producers. This generated a certain ambivalence towards any rebellious 'mob', especially amongst the gentry, who dominated the eighteenth-century magistracy. Where movements of protest were directed against the 'landed aristocracy' or 'commercial and industrial interests', magistrates tended to hold back from immediate intervention and gave varying degrees of covert encouragement to protesters.[36]

The illusions behind such local policies were finally dispelled in the later part of the eighteenth century. A more acute perception of the broader implications of local attacks on property and proprietorial rights became translated into a more standardised repressive approach, in which the final stage would invariably involve the calling in of the military. In the early nineteenth century, too, this remained 'a pattern which had become an established feature of English life . . . The outbreak of disturbances quickly led to a heavy demand for troops.'[37] Usually regular soldiers were employed, with the mounted (gentry-)yeomanry playing a greater role than the militia. Officially, the power to define the situation lay with the civil authorities – magistrates or justices of the peace. However, during the protest movements of the 1830s and 1840s (Captain Swing, the Chartists), regional military commanders could decide on their own initiative whether troops should go into action in those factory districts under military occupation.[38] Troops were also used in the policing of 'minor episodes' in rural areas at least until the middle of the century.[39] There were considerable regional differences in requisitioning procedures and responsibilities: in Warwickshire between 1830 and 1870 the justices of the peace kept these powers very much in their own hands.[40] In contrast, although the Home Office had nominal command over the *c.* 17,000 troops stationed in Wales, the North and the North Midlands, in practice their intensive deployment was decided on by the military.[41]

The nationwide introduction of the new police in the late 1850s marked a change of direction. This professionalised institution was able to combine a physical presence, which the military could not have matched in terms of numbers of men deployed, with an accurate knowledge of the locality and its potential 'dangerous classes'.[42] This allowed both a preventive and low-key approach as well as more robust and violent methods to be used – military tactics without the military.

As in Prussia, the low institutional density[43] of the bureaucratic apparatus of domination and coercion in England meant that, even under conditions of developed industrialisation, intermittent, local but massive force continued to be the sole response of both local and ministerial authorities to any apparently threatening movements of the 'dangerous classes'. However, unlike the situation in Prussia the military's power of definition was not simply assumed: bouts of acute mistrust of the army, and judicially backed reproofs against individual operations prevented any explicit, or officially tolerated, claims by the military to exercise the final power of definition on the ground.[44]

This was complemented by the hesitancy of the military itself, evident in its frequent procrastinations as to whether to intervene (as in the 1780 Gordon Riots). On the other hand, the practice of pacification by the state reveals not only frequent resort to the military, but also frequent acceptance of military intervention, especially after the 1760s. In this respect, the traditional 'anti-standing army attitude'[45] of the late-seventeenth-century did not typify the practice of the holders of government, judicial or county authority.[46] This was also indirectly evidenced by the continued lack of interest in the 'new police' until the second half of the nineteenth century. Tacitly, at least, the army was accepted as a 'constabulary force' (Janowitz, *The Military in the Development of New Nations*).

The functional link between the civil authority and the military in the exercise of pacification was bolstered by the social links between the officer corps and the local ruling class. Common interests were transmitted through family networks, and reinforced, for males, by common educational experiences – in the alternation between military service as an officer and attendance at university.[47]

The differences between England and Prussia should not be forgotten, however. In contrast to Prussia, England did not exhibit the conflict latent in the tension between the army and a professional bureaucracy. The general role of the army in society should also be remembered. In Prussia, the need to safeguard the capacity for military mobilisation, which shaped and bound together the perspectives and interests of ruling groups under the dual pressures of internal revolution and external power politics, took a different form to that in England. Here there was no comparable overlapping of the fear of both internal *and* external threats to the existence of the state and society. The military in England – or more precisely the army – had correspondingly less opportunity to display its indispensability to the existence of the system as such, or meet with approval were it to behave in such a way.

The preference of the English ruling class for preserving its existing institutions and interests, but primarily its wish to avoid the local additional cost, held up the implementation of laws requiring the introduction of a full-time professional police in rural areas (1839 and 1842) until central government threatened the immediate and massive withdrawal of troops.[48] The lack of permeation of military standards into civilian modes of domination was not, therefore, solely a product of the fact that the English army packed less social and political force than the Prussian, but also of the institutional separation of civil and military authority, aided by the lack of an all-pervasive military presence in everyday life.

France

At first glance France seems to exhibit a number of parallels to Prussian institutions, patterns and practices. However, there are two significant differences. Firstly, although a militarily organised, but civilian-led, control and intervention force had existed since the late seventeenth century (the *Maréchaussée*, after 1791 the *Gendarmerie*),[49] local affinities and low numbers prevented it from being anything other than sporadically effective.[50]

Secondly, in contrast to Prussia, the main role of the French civil administration under the *ancien régime* was not that of an auxiliary instrument in the pursuit of the state's military objectives. Its range of tasks was traditionally – and certainly from the middle of the seventeenth century – much broader. And, in particular, it operated to secure positions of power and influence for the aristocracy. But it also supported, and facilitated, economic expansion in the interests of the urban bourgeoisie and the crown. The duality of the administration – aristocratic *officiers*, the *noblesse de robe* engaged in extensive trafficking in offices, and the new bureaucracy in charge of the economic and fiscal affairs of the crown, the *commissaires* (with various posts as *intendant*) – did not generate competition or attempts at control between the two social groups or two bureaucratic organisations. Rather, the *intendants* remained dependent on the *officiers*. Even the social development of the Intendancy was determined by the *noblesse de robe*: legal training in the *parlements* and purchase of office yielded both a social and professional convergence between the two.[51] Overall, the *noblesse de robe* continued to exercise considerable social and political influence on the commissary bureaucracy. Each branch lent support to the other, a corollary of the plethora of functions which they exercised within the complex political sphere.

In France, military intervention for the purposes of policing was an everyday occurrence in the garrison towns. Civil requests for punitive – or intimidatory – expeditions to non-garrison towns, perhaps lasting several days, were also not uncommon both before and after 1789. Nevertheless, cooperation between the civil administration and the military was not without its problems. During the 1820s their relationship was marked by frequent conflicts between Prefects and regional military commanders.[52] The particular circumstances were crucial in this respect. In 1848–51 regional civil and police authorities appeared to have cooperated with military commanders without major difficulty. At the same time, the overwhelmingly rural movements and secret organisations after 1849 revealed an unmistakable trend towards resistance to the urban bourgeoisie and its allied ruling apparatuses of bureaucracy and army on the part of small *rural* proprietors and the landless.[53] However, neither the conflicts nor cooperation provided the military with any opportunities to acquire a superarbitrium, or put a military stamp on the social and cultural standards of officials.

Aside from its insitutional weight, bureaucratic *esprit de corps* was also critically important in safeguarding the uniqueness and independence of the civil administration. This was developed and sustained less through explicit regulations than through hierarchy, combined with social isolation and an inward-looking perspective. In particular, the social outlook generated through the *esprit de corps* kept procedural conflicts over how to deal with 'trouble-makers' and 'revolutionaries' to a minimum. From the *ancien régime* onward, the administrative ideal for French society prescribed a form of 'order' which was in no respect any less rigorous than the military's demand for discipline and loyalty.[54] Both pre-revolutionary 'subjects' and post-revolutionary 'citizens' were subjected to a considerable level of physical violence from the civil authorities. This did not, however, imply the existence of a universal, physically violent presence. A comprehensive system of permanent police control and regulation, ultimately based on permanent and violent intervention, was not established until the police reforms under Napoleon III in 1850.[55] The use of the military therefore remained the norm until the middle of the nineteenth century (if one disregards the first few months after the 1830 July Revolution).[56] And in 1848 Cavaignac's troops pioneered the use of systematic planning and training to suppress riots and insurrection – including on an international scale. In 1852 the later head of the Prussian military cabinet, Edwin von Manteuffel, thought it worthwhile taking soundings as to whether the French army 'subscribed to a type of brotherhood of arms amongst all armies for this purpose [the maintenance of internal order]'.[57] However, this plan to eliminate the spectre of the 'Red International' by means of a 'State of Siege International' did not take root. Nevertheless, it is significant that one of the leaders of military and political reaction in Prussia regarded the French army as a vital ally, irrespective of any dynastic or passing superficial 'national' differences.

Résumé: on the conditions of 'citadel practice' in Prussia

The central difference between France and England on the one hand and Prussia on the other lay in the fact that the Prussian army acquired the legally sanctioned power to define the situation. Of course, such differences may have seemed of little consequence, if perceptible at all, to those on the receiving end, given the periodic non-military violent propensities of 'the state', and the frequency and intensity of actual military interventions. There are two factors of causal relevance: in France the considerable power possessed by the competing civil bureaucracies (which sought to possess a monopoly of force), and in England a complex structure of 'checks and balances', local vested interests, and also general socio-cultural standards prescribing a merely instrumental role for the army. In both England and France, these different configurations of social and socio-economic interests, socio-cultural standards and political procedures not only prevented any legal confirmation of a military final say, but also limited the extent to which the civil power was permeated by military standards of 'short shrift' – that is, they prevented the development of a French or English 'citadel practice'.

We therefore come back to the questions of the overall sweep of social development raised above. Prussia underwent a specific form of agrarian development in which the unique structure of the estate economy as the unity of economic and social domination was retained, in the process stabilising the bases of power of the Junkers as a class. This enabled leading groups within this class not only to preserve their specific standards of domination but to transport them into the state – a process little affected by the growing 'embourgeoisement' of estate ownership. In its efforts to creat 'mobile' property and establish a system of extended, market-based exchange, the state never abandoned a form of domination which, in moments of doubt, unfailingly opted for the punitive crushing of the oppressed.

The civil administration also furthered its own militarisation. Seeing 'convulsions' to the existing order and the supposed ubiquitous revolutionary unrest in every direction, local executive officials – and particularly the police on the spot – combined their own, highly ambivalent, maxims with traditional patterns of domination. The 'rule of law' became (or remained) little more than a highly pliable mask: even the advocates of fixed legal limits on the activities of the state were unable to find any principled reason for a threshold to constrain the daily, selective imposition of violent forms of domination – in fact, they didn't even seek to do so. Civil officialdom was utterly steeped in its experiences of and with violence: with 'citadel practice'.

In Prussia, the correspondence of Junker interests and administrative patterns of interpretation and forms of behaviour provided repeated opportunities for the massive application of direct physical violence by the state – either as military intervention or, more often, as the quasi-military actions of civilian 'state servants'.

7

State violence, bureaucratic action and domination

On the functionality of state violence

Our study has concentrated on a relatively early phase of one industrial society in the making. Our conclusions are correspondingly confined to the context of Prussian development. We saw not merely that specifically economic forms of coercion and psychological, self-imposed, control were intimately bound-up with extra-economic coercion, but could also observe how the extent to which the everyday experiences of the dependent producers and propertyless were shaped by the forms taken by extra-economic coercion: specifically, the physical violence meted out by officials of the state.

Prussian 'citadel practice' was untempered by any more general preventive state policies. Although the number of emergency public works rose between 1820 and 1850,[1] they never provided more than supplementary, and usually belated, relief: they certainly never came remotely near to lifting those who worked on them out of poverty. And any such localised provision of subsistence made little, if any, impression on the overall severity and arbitrariness of the administration's police methods. In fact, the advance of the industrial-capitalist organisation of labour was sometimes seen more as a favourable opportunity for intensifying control and discipline over the direct producers – whilst relieving the state of some of the burden of exercising this task. Naumann, *Regierungspräsident* in Arnsberg in 1850, typified such an approach. He felt that the population of Hagen was more of a threat than the 'factory population' of Iserlohn, despite the latter's revolt in 1849. For whereas the producers in Iserlohn were concentrated in workshops and factories, Hagen was still dominated by domestic industry. 'Scattered in their homes, they are exposed to every influence pressing upon them, are not under the watchful eye of the factory master, and cannot therefore heed his admonitions.'[2]

In the event, Naumann was wrong. The state's coercive apparatus did not regard the spread of factory industrialisation as a relief. Despite their diversity, manifestations of 'counter-power' – the strikes of 1857,[3] the miners' movements of 1869–74 and 1889, and the links between socialist organisations – merely reinforced the patterns of perception and conduct established in the decades prior to 1848/9. What changed was merely the rhetoric: instead of the pre-1848 *general* 'rule of law', the customary practices of police-administration now operated behind the specific rights of association, assembly and industrial combination.

At a local level this meant that the 'police authorities did not confine themselves merely to the combating of disorder'. Instead, and where necessary with force, they carried out 'measures . . . appropriate to those subjects deemed a danger to the community and deserving of public contempt' (to quote the *Regierungspräsident* of Trier in 1878).[4] During the years of the anti-socialist legislation between 1878 and 1890, this *preventive repression*[5] was supplemented both 'in theory' and in practice by the 'minor state of siege' (*kleiner Belagerungszustand*), which included the banning of public meetings and publications by the police, and the particularly devastating practice of excluding individuals from specific towns or localities.

The terminological distinction between the 'minor' and 'full' – that is, military – state of siege constituted a kind of military *pas de deux*. Whereas the 'full state of siege' hinted at severe measures with possible unpleasant consequences, the lesser variant implied conciliation and lent legitimacy to the entire schema. In essence, the 'minor' state was a 'political',[6] and more specifically, a 'social state of siege'.[7]

The permanent and aggressive 'police war'[8] waged with similar methods against Catholics and Polish 'enemies of the Reich' reveals the element of continuity in the exercise of physically violent political authority in Prussia–Germany – a form of political domination by no means confined to activities of the security police in the narrow sense of the term.

State violence and 'forms of habitus'

The control of public life through 'citadel practice' was not simply an expression of the bureaucracy as an 'agency of domination'. It simultaneously stunted the ability of state officials to analyse and locate their experiences of 'misdemeanours' and 'infringements' within the wider context of social transformation. This entailed a variety of expressions of conflict and the assertion of alternative interests: the insubordination of weavers and spinners who were particularly vulnerable to the pressure of factory competition; thefts from woods and fields from the urban and rural propertyless who were hardest hit by unreliable harvests and rising grain prices; protests by railway construction workers during the 1840s against arbitrary treatment at the hands of overseers; the growing number of strikes by factory workers which occasionally culminated in 'tumults', as in the case of foundry workers in Iserlohn in 1840 striking against wage cutting (the employment of women and children); 'walk outs' for better pay and conditions, as with the dyers in 1855 and 1857, the Silesian miners in 1869, the Ruhr miners in 1872; and the mass movement of miners in 1889. These forms of resistance were accompanied by more local protests against infractions of traditional rights and symbols (as in the 1846 riot in Aachen over increases in the price of 'Passover bread'). These very diverse expressions of inequality and injustice, together with resistance and the articulation of counter-interests, all became buried beneath the few crude categories of the police mind. The essentially military character of the police approach, with its Manichean view of friend and foe and the application of 'short shrift' and a 'strong hand', even remained impervious to the need to provide for the longer-term maintenance of the 'quiet and order' established, for the moment, by direct repression.

'Citadel practice' generated its own legitimation. By following its required and implied patterns of behaviour, police officers acquired a palpable sense of such abstract legal ideas as the 'preservation of public peace' within their own everyday routine. The routinised embodiment and application of state force, the 'sovereign' manner of presentation accompanied by the applause or silent consent and acquiescence of 'decent' citizens on the one hand, and the unconcealed hostility, frequently mixed with fear and submissiveness of its customary victims on the other, all enacted under the friendly and watchful eye of superiors, established a framework within which customary and newly acquired standards of perception, modes of interpretation and forms of conduct interacted to shape 'a form of habitus' within the bureaucracy which, following Bourdieu, may be termed a 'structuring structure'. This 'form of habitus' in turn regulated the self-image and image of others held by officials, and in particular by the 'executive' officers of the police and Gendarmerie, without need for further explicit reference. Naturally, this structuring principle required regular practical trial and application: hence, although 'citadel practice' could function without constant formal reiteration, it should not be seen as a spontaneous automatism.

One indication of the scope of the 'form of habitus', can be seen in an observation by a highly conservative contemporary professor of administrative and constitutional law, Freiherr von Stengel. In 1884 Stengel complained that direct force was used particularly in the administration of 'spheres which should be handled only with care'.[9] Military-style 'citadel practice' not only coloured the control of spectacular instances of confrontation but also put its stamp on the state regulation of the everyday 'production and reproduction of immediate life' (Engels, letter to J. Bloch, September 1890). Universal state education was enforced by the police in the form of compulsory school attendance; and in the 1890s similar methods were used to populate the growing number of lunatic asylums.[10] The demands of bourgeois society for intellectual and moral 'hygiene' were evidently inseparable from the exercise of violent policing.[11] The open use of force may well have been seen, both by its practitioners and the cultivated public, as the only means by which 'order' in the state as whole could be secured (a state which, under the 'rule of law', combined 'the common good' with individual advantage). And by reflecting the boundaries of social and political inequality, the application of force in turn gave a disciplinary edge to the idea of the 'rule of law'.

The selective application of direct force bolstered the self-esteem – and self-deception – of those classes which profited from and ruled bourgeois society. The visibility of force against the poor and propertyless, the 'direct producers', strikers, 'poor unfortunates' and 'tramps' confirmed them in two respects. Firstly, it highlighted their own privileges in the most direct way. And, secondly, it fostered the illusion that the self-discipline associated with such 'progressive' principles as 'hygiene' and 'school learning' was solely a matter of conscious self-discipline, pursued and acquired in their own case entirely voluntarily and without compulsion. Overt force, therefore, did not become outmoded or superseded. It remained fundamental to 'modern' means and practices of domination and augmented the workings of that 'gentle violence' constantly implied in the maxims of bourgeois life.

State violence: symbolic and physical force

'Acquiescence to order' (Weber, *Economy and Society*) did not reflect any silent consensual assumption on the part of the dominated; nor is it an expression of the intangible 'omnipresence'[12] of social relations of power. Rather, as we have seen, the position of the dominated was not determined simply by the violent *practice* through which power was wielded, but at the same time by the organisation and legitimation of this violence by the *state*. The issue of the theoretical necessity of state power, domination and violence can therefore be set to one side: the fact that it was *practised* and demanded is sufficient proof of its functionality in the securing of power over social resources, be this via the market under the title of 'property' or as non-marketable resources in the form of command positions in the apparatus of domination procured through 'honour' and reputation.

The operations of the state do not imply a constant and unwavering use of force but rather the constant threat of its use – symbolised in the forms of 'gentle violence'. In the Prussian case, the rhetoric of the 'rule of law' was not in itself sufficient to filter or obstruct resistance and the development of alternatives to 'acquiescence'. Nor could the incessant ritual identifications of commitment 'to the King', 'to Prussia' or the common 'Fatherland', or the pressure of economic forces – that is, survival on the basis of wage-labour through repeated episodes of unemployment and hunger – guarantee that domination would be *accepted*.

Rather, the acceptance of domination was the product of an ensemble of individual experiences – and first and foremost of the numerous and ubiquitous experiences of physical violence at the hands of the state or state-sanctioned authority. Here the state did not merely supplement the specific violence of private 'masters'. Access to and use of firearms, edged weapons and truncheons by the police created the space within which the increasing violence of craft masters, factory owners and foremen, peasants, or more often seigneurial proprietors or their agents could take place. Private and state violence shaped and conditioned the other. On estates, the infliction of physical suffering was as common as the first resort as it was as the last – not merely as punishment but also to 'improve' 'refractory' subjects, a responsibility shared between the police and the military. The bureaucratic organisation of state authority – frequently exercised with military severity – conserved private violence, not only in the sense that it enabled it to be held in reserve, but as a condition of its very existence. The particular virtue of state violence, of course, was that, far from being concealed, it could be put demonstratively on show.

The well-turned out – if not dashing – and ceremonial outward appearance of state authority aroused the delight not only of small children but also of many of the 'administered'. The external smartness of the police, and especially of the guards of the watch, was inseparable from the demonstrative presence of the physical means of enforcement. Truncheons, bayonets and firearms were visible at all times on every officer. And the mood could change accordingly – from displaying their dignity to beating, stabbing, slashing at, possibly even shooting, the doting public of a few moments before.

The, in many cases, uniformed agencies of the state were, at the same time, the symbol of an aspiration towards an unlimited and all-encompassing control. The force and authority of the state not only expressed its – supposedly – inexhaustible power and magnitude, but *simultaneously* served to define 'the dominated', and control and discipline them.[13] This 'grip' was also no longer confined to the local or municipal sphere. The fact that state authority visibly and palpably reared its head everywhere, or nearly everywhere, was a sign that the dominated consisted of that part of the population whose whole life and activity were delivered over to the judgement and sanction of the executive organs of the state. The corollary of this was that, firstly, the public sphere became a zone of control – and, moreover, one no longer strictly demarcated from areas or periods of private disposition, which were also shaped by the interventions of the state (and not simply on the East Elbian estates). And, secondly, this aspiration for complete control fostered and legitimated the *invisible* arm of the state – the spread of spying and informing.

The executive 'organs' of the state were not simply adept at ensuring that the 'costs' of the social process were borne by the direct producers. They also exercised this task with a surly brutality which inevitably had further ramifications for those on the receiving end. Wasn't the mark of their standards evident in 'private' social relations between spouses, parents and children, colleagues and associates, members of oppositional political parties, within the SPD and the trade unions? The unquestioning adoption of an outward military style, together with militarised forms of expression and action by the organised labour-movement, from the 'Revolutionary Army' to the well-rehearsed columns of 1 May demonstrations, provides telling evidence. To what extent did 'citadel practice' infiltrate, and possibly mortally damage, the political and, in particular, the social imagination of the dominated – in pubs, on the streets, at work, and also in the home and in bed, not only during the Wilhelmine period but also in the Weimar Republic and under German Fascism? Might not an understanding of 'citadel practice' help us better to understand later forms of expression and protest – and especially, the 'mass' capitulation and submission to authoritarian excesses, as in 1914 and 1933?

Put more generally, the presence and intervention of the apparatus of physical compulsion establishes the foundations for those experiences out of which the 'belief in legality' and attributions of legitimacy first arise. Seen in this light the 'system-limit' may be quite flexible; but it is nevertheless dependent on the *forms of state conduct* within which and with which those classes who control the employment of labour-power and its products assert their interests, modes of interpretation and demeanour.

The actions of the administration are thus two-sided. On the one hand the administration mediates the requirements for the *maintenance* of the status quo, whilst at the same time defining the effective social limits of this 'maintenance'. This capacity to define the situation both creates and demonstrates the power potential of the administration,[14] establishing its real power as a *bureaucracy* in a developed class society.

This does not eliminate contradictions within the bureaucracy – between the civil administration and the military, for example – or remove conflicts between the socially dominant classes. However, the particular power of the bureaucracy, as the totality of the state apparatuses of domination, lies in its capacity to displace such contradictions. The definition of the 'dominated' through both 'overt' and 'gentle' violence allows the 'costs' of bureaucratic rule and social inequality to be shifted onto the broad spectrum of 'direct producers' and the propertyless. Only when perceived 'from above' can bureaucracy appear as the embryo of a classless society, as the medium of social organisation free of domination, as an instrument for replacing 'rule over persons' by the 'administration of things'.[15]

Bureaucratic domination is *necessarily violent*. It simultaneously wields both physical coercion and symbolic authority. Its holders, in contrast to other social centres of power, have access to the maximum possible level of authority through this combination of force with verbal and symbolic legitimation. The social selectivity nourished by this association of brute violence and the purported pursuit of the 'common good' conceals the fine structure of society. First and foremost, its blanket 'short shrift' envelops those social classes whose allotted place in society systematically reduces their scope for the autonomous satisfaction of their needs.

Appendix 1

Extracts from Johann Heinrich Gottlobs von Justi, Grundsätze der Policeywissenschaft 3rd edn (*Göttingen, 1782*, pp. 4f, 14f)

Section 2

Police, in the broad understanding of the term, refers to all those measures in the internal affairs of a nation through which the wealth of the state may be more permanently established and multiplied, the forces of the state better used and, in general, the happiness of the commonalty promoted...

Section 3

Police, in the narrow sense of the term, refers to all that which is required for the proper condition of civil life, and in particular for the maintenance of good order and discipline amongst subjects, and those measures which promote the flourishing and growth of trade...

Section 17

If subjects are therefore to be constituted as is required by the ultimate aim of the happiness of the commonalty, then firstly their moral condition must be good so as to render them fit to match the obligations which social life imposes on them. Moreover, and depending on their civil condition, they must also be useful members of the commonalty so that each may be able to contribute his own to the common good depending on his station. However, because not all the inhabitants of a state are equally good, inner security must be maintained and evil and injustice kept in check. We can express this more concisely as follows. If subjects are to have those attributes and capacities which are in accord with the happiness of the state, they must be (1) reasonable, (2) useful and (3) not excessively burdensome members of the commonalty. In accordance with this maxim, the police have therefore to attend to (1) the moral condition of subjects, (2) civil order and (3) internal security and the control of evil and injustice.

Appendix 2

Extracts from 'Instruction on the Conduct of Business by District Governments in the Royal Prussian States, 23 October 1817'
(*Gesetzesammlung für die Kgl. Pr. Staaten*, pp. 248–52)

Section 1 On the scope of the District Governments and their Departments

The scope of business of the District Governments embraces all those objects of internal administration which are subject to our Chancellor of State, the Ministers of Foreign Affairs, of the Interior, of Spiritual and Cultural Affairs and Public Education, of War, of the Police, of Finance and Trade inasmuch as these objects (a) are amenable to administration by a territorial authority and, (b) are not assigned to specific administrative authorities or expressly transferred to other authorities.

Section 2

The First Department of the District Government shall embrace:

(1) internal matters of national sovereignty; matters pertaining to the constitution, the Estates, national borders, allegiance, departures and deportations; the issuing of permits to travel outside the country; the expulsion of alien subjects; censorship; the publication of statutes and orders in the Official Gazette;
(2) all policing of security and order, including the maintenance of public peace, safety and order; the prevention and quelling of riots, the detection and apprehension of criminals, the execution of searches; prisons; penitentiaries and houses of correction; the prevention of fire and unauthorised constructions; the restoration of buildings destroyed by fire; poorhouses, hospitals and the poor laws; and other matters connected with these objects;
(3) matters pertaining to medicine and health with respect to police, e.g. trade in medicaments;
(4) agricultural police, hence all matters pertaining to cultivation; division of common lands;
(5) the entire system of local government, inasmuch as a particular involvement of the state is entailed; moreover, the supervision of all corporations, societies and associations;
(6) spiritual and educational matters;
(7) Mennonite and Jewish matters;
(8) all military matters which entail the activity of the civil administration, such as recruitment, mobilisation, billeting, the construction of fortifications, provision for invalids etc.
(9) the collection of all statistical information;
(10 the censorship of all written materials, inasmuch as this is not the province of a particular authority;
(11) the supervision, and administration of the *Institutskasse*;
(12) buildings:

Section 3

In contrast, the following fall within the Second Department of the District Government:

(1) all matters pertaining to the revenues of the state and taxation, or which impinge on the administration of domains, forests and royal property inasmuch as no particular administrative authorities have been established for individual branches;
(2) the entire policing of trade, hence: (a) all matters of industry, factories, commerce, navigation, corporations and guilds; (b) weights, measures and currency; (c) public communication, roads and waterways, highways and harbours;
(3) the policing of forestry and the hunt;
(4) the inspection of buildings;
(5) the supervision and administration of the principal District Government Treasury.

Section 5

The division of the District Governments into two departments has been ordered merely for the purposes of simplifying, shortening and facilitating the conduct of business. As a consequence the departments do not constitute separate and independent authorities, but rather together constitute one college.

Appendix 3

Extracts from Service Instructions for the Inspector of Police *(Minden, Westphalia): StadtA IS, Bestand I, no. k9*

1

The Inspector of Police does not constitute a separate authority; he is to act and authorise as an organ of the municipal administration in its name and on its instruction.

2

In general he shall receive instructions only from this authority, which is his immediate superior. Instructions, orders, requisitions and petitions from other persons, officials and authorities must, without exception, be shown prior to their execution, or, in the case of imminent danger, immediately afterwards.

3

The Inspector of Police may not have any so-called official secrets as regards the head of the municipal administration, with the exception of all reports of occasional inquiries which are not connected with service and whose confidentiality is obligatory.

4

The Inspector is liable in law for his actions and omissions towards the state, the municipality and individual citizens; the administration shall represent him only if he acts and remains within the bounds of his commission. . .

5

Duty entails concern for and execution of the responsibility assigned to each individual officer.

The Inspector is hereby empowered to attend to any business occurring within the following boundaries of the administration on his own responsibility within the limits of the existing regulations and to regard these as his assigned sphere of activity:

A. Passport and Aliens Police,
B. general policing of the locality,
C. supervision of the execution of laws pertaining to state revenues,
D. supervision of municipal revenues and poor relief,
E. transport of prisoners, safekeeping of monies, special supervision of the military prison.

Since the matter of Trade Tax is associated with the state's revenues, it will be assigned at a later date when the Inspector has acquired the requisite knowledge.

6

On Passport and Aliens Police

I refer to the Passport Regulation and the appropriate official files. There are no more specific instructions to which reference can be made.

Note the following on the subject of the policing of aliens:

(1) No stranger, that is, any person not resident here, may stay overnight without the knowledge and consent [of the authorities]. The Notices of Strangers required to be submitted by landlords constitute notifications of such. Their acceptance without further observation constitutes consent for accommodation. Strangers seeking accommodation in taverns for members of the lower estates must obtain a night ticket: accommodation without such a ticket is punishable.

Families who accommodate strangers must also report them. If the families are entirely above suspicion and of the first rank, and have accommodated persons from the nearby areas, then strict enforcement could lead to considerable unpleasantness. In contrast, the greatest stringency must be employed against those who offer strangers accommodation on a commercial basis and generally evade police supervision.

The policing of aliens and strangers cannot be satisfactorily carried out from the police station. Suspicious persons evading police supervision must be pursued on the streets and in every nook and brought in for investigation; namely, persons who go from house to house, wander on the streets, and frequently ask for directions. Such people are beggars and thieves and the greatest stringency is necessary. If such persons cannot explain themselves through the possession of passports, official certification and testimony, they are suspicious. If they are nationals then, if not already punishable for a street misdemeanour, they must be sent to the *Landrat* as itinerants with an application for the issue of a compulsory permit. If they are foreigners, and cannot be regarded as vagabonds, they are to be taken immediately to the military prison and are to remain there until it is firmly established that they have committed no crime here, and then they should be expelled from the town. If they are in fact itinerants they are to be deported.

(2) This provision is to be observed to the letter on passport inspection, and where such cases are found, those concerned are to be ejected from the gates.

(3) The state is obliged to accommodate sick journeymen. Those afflicted with scabies shall be regarded as sick. Foreigners who are able to travel must be removed from the town, but nationals are to be accommodated and given medical treatment once a doctor has testified to the necessity of their stay. . .

7
On the general policing of the locality

This embraces:

A. Inspection of foodstuffs,
B. Supervision of the streets,
C. Supervision of the maintenance of safety by day and night,
D. ditto the brothel,
E. ditto weights and measures.

8

Inspection of foodstuffs will be executed through enactment of the regulations on weekly markets, cornering and pre-emption, and it must be noted that necessities must not be made more expensive through speculation and no unhygienic goods are to be sold.

9

Bakers are to be controlled as regards observation of standards. The following should be noted:

(a) a large number of bakers should not be checked on the same day. The day is lost for other business and any overlight bread disappears.

(b) The Inspector should quickly weigh bread whilst passing by a bakery and repeat this once or twice in another part of the town, let a couple of days pass, check 2–4 bakers and so forth. If he finds light bread he should weigh it again on the next or the following day after that. The baker must not be able to detect any pattern in the audit and must be kept in a state of uncertainty. The Inspector will soon ascertain where weighing is necessary and can carry this out...

(e) Bread from the previous day should not be used for checking purposes: one becomes embroiled in endless arguments about drying out. And this will require more frequent checking.

(f) Weighing is especially necessary in the case of bread traders. These receive 5 Groschen for every Thaler sold; the bakers offset this loss by giving short weight.

(h) Confiscated bread must be delivered to the Town Hall and the numbers reported to me so that I can determine those paupers who are to receive it.

20

The Inspector of Police will find the going hard at first. He should not lose heart. In order that we may mutually behave appropriately as far this time is concerned note that I find frequent questions disagreeable and a burden in view of the many interruptions to which I am subject . . .

23

Nothing should go unnoticed as long as you make a daily, hour-long, patrol of the town, observe those streets which can be observed, and instruct constables to make frequent patrols through your precincts. The main thing is to ensure wherever possible that any trouble is dealt with at once.

Police officers may not patrol, i.e. walk, where there is nothing to observe or investigate, and should go accompanied as seldom as possible, so that their eyes and ears can be fully devoted to their duties, and must devise a suitable way of combining duty, recreation and pleasure. Such a man will eventually become a nuisance to others, but nevertheless will have time to pursue his duties.

24

I particularly urge caution in conduct and way of life. Keep free of debt; debt produces dependency; distress can strike the strongest man, and leads to confusion. You will be offered gifts to obtain your favour. Refuse them – maintain your independence. In particular I must draw your attention to your position as regards the military. You had the status of a subordinate: now you occupy a special position. Extricate yourself from previous associations: you are now entirely a civilian and should avoid as much as possible the external appearance of a soldier. To each his own, and I therefore believe that you must present yourself as fully civilian. Half soldier and half citizen is a poor match.

Minden, 2 January 1831
The Mayor

Appendix 4

Instruction of 30 December 1798 'for the most precise determination of diverse provisions of the General Legal Code and the General Statutory Code, Section I, on the prevention of tumults and the punishment of their instigators and participants'
(Rönne and Simon, *Polizeiwesen*, vol. 1, pp. 666–8)

Observing that existing laws do not contain adequate provisions for the suppression of a developing tumult at its inception, from the experience that, contrary to the wishes of those who occasion them, such popular disorders often result in the greatest mischief, and, in accordance with our sovereign concern for the maintenance of the general peace and safety of our subjects, we therefore find it necessary to decree the following provisions upon this matter:

Article 1

In the event of a tumult, every householder, or anyone discharging this duty, is required to lock their house once they have received word of unrest, and as long as the unrest is not quelled to deny egress to any persons of whom it might be feared that they might add to the mass either out of curiousity or evil intent. All residents of the house are required, through observation of the provisions in Arts. 2 and 3 below, to assist the householder and enable him to meet his obligation. It must be ensured at all times that entrance is not denied to those returning home.

Article 2

Equally, parents, school-teachers and masters are obliged to restrain their children, charges and servants and on no account allow them to swell the mass.

Article 3

Factory entrepreneurs, manufacturers, and especially those with spinning mills shall be responsible for taking measures to ensure that their workers, journeymen, apprentices and day-labourers are prevented from leaving factory premises and dwellings.

Article 5

All persons offering wine, schnapps, liqueurs, beer or other drinks for sale, and all persons with dance-halls, must immediately close their stores, cellars or dwellings in the event of a tumult, and they may not reopen until the unrest is entirely suppressed. Within the proximity of the tumult such drinks may not be made available on any grounds to anyone, and even in districts further from the tumult they may be provided only to persons of whom one is convinced that they will not participate in the tumult. Anyone contravening this provision is liable to a fine or corporal punishment.

Article 6

In the event of any unlawful assembly any police officers in the vicinity are to proceed swiftly and without delay to the scene, ascertain the occasion of the unrest, detain any disturbers of the peace and earnestly indicate to the assembled mass that they should peacefully disperse immediately. If this is not heeded they must seek assistance from the nearest watch and at the same time ensure that the Governor, or other military commander in the town, and the Director of Police are promptly informed of the incident. In the meantime they are to join with the watch to prevent any mischief and quell the disturbance; they shall also make the necessary arrangements that those who wish to swell the unruly mob, either out of curiosity or for other reasons, are warned and restrained by the occupation of all points of access.

Article 7

The conduct of the military authorities in such incidents is governed by a special Instruction. At all times they are to hasten to the police to suppress any tumults and provide powerful reinforcement, where necessary double the watch, equip it with live ammunition and, should milder methods prove ineffective, employ force. They are also instructed that any persons who are encountered on the streets in the vicinity of a tumult, and who do not leave the area after appropriate warning, are to be seized and brought for arrest.

Should these subsequently be convicted of no punishable intent, they are to be subject to an appropriate fine or corporal punishment for their disobedience.

Article 8

The commanding officer or subaltern of the detachment ordered to quell the tumult is to call upon the assembled mob in a loud voice to be still and disperse immediately. This call must be repeated twice. Should the assembled mob be so large that this call is not audible, then the signal for dispersal shall be made by drum-beat or trumpet. Anyone who does not obey this signal immediately, and fails to leave the area, stands suspected of punishable intent, and unless able to prove their innocence, may be subject, depending on circumstances, to imprisonment, hard labour in a house of correction, or confinement in a fortress.

Article 9

If acts of violence are committed during a tumult, and persons or property injured or damaged, then those who occasioned the tumult, together with those who committed the acts of violence, are to be punished with hard labour in a fortress or house of correction, in the latter case made more severe with corporal punishment.

Article 10

Persons in authority and watches despatched to quell a tumult must be obeyed and abuse of the same must be refrained from on pain of corporal punishment. Should insubordination or assault take place then the penalties specified in Article 8 above are to be doubled, and depending on the circumstances may be increased to life imprisonment.

Article 11

The instigator of a riot, even if stirred up only through thoughtlessness or frivolity, shall, by virtue of the danger to which they have exposed their fellow-citizens, incur a proportionate term of imprisonment in a jail, house of correction or fortress, to be determined by a justice depending on the circumstances, and in particular the greater or lesser degree of danger.

Article 12

Malicious youths, who create unrest on the streets or elsewhere, or who commit acts of gross immorality which could induce a crowd to gather, may expect to be punished by an appropriate term of imprisonment, corporal punishment, or punishment in a house of correction.

Article 13

We assign to the local police authorities responsibility for the preliminary investigation against the instigators of a tumult, irrespective of rank or other exemption, with the exception of military personnel. This police authority is also empowered to make judgement and execute sentence if the matter involves a police penalty of fourteen days or less imprisonment; in such cases decision in the second instance lies with the justice immediately superior to this police authority.

. . .

Appendix 5

Cabinet Order concerning the respective powers and obligations of the military and civil authorities in citadels and other garrison towns as regards police matters (KA, 4 (1820). pp. 810–12)

Through my Cabinet Order of 29 October last year [1819] I decreed, on the basis of the report from the Ministries of the Interior and of War, under which circumstances the military and civil authorities in the citadels and other garrison towns shall be required to notify each other as regards police matters. Investigations of a number of instances of unrest which have taken place since then indicate, however, that these authorities are still in doubt as to the timing and limits of their mutual operations inasmuch as what began as insignificant brawls between drunken journeymen ought not to have culminated in more major excesses.

I therefore determine that as soon as the police have informed the Commander or other Military Officer in Command in the garrison of a brawl, unlawful assembly or any other commotion prejudicial to public quiet, as they are required to do on all occasions without delay in accordance with my Cabinet Order of 29 October of last year, the military authorities shall be required immediately to observe the course of the incident and undertake any necessary preparations. However, in general it shall be the duty of the civil authorities, with the help of the Gendarmerie, to suppress such disorders at the outset and maintain quiet, and as long as this is the case they shall retain sole leadership and command over these measures. However, they are also responsible for not confining themselves to these measures for any longer than they can in probability expect to achieve their purpose with the forces at their disposal. Once the danger threatens that these are no longer adequate, they are required to call on the intervention of the military: should this be the case then sole leadership and command in the matter will pass to the commanding officer and the civil authorities will be required to act only on his requisition until quiet has been fully restored and customary order re-established. If, on observing the disorder, the military commander considers in all duty and conscience, that the civil authorities have overly delayed in requisitioning military assistance, inasmuch as their forces no longer suffice to restore quiet, he is authorised and required to intervene without requisition from the civil authorities and to assume command to which the civil authorities shall then be subject. Each authority must pay special note to the appropriate moment at which its respective sphere of activity commences. Should disturbance to public quiet consist in an attack on or insubordination to military watches or patrols, or culminate in such, then the military commander is immediately required to take over the restoration of public quiet and the civil authorities are liable to meet his requests to this purpose until quiet and order is re-established. I hereby command you to communicate these regulations to the Corps Headquarters Staffs and Provincial Praesidia so that they may instruct the military and police authorities in the garrison towns accordingly.

Berlin, 17 October 1820
Friedrich Wilhelm

To the Ministries of the Interior and Police and the War Ministry.

Appendix 6

Resolution of 17 August 1835 on the maintenance of public order and the observation due to the law

As a supplement and more precise regulation of the existing law, and following consultation in Our Ministry of State, we decree the following:

Article 1

The punishment of malicious youths who incite disorder or commit acts of gross immorality on the streets or in public places is regulated by Art. 183, Tit. 20, Part II of the General Legal Code. In the event of mischief of this type, leading to a commotion through screaming or whistling, or possibly an unlawful assembly, the penalty shall generally be corporal punishment and at any event a term of imprisonment or hard labour. Depending on the nature of the circumstances, the punishment imposed may consist of repeated severe correction and detention in prison, workhouse or house of correction for a term of up to six months.

Article 5

Punishment imposable under Art. 8 [of the 1798 Instruction] for failure to act immediately on the instructions of the armed force and move on when requested shall be set between three and six months' imprisonment or penal labour. This will be doubled in the event of any injury to person or property during the course of a riot.

Article 6

The provisions of Art. 9 [of the 1798 Instruction] will be applied to any person who makes use of weapons or other dangerous implements, or who throws stones or other objects, or is discovered to have in his possession weapons, dangerous implements, stones or other projectiles. The minimum penalty shall be three years' detention in a house of correction or imprisonment in a fortress.

Article 7

In the event of physical insubordination to persons in authority or watches on their way to quell a riot, or assault and injury to the same, then the penalty will be doubled and, in accordance with Art. 10 [1798 Instruction] may, depending on circumstances, extend to the death penalty.

Article 8

If, in the event of a riot, the armed force intervenes to disperse the assembled mob and restore quiet, then the officer commanding the detachment or the subaltern officer shall instruct the mob to disperse and, if on the second repetition of his command, drum-beat or trumpet-sound the order is not obeyed, he shall enforce compliance through the use of weapons.

Article 9

In the event of physical resistance being offered to the armed force or even an attack on the same with weapons or other dangerous implements, or if stones or other objects are thrown at the same, then, on the instruction of their commander, the armed force is authorised to use firearms.

Article 10

The circumstances shall be established by an official report of the commander.

Article 11

Liability for any material damage which occurs during such events rests not only with the instigators but also jointly with all those who:

(a) are guilty of any illegal acts during such a riot,

(b) and all observers at the scene of the riot who have not dispersed following the intervention of the local or police authorities. No excuse of any observer will be respected if his presence has taken place after the intervention of an armed force.

Persons only in the latter category can seek to recover costs from those with them in that category in equal proportion to them, but may do so for the whole of the sum paid by them from the instigators and participants in the crime.

Article 12

Any investigation occasioned by these crimes should employ a shortened procedure.

Notes

Preface

1. E. von Oldenburg-Januschau, *Erinnerungen*, 2nd edn (Leipzig, 1936), pp. 208ff.
2. Arno Mayer, *The Persistence of the Old Regime. Europe to the Great War* (New York, 1981). Mayer extends the focus of the debate into a comparison of strategies for the maintenance of aristocratic dominance in nineteenth-century Europe.
3. D. Blackbourn and G. Eley, *The Peculiarities of German History. Bourgeois Society and Politics in Nineteenth-Century Germany* (Oxford and New York, 1984).
4. *Ibid.*, p. 126.
5. Hans Rosenberg, *Bureaucracy, Aristocracy and Autocracy. The Prussian Experience 1660–1815* (Cambridge, Mass., 1958).
6. H. Rosenberg, 'Die Pseudodemokratisierung der Rittergutsbesitzerklasse' in H. Rosenberg, *Probleme der deutschen Sozialgeschichte* (Frankfurt, 1969). See also his *Machteliten und Wirtschaftskonjunkturen* (Göttingen, 1978), pp. 83–101.
7. F. Engels, 'Die preußische Militärfrage und die deutsche Arbeiterpartei' (1865), *Marx–Engels Werke*, 16 (Berlin, 1962), 37–78, at 56.
8. Blackbourn and Eley, *Peculiarities*, p. 241.
9. T. Nipperdey, *Deutsche Geschichte 1860–1866. Bürgerwelt und starker Staat* (Munich, 1983), p. 333.
10. G. Craig, *The End of Prussia* (Madison and London, 1984), pp. 8ff, pp. 33f.
11. K. Eder, *Geschichte als Lernprozeß? Zur Pathogenese politischer Modernität in Deutschland* (Frankfurt, 1985), esp. pp. 389ff.
12. See C. Emsley, 'Detection and prevention: the old English police and the new 1750–1900', *Historical Social Research*, 37 (1986), 69–88; see also C. Emsley, *Policing and its Context 1750–1870* (London and Basingstoke, 1983), p. 147.

1 State domination in the transition to industrial capitalism

1. M. Weber, *Economy and Society* vol. 2 (New York, 1968), p. 909.
2. 'The state cannot be defined by its ends', M. Weber, 'Politics as a vocation', in H. H. Gerth and C. Wright Mills, *From Max Weber. Essays in Sociology* (London, 1970), p. 77.
3. *Ibid.*, p. 73.
4. The terms 'power' and 'domination' follow Weber's still influential usage; see Weber, *Economy and Society*, pp. 53f. and 213ff. However, in contrast to Weber's highly formalistic position, we favour an emphasis on the socialised subject, as proposed by K. O. Hondrich: see his *Demokratisierung und Leistungsgesellschaft. Macht- und Herrschaftswandel als sozio-ökonomischer Prozeß* (Stuttgart, 1972), pp. 24ff. Hondrich's approach is, nevertheless, primarily concerned with *decisions* about the satisfaction of needs, denial of such satisfaction, production and distribution. See C. Offe's introduction to the German edition of P. Bachrach and M. S. Baratz, *Poverty and Power* (1970), *Macht und Armut. Eine theoretisch-empirische Untersuchung* (Frankfurt, 1977),

pp. 7–34. Offe also clearly draws on S. Lukes, *Power – A Radical View* (London, 1974). In contrast Luhmann's approach, interpreting the control of the 'selectivity of the partner' as the opposite of force, does not advance beyond structural-functionalism: cf. N. Luhmann, *Macht* (Stuttgart, 1975). An identification of the social *sources* of power requires the type of approach adopted by D. Claessens in his important treatment *Kapitalismus als Kultur. Entstehung und Grundlagen der bürgerlichen Gesellschaft* (Cologne, 1973). The extent to which appropriated surpluses also, in fact primarily, serve as 'symbolic capital' is a problem tackled most notably by P. Bourdieu, *Outline of a Theory of Practice* (Cambridge, 1977), pp. 77ff.

5. A. W. Gouldner, *Patterns of Industrial Bureaucracy* (New York, 1954), p. 223.
6. See K. Polanyi, *The Great Transformation*, 2nd edn (Boston, 1957). Polanyi also establishes that this practice corresponds to a principle which inevitably seems deficient when compared with the cited 'logic'.
7. Typical of this approach is K. Eder, *Die Entstehung staatlich organisierter Gesellschaften. Ein Beitrag zu einer Theorie sozialer Evolution* (Frankfurt, 1976). The role of physical violence is also omitted in H.-U. Wehler's critical, but generally favourable, review of Almond's concept of 'political development', see H.-U. Wehler, *Modernisierungstheorie und Geschichte* (Göttingen, 1975).
8. K. Marx, *Capital*, vol. 1 (Harmondsworth, 1976), p. 899.
9. See most notably E. Pashukanis, *Law and Marxism* (London, 1978).
10. See A. Gramsci, 'The problem of political leadership in the formation and development of the nation and the modern state in Italy', in Q. Hoare and G. Nowell-Smith, *Selections from the Prison Notebooks of Antonio Gramsci* (London, 1971), pp. 55–90. As Gramsci's observation on the bourgeois state as 'dictatorship + hegemony' (*ibid*., p. 239) indicates, he did not ignore the coercive character of the bourgeois state.
11. N. Poulantzas, *Political Power and Social Classes* (London, 1973). Poulantzas goes further than the majority of analysts who focus exclusively on 'crises' (irrespective of their diverse origins) in that he does not confine repression to specific situations or individual political spheres and acute crises. Repression is 'always present'. However, 'the state' attempts to generate the appearance that it is 'in harmony with the general interest'. None the less, Poulantzas does not explore the mediations between this and other forms of state domination and control. Poulantzas also *asserts* the relationship between the 'economic' and the 'political' rather than *demonstrating* it: cf. E. Laclau, 'The specificity of the political', *Economy and Society*, 4 (1975), 87–110, especially 102ff; B. Blanke, U. Jürgens and H. Kastendiek, *Kritik der Politischen Wissenschaft*, vol. 2 (Frankfurt and New York, 1975), pp. 436ff. See too Blanke *et al*., 'On the current marxist discussion on the analysis of form and function of the bourgeois state', in J. Holloway and S. Piccioto (eds.), *State and Capital* (London, 1978). Blanke *et al*., *Kritik*, takes some first steps towards a more systematic concretisation by drawing a distinction between a 'system-limit' and an 'activity-limit'. The 'system-limit in the narrow sense', i.e. the 'sovereignty of capital within the process of production', is hardly touched by the activities of the state since there is an 'activity-limit' denoted by the 'process of production of surplus-value', that is the class constellation of any given society. This 'activity-limit' operates asymmetrically: the state's function of protecting private property serves to regulate labour-power much more than it intervenes in the sphere of capital –

that is, activity-limit and system-limit are virtually coterminous in the latter case.

12. K. Marx and F. Engels, *The German Ideology* (London, 1965), p. 46.
13. C. Offe, 'Klassenherrschaft und politisches System. Die Selektivität politischer Institutionen', in C. Offe, *Strukturprobleme des kapitalistischen Staates* (Frankfurt, 1972), pp. 65–105. In 'Crises of crisis management', *Contradictions of the Welfare State* (London, 1984), Offe points to 'welfare state services' as means to win 'mass loyalty'. In contrast, his 1979 contribution to the *Kongreß der Deutschen Vereinigung für Politische Wissenschaft* argues for the *material* incapacity of the social system and state apparatus to achieve legitimacy in a capitalist social formation: the only feasible form was 'legitimation through procedure' (Luhmann, *Zweckbegriff und Systemrationalität*). Cf. C. Offe, 'Überlegungen und Hypothesen zum Problem politischer Legitimation', in C. Offe, *Bürgerlicher Staat und Legitimation* (Frankfurt, 1976), pp. 88ff.
14. See the short but informative review in A. Wolfe, 'New directions in the marxist theory of politics', *Politics and Society*, 4 (1974), 157ff.
15. Bourdieu, *Outline*, pp. 183ff on 'gentle violence', pp. 72ff on 'habitus'.
16. *Ibid.*, p. 187.
17. For this and subsequent quotations see *ibid.*, pp. 189–91.
18. N. Elias, *Über den Prozeß der Zivilisation*, 2nd edn (Munich, Zurich, 1969), vol. 2, p. 320 (1st edn, 1936). English translation, *The Civilising Process* (Oxford, 1982), see pp. 292f.
19. For a paradigmatic analysis of the development of surveillance, the disciplinary and regulatory forms and instruments of 'extra-economic force' in the seventeenth and eighteenth centuries, see M. Foucault, *Discipline and Punish. The Birth of the Prison* (Harmondsworth, 1982). See too G. Rusche and O. Kirchheimer, *Sozialstruktur und Strafvollzug*, 2nd edn (Frankfurt, 1974), pp. 137ff, originally published in 1939.
20. See W. Trapp, 'Volksschulreform und liberales Bürgertum in Konstanz', in G. Zang (ed.), *Provinzialisierung einer Region* (Frankfurt, 1978), pp. 375–434, at pp. 383ff.; K. Goebel, *Schule im Schatten. Die Volksschule in den Industriestädten des Wuppertals um 1850* (Wuppertal, 1978).
21. J. Donzelot, *La police des familles* (Paris, 1977), is particularly succinct on this issue. See too D. Blasius, *Der verwaltete Wahnsinn. Eine Sozialgeschichte des Irrenhauses* (Frankfurt, 1980), pp. 92–123.
22. Bourdieu, *Outline*, p. 72; cf. p. 85.
23. For a useful résumé of the discussion on the state in the German Democratic Republic see H. Gerstenberger, 'Zur Theorie des bürgerlichen Staates. Der gegenwärtige Stand der Debatte', in V. Brandes (ed.), *Handbuch 5, Staat* (Frankfurt, Cologne, 1977), pp. 21–49, at pp. 41ff.
24. Such a position is not confined to marxist approaches; see, for example, 'property rights' in D. C. North and R. P. Thomas, *The Rise of the Western World* (Cambridge, 1973).
25. See V. Ronge and G. Schmieg, *Restriktionen politischer Planung* (Frankfurt, 1973); C. Offe, *Berufsbildungsreform* (Frankfurt, 1975).
26. K. Marx, 'The Eighteenth Brumaire of Louis Bonaparte', in K. Marx and F. Engels, *Collected Works*, vol. 11 (London, 1979), pp. 185–6. See Engels to Conrad Schmidt, letter of 27 October 1890, in Marx–Engels, *Selected Correspondence* (Moscow, 1975), pp. 398–9. However, this does not detract from the state's function of being 'the ideal collective body of all capitalists' – in fact, it requires its autonomy; cf. F. Engels, *Anti-Dühring* (London, 1934), p. 306.

For a systematic treatment of this question see Pashukanis, *Law and Marxism*. However, individual analyses are insufficient to prove a general, yet at the same 'particular estate-, class-, and group-interest of the bureaucracy'. See on this subject J. Kocka, 'Preußischer Staat und Modernisierung im Vormärz. Marxistisch-leninistische Intrepretationen und ihre Probleme', in H.-U. Wehler (ed.), *Sozialgeschichte heute* (Göttingen, 1974), Festschrift for Hans Rosenberg, pp. 211–27, at pp. 215, 221.

27. The concept of 'arenas', their succession or simultaneity is expounded by T. J. Lowi, 'Decision-making vs. policy-making', *Public Administration Review*, 30 (1970), 314–25.
28. A. Smith, *An Inquiry into the Nature and Causes of the Wealth of Nations* (London, 1776; reprint, 1966), p. 314. On the narrowing down of the concept of property in the wake of the development of the capitalist mode of production to 'rights in material things and revenues', see C. B. MacPherson, 'Capitalism and the changing concept of property', in E. Kamenka and R. S. Neale (eds.), *Feudalism, Capitalism and Beyond* (London, 1975), pp. 110ff. In the same study, R. S. Neale shows that the differentiation of the right of property and its flexible application was not associated with any 'bourgeois' achievement, but essentially with the transformation of landownership into ownership of capital – in considerable measure the background to Locke's work (*ibid.*, pp. 84–102, 'The bourgeoisie, historically, has played a most revolutionary part'). On this subject in general see H. Medick, *Naturzustand und Naturgeschichte der bürgerlichen Gesellschaft* (Göttingen, 1973), pp. 257ff.
29. The concept of the 'indebted fiscal state' was suggested by R. Goldscheid in 1917. See R. Hickel (ed.), *Die Finanzkrise des Steuerstaates. Beiträge zur politischen Ökonomie der Staatsfinanzen* (Frankfurt, 1976). More specifically on the subject under consideration here, see R. Braun, 'Taxation, sociopolitical structure, and state-building: Great Britain and Brandenburg-Prussia', in C. Tilly (ed.), *The Formation of National States in Western Europe* (Princeton, 1975), pp. 234–327, at pp. 316ff.
30. D. Hay, 'Property, Authority and Criminal Law', in D. Hay *et al.*, *Albion's Fatal Tree. Crime and Society in Eighteenth-Century England* (London, 1975).
31. E. P. Thompson, *Whigs and Hunters* (London, 1975), pp. 263, 266.
32. H. Harnisch, *Kapitalistische Agrarreform und industrielle Revolution. Untersuchungen über das ostelbische Preußen zwischen Spätfeudalismus und bürgerlich-demokratischer Revolution 1848/49 unter besonderer Berücksichtigung der Provinz Brandenburg* (Weimar, 1984).
33. On the long drawn out, and for the peasantry, 'decades of most harrowing expropriation and bondage' associated with the 'Prussian path' of the development of capitalist agriculture, see the brief formulation in V. I. Lenin, 'The agrarian programme of social democracy in the first Russian Revolution, 1905–1907', in Lenin, *Collected Works*, vol. 13 (London, 1962). See too, on the Prussian experience, H. Bleiber, *Zwischen Reform und Revolution. Lage und Kämpfe der schlesischen Bauern und Landarbeiter im Vormärz 1840–1847* (Berlin, GDR, 1966), especially pp. 11–56. The problem of development on the land is systematically discussed under this aspect in, R. Berthold, H. Harnisch, H. H. Müller, 'Der preußische Weg der Landwirtschaft und neuere westdeutsche Forschungen', *Jb. Wirtsch. G.*, 1970/II, 259–89. And by the same authors, 'Bürgerliche Umwälzung und kapitalistische Agrarentwicklung', *Zeitschrift für Geschichtswissenschaft*, 27 (1979), 140–4. Although the terminological differentiation between the extension and intensification of market links, 'com-

mercialisation', and the capitalist organisation of production itself is somewhat unsatisfactory, this differentiation is very clearly seen in the material analyses. Cf. on 'commercialisation' (and for a clear separation of both dimensions of the same process of transformation), H. Schissler, *Preußiche Agrargesellschaft im Wandel* (Göttingen, 1978), pp. 59ff. Barrington Moore has tackled this problem in his global studies of the conditions of parliamentary forms of rule, revolutionary peasant revolutions, and fascist dictatorships. However, he does not advance beyond very broad observations – drawn from the literature – which confine the actual transition since the middle of the 18th century to political and administrative 'conservative modernisation': see B. Moore jnr, *The Social Origins of Dictatorship and Democracy* (Harmondsworth, 1969), pp. 433ff.

34. For a survey and detailed discussion of this problem see P. Kriedte, H. Medick and J. Schlumbohm, *Industrialisation before Industrialisation* (Cambridge, 1981), pp. 135ff.

35. On developments in the eighteenth century see H. Krüger, *Zur Geschichte der Manufakturen und der Manufakturarbeiter in Preußen. Die mittleren Provinzen in der zweiten Hälfte des 18. Jahrhunderts* (Berlin, GDR, 1958); on questions relating to the demand and supply of labour see K. Hinze, *Die Arbeiterfrage zu Beginn des modernen Kapitalismus in Brandenburg-Preußen* (Berlin, 1927). A mostly statistical survey is provided by K.-H. Kaufhold, *Das Gewerbe in Preußen um 1800*, (Göttingen, 1978); for detailed data on local developments, see J. Kermann, *Die Manufakturen im Rheinland, 1750–1833* (Bonn, 1972), especially p. 611. On the development of factory industry see R. H. Tilly, 'Capital formation in Germany in the 19th century', in P. Mathias and M. M. Postan (eds.), *The Cambridge Economic History of Europe* (Cambridge, 1978), vol. 7, pp. 382–441, at pp. 419ff.

36. H. Medick, 'Plebeian culture and the proto-industrial family economy: articulation of needs and patterns of consumption', in Kriedte, Medick, Schlumbohm, *Industrialisation*, pp. 64ff.

37. Godelier, 'Anthropology and economics' in, Godelier, *Perspectives in Marxist Anthropology* (Cambridge, 1977), p. 49.

38. See the seminal H. Rosenberg, *Bureaucracy, Aristocracy and Autocracy* (Cambridge, Mass., 1958). Cf. too the critical discussion of Rosenberg's approach in H. C. Johnson, *Frederick the Great and his Officials* (New Haven and London, 1975). Johnson seeks to show that the bureaucracy neither exclusively represented the interests of the aristocracy nor was it a mere auxiliary for the army. Instead, Johnson lays stress on its relative independence. Specifically on the omnipresence and power of definition of the military see O. Büsch, *Militärsystem und Sozialleben im alten Preußen, 1713–1803* (Berlin, 1962). Less forthcoming on this question is the comparative work by J. A. Armstrong, *The European Administrative Elite* (Princeton, 1973). Cf. the author's review, A. Lüdtke, 'Genesis und Durchsetzung des "modernen Staates". Zur Analyse von Herrschaft und Verwaltung', *Archiv für Sozialgeschichte*, 20 (1980), 483ff. Perry Anderson has brought state domination and its apparatuses into the framework of the mode of production and its dynamics; cf. P. Anderson, *Lineages of the Absolutist State* (London, 1974), especially pp. 195ff, 236ff. See my review, pp. 474–9, for a detailed discussion.

39. See J. Schlumbohm, 'Excursus: the political and institutional framework of proto-industrialisation', in Kriedte, Medick and Schlumbohm, *Industrialisation*, pp. 127ff.

40. I. Mittenzwei, *Preußen nach dem Siebenjährigen Krieg. Auseinandersetzungen*

zwischen Bürgertum und Staat um die Wirtschaftspolitik (Berlin, GDR, 1979) uses a good deal of empirical material to capture the differences and nuances, especially within the bourgeois anti-monarchist opposition.

41. E. Kehr, 'Zur Genesis der preußischen Bürokratie und des Rechtsstaates. Ein Beitrag zum Diktaturproblem', in E. Kehr, *Primat der Innenpolitik* ed. by H.-U. Wehler (Berlin, 1965), pp. 31–52, at p. 46. Kehr concentrates on the generally neglected background to and interaction between fiscal and financial policies. For an examination in greater depth, and with a more systematically critical approach, see Rosenberg, *Bureaucracy*, pp. 175ff. For a history of officialdom, together with its 'policies' on the constitution, law and society after 1815, see the much broader and more empirical study by R. Kosselleck, *Preußen zwischen Reform und Revolution. Allgemeines Landrecht, Verwaltung und soziale Bewegung von 1791–1848*, 1st edn (Stuttgart, 1967). Koselleck tends to give too much weight to the self-image of the bureaucracy. He initially overestimates their capacity to direct events (the drive for comprehensive social transformation) and overlooks the dimension of 'domination' and of the 'dictatorship of the bureaucracy' raised in particular by Kehr. Although he does ultimately acknowledge the bureaucracy's limited powers of control, he does not, however, explain them. Helplessness in the face of their own creation thus appears as the prime cause of the revolutionary movement of 1848–49: cf. pp. 48ff, 621. The restrictive conditions, and in particular the Junker nobility ('the beneficiaries'), are dealt with scrupulously but treated as the results of bureaucratic failure, and not systematically set in the context of the question of what social paths of development were in fact available. Thus, on the issue of the reasons behind the failure of the bureaucracy, the study does not go beyond references to social and institutional isolation or a desultory 'management' which became entangled in its own activity.
42. In his discussion of Marxist–Leninist approaches, Kocka stresses the 'interest of the bureaucracy in domination and self-preservation', against the view that the bureaucracy was merely an instrument of the 'feudal' aristocracy (an argument Kocka also directs against Koselleck): see J. Kocka, 'Rezension zu: Koselleck, Preußen zwischen Reform und Revolution', VSWG, 57 (1970), 121–5; cf. J. Kocka, 'Preußischer Staat', pp. 211–27. Vogel has emphasised the 'independence' of officialdom in another way, in the context of an organisational-sociological perspective which properly underlines the importance of occupational socialisation: group behaviour cannot be cogently explained by a breakdown according to social origins (noble or bourgeois families). In fact, such a general argument cannot fully express the 'life-world' of the bureaucracy. See B. Vogel, 'Die "allgemeine Gewerbefreiheit" als bürokratische Modernisierungsstrategie in Preußen', in D. Stegmann and P.-C. Witt (eds.), *Industrielle Gesellschaft und politisches System* (Bonn, 1978), p. 68. For a general and comparative study see B. Moore jnr, *Social Origins of Dictatorship and Democracy* (Harmondsworth, 1969).
43. Cf. G. F. Knapp, *Die Bauernbefreiung . . . in den älteren Teilen Preußens* (Leipzig, 1927), vols. 1 and 2. On social structure at the end of the eighteenth century and on legislation (but not its implementation) see H. Schissler, *Preußische Agrargesellschaft im Wandel* (Göttingen, 1978). On economic development from the aspect of the development of productivity see R. A. Dickler, 'Organisation and change in productivity in Eastern Prussia', in W. N. Parker and E. L. Jones (eds.), *European Peasants and their Markets* (Princeton, 1975), pp. 269–92.
44. R. Robin, 'Der Charakter des Staates am Ende des Ancien Régime: Gesellschafts-

formation, Staat und Übergang' in E. Schmitt (ed.), *Die Französische Revolution* (Cologne, 1976), pp. 202–29, at pp. 213 and 218.

45. See H. Bleiber, 'Staat und bürgerliche Umwälzung in Deutschland. Zum Charakter besonders des preußischen Staates in der ersten Hälfte des 19. Jahrhunderts', in *Universalhistorische Aspekte und Dimensionen des Jakobinismus* (Berlin, GDR, 1976), Reports of the Session of the Academy of Science of the German Democratic Republic, pp. 201–39. Marx– Engels quote is from the *Manifesto of the Communist Party* (Moscow, 1967), p. 44.

46. See I. Mittenzwei, *Preußen nach dem Siebenjährigen Krieg*, (Berlin, GDR, 1979), pp. 71–100. See also Sidney Pollard, *Peaceful Conquest. The Industrialization of Europe 1760–1970* (Oxford, 1981).

47. See the short outline of the problem in H.-J. Puhle, 'Preußen: Entwicklung und Fehlentwicklung', in H.-J. Puhle and H.-U. Wehler (eds.), *Preußen im Rückblick* (Göttingen, 1980), pp. 11–42. The experiences of the dominated and their 'costs' are left until a very general concluding paragraph.

48. H. Bleiber, 'Staat und bürgerliche Umwälzung', p. 228. Cf. too W. Schmidt, 'Zu einigen Problemen der bürgerlichen Umwälzung in der deutschen Geschichte', in H. Bleiber *et al.* (eds.), *Bourgeoisie und bürgerliche Umwälzung in Deutschland, 1789–1871* (Berlin, GDR, 1977), Festschrift for K. Obermann.

49. J. G. Hoffmann, *Nachricht über die Vorträge und die Anordnung derselben des Dr. J. G. Hoffmann* (Berlin, 1823), p. 31, for both this and subsequent quotation.

50. Anon, *Über Handhabung der Sicherheitspolizei durch Gendarmerie* (Karlsruhe, 1831), p.10.

51. M. K. F. W. Grävell, *Über höhere, geheime und Sicherheitspolizei* (Sonderhausen and Nordhausen, 1820), p. 188, for both this and subsequent quotation.

2 Bureaucracy as an apparatus of domination

1. See the comprehensive treatment of this field in R. Koselleck, *Preußen zwischen Reform und Revolution. Allgemeines Landrecht, Verwaltung und soziale Bewegung von 1791–1848*, 1st edn (Stuttgart, 1967), especially pp. 163ff and 217–83. F. L. Knemeyer, *Regierungs- und Verwaltungsreformen in Deutschland zu Beginn des 19. Jahrhunderts* (Cologne and Berlin, 1970) provides a comparative overview of the German states, albeit from a narrow institutional-historical perspective. For texts of the principal provisions see H. Gräff, L. von Rönne and H. Simon (eds.), *Ergänzungen und Erläuterungen der Preußischen Rechtsbücher*, 3rd edn (Breslau, 1849), vol. 4, pp. 252–373, 430ff. Implementation of the reforms took place crucially at provincial and regional (*Bezirk*) level. Until recently, access to the 'inside' experiences of those staffing these levels of administration has been very limited. One of the few sources, the voluminous diaries of *Oberpräsident* Ludwig Freiherr von Vincke have now been rendered more accessible, at least in part, through a modern edition: *Die Tagebücher des Oberpräsidenten Ludwig Freiherrn Vincke 1813–1818*, edited by L. Graf von Westphalen (Münster, 1980).

2. J. R. Gillis, *The Prussian Bureaucracy in Crisis, 1840–1860. Origins of an Administrative Ethos* (Stanford, 1971), p. 25. 'The manner in which decisions were arrived at indicated the prevalence of collective over individual norms, for although personal initiative was encouraged, it was the will of the group that was decisive. The stability of the collegiate system was reinforced by the fact

that the college was the officials' primary source of social identity. The authority of the senior members of the college was partially a function of the paternalistic social relationships between the younger and older members of the profession, which prevailed throughout the nineteenth century. Procedures were cooperative but nondemocratic, and authoritarianism flourished, for age meant more than merit or achievement. This particular deference pattern was reflected in the seniority rules, under which age ordinarily determined the individual's rank in the hierarchy of authority' (*ibid.*).

3. See the Cabinet Order of 31 December 1825 and the Instruction to the District Governments of the same day on the strengthening of the position of the *Regierungspräsident* and the abolition of the three-member *Präsidium*: cf. Gräff *et al.*, *Ergänzungen und Erläuterungen*, vol. 4, pp. 353ff, 357ff. However, the relevant preceding Instruction of 17 October 1817 (Section 40) had already specified that, 'The *Präsident* is the fulcrum of the entire administration of the Government' (*ibid.*, p. 342). See too Koselleck, *Preußen*, pp. 249ff.
4. See Koselleck, *Preußen*, pp. 177ff and 220ff on the protracted and vehement confrontations within the bureaucracy.
5. W. Bleek, *Von der Kameralausbildung zum Juristenprivileg* (Berlin, 1972), pp. 104, 124ff; D. Wegmann, *Die leitenden staatlichen Verwaltungsbeamten der Provinz Westfalen, 1815–1918* (Münster, 1969) provides a socio-biographical complementary study for an individual province. On the problems of recruitment, acceptance and promotion after the late 1830s see Gillis, *Prussian Bureaucracy*. On discipline within the service see Koselleck, *Preußen*, pp. 407–14 (in particular on the Cabinet Order of 21 February 1823, the secret decree of 16 August 1826, which provided for summary dismissal without legal grounds, and the Disciplinary Statute of 29 March 1844). The report by the acting *Oberpräsident* of Westphalia, Karl von Bodelschwingh, to the Interior Minister of 1 December 1848 reveals some of the differences and suspicions between the internal administration and the judiciary as regards political reliability in the years prior to the events of 1848, and during 1848–9 itself. 'It should be noted particularly that for the most part it is officials, especially those from the judiciary, who distinguish themselves in popular meetings as leaders and speakers and become doubly dangerous by virtue of their official character and knowledge of the law. The latter generally protects them from contravening the penal law, whilst the former contributes to the success and influence of their free-thinking and seditious talk and actions amongst the lower classes.' Bodelschwingh went on to complain about the judicial '*Referendarien*, *Assessoren* and judicial commissaries' and the inactivity and 'excuses' of the *Präsident* of the Provincial Court in Hamm: the younger officials were not being 'adequately supervised' by their superiors (GStA/PK 84a, no. 8209, fol. 142).
6. These figures are from A. Lotz, *Geschichte des Deutschen Beamtentums* (Berlin, 1909), p. 371, and apply to the period immediately after 1815. Koselleck suggests a figure of 'around six hundred' senior officials in the District Governments and offices of the *Oberpräsidenten* at provincial level; this fell to 'below five hundred' by the mid 1820s. In contrast to Lotz, Koselleck does not specify what proportion of this number were technical officials, such as those in construction, for example.
7. Freiherr von Zedlitz, *Die Staatskräfte der Preußischen Monarchie unter Friedrich Wilhelm III*, vol. 2 (Berlin, 1828), pp. xi, xxff.
8. Cf. the 'rankings' issued on 7 February 1817, summarised in Lotz, *Geschichte des Deutschen Beamtentums*, p. 376.

9. Cf. the Instruction for *Oberpräsidenten*, 31 December 1825, GS 1826, pp. 1–5, especially p. 1f (Sections 1 II, 4).
10. In general on this see Koselleck, *Preußen*, pp. 243f.
11. 'Formally merely constituted as the "uppermost advisory authority" of the King, in practice the Council of State was the representative of Prussian officialdom. No monarch would have felt able to push through legislation against its recommendations. The Council of State consisted of princes, senior members of the military, high officials and judges – increasingly the latter. The appointment of the numerous other officials, at the behest of the King, was to a considerable extent cooption by the Council itself. This, the most intelligent body in Europe as the publisher Perthes once described it, resembled an intra-administrative parliament. Its method of working was organised such that the various departmental interests of the Ministries met in the committees, with completely equal status for all members irrespective of service rank' (Koselleck, *Preußen*, p. 267).
12. See the Appendix in Koselleck, *Preußen* on the relative proportions of nobles and bourgeois in the provincial administration and office of *Landrat* ('Anhang IV: Anteil des Adels und der Bürger an der Provinzialverwaltung und an den Landratsstellen', *ibid.*, pp. 680–90. H. Reif, *Westfälischer Adel 1770–1860. Vom Herrschaftsstand zur regionalen Elite* (Göttingen, 1979), pp. 378–91, exposes the hesitancy, rejection and resignation on the part of the nobility towards a career in the bureaucracy in one of the new provinces, Westphalia.
13. D. Poestges, 'Die preußische Personalpolitik im Regierungsbezirk Aachen von 1815 bis zum Ende des Kulturkampfes', Doctoral thesis (Aachen, 1975).
14. J. D. F. Rumpf, *Handbuch für Landräte* (Berlin, 1835), pp. vf, quoting the Potsdam *Regierungsrat* Wehnert, *Über den Geist der preußischen Staatsorganisation und Staatsdienerschaft* (Potsdam, 1833).
15. See 'Über Interessen', in J. Mittelstrass, *Methodologische Probleme einer normativ-kritischen Gesellschaftstheorie* (Frankfurt, 1975), pp. 133ff.
16. Cf. the reports of the *Landrat* and the Commissary of the Arnsberg District Government to the *Oberpräsident*, StAMS Oberpräs., no. 680.
17. On the 'dual constitution of social reality' mediated and realised in 'social situations' see L. Hack *et al.*, 'Klassenlage und Interessenorientierung', *Zeitschrift für Soziologie*, 1 (1972), 15–130, especially 18, 24f. The work of Goffman remains extraordinarily stimulating on attempts to understand interaction not simply as 'mere forms of appearance'; cf. E. Goffmann, *Relations in Public* (New York, 1971) and *Frame Analysis* (New York, 1974). The situative approach attempted here in Chapters 3–5 below explains our concentration on local and regional authorities and archives. The refusal of the authorities in the German Democratic Republic to permit me to consult the documents of the Ministry of the Interior and Cabinet in the *Zentrales Staatsarchiv des DDR*, Merseburg, was not therefore too damaging to the central focus of the study.
18. C. Geertz, 'Thick description. Towards an interpretive theory of culture', in Geertz, *The Interpretation of Cultures* (New York, 1973), p. 7. It should be noted that Geertz isolates this dimension and does not advance to the issue of mediation.
19. Reproduced in H. Scheel (ed.), *Das Reformministerium Stein. Akten zur Verfassungs- und Verwaltungsgeschichte aus den Jahren 1807/8* (Berlin, GDR, 1968), vol. 3, p. 836.
20. See 'Bibliotheksverzeichnis Regierungspräsidium Minden', Landesbibliothek Detmold.

21. P. von Oertzen, *Die soziale Funktion des staatsrechtlichen Positivismus* (Frankfurt, 1974), pp. 67, 105ff, characterises Rönne's work and his position as 'practical' or 'open' positivism, which cannot be detached from the basic supposition of a pre-governmental 'moral legal order'.
22. L. von Rönne, *Das Staatsrecht der Preußischen Monarchie*, 3rd edn, Part 2, vol. 2, (Berlin, 1872), pp. 108, and 109 for the subsequent quotations.
23. See T. Foerstemann, *Prinzipien des preußischen Polizeirechts. Dargestellt und in ihren Grundlagen geprüft* (Berlin, 1969). In contrast to Rönne's or Heyde's compendia, Foerstemann took a clear position against orders, decrees and official interpretations (in 'rescripts'), which he regarded as encroachments by the police authorities on the judiciary.
24. *Allgemeines Landrecht für die Preußischen Staaten von 1794* (Frankfurt and Berlin, 1970), Teil II, tit. 17, para. 10 (p. 602), subsequently referred to in the text as the Prussian Legal Code.
25. H. Rosin, *Polizeiverordnungsrecht* (Berlin, 1882), pp. 96ff. See too the Crown Prince Lectures by Svarez, in C. G. Svarez, *Vorträge über Recht und Staat*, ed. H. Conrad and G. Kleinheyer (Cologne and Opladen, 1960), p. 38. The 'Kreuzberg Judgement' of 1882 was important for the subsequent course of events, i.e. the judicial curtailment of police powers; cf. *Entscheidungen des Preuß. Oberverwaltungsgerichts*, vol. 9, pp. 353ff. The judgement by the Prussian Administrative Court prohibited a building regulation issued by the 'Building *Polizey*' for a building line in Berlin-Kreuzberg on the grounds that it had been given on aesthetic grounds, and hence concerned the 'welfare' rather than the 'safety' of the district's future residents. On the legal consequences see K. H. Friauf, 'Polizei- und Ordnungsrecht', in I. von Münch (ed.), *Besonderes Verwaltungsrecht* (Bad Homburg, 1969), p. 146.
26. 'Verordnung wegen verbesserter Einrichtung der Provinzial-, Polizei- und Finanz-Behörden, vom 26. Dezember 1808', in *Sammlung der für die Königlich Preußischen Staaten erschienen Gesetze und Verordnungen 1806–1810* (Berlin, 1822), pp. 464ff, esp. 465f (section 3). 'Instruktion zur Geschäftsführung der Regierungen in den Königlich Preußischen Staaten', vom 23. Oktober 1817, in GS, 1817, pp. 248ff.
27. K. Wolzendorff, 'Die Entwicklung des Polizeibegriffs im 19. Jhdt', Doctoral thesis (Marburg, 1905), pp. 27–30, 39. See too K. Wolzendorff, *Der Polizeigedanke des modernen Staats* (Breslau, 1918), p. 264. On the subject in general, see W. Damkowski, *Die Entstehung des Verwaltungsbegriffs. Eine Wortstudie* (Cologne, 1969), pp. 143f (on the ALR, Teil II, tit. 13, para. 3).
28. W. G. von der Heyde, *Polizei-Verwaltung bezüglich auf den Inbegriff der Landes- und Lokal-Polizeiverwaltung, auf die Landes- und Lokal-Polizeibehörden, und auf deren Wirkungskreis und Geschäftsführung* (Magdeburg, 1843), vol. 1, p. 1. Between 1827 and 1855 Heyde wrote or published over seventy such 'Manuals'. P. Zeller, *Systematisches Lehrbuch der Polizeiwissenschaft nach preußischer Edicten . . . sowohl zum Unterricht der Regierungsreferendarien . . . als auch zur Hülfe für die Kgl. Preuß. Regierungsräthe, Landräthe, Polizeipräsidenten, Polizeiräthe, Bürgermeister* (Quedlinburg and Leipzig, 1828), p. 1, cites the police section from the Prussian Legal Code, however.
29. G. A. Bielitz, *Darstellung der Verfassung und Verwaltung der Polizei in Preußen. Ein Hülfsbuch für Landräthe, Magistratspersonen und Polizeibeamte . . . in Preußen* (Leipzig, 1841), pp. iii, 44.
30. Cf. 'Instruktion für die Geschäftsführung der Regierungen, vom 23. Oktober 1817', GS 1817, pp. 248ff, section 7.

31. Cf. J. Hart, 'Nineteenth-century social reform. A Tory interpretation of history', in *Past and Present*, 31 (1965), 39–61, at 47. The influence of Bentham's ideas on legislative practice and the conduct of state authorities in the first half of the nineteenth century continues to be a topic of controversy; cf. O. MacDonagh, *Early Victorian Government 1830–1870* (London, 1977), pp. 34–41.
32. G. W. F. Hegel, *Die 'Rechtsphilosophie' von 1820 mit Hegels Vorlesungsnotizen 1821–25*, ed. K.-H. 'Ilting (Stuttgart-Bad Cannstatt, 1974), pp. 692, 701, 708f.
33. T. Janke, *Preußen 1807 und jetzt, oder: Was ist in Preußen seit dem Jahre 1807 ausgeführt, um den gesellschaftlichen Zustand zu verbessern und zu erheben? Eine kurze, den Freunden des Preußischen Vaterlandes geweihte Abhandlung* (Berlin, 1831), p. 31. And primarily the *Preisschrift* by the Potsdam *Regierungsrat* Wehnert, *Über den Geist der Preußischen Staatsorganisation und Staatsdienerschaft* (Potsdam, 1833).
34. J. G. Schlosser, *Briefe über die Gesetzgebung überhaupt und den Entwurf des preußischen Gesetzbuches* (Frankfurt, 1789), pp. 11f.
35. Cf. E. R. Huber, *Deutsche Verfassungsgeschichte seit 1789*, vol. 2 (Stuttgart, 1960), pp. 16–19, on the 'statutory state'. This is a reference to the *relative* automony of the judiciary, although it remained at bottom dependent on the conduct and 'grace' of the monarch, including in individual cases. In effect, it meant dependency on the monarch's immediate advisers even where French law applied. Huber correctly draws attention to the fact that the principle of 'order' took precedence over 'freedom' in administrative practice. Although the 'programme' of furthering the common good may have legitimated state-administrative domination under the conditions of pre-constitutional government, it would be mistaken to see this as the only type of legitimation; cf. N. Luhmann, *Zweckbegriff und Systemrationalität*, 2nd edn (Frankfurt, 1973), pp. 93ff, especially 105.
36. See W. Rüfner, *Verwaltungsrechtsschutz in Preußen von 1749 bis 1842* (Bonn, 1962), pp. 154ff, 175ff. On self-protection in complaints procedures see E. von Bülow-Cummerow, *Preußen, seine Verfassung, seine Verwaltung, sein Verhältnis zu Deutschland* (Berlin, 1842), p. 125, or from a more 'radical' perspective, E. Dronke, *Berlin*, 2nd edn (Neuwied and Darmstadt, 1974), first published 1846, pp. 295, 306ff, and, by the same author, *Polizei-Geschichten* (Leipzig, 1846), pp. 133ff, describing the course of an unsuccessful appeal.
37. Cf. K. H. Hagen, *Von der Staatslehre und der Vorbereitung zum Dienste in der Staatsverwaltung. Aufsätze, gerichtet an angehende Kameralisten, zunächst an seine Herren Zuhörer* (Königsberg, 1839), pp. 457f.
38. K. Marx, 'Contribution to the Critique of Hegel's Philosophy of Law', in K. Marx and F. Engels, *Collected Works*, vol. 3 (London, 1975), p. 46. Marx's critique is confirmed by Hegel's characterisation of 'police' administration; G. W. F. Hegel, *Die 'Rechtsphilosophie' von 1820*, pp. 676f (section 234), 685–7 (section 249); cf. pp. 726–8 (section 272); see too, M. Riedel, *Bürgerliche Gesellschaft und Staat* (Neuwied and Berlin, 1970).
39. W. G. von der Heyde, *Polizei-Strafgewalt in den Königlich-Preußischen Staaten*, Part I (Magdeburg, 1837), pp. 1–3.
40. The 'means of coercion and punishment' were regulated by Section 48 of the Order of 26 December 1808; the 1817 Instruction reproduces these paragraphs unchanged in the Appendix (see GS 1817, p. 288). Section 11 of the Order of 30 April 1815 gave the District Governments the power 'to give weight to their decisions if needs be through legal means of coercion and punishment'.
41. M. Müller-Blattau, 'Die deutsche Polizei an der Wende vom Polizeistaat zum bürgerlichen Rechtsstaat', Doctoral thesis (Heidelberg, 1961), pp. 173ff.

42. Memorandum, 29 August 1808, to Minister Freiherr v. Schroetter, in Scheel, *Reformministerium Stein*, vol. 3, pp. 801–4, at 801.
43. Cf. Rosin, *Polizeiverordnungsrecht*, p. 97.
44. H. A. Zachariae, *Deutsches Staats- und Bundesrecht*, 1st edn, vol. 2 (Göttingen, 1842), p. 268. 'Wherever the issue becomes one of securing civil order in general, including in a certain respect *religion* and *morals*, against injury, and surmounting existing or potential dangers, the use of means of coercion is justified' (*ibid.*).
45. M. K. F. W. Grävell, *Wie darf die Verfassung Preußens nicht werden?* (Leipzig, 1819), p. 117.
46. *Ibid.*
47. G. Zimmermann, *Die deutsche Polizei im neunzehnten Jahrhundert*, vol. 3 (Hannover, 1849), p. 161.

3 'Common good', property and 'honour'

1. See W. Abel, *Massenarmut und Hungerkrisen im vorindustriellen Europa* (Hamburg and Berlin, 1974), pp. 314ff., 359ff.
2. For a detailed study see J. Mooser, *Ländliche Klassengesellschaft 1770–1848. Bauern und Unterschichten, Landwirtschaft und Gewerbe im östlichen Westfalen* (Göttingen, 1984), esp. pp. 146ff, 246ff: the main branch hit by crisis was hand-spinning.
3. For overall figures for the entire state, see C. F. W. Dieterici, 'Statistische Übersicht der im Preußischen Staat zu den sogenannten Arbeiterklassen gerechneten Personen überhaupt . . .', *Mitteilungen des statistischen Büros in Berlin*, 1 (1848), pp. 68ff. The figures reveal a disproportionately high growth in 'workers' between 1816 and 1846, with the exception of servants (*Gesinde*). See the discussion on migration on pp. 79ff below.
4. The 'Brandenburg nobleman', F. A. L. von der Marwitz, may well have been typical of this type of self-image; his defiant obstinacy is particularly indicative of the feudal character of the Prussian rural aristocracy in the first third of the nineteenth century. See F. A. L. von der Marwitz, *Lebensbeschreibung* (Berlin, 1908), edited by H. Meusel, vol. 1, pp. 44–7.
5. See J. Habermas, *Strukturwandel der Öffentlichkeit* (Neuwied, 1962), pp. 17ff, esp. 19f. Habermas denies that this public sphere is, or was, a 'sphere of political communication' (*ibid.*, p. 20).
6. It is not possible to provide a systematic study of the 'social circles' of public officials for the period under consideration here. Nevertheless, some leads can be found in individual references, such as memoires, e.g. the diaries of *Oberpräsident* Vincke. Bourdieu's observations on the interlinking and synchronicity of 'economic' and 'symbolic' actions and interests also provide some systematic points of reference: see P. Bourdieu, *Outline of a Theory of Practice* (Cambridge, 1977), pp. 176–7.
7. Report of tour of inspection by *Regierungspräsident* von Itzenplitz, no date, entry 18 July 1845, StAMS, Reg. Arnsberg Pr., no. 22.
8. R. von Delbrück, *Lebenserinnerungen*, vol. 1 (Leipzig, 1905), p. 194.
9. A. von Ernsthausen, *Erinnerungen eines preußischen Beamten* (Bielefeld and Leipzig, 1894), p. 133.
10. Huber supplies potted biographies for most of the members of the 'reform group' within the bureaucracy; see E. R. Huber, *Deutsche Verfassungsge-*

schichte seit 1798, vol. 1 (Stuttgart, 1957), pp. 127–35. *Ibid.*, pp. 138–45, on the members of the 'restoration party'. In addition to edited correspondence by individuals such as Stein, two (not complete) publications of documentary material are indispensable for any analysis of the advisory and decision-making procedures, and how influence was exercised; see G. Winter (ed.), *Die Reorganisation des preußischen Staates unter Stein und Hardenberg*, Part 1, vol. 1 (Leipzig, 1931), which covers all published material on civil administration between the early part of 1806 and July 1807; and H. Scheel (ed.), *Das Reformministerium Stein*, vols. 1–3 (Berlin, GDR, 1967–8).

11. See H. Schissler, *Preußische Agrargesellschaft im Wandel* (Göttingen, 1978), pp. 59–71, 106; see too H.-H. Müller, *Märkische Landwirtschaft vor den Agrarreformen von 1807. Entwicklungstendenzen des Ackerbaus in der zweiten Hälfte des 18. Jhdt.s* (Potsdam, 1967); H. Harnisch, *Die Herrschaft Boitzenburg* (Weimar, 1968), ch. 4.
12. Detailed proof in H. Harnisch, 'Die agrarpolitischen Reformmaßnahmen der preußischen Staatsführung in dem Jahrzehnt vor 1806/7', *Jahrbuch für Wirtschaftsgeschichte* (1977/III), 129-53. On Silesia see J. Ziekursch, *100 Jahre schlesische Agrargeschichte*, 2nd edn (Breslau, 1927), pp. 227ff (1792–3), 244ff (1798).
13. For more detail on this problem see E. Klein, *Von der Reform zur Restauration. Finanzpolitik und Reformgesetzgebung des preußischen Staatskanzlers K. A. von Hardenberg* (Berlin, 1965).
14. Obenaus has drawn attention to one of the 'cost factors': the granting of representative organs and constitutional limits in order to strengthen the 'confidence' in 'state credit' required to manage the national debt; see H. Obenaus, 'Finanzkrise und Verfassungsgebung. Zu den sozialen Bedingungen des frühen deutschen Konstitutionalismus', in G. A. Ritter (ed.), *Gesellschaft, Parlament und Regierung* (Düsseldorf, 1974), pp. 57–75.
15. 'Denkschrift des Kammerpräsidenten Frhr. v. Vincke über "Zwecke und Mittel der preußischen Staatsverwaltung, welche dieselbe verfolgen, deren dieselbe sich bedienen durfte", vom 3. August 1808', in Scheel, *Das Reformministerium Stein*, vol. 3, pp. 704–17, at 706. On Vincke's later activities as *Oberpräsident* in Westphalia see S. Bahne, *Die Freiherren Ludwig und Georg Vincke im Vormärz* (Dortmund, 1975), pp. 39–64.
16. Nevertheless, Vincke was careful not to put the post-1815 road-building programme, of which he was a vigorous advocate, into the hands of private interests; see Bahne, *Vincke*, pp. 58ff.
17. On the conceptual changes see D. Schwab, 'Eigentum', in *Geschichtliche Grundbegriffe*, vol. 2 (Stuttgart, 1975), pp. 65–115, esp. 84ff and 94ff. On one of the stages in the reformulation of the legal concept of property see U. J. Heuer, *Allgemeines Landrecht und Klassenkampf. Die Auseinandersetzungen um die Prinzipien des Allgemeinen Landrechts als Ausdruck der Krise des Feudalsystems in Preußen* (Berlin, GDR, 1960), esp. pp. 126–33.
18. For the original texts see GS, pp. 79ff (Trade Tax Edict, 2 November 1810) and pp. 263ff (Trade Police Edict, 7 September 1811). A résumé of both pieces of legislation can be found in Huber, *Verfassungsgeschichte*, vol. 1, pp. 206–8. The 'Edict concerning the regulation of the situations of lords and peasants', GS, pp. 281ff; the 'Declaration' of 29 May 1816, GS, pp. 154ff. On the origins of the agrarian reform laws, see G. F. Knapp, *Die Bauernbefreiung und der Ursprung der Landarbeiter in den älteren Theilen Preußens*, 2nd edn, vol. 2 (Berlin, 1927), pp. 226ff, 353ff.

19. According to Altenstein, in his Riga Memorandum, 11 September 1807, to Hardenberg; cf. G. Winter (ed.), *Die Reorganisation des Preußischen Staates*, Part 1, pp. 364–566, at p. 439.
20. On the 'gross inaccuracies' in the October Edict, and the 'incompetence' of Hardenberg's and Altenstein's financial planning, see Schissler, *Preußische Agrargesellschaft*, pp. 117, 119ff. On the meagre extent to which these Edicts actually achieved any of their sought-for social effects see Knapp, *Bauernbefreiung*, vol. 2, pp. 353ff; also Klein, *Von der Reform zur Restauration*, p. 160. Koselleck, *Preußen*, is a key text on the entire complex; cf. too B. Vogel, 'Die Preußischen Reformen als Gegenstand und Problem der Forschung' in B. Vogel (ed.), *Preußische Reformen 1807–1820* (Königstein, Taunus, 1980), pp. 1–27. Vogel, correctly, argues for 'greater emphasis on the close link with the French revolution' (*ibid*., p. 16) as regards the initiatives for reform: in Prussia the issue was less one of a 'conservative' (B. Moore jr, *Social Origins*, p. 438.) as of a 'defensive modernisation'. And, given the narrowness of the reform group, Vogel suggests that the term 'bureaucratic revolution' is more apt than 'revolution from above' (*ibid*., p. 17).
21. E. F. Klein, *Freiheit und Eigentum, abgehandelt in acht Gesprächen über die Beschlüsse der Französischen Nationalversammlung* (Berlin, 1790), p. 41. A scrupulous and balanced interpretation is provided by G. Birtsch, 'Freiheit und Eigentum. Zur Erörterung von Verfassungsfragen in der deutschen Publizistik im Zeichen der Französischen Revolution', in R. Vierhaus (ed.), *Eigentum und Verfassung. Zur Eigentumsdiskussion im ausgehenden 18. Jh.* (Göttingen, 1972), pp. 179–92.
22. This expression was coined in 1799 by a Prussian Minister, von Struensee: the 'salutary revolution' would proceed in Prussia 'slowly, from above downwards'; see W. Sauer, 'Das Problem des deutschen Nationalstaates', in H.-U. Wehler (ed.), *Moderne deutsche Sozialgeschichte*, 2nd edn (Cologne, 1968), pp. 407–36, 544–50, at 418. Cf. Altenstein's Riga Memorandum in Winter, *Die Reorganisation des Preußischen Staates*, pp. 389ff, esp. p. 396. The state was 'to effect a revolution within itself such that the beneficial consequences of such a revolution can take place without the painful convulsions of a revolution which takes place by itself'.
23. *Allgemeines Landrecht für die Preußischen Staaten von 1794* (Berlin, 1970), p. 98, Teil 1, tit. 8, para. 13; cf. Heuer, *Allgemeines Landrecht*, pp. 128f.
24. Altenstein in Winter, *Die Reorganisation des Preußischen Staates*, pp. 433, 389.
25. Vogel seeks to show that, as a 'strategy of modernisation' pursued by a relatively small group of reforming ministerial officials, economic liberalisation was to a large extent a success: B. Vogel, 'Die Allgemeine Gewerbefreiheit als bürokratische Modernisierungsstrategie', in D. Stegmann and P.-C. Witt (eds.), *Industrielle Gesellschaft und politisches System*, (Bonn, 1978), p. 77.
26. See R. Braun, 'Zur Einwirkung sozio-kultureller Umweltbedingungen auf das Unternehmerpotential und das Unternehmerverhalten', in W. Fischer (ed.), *Wirtschafts- und sozialgeschichtliche Probleme der frühen Industrialisierung* (Berlin, 1968), pp. 247–84; F. Redlich, 'Frühindustrielle Unternehmer und ihre Probleme im Lichte ihrer Selbstzeugnisse', in *ibid*., pp. 339–412, 386–93.
27. On overall economic growth trends and trade cycles see K. Borchardt, 'Wirtschaftliches Wachstum und Wechsellagen 1800–1914', in H. Aubin and W. Zorn (eds.), *Handbuch der deutschen Wirtschafts- und Sozialgeschichte*, vol. 2 (Stuttgart, 1976), pp. 198–275. For a sectoral analysis see R. Spree, *Die Wachs-*

tumszyklen der deutschen Wirtschaft von 1840–1880, mit einem konjunkturstatistischen Anhang (Berlin, 1977), pp. 129ff: Schissler, *Preußische Agrargesellschaft*, esp. pp. 148ff and 153ff. On political conduct see principally H. Rosenberg, 'Die Pseudodemokratisierung der Rittergutsbesitzerklasse', in H. Rosenberg, *Probleme der deutschen Sozialgeschichte*. On industrial development see J. Kermann, *Die Manufakturen im Rheinland, 1750–1833* (Bonn, 1972); L. Baar, *Die Berliner Industrie in der Industriellen Revolution* (Berlin, GDR, 1966); O. Büsch, *Industrialisierung und Gewerbe im Raum Berlin/Brandenburg 1800–1850* (Berlin, 1971). On socio-cultural 'implementation' and motivation, see F. Zunkel, *Der Rheinisch-Westfälische Unternehmer, 1834–1879* (Cologne, 1962). On the minimal or absent link between 'capitalists' see Koselleck, *Preußen*, p. 327.

28. Knapp, *Bauernbefreiung*, vol. 1, pp. 184ff.
29. For numerous instances of this see Koselleck, *Preußen*, *passim*, esp. chs. 2–3.
30. See Koselleck's convincing interpretation, *ibid*., pp. 78ff.
31. Martiny has vividly depicted the social 'embourgeoisement' of estate ownership prior to 1806, accompanied and exacerbated by the 'excessive multiplication' of Junkers: F. Martiny, *Die Adelsfrage in Preußen vor 1806 als soziales und politisches Problem* (Stuttgart, 1938).
32. The Gendarmerie Edict of 30 June 1812 was suspended in March 1814 following massive objection, in particular from the Silesian Estates (*Stände*) and 'conclaves' of estate owners; see Koselleck, *Preußen*, pp. 203ff. On regional differences in estate-owner opposition see Schissler, *Preußische Agrargesellschaft*, pp. 123ff.
33. See Koselleck, *Preußen*, pp. 525f.
34. See references to payments and concessions by large parts of the provincial bureaucracy in Schissler, *Preußische Agrargesellschaft*, pp. 132ff. These reveal the limits of even such a celebrated reformer as von Schön (cf. Koselleck, *Preußen*, p. 370).
35. J. Hansen, *Preußen und Rheinland von 1815 bis 1915* (Bonn, 1918); see too K.-G. Faber, *Die Rheinlande zwischen Restauration und Revolution. Probleme der rheinischen Geschichte von 1814 bis 1848 im Spiegel der zeitgenössischen Publizistik* (Wiesbaden, 1966). The views of David Hansemann, an Aachen merchant, could be seen as typical of the rising bourgeoisie: see his published works, dealt with by Faber, and his unprinted or undelivered memoranda (e.g. to the King of Prussia, 31 December 1830 and of the late summer of 1840) in J. Hansen (ed.), *Rheinische Briefe und Akten zur Geschichte der politischen Bewegung 1830–1850*, vol. 1 (Essen, 1919), pp. 11ff; cf. too Koselleck, *Preußen*, pp. 574ff. On the positions and behaviour of the Rhenish bourgeoisie on the issue of penal reform in the period 1815–48, see D. Blasius, *Bürgerliche Gesellschaft und Kriminalität. Zur Sozialgeschichte Preußens im Vormärz* (Göttingen, 1976), pp. 115–26. The 'convergence' of bourgeois liberalism and particularistic *Stand* 'civil' interests amongst the Estates of East Prussia should not be overlooked in any consideration of the constitutional movement of the 1840s. This was quite certainly not based solely on the direction of the self-assured *Oberpräsident*, Theodor von Schön, who occupied the office until 1841, but principally on the fairly considerable degree of social 'embourgeoisement' of those large-scale landowners eligible for membership of the *Land* Diet; cf. Koselleck, *Preußen*, pp. 366, 369f. See too Schissler, *Preußische Agrargesellschaft*, pp. 161, 166 (although no detailed breakdown is provided).

However, anti-bureaucratic initiatives and groupings with constitutionalist aims were not confined to the rising Rhenish bourgeoisie or East Elbian *Stände*. Up until the mid 1820s the Lower Rhenish, and especially Westphalian, nobility of knightly origin – more precisely a small group around Stein – played the major role in the 'constitutional issue'; see A. H. von Wallthor, *Die landschaftliche Selbstverwaltung Westfalens in ihrer Entwicklung seit dem 18. Jahrhundert*, Part 1 (Münster, 1965); H. Lademacher, 'Der niederrheinische und westfälische Adel in der preußischen Verfassungsfrage', *Rheinische Vierteljahrsblätter*, 31 (1966–7), 442–54; cf. too R. K. Weitz, 'Der niederrheinische und westfälische Adel im ersten preußischen Verfassungskampf 1815–1823/24. Die verfassungs- und gesellschaftspolitischen Vorstellungen des Adelskreises um den Freiherrn v. Stein', Doctoral thesis (Bonn, 1970).

36. Blasius overestimates the degree of permeation of the ideal of 'acquiring property', formulated in the Edicts of 9 October 1807 and 14 September 1811, especially as a motive for 'illegal' acquisition, e.g. theft: Blasius, *Bürgerliche Gesellschaft und Kriminalität*, p. 51.
37. Klein, *Freiheit*, p. 159.
38. C. G. Svarez, *Vorträge über Recht und Staat*, ed. H. Conrad and G. Kleinheyer (Cologne and Opladen, 1960), p. 37.
39. Cf. the definition of 'property' in the Prussian Legal Code as disposition over the 'substance of a thing or of a right' (*Allgemeines Landrecht*, Teil 1, tit. 8, para 1).
40. 'Geschäftsinstruktion für die Regierungen, vom 17. Oktober 1817', GS 1817, pp. 248. Cf. H. Gräff *et al.* (eds.), *Ergänzungen und Erläuterungen der Preußischen Rechtsbücher*, vol. 4 (3rd edn, 1849), pp. 326ff.
41. Instruction, 12 October 1818, approved by Police Minister von Wittgenstein and quoted in H. Nollau, *Die Entwicklung der Kgl. Preußischen Polizei-Behörde zu Aachen 1818–1910* (Aachen, 1910), pp. 23f.
42. See 1817 Instruction, Article 7. This ranking can also be found in a proposal drawn up by a Chief Superintendent of Police (*Kriminalrat*), Brand, in a 'Concluding Remark' to a document on the municipal constitution in Königsberg, 24 August 1808: 'Since the safeguarding of property and of persons is the sole purpose of the state . . .', in Scheel, *Das Reformministerium Stein*, vol. 3, p. 791.
43. L. Krug, *Betrachtungen über den Nationalreichtum des preußischen Staates und über den Wohlstand seiner Bewohner*, Part 2 (Berlin, 1805), reprinted Aalen, 1970, p. 218. The following quote is from *ibid.*, p. 705; cf. *ibid.*, pp. 158ff, 706ff on 'luxury'.
44. Altenstein, in Winter, *Die Reorganisation des preußischen Staates*, pp. 449; cf. p. 435.
45. M. K. F. W. Grävell, *Über höhere, geheime und Sicherheitspolizei* (Sondershausen and Nordhausen, 1820), pp. 54, 62ff.
46. J. G. Hoffmann, *Das Verhältnis der Staatsgewalt zu den Vorstellungen ihrer Untergebenen* (Berlin, 1842), pp. 101f.
47. For instances from the reports of provincial court authorities see Blasius, *Bürgerliche Gesellschaft und Kriminalität*, p. 50.
48. Blasius, *Bürgerliche Gesellschaft und Kriminalität*, p. 47. Up until 1898, the peasantry received only 14 per cent, or 2.4 million *Morgen* (1 *Morgen*=*c.* 0.75 acre), of the total of 17 million *Morgen* detached from the commons; it should be noted, however, that this process of separation did not begin immediately after the reform period, and, in the case of smallholders, until the second half of the nineteenth century; see D. Saalfeld, 'Zur Frage des bäuerlichen Landverlustes im Zusammenhang mit den preußischen Agrarreformen', *Zeitschrift*

für Agrargeschichte und Agrarsoziologie, 11 (1963), 163–71, at 166 and 170.

49. On the genesis of pauperism see P. Kriedte in P. Kriedte, H. Medick and J. Schlumbohm, *Industrialisation before Industrialisation* (Cambridge 1981), p. 310ff.
50. Von Lüttwitz, a *Regierungspräsident*, wasted little time in advocating disciplinary measures to combat poverty, for example: Frhr. von Lüttwitz, *Über Verarmung, Armengesetze, Armen-Anstalten und ins Besondere über Armen-Colonien mit vorzüglicher Rücksicht auf Preußen* (Breslau, 1834), esp. pp. 65f, 73f. On the proposal to concentrate the unemployed in 'work detachments' as 'forced labourers', deprived of the right to live with their families, see H. Graf Dohna, *Die freien Arbeiter im preußischen Staate* (Leipzig, 1847), pp. 110–15.
51. See Blasius, *Bürgerliche Gesellschaft und Kriminalität*, pp. 44f.
52. See Mooser, *Ländliche Klassengesellschaft*, p. 155. In 1839, 28 per cent of the families in the county of Paderborn were spinners.
53. See the biographical entry on Klemens Frhr. von Wolff gen. Metternich (II) in D. Wegmann, *Die leitenden staatlichen Verwaltungsbeamten* (Münster, 1969), p. 349. Wolff was appointed *Landrat* in 1834 at the age of 31; he was a Catholic, an estate owner, but had passed through the relevant examinations and stages for a career in the administration. His father was *Landrat* in the neighbouring county of Höxter until 1845. (On the extremely positive assessment of Wolff-Metternich by the District Government in Minden, see StAMS Oberpräs., no. 1364^{I}, fols. 133ff.)
54. Wilhelm von Hiddessen (II), also a Catholic landowner. Born in 1797 he was six years older than Wolff; see Wegmann, *Die leitenden Verwaltungsbeamten*, p. 285. His father was his predecessor in office; see StAMS Oberpräs., no. 1364^{I}, fols. 133ff.
55. Report 23 February 1836, StADT Reg. Minden I P, no. 960.
56. One of the rare counter-examples of a detailed and non-moralistic study of living and working conditions, incomes and indebtedness is represented by a report 'On the conditions of the working classes in the countryside', drafted by the *Landrat* in Altena, von Holtzbrinck, and submitted to the District Government in Arnsberg on 30 October 1848: StAMS Reg. Arnsberg I, no. 1270, fols. 8–11.
57. This was despite the fact that accurate information was available to the authorities, and had already been intensively discussed in a conference of administrative and judicial officials, merchants and clerics from the affected countries, held on 13 March 1832, see note 65 below. Vincke had made a similar effort in 1820, albeit a less traumatic year for the weavers and spinners; see StADT Reg. Minden I S, no. 3.
58. See Mooser, *Ländliche Klassengesellschaft*, pp. 247, 266ff.
59. One indicator of the difficulties, but also of the complacency and ignorance, of local officials was the relief expressed by the senior local offical in Delbrück, Prasso, in a report to the *Landrat* in Paderborn, von Spiegel: he was pleased at not having to submit figures on the numbers and trade situation of spinners and weavers as he was 'utterly lacking' in such information (StAMS Oberpräs., no. 370, fol. 19r).
60. StAMS Oberpräs., no. 370, fols. 61v, 63r, 65v. The data on population and its economic position clearly show that Paderborn had, relative to other counties, the lowest share of the core group of yarn-spinners, the *Heuerlinge* (in 1832, *c.* 21 per cent of the population, compared with 60 per cent in Halle, Bielefeld and Bünde). Importantly, these tables, based on figures supplied by the *Landräte*, also

provide data on annual average incomes and requirements for *Heuerling* families. The variations in family income during the course of the family life-cycle were crucial in determining disposable income: see the detailed study of Oberlausitz in Saxony in F. Schmidt, *Untersuchungen über Bevölkerung*, (Leipzig, 1836) pp. 298f.

61. On the maximisation of family labour, see Medick, in Kriedte, Medick, Schlumbohm, *Industrialisation*, p. 125.
62. This proposal came from a long-serving *Landrat* (in office since 1817), Franz von Borries, a Junker, a Protestant with administrative training; see Wegmann, *Die leitenden Versaltungsbeamten*, p. 259, no. 27. Von Borries had already made a detailed submission of the plan on 18 December 1831, which Vincke had immediately forwarded to Berlin. The 'net loss' to the state was put at 3,600 Thaler; this would have been sufficient to support 1,200 families for 6–8 months. The rejection from the Interior Minister von Schuckmann – who had obtained the agreement of the King – was received as early as 1 January 1832. The proposal was deemed 'inappropriate', since it would have implied the purchase of goods 'for which there was no demand' which would merely 'perpetuate the present situation' (StAMS Oberpräs., no. 370, fols. 38–44, 45f).
63. See the unhurried, brief – almost brusque – reply from the Minister of the Interior, 6 December 1832. Factory owners in Barmen and Elberfeld were to be called on to place the working of their thread in Eastern Westphalia (in Prussia) rather than Eichsfeld (in Hanover); but there was no need to raise quality, as this would merely encourage the perpetuation of what he regarded as an anyway doomed industry. At the same time *Heuerling* tenants should be given the opportunity to buy small plots when common land was divided; this, and the establishment of village handicrafts, could receive financial support from the Provincial Assistance Fund (StAMS Oberpräs., no. 370, fols. 78f).
64. Report, 21 May 1838, StADT Reg. Minden Präs., no. 714/1.
65. Cf. the note in the conference minutes, 13 March 1832, that spinning and weaving 'accords more or less exclusive or full-time labour to different degrees in the counties and individual parishes' (StAMS Oberpräs., no. 370, fol. 62r).
66. StADT Reg. Minden Präs., no. 714/1, 5 May 1838.
67. H. A. Fregier, *Über die gefährlichen Classen der Bevölkerung und die Mittel sie zu bessern* (Koblenz, 1840), p. 199.
68. David Hansemann in a memorandum which was despatched to the King, 31 December 1830 in J. Hansen (ed.), *Rheinische Briefe und Akten*, vol. 1 (Essen, 1919), p. 13.
69. Compare the argument employed by the *Regierungsräte* in Minden with that of Hansemann (according to an unsent memorandum of August/September 1840) cited in Hansen, *Rheinische Briefe*, vol. 1, p. 221, section 32.1; 'Machinery. On the one hand it multiplies the number of destitute persons who live merely from day to day. On the other, it reduces the price of manufactures and the evident differences between those of fine and those of lesser quality, such that clothing or external appearance promotes the equalisation or convergence of social ranks.' However, Hansemann was clearly more sceptical about these political consequences than the *Regierungsräte*: this 'irrefutable' development provided one of the central causes of the 'development and strengthening of the democratic element, together with its dangers'.
70. The 1817 Government Instruction emphasised the 'sense of honour' of officials as the primary regulator of their obedience and dutiful conduct. Superiors were to 'devote particular attention to this feeling', and were to know 'how to awaken

and stimulate it'. Punishments were to be imposed only 'if the prime method has been tried in vain, or if malevolent intent is apparent': 'Instruktion zur Geschäftsführung der Regierungen vom 23. Oktober 1817', GS 1817, Article 38, pp. 272f. This Instruction is also reprinted in full in J. G. Schoefert, *Der preußische Beamte oder die Kenntnis der preußischen Gesetze und Verordnungen über die Befähigung der höheren und niedern Verwaltungs-, Justiz-, Bau-, und Eisenbahnbeamten*, 2nd edn (Glogau, 1852), pp. 85f. B. Wunder, *Privilegierung und Disziplinierung. Die Entstehung des Berufsbeamtentums in Bayern und Württemberg (1780–1825)* (Munich and Vienna, 1978), pp. 227–30, stresses the disciplinary, but hardly identity-forming, aspect of 'official honour' in the case of constitutional officialdom in Bavaria. Koselleck regards the 'state rank ethos, which clung to aristocratic forms' merely 'from above', that is, as functional for the 'fusion' of the nobility and 'upper bourgeoisie' within senior officialdom, as he shows using recruitment data from the 1820s: Koselleck, *Preußen*, p. 245. His reference to the comparatively spectacular incident in the District Government of Cologne, when, in 1816, members of the government college excluded a bourgeois member for refusing to fight an (illegal!) duel, illustrates the extent to which accommodation to Junker-aristocratic standards could go; the Ministers of the Interior and Justice, Schuckmann and Bülow, dared not interfere (Koselleck, *Preußen*, p. 101, note 84).

As with many other issues, Weber provides the *locus classicus*; however, his comments on 'social honour' adapted to officialdom are not especially fruitful. He notes, 'the official always strives and usually enjoys a distinct, elevated "social" [*ständische*] esteem vis-à-vis the governed' (from Max Weber, *Essays in Sociology*, ed. H. H. Gerth and C. Wright Mills (Oxford, 1946), p. 197).

Hintze's outline of the *Beamtenstand* tends to be somewhat vague on this question. Unfortunately, he does not pursue his own suggestion that the 'character of domination in our state' could also be seen in the conduct of its officials: O. Hintze, 'Der Beamtenstand' in Hintze, *Soziologie und Geschichte*, *Gesamte Abhandlungen*, vol. 1, (Göttingen, 1964), ed. G. Oestreich, pp. 66–125, at 76f.

71. APW Rej. Op. Pr. B., no. 736, fols. 68ff.
72. *Ibid.*, fol. 15. Ewald entered the administration in 1805 at the age of 20.
73. *Ibid.*, fols. 74–90. Pückler was very prolific. The files consulted here contain numerous notes in his own hand, always very detailed and filling several sides each.
74. Pückler was the lord of the manor of Schedlau and Groditz, two estates lying 10 and 7 kilometers respectively west of Oppeln. The projected line of rail ran 3 kilometers north of the two villages. Pückler also owned an iron works; see H. Wutzmer, 'Die Herkunft der industriellen Bourgeoisie Preußens in den vierziger Jahren des 19. Jahrhunderts', in H. Mottek *et al.*, *Studien zur Geschichte der industriellen Revolution in Deutschland* (Berlin, GDR, 1960), pp. 145–63, at 155.
75. Also relevant to the politics of the *Regierungspräsidium* was the fact that an *Assessor*, von Seydel, who was a member of the District Government, joined the Board of Directors of the Upper Silesian Railway Company in 1843; see APW Rej. Op. Pr. B., no. 736, fol. 221. Such a situation was by no means unique to Silesia, as the involvement of *Regierungsräte* Ritz and Steffens from Cologne in the Rhenish Railway Company shows: StAMS Oberpräs., no. 1140, fol. 36.
76. A proven case of false reporting of the facts – which could have earned either Pückler or Ewald a ministerial reprimand – had previously earned a rebuke for

having undermined 'the credibility of government'; see Ministry of the Interior to *Regierungsrat* Benda, District Government of Oppeln, 1 January 1829, APW Rej. Op. Pr. B., no. 625, fols. 52ff.

77. Order, 11 May 1843, APW Rej. Op. Pr. B., no. 736, fols. 167–72.
78. *Ibid.*, fols. 169r ff.
79. On the upswing in this branch after 1842 cf. R. Spree, *Die Wachstumszyklen der deutschen Wirtschaft* (Berlin, 1977), pp. 178ff, 184f. For the officials in Oppeln, it was especially disturbing that one of the technically most advanced iron smelters, the Bethlen-Falva-Hütte, built as recently as 1832, was lying idle.
80. Ewald to Pückler, 25 May 1843; Pückler's marginalia, 13 June 1843, APW Rej. Op. Pr. B., no. 736, fols. 173–9.
81. Import duties were relatively low in the external tariff set in 1818 and 1821; pig iron was entirely free of tariff since it was regarded as a vital raw material. The 1839 customs union (*Zollverein*) continued this practice. However, the slump in late 1842 and the increased supply of cheap goods from England and Scotland led to the introduction of a tariff on pig iron in 1844, followed in 1845 by the raising of duties on other goods; see *Handwörterbuch der Staatswissenschaften*, vol. 3 (Jena, 1890), p. 682.
82. On the figures, see APW Rej. Op. Pr. B., no. 736, fols. 176f; between 1840 and 1843 there were *c.* 450–500 applications for passports from various groups of workers each spring, of which *c.* 80 per cent were building workers and day-labourers rather than smiths or smelters, with regional concentrations in the Rosenberg and Ratibor government districts.
83. There are no precise data on workers in the smelters. Schofer makes reference to the decline in real wages in the first half of the nineteenth century, and the small number of workers in each enterprise. He also notes that the majority were 'Poles' (although it is unclear whether he is referring to Polish-speaking Prussian subjects or subjects of the Austrian or Russian empires): L. Schofer, *The Formation of a Modern Labor Force. Upper Silesia 1865–1914* (Berkeley, 1975), pp. 63f. Market prices in Breslau might also give some idea of economic conditions for workers: for rye and potatoes they fell by *c.* 15 per cent between 1840 and 1843. However, such figures do not take into account local prices some 100–150 kilometres south east of Breslau, nor the evident drastic cuts in money wages; see H. Henning, 'Preußische Sozialpolitik im Vormärz', *Vierteljahrschrift für Sozial- und Wirtschaftsgeschichte*, 52 (1965), 485–539, at 539.
84. APW Rej. Op. Pr. B., no. 736, fol. 170r.
85. The fact that the commitment of most officials to the interests of the 'proprietors' was not accompanied by any corresponding knowledge of industry or economic theory was later the subject of much complaint by the *Assessor/Regierungsrat* dealing with tariff policy in the Ministry of Finance, and after 1844 in the Office of Trade, R. von Delbrück: see his *Lebenserinnerungen*, vol. 1 (Leipzig, 1905), p. 144. In the period prior to 1848 the only exceptions he noted were the *Oberpräsident* in Silesia (von Merckel) and in Westphalia (von Vincke), and the competent *Regierungsräte* in Liegnitz and Düsseldorf (von Minutoli and Quentin). Cf. too A. Zimmermann, *Blüthe und Verfall des Leinengewerbes in Schlesien* (Breslau, 1885), pp. 336ff, 374ff (on Minutoli), 34ff (on Merckel). Kaelbe shows for Berlin that the 'state administration' stopped insisting that its officials 'display specialised knowledge for all economic spheres' after the 1820s: H. Kaelble, *Berliner Unternehmer während der frühen Industrialisierung* (Berlin and New York, 1972), p. 255. In 1852 the *Regierungspräsident* in Düsseldorf, one of the most intensively industrialised Government

Districts, was concerned enough to report to the Ministry of the Interior that 'the shortage of senior officals for the administering of industrial matters in the Royal District Governments with an accurate knowledge of machinery and industry becomes increasingly evident with the passage of time': von Massenbach, 21/22 September 1852, HStAD Reg. Düsseldorf Präs., no. 134, fol. 115v.

86. Nevertheless, Delbrück spoke of the 'pride' of the administration at their creation, the *Zollverein*: Delbrück, *Lebenserinnerungen*, vol. 1, p. 183.
87. See C. Garve for a detailed and highly critical description of lord–peasant relations in the late eighteenth century: *Über den Charakter der Bauern und ihr Verhältnis gegen die Gutsherrn und gegen die Regierung* (Breslau, 1786–96), reprinted in C. Garve, *Popularphilosophische Schriften*, vol. 2 (Stuttgart, 1974), ed. K. Wölfel, pp. 799–1026, 889.
88. On Minutoli's unremitting efforts see Zimmermann, *Blüthe und Verfall des Leinengewerbes*, pp. 374ff, and Minutoli's own description on the preface to the edition of his memoranda and reports: A. von Minutoli, *Die Lage der Weber und Spinner im schlesischen Gebirge und die Maßregeln der preußischen Staatsregierung zur Verbesserung ihrer Lage* (Berlin, 1851), esp. pp. 5ff.
89. See L. Krug, *Abriß der Staatsökonomie* (Berlin, 1808), pp. 241ff.
90. On the perceptions and interpretations of regional and local officials, see the report by an *Assessor*, Schneer: A. Schneer, *Über die Zustände der arbeitenden Klassen in Breslau* (Berlin, 1845): security was the prime concern. On the problems of the administration of the Poor Law (*Armenpolizei*) see Koselleck, *Preußen*, pp. 631–4.
91. These were the terms used by the relevant ministers in 1844 to specify the behaviour expected of senior officials and subordinates; the occasion was Ewald's attack on a *Regierungsrat*, Bauer; 'Erlaß vom 11. Juni 1844), APW Rej. Op. Pr. B., no. 736, fol. 221r.
92. Cf. the exemplary case of *Regierungsrat* Count Fermemont, whose 'civil and official honour' was regarded as having been compromised 'to the highest degree' because he had been transferred from Danzig to Oppeln with debts amounting to several hundred Thalers in 1819 and in 1822 had owed the Louisen-Verein, under the governorship of the Minister of Finance, the sum of 200 Thalers for over five years. For the reporting head of the Department I in Oppeln, Commissary President von Schroetter, the critical issue was that Fermemont was actually paid only half his salary (1,200 Thalers per annum) and was therefore exposed to the danger of being unable 'to subsist on such a diminished salary in the manner befitting his rank, and the needs of his family'. He would simply run into further debt 'through which he would lose respect amongst his colleagues and subordinates and the public, where we must regrettably acknowledge that his chaotic circumstances are already only too well-known and that the matters under consideration here cannot be concealed' (the latter remark referred to an accusation of deception of which Fermemont was found not guilty in February 1842 on grounds of insufficient evidence; he was, however, compelled to pay costs): APW Rej. Op. Pr. B., no. 742, fols. 14, 17f (Order of the Interior Ministry, 20 September 1822, Schroetter's report, 19 November 1822); APW Rej. Op. Pr. B., no. 743, fol. 44. A few months previously Fermemont had also 'compromised his superior authority and the civil service' during a visit by Tsar Alexander I. Fermemont had accompanied the welcoming delegation as far as the border and – this was the *point d'honneur* – sought permission to do so from the Commanding General instead of civilian superiors,

impermissible behaviour as far as the relevant Instructions were concerned. This had represented a 'compromising of the civil service', as the Vice-President in Breslau had furiously reprimanded him on the order of von Merckel, the province's *Oberpräsident*, adding that the entire District Government was affected.

The District Government in Oppeln of necessity had to protect their member since the intervention of the *Oberpräsident* could be seen as interference in 'detail administration' and hence beyond his powers. And, as Schroetter wrote to the *Vice-President* Richter, on 13 September 1822, and directly to the Minister of the Interior on 9 October, the *Oberpräsident*'s action also represented 'unfair treatment and an undeserved reproof' for a 'most respectable colleague': APW Rej. Op. Br., no. 743, fols. 81–4. This incident, or rather the solidarity forced from Fermemont's fellow *Räte*, was given additional spice by the fact that he had also accepted a gold watch from the Tsar which, contrary to regulations, he had not declared. The rumour had spread as far as the Minister of the Interior that Fermemont had even proposed the gift himself (*ibid*., fols. 85–8): he left office, without a pension, in 1827. A final report to the Ministry from the new *Präsident*, von Hippel, noted that Fermemont not only possessed 'capabilities and much propriety, but had also performed excellent work at times' (APW Rej. Op. Pr. B., no. 743, fol. 169, 3 January 1827). However, Hippel also recorded his relief at the manner of Fermemont's departure, and his positive words should not therefore be taken as proof that he took a viewpoint radically different from that of his predecessor.

93. APW Rej. Op. Pr. B., no. 736, fols. 44f, 24 July 1839.
94. See Pückler's handwritten memo, 6 September 1841, 'Notizen über die Geschäftsführung des Oberregierungsrates Ewald', *ibid*., fols. 140–2.
95. Decree, 11 June 1844, *ibid*., fols. 220f.
96. Ewald became a Director (*Dirigent*) fairly late in his career. In 1843, for example, the Director of the Interior Department in Trier, *Oberregierungsrat* Birck, had already been in an office for seven and a half years which he had acquired at the age of 31, after ten years in the service (StAK 442, no. 3403, fols. 3ff).
97. With an annual salary of 2,200 Thalers, Ewald was the highest-paid *Regierungsrat* in Oppeln. The Director of Department II, *Oberregierungsrat* Kieschke, received 1,900 Thalers, for example; he was five years younger than Ewald and had incidentally been a member of Ewald's department in Königsberg until 1837. When Ewald assumed his post in Oppeln Kieschke had been awarded the unusually high decoration of Order of the Red Eagle, 2nd class, with oak leaves. On Kieschke see APW Rej. Op. Pr. B., no. 858 (he had 'no property', 2 children also without means in 1837, and with the exception of 1838–41 was given an annual *ex gratia* payment after 1837 of 150 Thalers as an expression of 'satisfaction' with his conduct). On Ewald see StAK 442, no. 340, fol. 15, and APW Rej. Op. Pr. B., no. 735, which reveal Ewald's persistent efforts to obtain permanent 'remuneration' as Director of a Department. In his view he had 'sacrificed enough nights' without due recompense, and *Räte* in corresponding positions in the Commission of Audit or judiciary had been receiving their due salaries for some considerable time (18 December 1837, fol. 38). On 8 January 1838 the provincial *Oberpräsident* von Schön submitted a request on Ewald's behalf to the Minister of the Interior (fols. 59f) which was overtaken by Ewald's transfer: on Ewald's work in Königsberg see H.-J. Belke, *Die preußische Regierung zu Königsberg, 1808–1850* (Cologne and Berlin, 1976), pp. 48f, 103. Ewald clearly campaigned a good deal on his own behalf, and was not easy to get on with (see his frictions with the *Stadtbaurat* Eichholz

in Königsberg). In addition to the Order of the Red Eagle, 4th class, Ewald had also been decorated with the Iron Cross, 2nd class, in the 1813–15 war (as was Kieschke) and received the 1813–14 campaign medal. (See Wegmann, *Die leitenden Verwaltungsbeamten*, pp. 153ff on the 'standards' used to award decorations.) On the general environment within the District Government in Oppeln, it should be added that Ewald's predecessor, *Oberregierungsrat* von Schroetter, had made great play of celebrating his fifty years in service in August 1837. Schroetter's circumstances also indicate what the term 'means' concealed: according to his personnel file, he had assets of some 80–100,000 Thalers; see APW Rej. Op. Pr. B., no. 1088; on the anniversary no. 1089.

98. Freiherr vom Stein, letter to Freiherr von Spiegel-Desenberg, Frankfurt, 2 March 1822 in Frhr. vom Stein, *Briefe und amtliche Schriften*, vol. 6 (Stuttgart, 1965), p. 485. Cf. Hansemann's unsent memorandum of August/September 1840, Section 15.4: 'The practical separation of officials from those they administer means that it is difficult for the former to understand and determine matters with any practical understanding', in Hansen, *Rheinische Briefe*, vol. 1, p. 208.
99. C. Garve, *Abhandlung über die menschlichen Pflichten*, 4th edn (Breslau, 1792), p. 179. On Garve's empirical interests, see his studies of the peasantry: 'Über den Charakter der Bauern'.

4 The organs of coercion at work

1. This and the quotation in the following sentence are taken from a letter from Duke Carl to his brother Georg, 16 April 1833, BA, Briefsammlung Strelitz, no. 253, pp. 235f. Cf. for a more comprehensive discussion of the relationship between the military and the civil administration: A. Lüdtke, ' "Wehrhafte Nation" und "innere Wohlfahrt": Zur militärischen Mobilisierbarkeit der bürgerlichen Gesellschaft. Konflikt und Konsens zwischen Militär und ziviler Administration in Preußen, 1815–1860', *Militärgeschichtliche Mitteilungen*, 30 (1981), issue 2, 7–56.
2. Undated note by the Duke, evidently in the early 1830s, BA, Briefsammlung Strelitz, no. 952, pp. 416–505, at 446 and 437.
3. L. von Rönne, *Das Staatsrecht der Preußischen Monarchie*, Part 1, vol. 2 (Leipzig, 1870), p. 108.
4. H. A. Fregier, *Über die gefährlichen Classen* (Koblenz, 1840), p. 199.
5. To quote the *Landrat* of Meschede, Pilgrim, in a memo to the *Regierungspräsidium*, 25 February 1821, StAMS, Reg. Arnsberg I, no. 1466.
6. Article 11 of the Order of 23 October 1817 (in connection with Article 48 of the Verordnung, 26 December 1808) in GS 1817, pp. 354ff (cf. Appendix 5). For a detailed discussion of police 'powers' see T. Foerstemann, *Prinzipien des Preußisches Polizeirechts* (Berlin, 1869).
7. H. Gräff, L. von Rönne, H. Simon (eds.), *Ergänzungen und Erläuterungen*, 3rd edn, vol. 5, p. 318.
8. See Circular (*Runderlaß*) from the Arnsberg District Government, 5 March 1838, StAMS, Krs. Hagen, LRA no. 117.
9. See C. G. Svarez, *Vorträge über Recht und Staat* (Cologne and Opladen, 1960), p. 41.
10. See Rönne, *Staatsrecht*, pp. 108f.
11. Taken from the report of *Landrat* Pilgrim, 25 February 1831, StAMS, Reg. Arnsberg I, no. 1466.

12. On the political police in general see the outline in E. R. Huber, 'Zur Geschichte der politischen Polizei im 19 Jhdt', in E. R. Huber (ed.) *Nationalstaat und Verfassungsstaat* (Stuttgart, 1965), pp. 144–67. On the 'persecution of demagogues' see E. Büssem, *Die Karlsbader Beschlüsse von 1819* (Hildesheim, 1974), pp. 452ff; E. Weber, *Die Mainzer Zentraluntersuchungskommission* (Karlsruhe, 1970); W. Siemann, 'Die Protokolle der Mainzer Untersuchungskommission von 1819 bis 1828', in F. Quarthal and W. Setzler (eds.), *Stadtverfassung–Verfassungsstaat–Pressepolitik*, Festschrift E. Naujoks (Sigmaringen, 1980), pp. 301–17. On the sometimes considerable differences in the perception of this task amongst senior officials see the comprehensive edition of the reports of E. T. A. Hoffmann, who became a member of the Prussian *Immediat Untersuchungs-Kommission* in 1819, Hoffmann, *Juristische Arbeiten*, ed. F. Schnapp (Munich, 1973). On Prince Wittgenstein, see H. Branig, *Fürst Wittgenstein. Ein preußischer Staatsmann der Restaurationszeit* (Cologne and Vienna, 1981), esp. pp. 101ff: the quote is taken from p. 114 (October 1818). On the *Bundeszentralbehörde* in Frankfurt am Main (1833–42) see W. Kowalski (ed.), *Vom kleinbürgerlichen Demokratismus zum Kommunismus* (Vaduz, 1978).
13. Fregier, *Über die gefährlichen Classen*, p. 19. Cf. the drastic sharpening of provisions in the Legal Code for the protection of property under the impact of the movements of the 1790s; see too the Regulation and Instruction 'on account of punishment and thefts' directed in particular against 'common crimes' against property, 26 February 1799, NCC 10, Spalte 2235ff.
14. See the statements by the director of the Office of Statistics, J. G. Hoffmann, *Das Verhältnis der Staatsgewalt zu den Vorstellungen ihrer Untergebenen* (Berlin, 1842), p. 102.
15. J. Lasker, *Das Auge der Polizei. Aus dem Leben Berlins* (Berlin, 1844), p. 53.
16. E. Dronke, *Berlin*, 2nd edn (Darmstadt and Neuwied, 1974), p. 293.
17. See the report of the head of the *Bürgergarde*, 2 September 1830, HistA Köln 400, I-9D, no. 10, pp. 42–5.
18. H. Ostermann, *Die gesamte Polizei-, Militär-, Steuer-, und Gemeindeverwaltung in den Kgl. Preuß. Staaten*, Part 1 (Coesfeld, 1836), p. 35, lists 'Gendarmes, police sergeants, police constables (*Polizei-Diener*), night-watchmen . . . and special night watches and night patrols'. More precise terms, corresponding with those used by the ministeries, are listed by Rönne, *Staatsrecht*, Part 2, vol. 2, p. 110: 'Police commissaries, inspectors, sergeants and constables'.
19. StAMS, Reg. Münster, no. 318, 6 April 1840, fol. 162r.
20. In the towns police authority lay with the crown or state: their authority was then exercised 'in accordance with their commission' by the municipal executive (*Magistrat*) or Mayor. In rural areas in the 'old provinces' (Posen, East and West Prussia, etc.) police powers were 'granted' to the seigneurial lords, the *Junker*, under the supervision of the *Landräte*. The *Land* Burgomasters were responsible for police administration in the Rhineland; cf. L. von Rönne, *Die preußischen Städteordnungen*, (Breslau, 1840), pp. 195ff; M. Bär, *Die Behördenverfassung der Rheinprovinz seit 1815* (Bonn, 1919), pp. 323ff; L. von Rönne and H. Simon, *Das Polizeiwesen des Preußischen Staates* (Breslau, 1840–1), vol. 2, pp. 490ff; see too H. Heffter, *Die deutsche Selbstverwaltung im 19. Jhdt* (Stuttgart, 1950), pp. 314ff., 330ff.
21. On appointment of officers: KA 18 (1834), pp. 126f. On incomes cf. the example cited in StAMS, Krs. Hagen, LRA, no. 117; cf. HStAD, Reg. Düsseldorf, no. 8797, 10 March 1834; see too C. W. Zimmermann, *Die Diebe in Berlin*

(Berlin, 1847), p. 393. On the wages of journeymen and day-labourers see W. Abel, *Massenarmut und Hungerkrisen* (Hamburg and Berlin, 1974), pp. 373ff.

22. StAMS, Krs. Iserlohn, LRA no. 146, 28 April 1854. On personal circumstances and biographies cf. StadtA IS, K 5.
23. L. Hoffmann, 'Vorbericht', *Polizei-Archiv für Preußen*, 1 (1817), 2.
24. According to the local government constitution (*Kommunalverfassung*), municipalities and local authorities were responsible for the costs of policing 'as required to do so' by the appropriate member of the *Magistrat*. The law of 11 March 1850 increased the burden on local authorities by additionally encumbering them with the material costs of the state police, as applied prior to the 1820 Tax Code; cf. Rönne, *Staatsrecht*, p. 348, notes 1 and 2. Exact figures are available only for individual authorities; nevertheless, Benzenberg did manage to compile a total for the Government District of Düsseldorf; Benzenberg, *Die Gemeinde-Ausgaben der Städte Düsseldorf*, 2nd edn (Bonn, 1835), p. 9.
25. Hoffmann, 'Vorbericht', p. 2.
26. Cf. *Landrat* von Bolschwingh, Neuss, 10 March 1834, HStAD, Reg. Düss., no. 8797; many instances can be found for the District Government in Münster in the 1830s: StAMS, Reg. Münster, no. 318, *passim*.
27. Circular from the District Government, Arnsberg, 11 June 1838, StadtA IS, K 12.
28. Report of the Mayor, 28 December 1923, StadtA IS, K 6; for the permission of the *Landrat*, 24 January 1824, *ibid.*
29. Instructions of 8 August 1843, StadtA IS, K 5.
30. Order of Mayor Franz, 1 July 1839, StadtA IS, K 5.
31. *Ibid.*
32. Order of Mayor Franz, 2 May 1845, *ibid.*
33. Order of 27 February 1834, StadtA TR, no. 400.
34. Duty Instructions for the Inspector of Police, Minden, 2 January 1831, StadtA IS, K 9.
35. Hoffmann, 'Vorbericht', p. 2.
36. Report of Mayor Mitsdörffer, Schwelm, 27 April 1818, StadtA DO, LRA DO, 246/2.
37. StAMS, Krs. Iserlohn, LRA no. 141. The expression 'insubordination towards an officer' offered every conceivable legal and normative protection for an officer's actions: cf. C. F. Koch, *Allgemeines Landrecht für die preußischen Staaten. Kommentar mit Anmerkungen*, Part 2, vol. 2 (Berlin, 1854), pp. 960ff.
38. Administrative Report of the District Government in Königsberg, 1827, issued 21 July 1828, GStA/PK, Rep. 2[I], tit. 40, no. 10, vol. 2, fol. 277.
39. Report by Constables Knieper and Krüger, 9 December 1845, StadtA IS, K 36.
40. StAMS, Krs. Hagen, LRA, no. 117; there were several cases in 1836.
41. StAK 403, no. 2345, Report of 24 September 1839, p. 568.
42. Stadtarchiv Saarlouis, XII 369, memo from the Commander to the Mayor, 29 March 1816.
43. StadtA AC, OB 16/1; 18/2. On the toils and ineffectiveness of the civilian militias and watches see HStAD, Polizei-Präsidium Aachen, no. 7I and 7II, the *Bürgermiliz* and *Bürgerwache*, 1819–24, 1825. Up until 1819, members of the *Landsturm* were still called out for watch duties as auxiliaries or stand-ins in some parts of Westphalia and the Rhenish Government District of Düsseldorf: cf. StADT, Reg. Minden IC, no. 80, and file no. 792.
44. The only towns with an uninterrupted record of state administration of the police were Cologne, Aachen, Magdeburg, Posen, Stettin, Breslau, Potsdam,

Königsberg, Danzig and – partly in connection with national government matters – Berlin; apart from Cologne and Aachen, all were seats of court and provincial capitals (of which only the smallest, Münster and Koblenz, were left out). By 1855 a further twenty-five had been added, although this was often merely for a few years, e.g. Krefeld, Trier, Elberfeld-Barmen, Düsseldorf, Wesel and Koblenz: see Bär, *Die Behördenverfassung der Rheinprovinz* pp. 325ff.

45. See HistA Köln, 400, I-9D, no. 10.
46. ZStA II, Rep. 77, 11 Lit C, 67, fol. 47. I am especially grateful to Dr Dieter Dowe who offered me access to his microfilms of the respective files in ZstA II.
47. Report, 2 February 1844; ZStA II, Rep. 77, tit. 343 A, no. 32, fol. 17v.
48. On the organisation and powers of the Gendarmerie, which was instituted in 1812 but substantially reduced after 1820, see Rönne and Simon, *Polizeiwesen*, vol. 1, pp. 12–80. For an introduction to the situation in the Rhine Provinces see Bär, *Behördenverfassung*, pp. 473ff. In 1820 the Gendarmerie were reduced from *c.* 9,000 to 1,336 men (excluding officers); cf. Koselleck, *Preußen*, pp. 460f.
49. StAK 441, no. 17311, Circular issued by the Ministry of the Interior, 14 May 1851.
50. StAK 403, no. 2435, 7 July 1839, p. 553; 15 August 1839, p. 562, both reports drafted by Spiegel.
51. StAK 403, no. 2345, 24 April 1839, p. 524.
52. Department of the Interior (drafted by *Regierungsrat* Jacobi), 13 April 1853, to the Minster of the Interior, StAMS, Reg. Arnsberg 1, no. 1468. (Emphasis in original.)
53. On *Gesinde* see Rönne and Simon, *Polizeiwesen*, vol. 1, pp. 404ff. In the Rhine Provinces a comparably strict Servants Ordinance was not issued until 19 August 1844 (GS, pp. 410ff); on the real situation see the imaginary letters, drafted by Moses Heß, of a maidservant in his 'Gesellschaftsspiegel' 1845–6 (Issue 1, pp. 18ff; Issue 9, pp. 80ff; Issue 10, pp. 114ff). These provisions remained in force in essence until 1918; the right to inflict punishment was abandoned in the 1899 Civil Code, although often it was continued in practice.
54. On 'beggars, vagabonds and rogues' see Rönne and Simon, *Polizeiwesen*, vol. 1, pp. 521ff; cf. too the 'Law on the Punishment of Vagrants, Beggars and Malingerers', 6 January 1843, pp. 19f. On modes of perception of police officers and officials, see the Preface to a study by the long-serving Director of the Workhouse and House of Correction in Brauweiler (Rhine Province), J. B. Ristelhüber, *Leben und Schicksale zweier Strafgefangenen, nach der gekrönten Preisschrift 'Anton und Moritz' von L.P. de Jussieu frei übersetzt* (Hamburg, 1836). These views were not of course a Prussian speciality, and were evident in other bureaucratically organised 'modern states' (especially monarchies with a claim to absolute bureaucratic rule), and, in particular, in France: see R. Cobb, *The Police and the People. French Popular Protest 1789–1820* (London, 1970), pp. 13–37.
55. cf. Harnisch, *Kapitalistische Agrarreform und industrielle Revolution* (Weimar, 1984); K. Obermann, 'Die Arbeitermigrationen in Deutschland im Prozeß der Industrialisierung und der Entstehung der Arbeiterklasse in der Zeit von der Gründung bis zur Auflösung des Deutschen Bundes', *Jahrbuch für Wirtschaftsgeschichte* (1972/1), 135–81, at 146; on concentrations of workers in the wake of railway construction, *ibid.* pp. 150ff. On the floating poor in towns in the eighteenth and early nineteenth centuries, and the growth of the pauperised 'masses' in general see, K. Hinze, *Die Arbeiterfrage zu Beginn des modernen.* Kapitalismus in Brandenburg-Preußen (Berlin, 1927). Küther has attempted to calculate the number of itinerants in Bayern at the turn of the nineteenth

century, and estimates that 'vagrants' accounted for some 10 per cent of the population: C. Küther, *Räuber und Gauner in Deutschland. Das organisierte Bandenwesen im 18. und frühen 19. Jahrhundert* (Göttingen, 1976), p. 22.

56. For comparative figures for town populations in Prussia between 1840 and 1855, see 'Vergleichende Zusammenstellung der Einwohnerzahl der Städte des Preußischen Staates von 1840–1855' (1856), Heft 4, *Archiv für Landeskunde der Preußischen Monarchie*, pp. 228ff.
57. C. A. Dosse, *Die Polizei Berlins* (Berlin, 1847). On the allocation in 1830, see 'Berliner Polizei-Verwaltungs-Bezirk' (Berlin, 1830), GStA/PK 84a, no. 9254, fols. 160ff; cf. A. Glassbrenner, 'Berlin und die Berliner', in A. Glassbrenner, *Berliner Volksleben*, vol. 1 (Leipzig, 1847), pp. 17–56, especially 49 and 52: 'Only the people are observed; better society can do as it wishes.'
58. These figures from D. Bergmann, 'Die Berliner Arbeiterschaft in Vormärz und Revolution 1830–1850', in O. Büsch (ed.), *Untersuchungen zur Geschichte der frühen Industrialisierung vornehmlich im Wirtschaftsraum Berlin/Brandenburg* (Berlin, 1971), pp. 455–511, at 462ff; see too F. D. Marquardt, 'Sozialer Aufstieg, sozialer Abstieg und die Entstehung der Berliner Arbeiterklasse, 1806–1848', *Geschichte und Gesellschaft*, 1 (1975), 43–77, at 49; on servants, see, R. Engelsing, 'Das Häusliche Personal in der Epoche der Industrialisierung', in R. Engelsing, *Zur Sozialgeschichte deutscher Mittel- und Unterschichten* (Göttingen, 1973), pp. 225–61, at 251; figures for 'paupers' from A. Schück, 'Die Revision der preußischen Armengesetzgebung', *Archiv für Landeskunde der preußischen Monarchie* (1856), Heft 4, pp. 348–76, at 350. Difficulties in using these figures arise for several reasons: firstly, the breakdown of occupations excludes data on family members and their incomes, and, secondly, occupational statistics need to be read parallel to those recording individuals subject to Trade Tax (and those exempt), and in particular, the payers and non-payers of the Class (Income) Tax; see Koselleck, *Preußen*, pp. 534ff, esp. 538f (Class Tax), 600 (Trade Tax).
59. Obermann, 'Die Arbeitermigrationen in Deutschland', 171.
60. L. Baar, *Die Berliner Industrie in der Industriellen Revolution* (Berlin, GDR, 1966), pp. 171ff. Cf. the attempt by von Armin to give a more detailed picture of the situation of these groups in the Berlin suburb 'Vogtland', in B. von Arnim, 'Dies Buch gehört dem König' (1843), in B. von Arnim, *Werke und Briefe*, ed. G. Konrad (Frechen and Cologne, 1963), vol. 3, pp. 229ff; cf. W. Vordtriede (ed.), *Bettina von Arnims Armenbuch* (Frankfurt, 1969).
61. Schmidt, *Untersuchungen über Bevölkerung*, p. 251.
62. A. Schneer, *Über die Zustände der arbeitenden Klassen in Breslau* (Berlin, 1845), p. 16. Of the 1,014 individuals placed under police supervision in 1844, 532 (52 per cent) were registered in two out of the eight Police Districts (in the north and north east): p. 15.
63. APW, Mag. Wrocł, III, no. 1946.
64. See, for example, the annual Administrative Report of the District Government in Gumbinnen for 1835, issued 26 March 1836, GStA/PK, Rep. 2^{I}, tit. 40, no. 10, vol. 10, fol. 211r.
65. See the report by the *Regierungspräsident* in Trier, von Schaper, to the Minister of the Interior, 1 July 1840, on the subject of the Whitsun and Corpus Christi processions in Trier. 'Around' 4,500 people had entered the town prior to Whitsun to participate in the processions, 'including subjects of the Government Districts of Düsseldorf and Cologne'; some would have covered more

than 350 km. on the journey to and from home: cited in J. Hansen, *Rheinische Briefe und Akten*, vol. 1 (Essen, 1919), p. 184. On the 'processions of pilgrims who make an overnight stay' together with an incident in Krefeld in 1842, see HStAD, Reg. Düsseldorf, no. 253, fols. 36. On the 'masques' see the Cabinet Order of 5 August 1834, StadtA IS, K 2. This file also includes reports of penalties for contraventions of the provision; the usual punishment was a fine of up to 2 Thalers.

66. 'Publikandum des Oberbürgermeisters zu Elberfeld das Betragen der Knaben auf den Straßen betr.', 12 March 1822, in KA 6 (1822), pp. 139f.
67. HStAD, Reg. Düss., no. 754, fol. 252r, 12 November 1830.
68. Formulation used in Article 5 of the 'General Instruction appertaining to Residence Cards', 12 July 1817, in KA 1 (1817), Part 1, pp. 114–20, at 117.
69. Anonymous review of Merker's manual, 'Die Notwendigkeit des Paßwesens zur Erhaltung der öffentlichen Sicherheit; zugleich ein Versuch, die Reisenden mit den Unannehmlichkeiten dieser Einrichtung auszusöhnen' (Erfurt, 1818), in KA 2 (1818), pp. 1125–8, at 1225. On the Passport Edict, 22 June 1817, see Rönne and Simon, *Polizeiwesen*, vol. 1, pp. 294ff.
70. Review of Merker, *Handbuch für die ausübenden Polizei-Beamten* (Erfurt, 1818), p. 1226. See the regulations decreed by the District Governments on 'police vigilance over travellers, etc.' in the late summer of 1817, in accordance with Articles 17 and 18 of the Passport Law, 22 June 1817. See KA 1 (1817), Part 1, pp. 123–33 (i.e. District Governments in Oppeln, Stralsund, Cologne and Trier).
71. Order of 2 January 1831, StadtA IS, K 9.
72. StadtA IS, K 5.
73. StadtA DO, LRA DO, D. 246/2, Mayor Mitsdörffer, 1 September 1820, fol. 46.
74. Report by the *Landrat*, Wolff-Metternich, 23 February 1836, StADT, Reg. Minden I P, no. 960, fols. 21f.
75. See the report of the official tour of *Regierungsrat* Fasbender, 7 July 1839, StAK 403, no. 437, p. 289.
76. Cited in Rönne and Simon, *Polizeiwesen*, vol. 2, p. 366. (Emphasis in original.)
77. StAK 403, no. 437, the investigations of the communal budget in the Government District of Düsseldorf, pp. 186ff.
78. J. G. Hoffmann, *Die Bevölkerung des Preußischen Staates* (Berlin, 1839), p. 183, pp. 184ff. for following material.
79. Author's calculations, following Diederichs who cites 130 public houses for the Mayoral District (StAK 403, no. 437, p. 186).
80. F. Engels, 'Preußischer Schnapps im Deutschen Reichstag', in *Marx-Engels Werke*, 19, pp. 40f.
81. Diederichs, StAK 403, no. 437, p. 186.
82. Rönne and Simon, *Polizeiwesen*, vol. 1, p. 664.
83. Report of 27 March 1847, HStAD, Reg. Düsseldorf, no. 8900, fols. 30f. (Quotations in the next four paragraphs are from this source.)
84. On previous police experience of these festivals see reports by the Director of Police and subordinate officer, e.g. by Heister, 17 August 1836, and that of the Police Commissary von Gress, 11 August 1836, HStAD, Reg. Köln, no. 62, fols. 4–7 and 12–13; specifically on the 1846 festival, ZStA II, Rep. 77, tit. 505, no. 2, vol. 3. (Quotation in this and following two paragraphs from these sources.)
85. See the Instruction issued by the District Government in Potsdam for *Landräte*,

'concerning the better administration of the security police in smaller towns', 16 June 1822 (praised on 29 June as 'highly useful' by the Minister of the Police and Interior, with the recommendation that other areas should adopt it): KA 6 (1822), pp. 398–403.

86. See 'General-Instruktion für die allgemeinen und besonderen Vagabunden-Visitationen', 9 October 1817 (which was intended to replace an older Instruction issued on 20 November 1730), StAMS, Reg. Münster, no. 3760. The objection raised by several District Governments that the prescribed frequency (twice a year in each Government District, at least four times a year in each county) did more harm than good was not fully accepted by the Police Minister. He required that there had to be at least two searches a year at provincial level; see Kamptz's instruction to the District Government in Merseburg, 8 December 1817, StAMS, Reg. Münster, no. 3760.

87. The police were able to exploit licensing procedures to put pressure on landlords; see complaints about the 'administrative arbitrariness of the police', E. Lasker, *Zur Verfassungsgeschichte Preußens* (Leipzig, 1874), p. 201. For the relevant provisions, see Rönne and Simon, *Polizeiwesen*, vol. 1, pp. 364ff. Cf. too W. G. von der Heyde, *Der Gast- und Schankwirt oder Mitteilung der über den Gewerbsbetrieb und die polizeilichen Verhältnisse der Gast- und Schankwirte, so wie über den Handel mit Getränken bestehenden gesetzlichen Bestimmungen* (Magdeburg, 1841); also, H. Dennstedt and W. von Wolfsburg, *Preußisches Polizei-Lexikon*, vol. 5 (Berlin, 1856), pp. 236–51. Street lighting was also supposed to ease 'observation': H. Rösen, 'Öl- oder Gasbeleuchtung in den Straßen Krefelds? 1837–1847', *Die Heimat* 35 (1964), pp. 139ff, at p. 148.

88. Rescript of the Ministry of the Police and Interior to the *Polizeipräsidium*, Berlin 'on the establishment of aliens', KA 6 (1822), pp. 717–19, at 718, 20 July 1822.

89. This was the breakdown adopted in the 'summary report of beggars detained by the 8th Brigade of Gendarmes on their own initiative in the course of February 1831', 23 March 1831: HStAD, Reg. Düsseldorf, no. 8900.

90. See the figures in the annual Administrative Report for the Government District of Münster for 1837 and 1838, StAMS, Reg. Münster, no. 318, fols. 81f and 140.

91. See the 1839 Administrative Report by the District Government of Münster, issued 6 April 1840, StAMS, Reg. Münster, no. 318, fol. 166v; the following from fols. 272, 328.

92. See the 'summary report' of 23 March 1831, HStAD, Reg. Düsseldorf, no. 8900. The percentages are based on 1837 population figures: see Hoffmann, *Die Bevölkerung des preußischen Staates*, pp. 271–82. In the areas of the Rhine Province on the left bank of the Rhine, i.e. under the jurisdiction of the Cologne Court of Appeal, the *Code pénal* and *Code d'instruction criminelle*, all cases of police punishment were decided by special justices of the peace (appointed by the Minister of Justice). On the enormous increase in the number of police cases 'decided' in the area of the Cologne Court of Appeal between 1 November 1832 and 1 November 1833 and in 1844 see HStAD, Rep. 11, no. 1311, and D. Blasius, 'Der Kampf um die Geschworenengerichte im Vormärz', in H.-U. Wehler (ed.), *Sozialgeschichte heute* (Göttingen, 1974), pp. 156f: In 1832–3, 77,933 police cases were settled (69,046 with a conviction, 7,388 with acquittal and 1,499 with reference to other courts). In contrast, by 1844 the total had reached 127,778.

93. See C. F. W. Dieterici, 'Statistiche Übersicht der im Preußischen Staate', *Mit-*

teilungen des statistischen Büros in Berlin 1 (1848), 68–80 at 77. See also K. Tenfelde, 'Ländliches Gesinde in Preußen. Gesinderecht und Gesindestatistik 1810–1861', *Archiv für Sozialgeschichte*, 19 (1979), 189–229; T. Vormbaum, *Politik und Gesinderecht im 19. Jhdt* (Berlin, 1980), pp. 35–115.

94. On the legal and administrative provisions see W. G. von der Heyde, *Preußisches Gesinde-Recht mit dem Inbegriff der seit dem Jahre 1810 bis zum Jahre 1836 erschienenen Erläuterungen, Ergänzungen und Zusätze*, 5th edn (Magdeburg, 1836). On the extension of the Servants Ordinance to *Instleute* in the province of Prussia (Order of 8 August 1837), see H. Hübner and H. Kathe (eds.), *Lage und Kampf der Landarbeiter im ostelbischen Preußen (vom Anfang des 19. Jahrhunderts bis zur Novemberrevolution 1918/19)*, vol. 1 (Vaduz, 1977), pp. 89–92; on the introduction of service registers for servants (*Gesinde*) see *ibid.*, pp. 96–102 (Order of 29 September 1846). On the toughening up and encouragement of police action using 'means of coercion' against 'refractory' servants, see Hübner and Kathe (eds.), *Lage und Kampf der Landarbeiter*, pp. 90f. On the decision of the Ministry of the Interior, 18 December 1834 and the Rescript of 31 January 1843 approving the employment of 'intensified means of coercion', see W. Erdmann, (ed.), *Die Praxis der Polizeiverwaltung* (Berlin, 1892), p. 237, note 2; see too H. Plaul, *Landarbeiterleben im 19. Jahrhundert* (Berlin, GDR, 1979), pp. 311–20.

95. F. Weidemann, *Oberschlesische Zustände in freien Rasirspiegel-Scenen* (Leipzig, 1843), p. 64; in general, Koselleck, *Preußen*, pp. 643ff, 649ff.

96. Rönne, *Staatsrecht*, Part 1 (Leipzig, 1869), vol. 1, pp. 340ff, 345f.

97. A. Schäffle, 'Die Stellung der politischen Verwaltung im Staatsorganismus', *Zeitschrift für die gesamte Staatswissenschaft*, 27 (1871), 181–250, at 240.

98. In general, see S. Pollard, 'Factory discipline in the Industrial Revolution', *Economic History Review*, 16 (1963), 254–71; cf. E. Gruner, *Die Arbeiter in der Schweiz im 19. Jahrhundert. Soziale Lage, Organisation, Verhältnis zu Arbeitgeber und Staat* (Berne, 1968), pp. 97–103. On 'factory constitutions' see, H. Zwahr, 'Ausbeutung und gesellschaftliche Stellung des Fabrik- und Manufakturproletariats am Ende der Industriellen Revolution im Spiegel Leipziger Fabrikordnungen', in W. Jacobeit and U. Mohrmann (eds.), *Kultur und Lebensweise des Proletariats, Kulturhistorisch-volkskundliche Studien und Materialien*, 2nd edn (Berlin, GDR, 1974), pp. 85–136.

99. Report of 12 October 1812 in J. Kuczynski, *Darstellung der Lage der Arbeiter in Deutschland von 1789–1849* (Berlin, GDR, 1961), pp. 224f.

100. Lasker, *Das Auge der Polizei*, p. 61.

101. Dronke, *Berlin*, p. 297.

102. Report of 20 March 1837, StAMS, Reg. Münster, no. 318, p. 22.

103. Report of 10 March 1834, HStAD, Reg. Düsseldorf, no. 8797. Cf. too Ristelhüber, *Leben und Schicksale*.

104. H. Botzet, *Die Geschichte der sozialen Verhältnisse in Krefeld und ihre wirtschaftliche Zusammenhänge*, Doctoral thesis (Cologne, 1953), p. 86.

105. Report of 7 July 1839, StAK 403, no. 437, pp. 263f.

106. Report from the District Government of Minden to the Ministry of the Interior, 29 August 1818, StADT, Reg. Minden I C, no. 17.

107. Cabinet Order, 29 March 1833 (KA 17, 1833, p. 133); Rescript of the Minister of the Police and Interior, 16 September 1836, cited here from Gräff *et al.*, *Ergänzungen und Erläuterungen*, 2nd edn, vol. 6, p. 642 (where the 1833 Cabinet Order is incorrectly dated 1839).

108. Report of a tour of inspection in the county of Lennep, 27 February 1836, StAK 403, no. 437, p. 123.

109. E. Schmidt, *Einführung in die Geschichte der deutschen Strafrechtspflege*, 5th edn (Göttingen, 1965), pp. 269ff; D. Blasius, *Kriminalität und Alltag. Zur Konfliktgeschichte des Alltagslebens im 19. Jahrhundert* (Göttingen, 1978), p. 38.
110. The entire incident is dealt with in detail in the *Landrat*'s personnel files, APW, Rej. Op. Pr. B., no. 1180.
111. *Kriminal-Ordnung für die Königlich Preußischen Staaten* (Berlin, 1805), Article 288.
112. On the limit of fourteen days' imprisonment, twenty lashes or 5 Thalers – a limit often moved upwards by special legislation, e.g. Servants Ordinance – the regulations were somewhat vague, and often merely referred to the 'discretion' to punish within these limits: W. G. von der Heyde, *Polizei-Strafgewalt in den Königlich Preußischen Staaten*, Part 1 (Magdeburg, 1837); on p. 66, for example, 'transport of travellers into the Prussian states by hired coachmen or boatmen in contravention of a proscription', or on p. 67, 'accommodating illegal aliens' – each would earn 'severe reprimand from the police'.
113. Cf. the inquiry of by the District Government in Cologne, 6 April 1838, 'concerning police supervision of those workers employed on the railways'. The *Oberpräsident*, von Bodelschwingh, rejected an application from the Rhenish Railway Company (Rhine–Weser line) for the deployment of Gendarmes to maintain 'quiet and order' – at the state's expense: STAK 403, no. 2381, pp. 1f.
114. See the report of his successor, von Schaper, to the Minister of the Interior (von Eichhorn), 18 March 1843, *ibid.*, pp. 27f.
115. See R. Mohl, 'Über die Nachteile des fabrikmäßigen Betriebs der Industrie', *Archiv für politische Ökonomie und Polizeiwissenschaft*, 2 (1835), 141–203, at 157.
116. No date, but with an archival record, cited in K. Lärmer, 'Maschinenbau in Preußen', *Jahrbuch für Wirtschaftsgeschichte* (1975/II), 13–32 at 31.
117. StAMS, Reg. Arnsberg, Pr., no. 56, Report of the Interim *Präsident*, Naumann, 13 April 1850, 17 May 1850.
118. See J. Haalck, 'Die staatspolizeilichen Koordinierungsmaßnahmen innerhalb des Deutschen Bundes zwischen 1851 und 1866', *Wiss. Zeitschrift der Universität Rostock*, 9 (1959–60), Part 1, pp. 99–105.
119. See P. Schmidt, *Die ersten 50 Jahre der Kgl. Schutzmannschaft zu Berlin* (Berlin, 1898).
120. StAMS, Reg. Arnsberg 1, no. 1499, 5 November 1862.
121. L. Schücking, *Die Reaktion in der inneren Verwaltung* (Berlin, 1908), pp. 87ff. On the District Police Commissaries (*Bezirkspolizeikommissare*) in Gelsenkirchen, Bochum, Dortmund, Düsseldorf, Elberfeld and Essen, see StadtA DO 3, no. 61, and G. Knopp, *Die preußische Verwaltung des Regierungsbezirks Düsseldorf 1899–1919* (Cologne and Berlin, 1974), pp. 105f.
122. StAMS, Oberpräs., no. 2691, fol. 77, Decree of 27 April 1851. For quotations in the following paragraphs, StAMS, Reg. Arnsberg Pr., no. 75, fol. 219r, Circular to *Landräte*, 8 May 1857; HStAD, Reg. Düsseldorf, no. 8797, Decree of the Ministry of the Interior, 14 June 1859. For insight into the 'social question' see the report of the Police Director in Düsseldorf, von Falderen, 19 June 1851: ZStA II, Rep. 77, tit. 505, no. 1, vol. 3, fol. 20.
123. StAMS, Krs. Hagen LRA, no. 117, Circular to *Landräte*, 22 September 1877.
124. StAMS, Krs. Iserlohn LRA, no. 146, Circular from the Minister of the Interior to *Landräte*, 12 August 1898. On the military see W. Deist, 'Die Armee in Staat und Gesellschaft, 1890–1914', in M. Stürmer (ed.), *Das kaiserliche Deutschland* (Düsseldorf, 1970), pp. 312–39, at 319f.

125. StAMS, Krs. Hagen LRA, no. 118, Decree of the District Government in Arnsberg. On weapons see the 'confidential decree of the Ministry of the Interior to the *Regierungspräsident* in Erfurt', 22 June 1898, StADT, Krs. Lübbecke, no. 19. On the 'police war' of the 1890s, see K. Saul, 'Der Staat und die "Mächte des Umsturzes"', *Archiv für Sozialgeschichte*, 12 (1972), 293–350, esp. 299ff.
126. Von der Heyde, *Polizei-Strafgewalt in den Kgl.-Preußischen Staaten*, Part 1, p. 5.
127. See the Circular Rescript of the Minister of Police, 13 November 1817, in Gräff *et al.*, *Ergänzungen und Erläuterungen*, 2nd edn. vol. 6, pp. 665–8; see too Rönne and Simon, *Polizeiwesen*, vol. 2, pp. 557ff, 815ff. Generally on this subject, Rönne, *Staatsrecht*, Part 1, vol. 1, pp. 339ff.
128. See the Report to the King (*Immediat-Bericht*) of the Ministry of State, 21 March 1837, and the opinions of the Departments of the Interior and Justice in the Council of State, 19 October 1837 (on the powers of estate owners with police jurisdiction), GStA/PK 84a, no. 3719, fols. 128ff, fols. 130ff, here fol. 135.
129. Rescript of the Minister of Police and the Interior on the Testimony of witnesses, 21 November 1829 to the District Government in Magdeburg, in Gräff *et al.*, *Ergänzungen und Erläuterungen*, 2nd edn, vol. 6, p. 671.
130. C. G. Svarez, *Vorträge über Recht und Staat*, p. 41.
131. See *Allgemeines Landrecht*, Teil II, tit. 17, para. 12.
132. Report on the Departments of the Interior and Justice, 3 March 1826, GStA/PK 84a, no. 3718, fols. 234–47; the cases cited here are on fols 242v–r. On the Rhenish judiciary see Bär, *Die Behördenverfassung der Rheinprovinz*, pp. 384–415.
133. *Allgemeines Landrecht*, Teil II, tit. 20, para. 611 'concerning mild affront' by persons 'of lower rank to those of higher'.
134. Report of 3 March 1826, GStA/PK 84a, no. 3718, fol. 241.
135. Klein in an essay in his 'Annalen der Preussischen Gesetzgebung', vol. 4, pp. 326ff, cited in J. G. Schlosser, *Fünfter Brief über die Entwicklung des Preußischen Gesetzbuches* (Frankfurt, 1790), p. 49.
136. See O. Hintze, 'Preußens Entwicklung zum Rechtsstaat', in *idem*, *Regierung und Verwaltung*, vol. 3, 2nd edn (Göttingen, 1967), ed. G. Oestreich, pp. 158ff; H. Schrimpf, 'Die Auseinandersetzung um die Neuordnung des individuellen Rechtsschutzes gegenüber der staatlichen Verwaltung nach 1807', *Der Staat*, 18 (1979), 59–80, esp. 69–74.
137. Report of 3 March 1826, GStA/PK 84a, no. 3718, fol. 237.
138. In addition to the reports submitted to the Council of State, see the views of *Staatsrat* Friese, who was responsible for changes in departmental responsibilities, in Hintze, 'Preussens Entwicklung zum Rechtsstaat', p. 148.
139. Dronke, *Polizei-Geschichten*, pp. 132–40, esp. p. 136.
140. Report, 3 March 1826, GStA/PK 84a, no. 3718, fol. 242.
141. Declaration, 10 February 1827, in Gräff *et al.*, *Ergänzungen und Erläuterungen*, 3rd edn, vol. 5, p. 322. The Report of the Council of State, 3 March 1826, GStA/PK 84a, no. 3718, fols. 234ff, was drawn up in preparation for this Declaration. See too *Allgemeines Landrecht*, Teil II, tit. 17, paras. 74, 76.
142. Cited in the Council of State Report, GStA/PK 84a, no. 3718, fol. 243.
143. See the Report of the Ministry of State, 21 March 1837, GStA/PK 84a, no. 3719, fol. 128. See too J. Abegg, 'Zur sprachlichen Auslegung des Strafgesetzbuches, insbesondere der Bedeutung der Öffentlichkeit', *Archiv für preußisches Strafrecht*, 9 (1861), 1–23.

144. See the Report of the Ministry of State, 30 November 1827, GStA/PK 84a, no. 3718, fol. 358.
145. Cabinet Order in Gräff *et al.*, *Ergänzungen und Erläuterungen*, 2nd edn, vol. 6, p. 642.
146. This and next quotation from Report of 3 March 1826, GStA/PK 84a, no. 3718, fols. 241v–r.
147. This formula from 3 March 1826 Report (see note 146) occurs almost word for word in the Report to the King from the Ministry of State, 22 September 1825, GStA/PK 84a, no. 3718, fol. 232.
148. The formula used for practical application in Heyde, *Polizei-Strafgewalt*, Part 1, pp. 84f. This shorter version is based on the Circular Order, 30 December 1798, 'on the prevention of tumults and the punishment of their instigators and participants' in von Rönne and Simon, *Polizeiwesen*, vol. 1, pp. 666ff; cf. Appendix 4.
149. Von der Heyde, *Polizei-Strafgewalt*, Part 1, pp. 67–74, 312–18.
150. *Ibid.*, pp. 318f. See *Allgemeines Landrecht*, Teil II, tit. 8, para. 360 (Heyde incorrectly cites para. 359).
151. Heyde, *Polizei-Strafgewalt*, part 1, p. 86.
152. *Allgemeines Landrecht*, Teil II, tit. 20, paras. 182, 183.
153. *Ibid.*, para. 35.
154. Report of 3 March 1826, GStA/PK 84a, no. 3718, fol. 235.
155. GStA/PK 84a, no. 3718, fol. 327; *ibid.*, fol. 347.
156. The prohibition on 'self-help' was established in the Prussian Legal Code, *ALR* Teil II, tit. 20, para. 156. Cf. in general, Koselleck, *Preußen*, pp. 541–52.
157. Noted in the report of the Council of State, 19 October 1837, fol. 131; cf. fol. 128.
158. The formulation used in the Cabinet Order, 18 November 1834, to the Ministry of State requesting the Ministry to submit a report; see GStA/PK 84a, no. 3719, fol. 128.
159. This and other quotations in this paragraph are from the Council of State, minutes of the session 22 November 1836, cited in Reports of the Departments of Justice and the Interior of the Council of State, 19 October 1837, GStA/PK 84a, no. 3719, fol. 132.
160. Heyde, *Polizei-Strafgewalt*, Part 1, pp. 365f (on Article 34 of the Servants Ordinance). Cf. Gräff *et al.*, *Ergänzungen und Erläuterungen*, 2nd edn, vol. 3, pp. 484ff, 656f, 672ff; see too Heyde, *Preußisches Gesinde-Recht* (p. 32 on Article 77, which remained in force until the abolition of the disciplinary rights of employers in the November 1918 Civil Code). In general on this issue see T. Vormbaum, *Politik und Gesinderecht, im 19. Jahrhundert* (Berlin, 1980), pp. 35ff.
161. Order of 31 March 1838, in Gräff *et al.*, *Ergänzungen und Erläuterungen*, 3rd edn, vol. 5, p. 323.
162. On representation, see Gräff *et al.*, *ibid.* Only female owners of estates were forced to nominate representatives: see Report of 3 March 1826, GStA/PK 84a, no. 3718, fol. 246.
163. See note of the Ministry of the Interior, 3 August 1828, and the reply from the Minister of Justice, 21 August, GStA/PK 84a, no. 3718, fols. 306, 309f. On the competence of the courts see Gräff *et al.*, *Ergänzungen und Erläuterungen*, 2nd edn, vol. 6, p. 647.
164. On the punishments for and distinctions between 'common theft', 'common theft under aggravating circumstances', 'repeated common theft', 'theft with

assault', theft with assault 'under aggravating circumstances', 'repeated theft with assault', 'robbery' (the distinctions turned on violence against persons, theft with assault, breaking and entering), see *Allgemeines Landrecht*, Teil II, tit. 20, paras. 1108ff. See also NCC 10, Sp. 2235–86 (and note 92 above).

165. Letter from Schuckmann, 2 September 1828, GStA/PK 84a, no. 3718, fols. 312–14.
166. Letter of 11 September 1828, GStA/PK 84a, no. 3718, fols. 317f.
167. See R. Wirtz, 'Zur Logik plebejischer und bürgerlicher Aufstandsbewegungen. Die gescheiterte Revolution von 1848', *Sozialwissenschaftliche Information für Unterricht und Studium*, 8 (1979), 83–8; J. Bergmann, 'Ökonomische Voraussetzungen der Revolution von 1848. Zur Krise von 1845–1848 in Deutschland', *Geschichte und Gesellschaft*, special issue 2 (1976), 254–87.
168. Koselleck, *Preußen*, p. 654.
169. Report of 27 November 1829, GStA/PK 84a, no. 3718, fol. 359r.
170. GStA/PK 84a, no. 3718, fols. 336–9. On the powers of the courts for theft involving a loss of less than 5 Thalers, see the Rescript of the Ministry of the Interior, 28 September 1828 in KA 2 (1818), p. 761; general sources in Gräff *et al.*, *Ergänzungen und Erläuterungen*, 2nd edn, vol. 6, p. 647.
171. GStA/PK 84a, no. 3718, fols. 301r–303.
172. Resolution of 9 September 1828, GStA/PK 84a, no. 3718, fol. 311.
173. Report of 21 July 1828, GStA/PK 84a, no. 3718, fol. 340. For the development of crimes against property, see Blasius, *Bürgerliche Gesellschaft und Kriminalität* (Göttingen, 1976), pp. 29ff, 140–6.
174. L. Hoffmann (anon.), 'Etwas über Prügel', *Polizei-Archiv für Preußen*, 3 (1819) issue 2, 227–36, 232. It should be borne in mind that 'lack of assets' meant that the mass of dependent producers and propertyless were simply not in a position to pay fines.
175. W. Obenaus, *Die Entwicklung der preußischen Sicherheitspolizei* (Berlin, 1940), p. 79.
176. Rescript of the Police and Interior Ministry, 31 December 1831 (to the Berlin *Polizeipräsidium*), in Gräff *et al.*, *Ergänzungen und Erläuterungen*, 2nd edn, vol. 6, pp. 641f.
177. Koselleck, *Preußen*, pp. 655f.
178. Report of 22 June 1795, cited in E. Lennhoff, *Das ländliche Gesindewesen in der Kurmark Brandenburg vom 16. bis zum 19. Jahrhundert* (Breslau, 1906), p. 69.
179. 'Etwas über Prügel', 232.
180. T. Brand, *Das Dorf-Buch für die Provinz Sachsen* (Glogau, 1838), p. 503.
181. See Gräff *et al.*, *Ergänzungen und Erläuterungen*, 2nd edn, vol. 6, p. 642.
182. Decree of 18 January 1796 to the (Judicial) *Regierungen* and *Oberlandesjustizkollegien* 'this side' – that is, east – of the Weser, cited in Lennhoff, *Das ländliche Gesindewesen*, p. 69.
183. See R. Lehmann, *Quellen zur Lage der Privatbauern in der Niederlausitz im Zeitalter des Absolutismus* (Berlin, GDR, 1957), p. 267; W. Boelcke, *Bauer und Gutsherr in der Oberlausitz* (Bautzen, 1957), p. 68. The usual course of 'running the gauntlet' is described in M. Lehmann, *Scharnhorst*, vol. 2 (Leipzig, 1887), pp. 100–3.
184. 'Etwas über Prügel', 234.
185. C. Garve, 'Über den Charakter der Bauern und ihr Verhältnis gegen die Gutsherren und gegen die Regierung' (Breslau, 1786–96), in C. Garve, *Popularphilosophische Schriften*, vol. 2, ed. K. Wölfel (Stuttgart, 1974), pp. 873, 907.
186. 'Etwas über Prügel', pp. 234ff, and subsequently, p. 235.

187. H. L. von Strampff, *Kritische Briefe über den Entwurf des Strafgesetzbuches* (Berlin, 1844), p. 81.
188. H. Bleiber, *Zwischen Reform und Revolution* (Berlin, GDR, 1966), p. 107.
189. 'Etwas über Prügel', pp. 233f.
190. E. Bauer, 'Die Reise auf öffentliche Kosten', *Die Epigonen* (1848), vol. 5, pp. 1ff, at p. 23.
191. Rönne, *Das Staatsrecht der Preußischen Monarchie*, Part 2, vol. 2, pp. 61ff.
192. W. Eichhoff, *Berliner Polizei-Silhouetten*, 4th series (London, 1861), p. 119. Cf. Reg. Minden, 20–21 April 1853 to the Ministry of the Interior. Corporal punishment was considered appropriate for youths and recidivist 'beggars and vagrants': StADT, Reg. Minden, IP. no. 765, fols. 27ff.
193. A. Ballhorn, 'Vorwort', *Archiv für Polizei-Gesetzkunde und polizeiliches Strafverfahren*, 1 (1855), unpaginated.
194. See Regulations for the District Work- and Poorhouse, Benningshausen, 15 December 1820, Articles 1 and 18, GStA/PK 84a, no. 8054, fols. 44ff; District Paupers Regulations for Hinter and Near Pomerania, 6 March 1799, *ibid.*, fols. 52ff; Ristelhüber, *Leben und Schicksale*, pp. vii ff; F. G. F. Schläger, *Der Bußfertige. Ein Erbauungsbuch für Schuldbeladene, für Sträflinge in Gefängnissen und öffentlichen Zuchtanstalten* (Hanover, 1828), pp. v ff.
195. T. Goldtammer, *Die Materialien zum Strafgesetzbuch für die Preußischen Staaten*, Part 1 (Berlin, 1851), pp. 218ff.
196. C. Sohm, *Die unbestimmte Verurteilung in Preußen unter der Herrschaft des Allgemeinen Landrechts* (Leipzig, 1939), esp. pp. 63ff. Rescript of the Interior Ministry to the District Government, Magdeburg, 11 December 1821 in KA 6 (1822), pp. 157f.
197. See GStA/PK 84a, no. 8043, fols. 154r–155v, Ministry of State, 10 March 1830; fols. 186f; fols. 194–203; and the 6 January 1843 law in GS 1843, pp. 19f.
198. Circular of 30 August 1823, cited in Rönne and Simon, *Polizeiwesen*, vol. 1, p. 506.
199. Article 1, in Rönne and Simon, *Polizeiwesen*, vol. 1, p. 499; cf. the entire relevant section, pp. 496–510.
200. Decree, 25 May 1824, KA 8 (1824), pp. 551f.
201. P. Zeller, *Systematisches Lehrbuch der Polizeiwissenschaft nach Preußischen Edicten*, Part 1 (Quedlingburg and Leipzig, 1828), pp. 48ff. See too the instructions to the Mayor of Ronsdorf (in the county of Lennep) in the 1830s–40s, StadtA, Wuppertal BM Ronsdorf, O II, no. 87. See also W. G. von der Heyde, *Hülfsschrift zum Gebrauch bei der Verwaltung der ausübenden Polizei* (Calbe, 1832), p. 22.
202. Decree, 26 November 1839, KA 23 (1839), p. 895.
203. See the Report of 27 May 1836 by the commissary *Landrat* in Iserlohn, Müllensiefen, StAMS, Krs. Iserlohn, LRA. no. 139.
204. Figures from W. Obenaus, *Preußische Sicherheitspolizei*, p. 78, note 3; on Posen, M. Laubert, *Die Verwaltung der Provinz Posen, 1815–47* (Breslau, 1923), p. 177, and Hoffmann's demographic statistics in his *Bevölkerung*, p. 17.
205. Rönne, *Staatsrecht*, part 2, vol. 2, pp. 138–42, esp. p. 141, note 5. On post-1851 judicial practice, see K. Fuhr, *Strafrechtspflege und Sozialpolitik* (Berlin, 1892), p. 179. On individual cases see StadtA, Wuppertal BM Ronsdorf, O II, nos. 89, 90. On the enforcement of the procedure towards 'those discharged from a house of correction' after detention in the 1850s, i.e. the required 'public parade' before the police inspector, and procession through the town, see HStAD, Reg. Düsseldorf, no. 30435.

206. Figures from 'Vergleichende Zusammenstellung der Einwohnerzahl'; on the distinction between civilian and military residents, see K. Weimann, 'Bevölkerungsentwicklung und Frühindustrialisierung in Berlin, 1800–1850', in O. Büsch (ed.), *Untersuchungen zur Geschichte der frühen Industrialisierung* (Berlin, 1971), pp. 150–90, at p. 184. The military were listed as an 'estate' (*Stand*) until 1867: we assume the presence of a garrison in company or squadron strength where the number of military residents exceeds 150.
207. The experiences of von Fransecky, then a Lieutenant and later an Infantry General, demolish the idea that watch duty combined comfortable inactivity with the undisturbed pleasures of exercising power and violence: see W. von Bremen (ed.), *Denkwürdigkeiten des preußischen Generals der Infanterie Eduard von Fransecky* (Bielefeld and Leipzig, 1901), pp. 95f. See note 27 on the citadels.
208. See Heyde, *Polizei-Verwaltung*, pp. 309ff; KA 1 (1817), Part 4, pp. 139ff.
209. On the location – usually isolated – of watches and associated building works, see *Über Militärwachen, Militärarreste und das Unterkommen der Militärsträflinge* (Berlin, 1840), esp. p. 5.
210. 'Regulation on the arrest of civil persons in the royal capital by military watches', Berlin, 16 March 1802, GStA/PK 84a, no. 2243, fols. 16f, esp. the 'preamble', Articles 4, 5 and 9.
211. L. Siegrist (pseud.), *Leben, Wirken und Ende weiland Sr. Exc. des Oberfürstlich Winkelkramschen Gen. d. Inf. Frhr. Leberecht von Knopf* (Darmstadt and Leipzig, 1869), p. 58.
212. StadtA TR 17, no. 222.
213. Report of 19 July 1824 to the Ministry of War, GStA/PK 84a, no. 2243, fols. 59–61.
214. Memorandum, 27 October 1807, submitted to the King and used by the Military Reorganisation Commission; cf. R. Vaupel (ed.), *Die Reorganisation des Preußischen Staates unter Stein und Hardenberg*, part 2, vol. 1 (Leipzig, 1938), pp. 108–19, at p. 111.
215. This was the position of some leading members of the military led by Prince Wilhelm (later Kaiser Wilhelm I) in a minority report on the issue of penalties for insults to officers. See GStA/PK 84a, no. 8035, Report of the Commission of the Council of State on the Reform of the Penal Law, 22 April 1846, pp. 138, 140.
216. Cabinet Order, 10 April 1845, in K. von Helldorf (ed.), *Dienst-Vorschriften der Kgl. Preußischen Armee*, 3rd edn, Part 2, section 3 (Berlin, 1874), p. 3.
217. GStA/PK 84a, no. 2243, fols. 45ff.
218. GStA/PK 84a, no. 2243, fols. 50f.
219. Letter to the Minister of War, 13 November 1821, GStA/PK 84a, no. 2243, fol. 56.
220. Annex to a report of the Law Commission, 6 February 1802, GStA/PK 84a, no. 2243, fol. 13. The figures from Magdeburg reveal a similar picture for the period between 1818 and the middle of 1821; according to a report from the local Regional High Court, 31 August 1821, there were twenty-five cases, i.e. about seven per year, GStA/PK 84a, no. 2243, fols. 45–7.
221. Letter from Lieutenant General von Tippelskirch to the Minister of Justice, von Danckelmann, 7 November 1829, GStA/PK 84a, no. 2243, fol. 109v.
222. Report of 22 June 1839, GStA/PK 84a, no. 2244, fols. 91ff.
223. Report of 3 December 1829, GStA/PK 84a, no. 2243, fol. 110.
224. Report of 23 April 1839, GStA/PK, no. 2244, fols. 83f.
225. Report, 11 September 1838, GStA/PK 84a, no. 2243, fols. 261f.

226. Letter of 30 January 1831, GStA/PK 84a, no. 2243, fols. 125–7, at 125f.
227. Instruction of 14 January 1844, GStA/PK 84a, no. 2244.
228. Cabinet Order of 4 October 1810, GStA/PK 92 Nachlaß Vaupel, no. 48, fols. 14f.
229. Cabinet Order of 6 August 1820, StADT, Reg. Minden I C, no. 199, fol. 1; on the reductions cf. the complaints of the judicial authorities, GStA/PK 84a, no. 2220 *passim*.
230. Report of the Military, Interior, and Justice Departments of the Council of State, 23 January 1837, GStA/PK 84a, no. 2244, pp. 25f.
231. Law of 20 March 1837, Gräff *et al.*, *Ergänzungen und Erläuterungen*, 3rd edn, vol. 4, p. 380, esp. Article 10.
232. 'Observations of the Regulation Commission', GStA/PK 84a, no. 2244, fol. 199.
233. See 'Views of the Minister of War on the observations of the Commission for the preparation of a new service regulation for the army', 18 November 1843, GStA/PK 84a, no. 2244, fols. 200ff (marginal notes).
234. Instruction of 17 July 1828, GStA/PK 84a, no. 2244, fols. 200ff.
235. See the 'Views' cited in note 233 above.
236. Rochow to Mühler, 6 March 1840, GStA/PK 84a, no. 2244, fol. 228.
237. F. G. Graf von Waldersee, *Der Dienst des Preußischen Infanterie-Unteroffiziers*, 3rd edn (Berlin, 1848), p. 73.
238. T. Brand, *Volksthümlicher Soldaten-Katechismus für Preußen*, Breslau, undated (1830), pp. 44–7.
239. Report of the Military, Interior, and Justice Departments of the Council of State, 23 January 1837, GStA/PK 84a, no. 2244, p. 31 (of the printed version).
240. The difficulty in establishing the line of demarcation between physical 'insubordination' and disobedience was important here. Case law in the 1840s did not come to any firm conclusion as to whether solely the physical assault on a tax official, or in addition 'blocking the door through which the official has to pass to reach [the person to be distrained]' was to count as 'physical insubordination'. See Gräff *et al.*, *Ergänzungen und Erläuterungen*, 3rd edn, vol. 3, pp. 275–8, esp. pp. 276f.
241. Report of 23 January 1837, GStA/PK 84a, no. 2244, p. 36.
242. Report of the Department of the Interior to the Ministry of the Interior, 27 June 1839, StAK 441, no. 17274.
243. Letter from the Military Commander in Chief to the citadels of Koblenz and Ehrenbreitstein to the District Government, 2 March 1846, StAK 441, no. 17274.
244. For the case of Ottweiler in the Saarland in 1833, see StAK 442, no. 3870.
245. Cabinet Order, 11 July 1829, GStA/PK 84a, no. 2220, fol. 116.
246. See StAK 442, no. 3859; cf. StadtA TR 17, no. 222.
247. See Report of the Military and Interior Departments of the Council of State, 20 December 1820, GStA/PK 84a, no. 2220, p. 21 (of the printed report); see in the same vein the Minister of War to the Minister of Justice, 9 February 1821, *ibid.*, fol. 59.
248. Report of 9 October 1830, GStA/PK 84a, no. 2220, fol. 147.
249. Cf. Blasius. *Bürgerliche Gesellschaft und Kriminalität*, pp. 29ff, 104ff (only theft); Blasius, 'Der Kampf um die Geschworenengerichte im Vormärz', pp. 156f.
250. Report of the Justice and Military Departments of the Council of State, 12 March 1846, GStA/PK 84a, no. 2244, pp. 20f.

251. See the Cabinet Order of 14 June 1816 which included a section (Article 68) on police regulations for the citadel town of Koblenz, E. Baldus, 'Geschichte der Polizei-Direktion Koblenz', mimeo (Koblenz 1961), pp. 42f. The citadels between 1815 and the 1860s were as follows: in the east and middle provinces, Pillau, Danzig, Kolberg, Stralsund, Graudenz, Thorn, Posen, Kosel, Glogau, Küstrin, Stettin, Neiße, Glatz, Silberberg, Schweidnitz, Spandau, Torgau, Wittenberg, Magdeburg, Erfurt: in the west, Minden, Koblenz and Ehrenbreitstein, Cologne and Deutz, Wesel, Jülich, Saarlouis; cf. Freiherr von Zedlitz, *Die Staatskräfte der Preußischen Monarchie unter Friedrich Wilhelm III* (Berlin, 1830), vol. 3, p. 143.
252. Baldus, *Polizei-Direktion Koblenz*, p. 43.
253. Memorandum of 5 July 1808, in Vaupel, *Die Reorganisation des Preußischen Staates*, Part 2, vol. 1, pp. 501–3; cf. too G. H. Peertz, *Das Leben des Feldmarschalls Grafen Neithardt von Gneisenau*, vol. 1 (Berlin, 1864), pp. 351–4; Lehmann, *Scharnhorst*, vol. 2, p. 235, note 1.
254. Cf. Lehmann, *Scharnhorst*, vol. 2, p. 235 which refers to the customary practice based on the 1756 Instruction, under which an officer had been proposed for the post of commander for the citadel of Memel who was 'no longer sufficiently fit to be able to serve in the army'.
255. Undated draft, written after 25 November 1808, cited in Vaupel, *Die Reorganisation des Preußischen Staates*, Part 2, vol. 1, pp. 733–5.
256. The regulations were set out in a public announcement issued on 30 September 1830, 'On the cooperation and obligation of the civil authorities and chambers in the citadels and their districts in the event of enclosure and siege', StADT, Reg. Minden Präs., no. 139, fols. 6ff, Article 3.
257. *Ibid.*, Article 7.
258. Report of 22 February 1831, StAK 403, no. 1807, pp. 55f; following quote, *ibid.*
259. Conference, 1 August 1831, *ibid.*, pp. 139ff.
260. Minutes of meeting between Commander Major General von Othegrafen, *Regierungspräsident* von Reimann, and Mayor König, 13 August 1831, *ibid.*, pp. 171f; inquiry from the commander, 13 September 1832, *ibid.*, p. 312.
261. Report of the District Government in Cologne, 21 December 1832, StAK 403, no. 1807, pp. 353–6, at p. 353.
262. Letter from the Commanding General of the Observer Corps, von Müffling, to the *Oberpräsident*, 23 December 1832, *ibid.*, pp. 367–9, at p. 367.
263. See the file StAK 403, no. 11310.
264. L. Blesson, *Feld-Befestigungskunst für alle Waffen* (Berlin, 1825), p. 445. Although this passage does not apply directly to permanent fortresses, the idea is evidently analogous.
265. A passage from a later provision (1888) could well apply here: garrison duty, and first and foremost watch duty 'is only rarely an exercise, and rather consists of real duties': Garrison Service Regulations, 13 September 1888, cited in A. von Boguslawski, 'Das Heer' in J. von Pflugk-Harttung (ed.), *Die Heere und Flotten der Gegenwart*, vol. 1 (Berlin, 1896), p. 162.
266. W. von Kamptz, *Der Dienst der Infanterie bei der Vertheidigung der Festungen gegen gewaltsamen Angriff* (Potsdam, 1855), pp. 65f.
267. HStAD, Reg. Aachen 1, no. 1482, Circular Rescript, 11 May 1816.
268. This and subsequent quotations in this paragraph are from the Decree of the Commander General to the Office of the Commander (*Kommandantur*), 27 May 1830, HistA Köln 400, V-5C, no. 30.
269. See for an analysis of the social composition of the population in Cologne, P.

Ayçoberry, 'Probleme der Sozialschichtung in Köln im Zeitalter der Frühindustrialisierung', in W. Fischer (ed.), *Wirtschafts- und sozialgeschichtliche Probleme der frühen Industrialiseriung* (Berlin, 1968), pp. 512–28, esp. pp. 521ff.

270. Cf. in general E. Gothein, *Verfassungs- und Wirtschaftsgeschichte der Stadt Köln* (Cologne, 1916) vol. 1, *passim*; O. Büsch, 'Festungsstadt und Industrie. Zur Geschichte von Spandau und Siemensstadt im Zeitalter der Industrialisierung', *Jahrbuch für die Geschichte Mittel- und Ostdeutschlands*, 20 (1971), 161–82, at 169f. For a perception from the 'other side' i.e. the citizenry, cf. the resigned report by the municipal executive in Minden, 6 October 1849, to the District Government: 'We have no more information as to the conceptions which move the citadel commander', StADT, Reg. Minden 1 C, no. 81.

271. According to Hackländer 'an untranslatable term covering activities ranging from singing in the streets to knocking down signs and breaking windows and every other conceivable scandal': F. W. Hackländer, *Das Soldatenleben im Frieden* (Stuttgart, 1844), pp. 48f. During the 1830s Hackländer was a Prussian soldier with the garrison in Düsseldorf.

272. On the difficulties which the hunting laws created for the town concerned, see APW, Kłodzko (Glatz), no. 920; for Minden, StADT, Reg. Minden 1 C, no. 255.

273. On Cologne see Gothein, *Verfassungs- und Wirtschaftsgeschichte*, *passim*; on Magdeburg, von Stuckrad, *Geschichte des 1. Magdeburgischen Infantierieregiments*, no. 26, Part 1 (Berlin, 1888), pp. 166ff, 203ff.

274. See the Report by the Director of Police, Heister, 6 November 1838, HStAD, Reg. Köln, no. 62; also reproduced in F. von Keinemann, *Das Kölner Ereignis, sein Widerhall in der Rheinprovinz und in Westfalen* (Münster, 1974), Part 1, p. 158. Cf. too the Decree of 14 November 1838 to Commanders and Commanding Staffs, in Keinemann, *ibid.*, Part 2, p. 236.

275. HStAD, Rep. 11, no. 1310. The commander was Colonel von Hüser (appointed in March 1831); he had been a regimental commander stationed in Saarlouis since 1828, and in 1830/1 had organised the equipping of troops during mobilisation: see *Denkwürdigkeiten aus dem Leben des General d. Inf. v. Hüser* (Berlin, 1877), edited M.Q. For Hüser appointment to the post of commander was a painful blow. On the day of his appointment he noted a verse from Schiller's *Wallenstein*: 'The bloom has gone out of my life', *ibid.*, p. 213.

276. GStA/PK, 84a, no. 2244. On arrest, GStA/PK 84a, no. 2243, Decree to the President of the District Court in Saarbrücken, Bessel, 9 December 1836, fol. 302.

277. StADT, Reg. Minden 1 C, no. 199, Militärwachdienst.

278. *Ibid.* fols. 18ff, 9 September 1844.

279. Report of 15 July 1841, StAK 403, no. 381. During the debate on the conduct of civil officials in the event of a hostile invasion, Bodelschwingh – then *Regierungspräsident* in Trier – had stressed that 'the organisation of our state is principally *military*' (italics in original), StAK 403, no. 1807, p. 239.

5 Emergencies and the requisitioning of the military

1. For a typology of 'riotous assemblies' see the commentary in Rönne and Simon, *Polizeiwesen*, vol. 1 (Breslau, 1840), p. 664. Some of the material in this chapter is based on a previous paper: A. Lüdtke, 'Praxis und Funktion staatlicher

Repression: Preußen 1815–50', *Geschichte und Gesellschaft*, 3 (1977), 190–211, at 196ff.

2. See the file opened in the Ministry of the Interior on 'Police surveillance of the great assemblages of railway workers', ZStA II, Rep. 77, Lit. 258, no. 22, vol. 1.
3. Cf. A.Schweder, *Politische Polizei. Begriff und Wesen der politischen Polizei im Metternichschen System* (Berlin, 1937), pp. 44f.
4. Rönne and Simon, *Polizeiwesen*, vol. 1, p. 664.
5. Observation in the 'Vorbericht' (Preface) to Hoffmann's *Polizei-Archiv*, (1817), p. 1.
6. Cf. chapter 5 of R. Tilly, 'Protest and Collective Violence in Germany during Modernization (1800–1914)', mimeo (Münster, 1974).
7. C. Tilly *et al.*, *The Rebellious Century, 1830–1930* (Cambridge, Mass., 1975), pp. 50f.
8. See H. Medick, 'Plebeian culture and the proto-industrial family economy: articulation of needs and patterns of consumption', in P. Kriedte, H. Medick and J. Schlumbohm, *Industrialisation before Industrialisation* (Cambridge, 1982), pp. 64–73.
9. See Pestel to the *Landrat* in Kempen, 13 November 1830, HStAD, Reg. Düss. Präs., no. 754, fol. 283, and Pestel to the *Landrat* in Raes, *ibid.*, fols. 93ff.
10. Report of the District Government in Münster, Department of the Interior, 24 October 1833, ZStA II, Rep. 77, tit. 508, no. 2, vol. 1, fols. 135f.
11. Merker, *Handbuch für die ausübenden Polizei-Beamten* (Erfurt, 1818), pp. 63ff; see also G. A. Bielitz, *Darstellung der Verfassung* (Leipzig, 1841), p. 21; W. G. von der Heyde, *Polizei-Verwaltung* (Magdeburg, 1842), p. 23. The guidelines correspond to the Circular of 30 December 1798 and the Order of 17 August 1835, which merely confirmed the previous regulation: the texts are reproduced in Rönne and Simon, *Polizeiwesen*, vol. 1, pp. 666ff. See Appendices 4 and 6.
12. The German term 'possessionierten Bürger' was used in a report by the *Landrat* in Wevelinghofen, 8 September 1830, to the District Government in Düsseldorf, HStAD, Reg. Düss. Präs., no. 754, fol. 40v.
13. See the review of a number of writings on unrest in Germany in *Annalen der preußischen innern Staatsverwaltung*, 14 (1830), Part 3, 671–708.
14. See D. Eichholtz, 'Bewegungen unter den preußischen Eisenbahnbauarbeitern im Vormärz', *Beiträge zur deutschen Wirtschafts- und Sozialgeschichte des 18. und 19. Jahrhunderts* (Berlin, GDR, 1962), 251–87. Eichholtz lists 33 incidents for the period 1841–7. The military intervened in 11 instances, or were implicated in the event itself; during the construction of the Vohwinkler Railway, the *Regierungspräsident*, von Spiegel, expressly reserved the use of the military in an incident in Langenberg (9 April 1845): ZStA II, Rep. 77, tit. 258, no. 22, vol. 1, fol. 77v. Cf. W. Wortmann, *Eisenbahnbauarbeiter im Vormärz* (Cologne and Vienna, 1972).
15. See ZStA II, Rep. 77, tit. 258, no. 22, vol. 1, especially fol. 202v; fol. 247 (2 June 1846); on 'religious discipline' see StAK 403, no. 2381, pp. 33f.
16. Report of the *Landrat* in Ohlau, 25 November 1844, APW, Rej. Wrocł 1, no. 9077, fols. 13f.
17. See internal memoranda between October 1844 and June 1846, ZStA II, Rep. 77, tit. 258, no. 22, vol. 1, fols. 88ff, 165ff, 246ff.
18. At least according to the report of the *Landrat* in Iserlohn, P. E. Müllensiefen: P. E. Müllensiefen, *Ein deutsches Bürgerleben*, ed. F. von Oppeln-Bronikowski

(Berlin, 1931), p. 288. See too the description by the *Landrat* of Neumarkt, in Mid-Silesia, of a railway navvies' 'tumult' in the autumn of 1844, which 'was immediately suppressed by the determined presence of the court clerk, a former NCO from the war', APW, Rej. Wrocł. 1, no. 9077, report of incidents on 5 November 1844, fol. 16.

19. According to the report of Freiherr von Spiegel, *Regierungspräsident* in Düsseldorf, 15 August 1839, StAK 403, no. 2435, p. 562.
20. See StAK 402, no. 671, on 'the unrest which has broken out amongst factory workers in Eupen'.
21. See StAK 403, no. 2446, on an 'excess carried out on the occasion of troop mustering in Ahrweiler' by those liable for military service.
22. G. Zimmermann, *Die deutsche Polizei im 19. Jahrhundert*, vol. 3 (Hanover, 1849), p. 857.
23. On Berlin, see P. Clauswitz, *Die Städteordnung von 1808 und die Stadt Berlin* (Berlin, 1908), pp. 116ff. According to the 11 March 1850 law, payments for Gendarmes ceased (these were in fact moved out of Berlin with the establishment of the constabulary, the *Schutzmannschaft*).
24. Circular from the Ministry of the Police and Interior, 4 October 1830, Rönne and Simon, *Polizeiwesen*, vol. 1, pp. 83f.
25. HStAD, Reg. Aachen Präs., nos. 628, 692. See the events of 1847, StAK 403, no. 2358, pp. 44f, 75f, 93.
26. ZStA II, Rep. 77, tit. 500, no. 1, vol. 2, fols. 130ff, and undated memorandum from the *Polizeirat* F. W. Duncker (who was responsible for the criminal investigations during the weavers' rising in 1844). For the Order itself see GS 1846, p. 111.
27. For the text of the law, see GS 1848, pp. 289f. Cf. the reports from the *Landrat* in Minden, March 1849; the observations by his *Kreissekretär* in Paderborn are characteristic: 'In the open countryside the *Bürgerwehr* is regarded as a useless, superfluous, costly institution', which 'absorbs a good deal of money and effort', 13 March 1849, StADT, Reg. Minden I C, no. 81.
28. See the Order of 30 April 1815 and the Instruction to District Governments, 31 December 1825 (Section 11a). The Cabinet Order of 21 June 1815 established that the decision as to what measures to adopt was to lie with the military, at least in instances of 'imminent danger', GStA/PK 84a, no. 2196, fols. 22ff.
29. Circular from the District Government in Düsseldorf to *Landräte*, 15 October 1830, HStAD, Reg. Düsseldorf Präs., no. 752, on the 'securing of public order', fols. 44ff. Cf. too the circular from the Ministry of the Interior, 3 July 1844, which prescribed a direct report to be sent from *Landräte* or Mayors to the Ministry, HStAD, Reg. Düss. Präs., no. 753, fol. 126.
30. In 1848 there was an explicit Ministerial Order to this effect: the Ministry contended that the efficiency of the police could be jeopardised by the collegial structure of the District Governments, and hence officials 'on the spot' were to make the widest use of their powers to act independently. StAK 441, no. 23868, Circular decree, 17 July 1848.
31. Letter to his brother, 18 September 1830, BA, Briefsammlung Strelitz, no. 253, fols. 35f. Cf. the observation by the later Chief of the General Staff, Graf von Waldersee, where he noted that he would not allow these 'old guns' to be loaded since, if the bearer was careless in standing at ease, with the gun cocked the weapon could go off, injuring or even killing the bearer or those in the vicinity: see H. Mohls (ed.), *Generalfeldmarschall Alfred Graf von Waldersee in seinem militärischen Wirken*, vol. 1 (Berlin, 1929), p. 9.

32. Texts in Rönne and Simon, *Polizeiwesen*, vol. 1, pp. 666ff.
33. See StAK 403, no. 2358, von Brenn, 26 November 1832, fols. 37ff. On the following Instruction, 19 November 1846, StAK 403, no. 2358, pp. 67f.
34. StAMS Oberpräs., no. 680.
35. GS 1846, p. 60. Cf. the provision issued on 1 March 1850, GStA/PK 84a, no. 2244, fols. 169ff, Instruction to the Gendarmerie in Rönne and Simon, *Polizeiwesen*, vol. 1, pp. 19ff. The 4 February 1854 Cabinet Order confirmed that Article 28 also applied to 'executive police officers', including the constabulary (*Schutzmannschaft*); cf. *Ministerialblatt für die gesamte innere Verwaltung 1854*, p. 69. For an analysis see F. van Calker, *Das Recht des Militärs zum administrativen Waffengebrauch* (Munich, 1888); A. Wilfling, *Der administrative Waffengebrauch* (Vienna and Leipzig, 1909).
36. Cf. F. G. Graf von Waldersee, *Der Dienst des preußischen Infanterie-Unteroffiziers*, 3rd and 4th edns. (Berlin, 1848 and 1849). A similar difference can be noted in A. von Witzleben, *Grundzüge des Heerwesens und Infanteriedienstes der Kgl. Preuß. Armee* (Berlin, 1845; and also 9th edn, 1867).
37. Anon, 'Rezensionen', *Militär-Literatur-Zeitung* (1849), 165–79, and (1850), 9–15. Kliem notes that, 'according to the tactical considerations of the time', a ratio of one soldier to ten members of the public was regarded as essential, M. Kliem, 'Genesis der Führungskräfte der feudal-militärischen Konterrevolution 1848 in Preußen', Doctoral thesis (Berlin, GDR, 1966), p. 224.
38. See the Circular from the District Government in Breslau, 15 May 1847, APW, Mag. Kłodzka, no. 514. For 1848 cf. ZStA II, Rep. 77, tit. 508, no. 1, *passim*; StAK 441, no. 23868, *passim*. For 1839 in the Lower Rhenish area, H. von Brehn, *Geschichte des Westfälischen Ulanen-Regiments Nr. 5* (Düsseldorf, 1890), p. 43; on the origins and outbreak of the unrest in Cleves see F. Keinemann, *Das Kölner Ereignis, sein Widerhall in der Rheinprovinz und in Westfalen* (Münster, 1974), Part 1, pp. 191–7.
39. E. von Conrady, *Leben und Wirken des Gen. d. Inf. und Komm. Generals. des V. Armeekorps Carl von Grolman*, vol. 3 (Berlin, 1896), p. 122.
40. ZStA II, Pr. Br. H.A., Rep. 51e, no. 62f, fols. 59f.
41. See the numerous comments in the memoirs of contemporary officers, e.g. Anon, *Erinnerungen aus dem Dienstleben eines alten preußischen Offiziers der Kgl. Preuß. Armee* (Görlitz, 1875), p. 26, covering the 1820s–30s, and p. 27; F. Meinecke, *Das Leben des Gen.-Feldmarschalls Hermann von Boyen*, vol. 2 (Stuttgart, 1899), p. 506 (on the 1840s). Cf. too the memoirs of one particularly stigmatised outsider, the only Jewish officer in the pre-1848 army, Artillery Major Meno Burg: *Geschichte meines Dienstlebens*, 3rd edn (Leipzig, 1916), pp. 5, 127.
42. This homogeneity can be confirmed by looking at the army's annually published list of rankings; cf. Kliem, 'Genesis der Führungskräfte', pp. 171ff, esp. 176. The quote is from Edwin von Manteuffel, later Chief of the Military Cabinet (and centrally responsible for the make-up and ethos of the officer corps with direct access to the King), in 1841 in which he described the 'inner officer aristocracy' as the 'noblest in the army'.
43. H. Feldt, *Geschichte des Infanterie-Regiments Frhr v. Sparr (3. Westf.) Nr. 16* (Berlin, 1905), p. 157; O. Paulizky and A. von Woedtke, *Geschichte des 4. Rhein. Inf.-Regiments Nr. 30*, Part 1, 1815–84 (Berlin, 1884), p. 135.
44. See C. Friccius, *Das Preußische Militärstrafrecht* (Berlin and Elbing, 1835).
45. Zychlinski, *Geschichte des Preuß. Inf.-Regiments Nr. 24* (Berlin, 1857), p. 102; cf. too p. 133.

46. According to a report from the *Oberpräsident* in Koblenz, von Schaper, 24 March 1844 to the Minister of the Interior, ZStA II, Rep. 77, tit. 343 A, no. 32, fol. 19.
47. The group of *Frühsozialisten* and Communists which got together in the artillery after 1841 was unrepresentative in this respect: J. Hansen (ed.), *Rheinische Briefe und Akten*, vol. 2 (Bonn, 1942), pp. 385ff; F. Anneke, *Ein ehrengerichtlicher Prozeß* (Leipzig, 1846); von Willich, *Im preußischen Heere* (Mannheim, 1848). We should not overlook the refusals to obey orders amongst soldiers, including combat troops (principally the infantry) in 1848. However, they were not crucial when matters became 'critical'; cf. E. Czóbel, 'Zur Geschichte des Kommunistenbundes. Die Kölner Bundesgemeinde vor der Revolution', *Archiv für die Geschichte des Sozialismus und der Arbeiterbewegung*, 11 (1925), 299–335, at 320ff; H. Peters, 'Erfurt im Jahre 1848', Doctoral thesis (Berlin, GDR, 1966), p. 223.
48. Noted, without a precise date, in Kliem, 'Genesis der Führungskräfte', p. 191.
49. See *ibid.*, and Meinecke, *Boyen*, vol. 2, p. 256: the Cabinet Orders dated from 31 December 1846 and 24 July 1847 (Kliem does not cite the latter).
50. See C. Jany, *Die Kgl. Preuß. Armee, Geschichte der Kgl. Preuß. Armee*, vol. 4 (Berlin, 1933), pp. 152ff. The 'Observation Corps' (1830–2) was basically formed from the 4th Army Corps.
51. R. von Leszcynski, *Fünfzig Jahre Geschichte des Kgl. Preuß. 2. Posensche Inf.-Regiments Nr. 19*, 1813–63 (Luxemburg, 1863), p. 205.
52. See Kliem, 'Genesis der Führungskräfte', pp. 171f.
53. See the comprehensive report on the security situation in the Government District, 17 May 1850, StAMS, Reg. Arnsberg Pr., no. 56.
54. Anon, *Westfälische Zustände*, 2nd edn (n.p., 1842), p. 64. The fact that the author had the control of riots in mind is evidenced by his observation that 'revolts and riots would then be out of the question'.
55. See the memos from the Commanding General, von Borstell, to the Mayor and Municipal Executive in Neuß, and the *Oberpräsident* of the Province, von Bodelschwingh, both dated 2 March 1839, StAK 403, no. 2523[1], pp. 295–9, 329f; both are reproduced in F. Keinemann, *Das Kölner Ereignis*, Part 2, pp. 273–5.
56. See the collection of documents on the incidents in H. Rösen, 'Der Aufstand der Krefelder "Seidenfabrikarbeiter" 1828 und die Bildung einer "Sicherheitswache"', *Die Heimat* (1965), 32–61. On the events of 10 and 25 October, the orders from the *Landrat* to the Mayor, 25 October, and the District Government in Düsseldorf, 28 October, see Rösen, *ibid.*, p. 33.
57. On the structure of the silk-cloth industry in Krefeld see J. Kermann, *Die Manufakturen im Rheinland, 1750–1833* (Bonn, 1872), pp. 284–90, 716ff. Kermann's work concentrates on manufacture and mechanical production ('machinofacture'). See too H. Botzet, 'Die Geschichte der sozialen Verhältnisse in Krefeld und ihre wirtschaftlichen Zusammenhänge', Doctoral thesis (Cologne, 1953), p. 70; and A. Thun, *Die Industrie am Niederrhein und ihre Arbeiter*, vol. 1 (Leipzig, 1879), pp. 102–20.
58. According to a report by the *Landrat*, 14 November 1828, Rösen, 'Der Aufstand', 41.
59. Report, 6 November, 1828, Rösen, *ibid.*, 35.
60. Rönne and Simon, *Polizeiwesen*, vol. 1, p. 664.
61. *Ibid.*
62. *Ibid.*, p. 665.

63. Orders of the 28 October 1828, Rösen, 'Der Aufstand', 33 and 33f.
64. Report, 5 November 1828, 2.45 p.m., Rösen, *ibid.*, 34.
65. See the detailed report of 24 December by the District Government, which brought together all official information on the incidents, Rösen, *ibid.*, 54–7. Thun's observation that the lower rates had already been paid on the 3rd is clearly off the mark: Thun, *Industrie am Niederrhein*, vol. 1, p. 102.
66. Report by the *Regierungspräsident*, von Pestel, to von Schuckmann, Minister of the Interior, 6 November 1828, Rösen, 'Der Aufstand', 34f.
67. Report, 24 December 1828, Rösen, *ibid.*, 54ff. Quotations in this and subsequent two paragraphs from this source.
68. Report, 10 November 1828, Rösen, *ibid.*, 37f.
69. Diary of C. R. Vogelsang (MSS in Stadtarchiv, Krefeld), fol. 18, entry for 4 November 1828, Rösen, *ibid.*, 34.
70. Notice issued by the Mayor, 5 November, and proclamation from Superintendent Walther, also 5 November, Rösen, *ibid.*, 34.
71. See the Circular for the 'more precise specification of diverse provisions in the General Legal Code and the General Statutory Code, Section 1, on the prevention of tumults and the punishment of their instigators and participants', in Rönne and Simon, *Polizeiwesen*, vol. 1, pp. 666ff. Appendix 4 below contains an abridged version of this provision.
72. Cabinet Order, 17 October 1820, in KA 4 (1820), pp. 810ff.
73. Order reproduced in Rönne and Simon, *Polizeiwesen*, vol. 1, pp. 666ff, here Sections 6, 7.
74. See Section 48 of the Order of 26 December 1808, which was added without amendment to the Instructions to District Governments of 23 October 1817, GS 1817, p. 288.
75. In the *Vormärz* period, messages by courier were expected to travel 30–40 German miles – 210–280 km – a day; assuming a short preparation time in Koblenz, theoretically a message sent in the morning could be responded to by that same evening. Cf. on these figures Born, 'Die Entwicklung der Kgl. Preußischen Ostbahn', *Zeitschrift für Eisenbahnwesen*, 34 (1911), 879ff, 885.
76. Figures taken from District Government Report, 10 November 1828, Rösen, 'Der Aufstand', 55.
77. Minutes of the Municipal Council (*Gemeinderat*), 7 November, Rösen, *ibid.*, 45.
78. District Government Order to the *Landrat*, 21 November, Rösen, *ibid.*, 45.
79. Minutes of a meeting between the Mayor, a number of angry citizens and the Superintendent of Police, 24 November, Rösen, *ibid.*, 46; Order of the *Landrat*, 3 December, *ibid.*; order of the District Government, also 3 December, *ibid.*
80. Report, 7 November 1818, Rösen, *ibid.*, 35.
81. Order of the *Landrat*, 9 November 1828, Rösen, *ibid.*, 38f.
82. Order of *Regierungspräsident* von Pestel, 10 November 1828, Rösen, *ibid.*, 38ff.
83. Letter of 8 November 1828, Rösen, *ibid.*, 35f.
84. Letter from Corps Headquarters Staff to the *Oberpräsident*, 11 November, Rösen, *ibid.*, 40f; cf. too the letter from Corps Headquarters Staff, 17 November, Rösen, *ibid.*, 44; notification of the *Oberpräsidium*'s assent to the proposed troop withdrawal to the District Government in Düsseldorf, 16 November, Rösen *ibid.*, 41.
85. These dates are maintained by Cappe in his report to the District Government, 14 November, Rösen, *ibid.*, 41. However, there is no mention of this in the 7 November Report.

86. Report, 14 November, Rösen, *ibid.*, 41.
87. Letter to the Division, 16 November 1828, Rösen, *ibid.*, 42; and to the *Oberpräsident* on the same day, Rösen, *ibid.*, 43.
88. Letter, 17 November 1828, Rösen, *ibid.*, 44.
89. Marginal note, 17 November 1828, Rösen, *ibid.*, 44.
90. Letter, 18 November 1828, Rösen, *ibid.*, 44f.
91. Order, 18 November, 1828, Rösen, *ibid.*, 44.
92. Letter, 30 November, Report of 1 December 1828, Rösen, *ibid.*, 47.
93. Letter, 15 December 1828, Rösen, *ibid.*, 52.
94. Rösen, *ibid.*, 54–7.
95. Order of the Minister of the Interior and Police, 27 January 1829, Rösen, *ibid.*, 59; Order on a bonus payment was issued on 9 March, and forwarded from the District Government to the *Landrat* on 25th, Rösen, *ibid.*, 59.
96. Application by Walther, 23 December 1828, Rösen, *ibid.*, 54; decision of the Municipal Council, 14 January (notified to the *Landrat* on 22 January); approval by the District Government, 18 February 1829, Rösen, *ibid.*, 49.
97. Rösen, *ibid.*, 60f.
98. Drawing on documentary evidence in Krefeld, Rösen adds that this individual was pardoned three months before the end of his punishment, and following a petition in March 1840 was eventually exempted from police supervision by Royal Pardon on 12 October 1840, *ibid.*, p. 61, note 42.
99. Decree of 1 November 1816, StAK 441, no. 24087.
100. H. Ostermann, *Die Gesamte Polizei-, Militär-, Steuer- und Gemeindeverwaltung*, Part 1 (Coesfeld, 1836), p. 52.
101. Heyde, *Polizei-Verwaltung*, p. 22.
102. Ministerial Decree, 4 November 1830, HStAD, Reg. Düsseldorf Präs., no. 754.
103. GStA/PK 181, no. 1455, 18 October 1848, Marg. p. 78 (Nordenflycht became *Regierungspräsident* in 1831, but had administered the office as Commissary since 1830).
104. The entire episode is contained in HStAD, Oberpräs. Köln, no. 494.
105. Text in KA 4 (1820), pp. 810ff.
106. Cf. the Cabinet Order to Minister Count Dohna and Generals von Scharnhorst and von Hake, 18 October 1810, occasioned by a military intervention in a tumult in Electoral Brandenburg: there was 'not as yet agreement as to the principles (by which) such police measures were to be effectively executed', GStA/PK 92, Nachl. Vaupel, no. 50, fols. 39f.
107. In general, see W. Abel, *Massenarmut und Hungerkrisen*, (Hamburg and Berlin, 1974), pp. 314ff; see too Chapter 3 above.
108. More detail in A. Lüdtke, ' "Wehrhafte Nation" und "innere Wohlfahrt" ', *Militärgeschichtliche Mitteilungen*, 30 (1981), Heft 2, 7–56.
109. E. Sterling, *Judenhaß. Die Anfänge des politischen Antisemitismus in Deutschland (1815–50)* (Frankfurt, 1969).
110. Cabinet Order, 17 October 1820 in KA 4 (1820), pp. 810ff. Cf. the Instruction issued by the Minister of the Interior, 19 November 1846, StAK 403, no. 2358, pp. 67f.

6 Citadel practice

1. For political and ideological developments, though only within the Berlin centre, see W. M. Simon, *The Failure of the Prussian Reform Movement, 1807–19* (Ithaca, 1955).

2. The continuity of this practice is reflected in an order of the day given by the Commander General of the 8th Corps, von Hake, on 4 August 1818: in the event of 'excesses' officers 'should consider only those military persons involved. You are therefore to refrain from any orders to civil persons, who are to be entrusted at all times to the local executive or police officers. In fact, you should ensure that a [civil] police officer is fetched as swiftly as possible', HStAD, Reg. Köln, no. 1692, fol. 3.
3. See the autobiographical account by Wehnert, a *Regierungsrat* in Potsdam, *Über den Geist der preußischen Staatsorganisation und Staatsdienerschaft* (Potsdam, 1833), pp. 24f, 28f, 61. Wehnert refers to his colleagues as the 'guardians . . . of the subjects'.
4. *Ibid*., p. 24.
5. The 'superarbitrium', in the sense referred to here, was made a subject of debate by the then Minister of the Interior, O. von Manteuffel, in the ministerial debate on the law regulating the state of siege, which came into force on 4 June 1851; see his memo to the Ministers of Justice and of War, 22 December 1850, GStA/PK 84a, no. 2106, fol. 5. Manteuffel's reservations expressed here were ignored, however. Art. 2, Para. 2 of the law specified that in the event of 'imminent danger', the local or regional military commander could act without application from the civil authorities; see E. R. Huber, *Dokumente zur deutschen Verfassungsgeschichte*, vol. 1 (Stuttgart, 1961), no. 169.
6. Quoted from the *Landrat* in Iserlohn, Schütte, to a subordinate, 12 April 1846, StAMS, Krs. Iserlohn Landratsamt, no. 165.
7. Präs. Naumann, 17 May 1850, StAMS, Reg. Arnsberg Pr., no. 56.
8. On a vain attempt by the *Landrat* in Hagen to retain a Gendarme with local knowledge and prevent him being transferred for the Austro-Prussian War, 30 May 1866, see StAMS, Reg. Arnsberg I, no. 1499.
9. See the order of Police Minister von Brenn, 5 June 1831, to the District Government in Bromberg on the occasion of the tumult in Inowrocław already noted on pp. 162. The District Government was to 'pursue its first and most sacred duty, the maintenance of public quiet', APP, Nadprez., no. 1012, p. 88.
10. StAK 403, no. 2514, p. 3.
11. Spiegel's memorandum, 29 April 1839, StAK 403, no. 2435, pp. 541ff. The appeal by von Ingersleben, *Oberpräsident* in the Rhine province, on 1 September 1830 – in the aftermath of the riots in Aachen – was also unsuccessful, HStAD, Reg. Düss. Präs., no. 754, fol. 11v.
12. Report to Minister of the Interior, von Rochow, 24 April 1839, StAK 403, no. 2435, pp. 515–30.
13. M. Laubert, 'Skizzen zur Posener Stadtgeschichte vor 100 Jahren', *Deutsche wiss. Zeitschrift im Wartheland* (1940), 68–128, esp. 99f.
14. Spiegel in a memorandum to the Commander General of the 7th Army Corps (Münster), 29 April 1839, StAK 403, no. 3245, pp. 541–59.
15. Report from the provincial authorities in Koblenz, 24 June 1816, on the decision as to whether the Gendarmerie established in the Rhine province ought to be dissolved, StAK 402, no. 609, pp. 41ff. Cf. too R. Koselleck, *Preußen zwischen Reform und Revolution* (1st edn, Stuttgart, 1967).
16. Report from the Dept of the Interior in the Koblenz District Government, 5 October 1848, StAK 403, no. 2358, pp. 113ff.
17. See the 'Rescript' from the Ministry of the Interior to the District Government in Minden, 26 March 1837, on 'mutual notifications between the local police and military authorities' (KA 21 (1837), no. 128), which, by way of example, cites the possible – but, with prompt notification, avoidable – disturbance to a funeral

procession by a military alarm. The problems of command during the Martinmas events in Cologne occasioned a Cabinet Order (29 September 1846) regulating such 'crisis situations', in which the key point had first been mooted in an internal ministerial report – namely, that in the event of conflict only the military were to issue orders and corresponding proclamations: ZStA II Rep., tit. 500, no. 1, vol. 1.

18. On the concept of 'symbiosis' see L. Machtan and D. Milles, *Klassensymbiose und Bonapartismus. Zu einer materialistischen Analyse der gesellschaftlichen und politischen Herrschaftsverhältnisse in Preussen-Deutschland (1850–1878/79)* (Frankfurt, 1980).
19. Report, 7 May 1847, StAK 441, no. 17274.
20. Spiegel's memorandum, 29 April 1839, StAK 403, no. 2435, pp. 541ff. Cf. the application for police reinforcements made by the Mayor of Elberfeld, von Carnap, 24 January 1839, StadtA Wuppertal Oberbürgermeisteramt Elberfeld O V, no. 8.
21. In general on censorship and the provisions within the German Confederation, see E. R. Huber, *Deutsche Verfassungsgeschichte, seit 1789*, vol. 1 (Stuttgart, 1957), pp. 742ff, vol. 2 (Stuttgart, 1960), pp. 163, 182. On the phase of 'limited freedom of the press' between May 1842 and January 1843, see G. Mayer, 'Die Anfänge des politischen Radikalismus im vormärzlichen Preussen (1913)', in G. Mayer, *Radikalismus, Sozialismus und bürgerliche Demokratie*, ed. H.-U. Wehler (Frankfurt, 1969), pp. 7–107, esp. 24ff. For one individual, and important, instance see U. Radlik, 'Heine in der Zensur der Restaurationsepoche', in J. Hermand and M. Windfuhr (eds.), *Zur Literatur der Restaurationsepoche, 1815–1848* (Stuttgart, 1970), pp. 460–89.
22. K. Heinzen, *Die Preußische Bürokratie* (Darmstadt, 1845), p. 105; the succeeding quote is also from Heinzen, pp. 102, 104. For a synopsis of the contemporary critique of the bureaucracy see R. Mohl, 'Über Bureaukratie', *Zeitschrift für die gesamte Staatswissenschaft*, 3 (1846), 340–64.
23. T. Fontane, 'Preussen – ein Militär- oder Polizeistaat?', in T. Fontane, *Politik und Geschichte* (Munich, 1969), *Sämtliche Werke*, vol. 19, pp. 70–4.
24. Report, 28 January 1849, HStAD, Reg. Düsseldorf Präs., no. 814, fols. 619f. This institution, established by statute in 1849–51, transferred 'executive authority' to local or regional military commanders, i.e. the direction of the administration and certain areas of criminal jurisdiction, such as incendiarism. On the relevant statute, see Huber, *Dokumente zur deutschen Verfassungsgeschichte*, vol. 1, no. 169, Law of 4 June 1851; cf. *ibid.*, no. 157, General Wrangel's Order of 12 November 1848 which imposed a state of siege on Berlin. On the Order of 10 May 1849 and the declaration of 4 July 1849 see GS 1849, pp. 165 and 250.
25. A. Ballhorn, *Das Polizeipräsidium zu Berlin* (Berlin, 1852), p. iii; Ballhorn was a *Regierungsassessor* in the Police Presidium in Berlin. The enormous brutality exhibited by the Berlin police towards both people and personal property during housing riots in July and August 1872 gives some idea of the nature of this 'war': see P. Kampffmeyer and B. Altmann, *Vor dem Sozialistengesetz. Krisenjahre des Obrigkeitsstaates* (Berlin, 1928), p. 100; A. Lange, *Berlin zur Zeit Bebels und Bismarcks* (Berlin, GDR, 1972), pp. 134–8. The rate of police actions against strikes gives one, quantitative, index for the years around the turn of the century: this rose from 21.6 per cent in 1904, to 27.2 per cent in 1910 and then jumped to 35.9 per cent in 1912 and 33.9 per cent in 1913; cf. H. Bleiber, 'Die Moabiter Unruhen 1910', *Zeitschrift für Geschichtswissenschaft*, 3 (1955), 173–211, 182.

26. On Königshütte, see *Volksstaat*, no. 55, 8 July 1871. On Bielefeld see W. Hofmann, *Die Bielefelder Stadtverordneten* (Stuttgart, 1964), p. 25.
27. See D. Groh, *Negative Integration und revolutionärer Attentismus. Die deutsche Sozialdemokratie am Vorabend des Ersten Weltkriegs* (Frankfurt, 1973), p. 126, note 150.
28. See W. Deist, 'Die Armee in Staat und Gesellschaft 1890–1914', in M. Stürmer (ed.), *Das kaiserliche Deutschland. Politik und Gesellschaft 1870–1918* (Düsseldorf, 1970), pp. 312–39; cf. too, Deist, *Militär und Innenpolitik im Weltkrieg 1914–1918*, Part 1 (Düsseldorf, 1970), pp. xxxi ff. See additionally M. Stürmer, 'Staatsstreichgedanken im Bismarckreich', *Historische Zeitschrift*, 209 (1969), 566–615, 615; H. Boldt, *Rechtsstaat und Ausnahmezustand. Eine Studie über den Belagerungszustand des bürgerlichen Rechtsstaates im 19. Jahrhundert* (Berlin, 1967).
29. See H.-U. Wehler, 'Symbol des halbabsolutistischen Herrschaftssystems. Der Fall Zabern von 1913/14 als Verfassungskrise des Wilhelminischen Kaiserreichs', in H.-U. Wehler, *Krisenherde des Kaiserreichs*, 2nd edn (Göttingen, 1970), pp. 70–88.
30. The following is a revised and extended version of my paper 'The role of state violence in the period of transition to industrial capitalism: the example of Prussia from 1815 to 1848', *Social History*, 4 (1979), 175–221, at 216–20.
31. E. J. Hobsbawm, *Industry and Empire* (Harmondsworth, 1968); D. H. Aldcroft and P. Fearon (eds.), *British Economic Fluctuations 1730–1939* (London, 1972).
32. D. L. Keir, *The Constitutional History of Modern Britain since 1485*, 6th edn (London, 1960), esp. pp. 389ff.
33. A. S. Milward and S. B. Saul, *The Economic Development of Continental Europe, 1780–1870* (London, 1973), pp. 307ff; M. Lévy-Leboyer, 'La Croissance économique en France au XIXe Siècle', *Annales*, 23 (1968), 788–807.
34. P. Goubert, *L'Ancien Régime*, vol. 2 (Paris, 1973), pp. 15ff.
35. See L. Radzinowicz, *A History of English Criminal Law and its Administration from 1750*, vol. 4 (London, 1968); on 1856 see pp. 191ff. See too J. Brewer and J. Styles (eds.), *An Ungovernable People. The English and their Law in the Seventeenth and Eighteenth Century* (London, 1980).
36. See W. L. Shelton, *English Hunger and Industrial Disorders. A Study of Social Conflict during the First Decades of George III's Regime* (London, 1973), pp. 95ff, 107, 204.
37. F. C. Mather, *Public Order in the Age of the Chartists* (New York, 1967), p. 141.
38. *Ibid.*, pp. 57f.
39. J. P. D. Dunbabin, *Rural Discontent in 19th Century Britain* (London, 1974), p. 310.
40. R. Quinault, 'The Warwickshire county magistracy and public order', in R. Quinault and J. Stevenson (eds.), *Popular Protest and Public Order* (London, 1974), pp. 181–214, at 211.
41. J. V. Jones, 'Law enforcement and popular disturbances in Wales 1793–1835', *Journal of Modern History*, 42 (1970), 496–523; Mather, *Public Order*, *passim*.
42. See R. D. Storch, 'The policeman as domestic missionary. Urban discipline and popular culture in northern England, 1850–80', *Journal of Social History*, 9 (1975–6), 481–509; Storch, 'The plague of the blue locusts. Police reform and popular resistance in Northern England, 1840–57', *International Review of Social History*, 20 (1975), 61–90. W. R. Miller suggests the more pointed view that the 'new police' in London acquired 'authority' after the 1860s because

officers, or at least their superiors, rejected or did not employ 'pure repression'; see his comparison of policing practice in London and New York, although this only touches on the 'violence standards' in each city: *Cops and Bobbies. Police Authority in New York and London, 1830–1870* (Chicago and London, 1977). See too, S. H. Palmer, *Police and Protest in England and Ireland 1780–1850* (Cambridge, 1988).

43. Radzinowicz, *English Criminal Law*, p. 247 (on institutional diversity in the 1840s) and p. 287 (on police strength).
44. *Ibid.*, pp. 118, 124, 141ff.
45. L. G. Schwoerer, *'No Standing Armies!' The Antiarmy Ideology in Seventeenth Century England* (Baltimore and London, 1974), p. 195.
46. Radzinowicz, *English Criminal Law*, pp. 153ff.
47. G. Harries-Jenkins, *The Army in Victorian Society* (London, 1977), pp. 153ff, 179ff, 247ff.
48. Radzinowicz, *English Criminal Law*, pp. 281ff.
49. See the somewhat sparse references in the, on the whole, unsatisfying treatment in D. H. Bayley, 'The police and political development in Europe', in C. Tilly (ed.), *The Formation of National States in Western Europe* (Princeton, 1975), pp. 343ff. Bayley seeks to compare Germany, England, France and Italy; in the case of England and Germany he is either insufficiently informed or suggests hypotheses of crude generality, such as the 'non-punitive character' of the English 'new police', p. 357.
50. I. A. Cameron, 'The police of eighteenth century France', *European Studies Review*, 7 (1977), 47–75; A. Farge, *Vivre dans la rue à Paris au XVIIIe siècle* (Paris, 1979), pp. 196ff, 208ff; A. Williams, *The Police of Paris, 1718–89* (Baton Rouge, La., 1979).
51. W. Fischer and P. Lundgreen, 'The recruitment and training of administrative and technical personnel', in C. Tilly (ed.), *The Formation of National States in Western Europe* (Princeton, 1975), pp. 456–561, at pp. 490–509.
52. See, for the 1820s, A. B. Spitzer, 'The bureaucrat as proconsul. The Restoration Prefect and the *Police Générale*', *Comparative Studies in Society and History*, 7 (1964), 371–92, at 389.
53. T. W. Margadant, *French Peasants in Revolt. The Insurrection of 1851* (Princeton, 1979), pp. 187–227.
54. R. Cobb, *The Police and People* (London, 1970), esp. pp. 13–45; on repression in the 1790s and early 1800s, pp. 165–8. On the nineteenth century in general see too Margadant, *French Peasants*, pp. 187ff; H. C. Payne, *The Police State of Louis Napoleon Bonaparte, 1851–60* (Seattle, 1966). See too, Ph. Vigier *et al.*, *Maintien de l'ordre et polices* (Paris, 1987); J. Aubert, *L'Etat et sa police en France (1780–1914)* (Geneva, 1979)
55. Payne, *ibid.*, pp. 206ff.
56. R. D. Price, 'The French army and the revolution of 1830', *European Studies Review*, 3 (1973), 243–67; on 1849–51 see Margadant, *French Peasants*, pp. 203–14.
57. Letter to the then Major August Freiherr Hiller von Gaertringen, 10 August 1852; Hiller wanted to ascertain before travelling to France whether the French army 'believed in a type of brotherhood of arms', GStA/PK 92, Nachlass Hiller von Gaertringen. On the suppression of 'unruly elements' in France before Louis Napoleon's coup see J. M. Merriman, *The Agony of the Republic* (New Haven and London, 1978) and Margadant, *French Peasants*, pp. 187ff; in general, Payne, *Police State*.

7 State violence, bureaucratic action and domination

1. See K. Borchardt, 'Staatsverbrauch und öffentliche Investitionen 1780–1850', Doctoral thesis (Göttingen, 1968), p. 176. The budget of the ministerial department and the Ministry of Trade, Industry and Public Works rose fourfold in money terms between 1821 and 1850 from 1.5 to 6.6 million Thalers.
2. Report to the *Oberpräsident*, 17 May 1850, StAMS, Reg. Arnsberg Pr., no. 56.
3. See T. Offermann, *Arbeiterbewegung und liberales Bürgertum in Deutschland 1850–1863* (Bonn, 1979), pp. 146–63, esp. 152.
4. Report of the *Regierungspräsident* in Trier, von Wolff, 15 July 1878 to the *Oberpräsident*, quoted from H. Pelger, 'Zur sozialdemokratischen Bewegung in der Rheinprovinz nach dem Sozialistengesetz', *Archiv für Sozialgeschichte*, 5 (1965), 377–406, at 377ff, 385. Cf. G. Bergmann, *Das Sozialistengesetz im rechtsrheinischen Industriegebiet* (Hanover, 1970), p. 100 and *passim*.
5. See the résumé by one of the leading political scientists of the Wilhelmine period, Adolf Wagner, written in 1892: 'It should be appreciated that often it is only the increased, refined, large-scale organisation of the preventive activity of the state in the police, in the organs of the judicial authorities and in its armed power which brings about a reduction in breaches of the law': *Grundlegung der politischen Ökonomie*, 3rd edn (Leipzig, 1892), p. 899.
6. C. T. Welcker, 'Belagerungszustand', in *Staatslexikon*, 3rd edn, vol. 2 (Leipzig, 1858), p. 558. The fact that this concept is not dealt with in the first two editions of the *Lexikon* is explained by the pre-constitutional situation in the German Confederation.
7. L. von Stein, *Handbuch der Verwaltungslehre*, 3rd edn, vol. 1 (Stuttgart, 1888), p. 227.
8. K. Saul, 'Der Staat und die "Mächte des Umsturzes" ', *Archiv für Sozialgeschichte*, 12 (1972), 293–350, at 299ff.
9. K. Freiherr von Stengel, *Die Organisation der Preußischen Verwaltung nach den neuen Reformgesetzen* (Leipzig, 1884), p. 5. The full quote reads as follows: 'On the one hand even the careful acts of the organs of administration [appear] to be of a policing character . . . and, on the other, actions based on coercion which should be reserved for the most extreme instances are also applied in spheres which should only be dealt with carefully.' Existing literature on the 'breadth' of state administration gives few further references; cf. the series of dissertations under the supervision of W. Hubatsch on the Prussian provincial Government Districts, e.g. I. Berger, *Die preußische Verwaltung des Reg.-Bez. Bromberg 1815–47* (Cologne and Berlin, 1966); H. Mies, *Die preußische Verwaltung des Reg.-Bez. Marienwerder 1830–70* (Cologne and Berlin, 1972); R. Engels, *Die preußische Verwaltung von Kammer und Regierung Gumbinnen 1724–1870* (Cologne, Berlin, 1974). The issue of compulsory school attendance, of some importance in our context, is dealt with by Engels (*Gumbinnen*, pp. 71f) only from the aspect of the competing interests of different bureaucracies, such as the school administration vs. the internal administration – the question of force is left unposed. One work which highlights the violence intrinsic to state policy passes over the actual practice of the bureaucracy on the spot; cf. P. Kunze, *Die preußische Sorbenpolitik 1815–1847. Eine Studie zur Nationalitätenpolitik im Übergang vom Feudalismus zum Kapitalismus* (Bautzen, 1978).
10. See D. Blasius, 'Bürgerliche Gesellschaft und bürgerliche Ängste – Der Irre in

der Geschichte des 19. Jahrhunderts. Eine Skizze', *Sozialwissenschaftliche Information für Unterricht und Studium*, 8 (1979), issue 2, 88–94, at 92ff.

11. J. Donzelot, *La police des familles* (Paris, 1977).
12. M. Foucault, *History of Sexuality*, vol. 1 (Harmondsworth, 1979), p. 93; see too pp. 92–102.
13. Foucault sees this as a dichotomy and historical succession (on the one hand, direct sanction through visible power; on the other, 'over the last few centuries' power has increasingly asserted itself 'by making itself invisible'): cf. M. Foucault, *Discipline and Punish. The Birth of the Prison* (Harmondsworth, 1983), p. 201.
14. U. K. Preuss runs up against parallel problems in his analysis of the juridical forms of the bourgeois state. However, he does not take up the question of the constitutive significance of administrative and bureaucratic practice itself: U. K. Preuss, *Legalität und Pluralismus* (Frankfurt, 1973), pp. 71, 81, 83.
15. See my review, 'Genesis und Durchsetzung des "modernen Staates" ', *Archiv für Sozialgeschcihte*, 20 (1980), 470–91, at 473, note 16.

Bibliography

Abegg, J. 'Zur sprachlichen Auslegung des Strafgesetzbuches, insbesondere der Bedeutung der Öffentlichkeit', *Archiv für Preußisches Strafrecht*, 9 (1861), 1–23.

(ed.). *Die Polizei in Einzeldarstellungen.* Berlin, 1926.

Abel, W. *Massenarmut und Hungerkrisen im vorindustriellen Europa.* Hamburg and Berlin, 1974.

Aldcroft, D. H., and Fearon, P. (eds.). *British Economic Fluctuations 1790–1939.* London 1972.

Allgemeines Landrecht für die Preußischen Staaten von 1794, edited by H. Hattenhauer and G. Bernet. Frankfurt and Berlin, 1970.

Anderson, P. *Lineages of the Absolutist State.* London, 1974.

Annalen der preußischen inneren Staatsverwaltung (Kamptz' Annalen). Berlin, 1 (1817)ff.

Anneke, F. *Ein ehrengerichtlicher Prozeß.* Leipzig, 1846.

Anon. *Erinnerungen aus dem Dienstleben eines alten preußischen Offiziers der Kgl. Preuß. Armee.* Görlitz, 1875.

Anon. 'Rezension' (of Merker, *Die Notwendigkeit des Paßwesens*), *Kamptz Annalen der preußischen inneren Staatsverwaltung*, 2 (1818), 1225–8.

Anon. 'Rezensionen', *Militär-Literatur-Zeitung* (1849 and 1850).

Anon. *Über Handhabung der Sicherheitspolizei durch Gendarmerie.* Karlsruhe, 1831.

Anon. *Westfälische Zustände*, 2nd edn. N.p., 1842.

Armstrong, J. A. *The European Administrative Elite.* Princeton, 1973.

Arnim, B. von. 'Dies Buch gehört dem König' (1843), in B. von Arnim, *Werke und Briefe*, vol. 3, ed. by G. Konrad. Frechen and Cologne, 1963, 7–254.

Aubert, J. *L'Etat et sa police en France (1780–1914).* Geneva, 1979.

Ayçoberry, P. 'Probleme der Sozialschichtung in Köln im Zeitalter der Frühindustrialisierung', in W. Fischer (ed.), *Wirtschafts- und sozialgeschichtliche Probleme der frühen Industrialisierung*, pp. 512–28. Berlin, 1968.

Baar, L. *Die Berliner Industrie in der Industriellen Revolution.* Berlin, GDR, 1966.

Bachrach, P., and Baratz, M. S. *Macht und Armut. Eine theoretisch-empirische Untersuchung.* Frankfurt, 1977.

Bahne, S. *Die Freiherren Ludwig und Georg Vincke im Vormärz.* Dortmund, 1975.

Baldus, E. 'Geschichte der Polizei-Direktion Koblenz', mimeo. Koblenz, 1961.

Ballhorn, A. *Das Polizeipräsidium zu Berlin.* Berlin, 1852.

'Vorwort', *Archiv für Polizei-Gesetzkunde und polizeiliches Strafverfahren*, 1 (1855).

Bär, M. *Die Behördenverfassung der Rheinprovinz seit 1815.* Bonn, 1819.

Bauer, E. 'Die Reise auf öffentliche Kosten', *Die Epigonen*, 5 (1848), 1ff.

Bayley, D. H. 'The police and political development in Europe', in C. Tilly (ed.), *The Formation of National States in Western Europe*, pp. 328–79. Princeton, 1975.

Belke, H.-J. *Die preußische Regierung zu Königsberg, 1808–1850.* Cologne and Berlin, 1976.

Benzenberg, *Die Gemeinde-Ausgaben der Städte Düsseldorf*, 2nd edn. Bonn, 1835.

Berger, I. *Die preußische Verwaltung des Reg.-Bez. Bromberg, 1815–47.* Cologne and Berlin, 1966.

Bergmann, D. 'Die Berliner Arbeiterschaft in Vormärz und Revolution 1830–1850', in O. Büsch (ed.),
Untersuchungen zur Geschichte der frühen Industrialisierung vornehmlich im Wirtschaftsraum Berlin/Brandenberg, pp. 455–511. Berlin, 1971.
Bergmann, G. *Das Sozialistengesetz im rechtsrheinischen Industriegebiet*. Hanover, 1970.
Bergmann, J. 'Ökonomische Voraussetzungen der Revolution von 1848. Zur Krise von 1845–1848 in Deutschland', *Geschichte und Gesellschaft*, special issue 2 (1976), 254–87.
Berthold, R., Harnisch, H. and Müller, H. H. 'Der preußische Weg der Landwirtschaft und neuere westdeutsche Forschungen', *Jb. Wirtsch. G.*, 1970/II, 259–89.
Berthold *et al.* 'Bürgerliche Umwälzung und kapitalistische Agrarentwicklung', *Zeitschrift für Geschichtswissenschaft*, 27 (1979), 140–4.
Bielitz, G. A. *Darstellung der Verfassung und Verwaltung der Polizei in Preußen. Ein Hülfsbuch für Landräthe, Magistratspersonen und Polizeibeamten in Städten, Gutsherrschaften und Polizei-Schulzen auf dem Lande, und Gendarmen in Preußen*. Leipzig, 1841.
Birtsch, G. 'Freiheit und Eigentum. Zur Erörterung von Verfassungsfragen in der deutschen Publizistik im Zeichen der Französischen Revolution', in R. Vierhaus (ed.), *Eigentum und Verfassung. Zur Eigentumsdiskussion im ausgehenden 18. Jahrhundert*, pp. 179–92. Göttingen, 1972.
Blackbourn, D., and Eley, G. *The Peculiarities of German History. Bourgeois Society and Politics in Nineteenth-Century Germany*. Oxford and New York, 1984.
Blanke, B., Jürgens, U., and Kastendiek, H. *Kritik der Politischen Wissenschaft*, vol. 2. Frankfurt and New York, 1975.
Blanke, B., Jürgens, U., and Kastendiek, H. 'On the current marxist discussion on the analysis of form and function of the bourgeois state', in J. Holloway and S. Piccioto (eds.), *State and Capital*. London, 1978.
Blasius, D. 'Der Kampf um die Geschworenengerichte im Vormärz', in H.-U. Wehler (ed.), *Sozialgeschichte heute*. Festschrift for Hans Rosenberg, pp. 148–61. Göttingen, 1974.
Bürgerliche Gesellschaft und Kriminalität. Zur Sozialgeschichte Preußens im Vormärz. Göttingen, 1976.
Kriminalität und Alltag. Zur Konfliktgeschichte des Alltagslebens im 19. Jahrhundert. Göttingen, 1978.
'Bürgerliche Gesellschaft und bürgerliche Ängste – Der Irre in der Geschichte des 19. Jahrhunderts. Eine Skizze', *Sozialwissenschaftliche Informationen für Unterricht und Studium*, 8 (1979), issue 2, 88–94.
Der verwaltete Wahnsinn. Eine Sozialgeschichte des Irrenhauses. Frankfurt, 1980.
Bleek, W. *Von der Kameralausbildung zum Juristenprivileg. Studium, Prüfung und Ausbildung der höheren Beamten des allgemeinen Verwaltungsdienstes in Deutschland im 18. und 19. Jahrhundert*. Berlin, 1972.
Bleiber, H. 'Die Moabiter Unruhen 1910', *Zeitschrift für Geschichtswissenschaft*, 13 (1955), 173–211.
Zwischen Reform und Revolution: Lage und Kämpfe der schlesischen Bauern und Landarbeiter im Vormärz 1840–1847. Berlin, GDR, 1966.
'Staat und bürgerliche Umwälzung in Deutschland. Zum Charakter besonders des preußischen Staates in der ersten Hälfte der 19. Jahrhunderts', in *Universalhistorische Aspekte und Dimensionen des Jakobinismus*. Berlin, GDR, 1976.

Reports of the Session of the Academy of Science of the German Democratic Republic, pp. 201–39.

et al. (eds.), *Bourgeoisie und bürgerliche Umwälzung in Deutschland, 1789–1871.* Berlin, GDR, 1977. Festschrift for K. Obermann.

Blesson, L. *Feld-Befestigungskunst für alle Waffen.* Berlin, 1825.

Boelcke, W. *Bauer und Gutsherr in der Oberlausitz.* Bautzen, 1957.

Boguslawski, A. von. 'Das Heer', in J. von Pflugk-Harttung (ed.), *Die Heere und Flotten der Gegenwart*, vol. 1. Berlin, 1896.

Boldt, H. *Rechtsstaat und Ausnahmezustand. Eine Studie über den Belagerungszustand des bürgerlichen Rechtsstaates im 19. Jahrhundert.* Berlin, 1967.

Borchardt, K. 'Wirtschaftliches Wachstum und Wechsellagen 1800–1914', in H. Aubin and W. Zorn (eds.) *Handbuch der deutschen Wirtschafts- und Sozialgeschichte*, vol. 2 (Stuttgart, 1976), pp. 198–275.

'Staatsverbrauch und öffentliche Investitionen in Deutschland, 1780–1850', Doctoral thesis. Göttingen, 1968.

Born, 'Die Entwicklung der Kgl. Preußischen Ostbahn', *Zeitschrift für Eisenbahnwesen*, 34 (1911), 879ff.

Botzet, H. 'Die Geschichte der sozialen Verhältnisse in Krefeld und ihre wirtschaftlichen Zusammenhänge', Doctoral thesis. Cologne, 1953.

Bourdieu, P. *Outline of a Theory of Practice.* Cambridge, 1977.

Brand, T. *Volksthümlicher Soldaten-Katechismus für Preußen.* Breslau, undated (1830).

Das Dorf-Buch für die Provinz Sachsen. Glogau, 1838.

Branig, H. *Fürst Wittgenstein. Ein preußischer Staatsmann der Restaurationszeit.* Cologne and Vienna, 1981.

Braun, R. 'Zur Einwirkung sozio-Kultureller Umweltbedingungen auf das Unternehmerpotential und das Unternehmerverhalten', in W. Fischer (ed.), *Wirtschafts- und sozialgeschichtliche Probleme der frühen Industrialisierung*, pp. 247–84. Berlin, 1968.

'Taxation, sociopolitical structure, and state-building. Great Britain and Brandenburg-Prussia', in C. Tilly (ed.), *The Formation of National States in Western Europe*, pp. 234–327. Princeton, 1975.

Brehn, H. von. *Geschichte des Westfälischen Ulanen-Regiments Nr. 5.* Düsseldorf, 1890.

Bremen, W. von (ed.). *Denkwürdigkeiten des preußischen Generals der Infanterie Eduard von Fransecky.* Bielefeld and Leipzig, 1901.

Brewer, J., and Styles, J. (eds.). *An Ungovernable People. The English and their Law in the Seventeenth and Eighteenth Century.* London, 1980.

Bülow-Cummerow, E. von. *Preußen, seine Verfassung, seine Verwaltung, sein Verhältnis zu Deutschland.* Berlin, 1842.

Burg, M. *Geschichte meines Dienstlebens*, 3rd edn. Leipzig, 1916.

Büsch, O. *Militärsystem und Sozialleben im alten Preußen, 1713–1807.* Berlin, 1962.

'Festungsstadt und Industrie. Zur Geschichte von Spandau und Siemensstadt im Zeitalter der Industrialisierung', *Jahrbuch für die Geschichte Mittel- und Ostdeutschlands*, 20 (1971), 161–82.

Industrialisierung und Gewerbe im Raum Berlin/Brandenburg 1800–1850. Berlin, 1971.

Büssem, E. *Die Karlsbader Beschlüsse von 1819. Die endgültige Stabilisierung der restaurativen Politik im deutschen Bund nach dem Wiener Kongreß von 1814/15.* Hildesheim, 1974.

Calker, F. van. *Das Recht des Militärs zum administrativen Waffengebrauch*. Munich, 1888.

Cameron, I. A. 'The police of eighteenth century France', *European Studies Review*, 7 (1977), 47–75.

Claessens, D. *Kapitalismus als Kultur. Entstehung und Grundlagen der bürgerlichen Gesellschaft*. Cologne, 1973.

Clauswitz, P. *Die Städteordnung von 1808 und die Stadt Berlin*. Berlin, 1908.

Cobb, R. *The Police and the People. French Popular Protest 1789–1820*. London, 1970.

Conrady, E. von. *Leben und Wirken des Generals der Infanterie und Kommandierenden Generals der V. Armeekorps Carl von Grolmann*, vol. 3. Berlin, 1896.

Craig, G. *The End of Prussia*. Madison and London, 1984.

Czóbel, E. 'Zur Geschichte des Kommunistenbundes. Die Kölner Bundesgemeinde vor der Revolution', *Archiv für die Geschichte des Sozialismus und der Arbeiterbewegung*, 11 (1925), 299–335.

Damkowski, W. *Die Entstehung des Verwaltungsbegriffs. Eine Wortstudie*. Cologne, 1969.

Deist, W. 'Die Armee in Staat und Gesellschaft 1890–1914', in M. Stürmer (ed.), *Das kaiserliche Deutschland. Politik und Gesellschaft 1870–1918*, pp. 312–39. Düsseldorf, 1970.

Militär und Innenpolitik im Weltkrieg 1914–1918. Part 1. Düsseldorf, 1970.

Delbrück, R. von. *Lebenserinnerungen*, vol. 1. Leipzig, 1905.

Denkwürdigkeiten aus dem Leben des Generals der Infanterie von Hüser, edited by M. Q. Berlin, 1877.

Dennstedt, H., and Wolfsburg, W. von. *Preußisches Polizei-Lexikon*, vol. 5. Berlin, 1856.

Dickler, R. A. 'Organisation and change in productivity in Eastern Prussia', in W. N. Parker and E. L. Jones (eds.), *European Peasants and their Markets*, pp. 269–92. Princeton, 1975.

Dieterici, C. F. W. 'Statistische Übersicht der im Preußischen Staate zu den sogenannten Arbeiterklassen gerechtneten Personen überhaupt und besonders in Berlin', *Mitteilungen des statistischen Büros in Berlin*, 1 (1848), 68–80.

Dohna, H. Graf, *Die freien Arbeiter im preußischen Staate*. Leipzig, 1847.

Donzelot, J. *La police des familles*. Paris, 1977.

Dosse, C. A. *Die Polizei Berlins*. Berlin, 1847.

Dronke, E. *Berlin*, 2nd edn. Neuwied and Darmstadt, 1974. First published 1846.

Polizei-Geschichten. Leipzig, 1846.

Dunbabin, J. P. D. *Rural Discontent in 19th Century Britain*. London, 1974.

Eder, K. *Die Entstehung staatlich organisierter Gesellschaften. Ein Beitrag zu einer Theorie sozialer Evolution*. Frankfurt, 1976.

Geschichte als Lernprozeß? Zur Pathogenese politischer Modernität in Deutschland. Frankfurt, 1985.

Eichhoff, W. *Berliner Polizei-Silhouetten*. 4th series. London, 1861.

Eichholtz, D. 'Bewegungen unter den preußischen Eisenbahnbauarbeitern im Vormärz', *Beiträge zur deutschen Wirtschafts- und Sozialgeschichte des 18. und 19. Jahrhunderts*, pp. 251–87. Berlin, GDR, 1962.

Elias, N. *Über den Prozeß der Zivilisation*, vol. 2, 2nd edn. Munich and Zurich, 1969, 1st edn., 1936.

Emsley, C. *Policing and its Context 1750–1870*. London and Basingstoke, 1983.

'Detection and prevention: the old English police and the new 1750–1900', *Historical Social Research*, 37 (1986), 69–88.

Engels, F. 'Preußischer Schnaps im Deutschen Reichstag', 25 February 1876 in 'Volksstaat', in *Marx–Engels Werke*, 21, pp. 405–65.

'The origin of the family, private property and the state', in K. Marx and F. Engels, *Selected Works*, p. 449. London, 1970.

Anti-Dühring. London, 1934.

'Letter to Conrad Schmidt, 27 October 1890', in *Marx–Engels Selected Correspondence*, pp. 396–402. Moscow, 1975.

Engels, R. *Die preußische Verwaltung von Kammer und Regierung Gumbinnen 1724–1870*. Cologne and Berlin, 1974.

Engelsing, R. 'Das häusliche Personal in der Epoche der Industrialisierung', in R. Engelsing, *Zur Sozialgeschichte deutscher Mittel- und Unterschichten*, pp. 225–61. Göttingen, 1973.

Erdmann, W. (ed.). *Die Praxis der Polizeiverwaltung*. Berlin, 1892.

Ernsthausen, A. E. von. *Erinnerungen eines preußischen Beamten*. Bielefeld and Leipzig, 1894.

Faber, K.-G. *Die Rheinlande zwischen Restauration und Revolution. Probleme der rheinischen Geschichte von 1814 bis 1848 im Spiegel der zeitgenössischen Publizistik*. Wiesbaden, 1966.

Farge, A. *Vivre dans la rue à Paris au XVIIIe siècle*. Paris, 1979.

Feldt, H. *Geschichte des Infanterie-Regiments Frhr. v. Sparr (3. Westf.) Nr. 16*. Berlin, 1905.

Fischer, W., and Lundgreen, P. 'The recruitment and training of administrative and technical personnel', in C. Tilly (ed.), *The Formation of National States in Western Europe*, pp. 456–561. Princeton, 1975.

Foerstemann, T. *Prinzipien des Preußischen Polizeirechts. Dargestellt und in ihren Grundlagen geprüft*. Berlin, 1869.

Fontane, T. 'Preußen – eine Militär- oder Polizeistaat?' (1849), in T. Fontane, *Politik und Geschichte, Sämtliche Werke*, vol. 19, pp. 70–4. Munich, 1969.

Foucault, M. *History of Sexuality*. Harmondsworth, 1979.

Discipline and Punish. The Birth of the Prison. Harmondsworth, 1982.

Fregier, H. A. *Über die gefährlichen Classen der Bevölkerung und die Mittel sie zu bessern*. Koblenz, 1840; 1st edn., Paris 1839.

Friauf, K. H. 'Polizei- und Ordnungsrecht', in I. von Münch (ed.), *Besonderes Verwaltungsrecht*, pp. 137–207. Bad Homburg, 1969.

Friccius, C. *Das Preußische Militärstrafrecht*. Berlin and Elbing, 1835.

Fuchs, K. *Vom Dirigismus zum Liberalismus. Die Entwicklung Oberschlesiens als preußisches Berg- und Hüttenrevier*. Wiesbaden, 1970.

Fuhr, K. *Strafrechtspflege und Sozialpolitik*. Berlin, 1892.

Garve, C. 'Über den Charakter der Bauern und ihr Verhältnis gegen die Gutsherren und gegen die Regierung' (Breslau, 1786–96), reprinted in C. Garve, *Popularphilosophische Schriften*, vol. 2, ed. K. Wölfel, pp. 799–1026. Stuttgart, 1974.

Abhandlung über die menschlichen Pflichten, 4th edn. Breslau, 1792.

Geertz, G. 'Thick description. Towards an interpretive Theory of culture', in C. Geertz, *The Interpretation of Cultures*, pp. 3–30. New York, 1973.

Gerschenkron, A. *Economic Backwardness in Historical Perspective*. Cambridge, Mass., 1962.

Gerstenberger, H. 'Zur Theorie des bürgerlichen Staates. Der gegenwärtige Stand der Debatte', in V. Brandes (ed.), *Handbuch 5, Staat*, pp. 21–49. Frankfurt and Cologne, 1977.

Gerth, H. H., and Wright Mills, C. (eds.), *From Max Weber. Essays in Sociology*. London, 1970.

Gillis, J. R. *The Prussian Bureaucracy in Crisis, 1840–1860. Origins of an Administrative Ethos*. Stanford, 1971.

Godelier, M. *Perspectives in Marxist Anthropology*. Cambridge, 1977.

Glassbrenner, A. 'Berlin und die Berliner', in A. Glassbrenner, *Berliner Volksleben*, vol. 1. Leipzig, 1847.

Goebel, K. *Schule im Schatten. Die Volksschule in den Industriestädten des Wuppertals um 1850*. Wuppertal, 1978.

Goffman, E. *Relations in Public. Microstudies of the Public Order*. New York, 1971.

Frame Analysis. An Essay on the Organisation of Experience. New York, 1974.

Goltdammer, T. *Die Materialien zum Strafgesetzbuch für die Preußischen Staaten*. Part 1. Berlin, 1851.

Gothein, E. *Verfassungs- und Wirtschaftsgeschichte der Stadt Köln vom Untergange der Reichsfreiheit bis zur Errichtung des Deutschen Reiches*. Cologne, 1916.

Goubert, P. *L'Ancien Régime*, vol. 2. Paris, 1973.

Gouldner, A. W. *Patterns of Industrial Bureaucracy*. New York, 1954.

Gräff, H., Rönne, L. von, and Simon, H. (eds.). *Ergänzungen und Erläuterungen der Preußischen Rechtsbücher*, vol. 2, 2nd edn, 1844; vol. 4, 3rd edn, 1849; vol. 5, 2nd edn, 1844; vol. 5, 3rd edn, 1849; vol. 6, 2nd edn, 1844. Breslau.

Gramsci, A. 'The problem of political leadership in the formation and development of the nation and the modern state in Italy', in Q. Hoare and G. Nowell-Smith, *Selections from the Prison Notebooks of Antonio Gramsci*. London, 1971.

Grävell, M. K. F. W. *Wie darf die Verfassung Preußens nicht werden?* Leipzig, 1819.

Über höhere, geheime und Sicherheitspolizei. Sondershausen and Nordhausen, 1820.

Groh, D. *Negative Integration und revolutionärer Attentismus. Die deutsche Sozialdemokratie am Vorabend des Ersten Weltkriegs*. Frankfurt, 1973.

Gruner, E. *Die Arbeiter in der Schweiz im 19. Jahrhundert. Soziale Lage, Organisation, Verhältnis zu Arbeitgeber und Staat*. Berne, 1968.

Haalck, J. 'Die staatspolizeilichen Koordinierungsmaßnahmen innerhalb des Deutschen Bundes zwischen 1851 and 1866', *Wissenschaftliche Zeitschrift der Universität Rostock*, 9 (1959–60), Part 1, 99–105.

Habermas, J. *Strukturwandel der Öffentlichkeit*. Neuwied, 1962.

Hackländer, F. W. *Des Soldatenleben im Frieden*. Stuttgart, 1844.

Hack, L. *et al*. 'Klassenlage und Interessenorientierung', *Zeitschrift für Soziologie*, 1 (1972), 15–30.

Hagen, K. H. *Von der Staatslehre und der Vorbereitung zum Dienste in der Staatsverwaltung. Aufsätze, gerichtet an angehende Kameralisten, zunächst an seine Herren Zuhörer*. Königsberg, 1839.

Handwörterbuch der Staatswissenschaften, vol. 3. Jena, 1890.

Hansen, J. *Preußen und Rheinland von 1815 bis 1915*. Bonn, 1918.

Hansen, J. (ed.). *Rheinische Briefe und Akten zur Geschichte der politischen Bewegung 1830–1850*, vol. 1. Essen, 1919. vol. 2. Bonn, 1942.

Harnisch, H. *Die Herrschaft Boitzenburg*. Weimar, 1968.

'Die agrarpolitischen Reformmaßnahmen der preußischen Staatsführung in dem Jahrzehnt vor 1806/7', *Jahrbuch für Wirtschaftsgeschichte* (1977/III), 129–53.

Kapitalistische Agrarreform und industrielle Revolution. Untersuchungen über das ostelbische Preußen zwischen Spätfeudalismus und bürgerlich-demokratischer Revolution 1848/49 unter besonderer Berücksichtigung der Provinz Brandenburg. Weimar, 1984.

Harries-Jenkins, G. *The Army in Victorian Society*. London, 1977.

Hart, J. 'Nineteenth-century social reform. A Tory interpretation of history', *Past and Present*, 31 (1965), 39–61.

Hay, D. 'Property, authority and criminal law', in D. Hay *et al.*, *Albion's Fatal Tree. Crime and Society in Eighteenth-Century England*, pp. 17–63. London, 1975.

Heffter, H. *Die deutsche Selbstverwaltung im 19. Jahrhundert*. Stuttgart, 1950.

Hegel, G. W. F. *Die 'Rechtsphilosophie' von 1820 mit Hegels Vorlesungsnotizen 1821–25*, edited by K.-H. Ilting. Stuttgart-Bad Canstatt, 1974.

Heinzen, K. *Die Preußische Bürokratie*. Darmstadt, 1845.

Helldorf, K. von, (ed.). *Dienst-Vorschriften der Kgl. Preußischen Armee*, 3rd edn. Part 2. Berlin, 1874.

Henning, H. 'Preußische Sozialpolitik im Vormärz', *Vierteljahrschrift für Sozial- und Wirtschaftsgeschichte*, 52 (1965), 485–539.

Das westdeutsche Bürgertum in der Epoche der Hochindustrialisierung, 1860–1914. Soziales Verhalten und soziale Strukturen, vol. 1. Wiesbaden, 1972.

Heß, Moses. 'Briefe von Dienstmädchen', in M. Heß, *Gesellschaftsspiegel* (1845/6), nos. 1, 9, 10.

Heuer, U. J. *Allgemeines Landrecht und Klassenkampf. Die Auseinandersetzungen um die Prinzipien des Allgemeinen Landrechts als Ausdruck der Krise der Feudalsystems in Preußen*. Berlin, GDR, 1960.

Heyde, W. G. von der. *Hülfsschrift zum Gebrauch bei der Verwaltung der ausübenden Polizei*. Calbe, 1832.

Preußisches Gesinde-Recht mit dem Inbegriff der seit dem Jahre 1810 bis zum Jahre 1836 erschienenen Erläuterungen, Ergänzungen und Zusätze, 5th edn. Magdeburg, 1836.

Polizei-Strafgewalt in den Königlich-Preußischen Staaten. Ein Handbuch für Polizei- und Justizbeamten sowohl in den Provinzen, wo selbst das Allgemeine Landrecht Gültigkeit besitzt, als auch in den Provinzen, wo dasselbe nicht eingeführt ist. Part 1. Magdeburg, 1837. Part 3. Magdeburg, 1842.

Der Gast- und Schankwirt oder Mitteilung der über den Gewerbsbetrieb und die polizeilichen Verhältnisse der Gast- und Schankwirte, so wie über den Handel mit Getränken bestehenden gesetzlichen Bestimmungen. Magdeburg, 1841.

Polizei-Verwaltung bezüglich auf den Inbegriff der Landes- und Lokal-Polizeiverwaltung, auf die Landes- und Lokal-Polizeibehörden, und auf deren Wirkungskreis und Geschäftsführung, vol. 1. Magdeburg, 1842.

Hickel, R. (ed.). *Die Finanzkrise des Steuerstaates. Beiträge zur politischen Ökonomie der Staatsfinanzen*. Frankfurt, 1976.

Hintze, O. 'Der Beamtenstand' (1911), in O. Hintze, *Soziologie und Geschichte, Gesamte Abhandlungen*, vol. 1, pp. 66–125, edited by G. Oestreich. Göttingen, 1964.

'Preußens Entwicklung zum Rechtsstaat' (1920), in O. Hintze, *Regierung und Verwaltung, Gesamte Abhandlungen*, vol. 3, 2nd edn, pp. 97–16, edited by G. Oestreich. Göttingen, 1967.

Hinze, K. *Die Arbeiterfrage zu Beginn des modernen Kapitalismus in Brandenburg-Preußen*. Berlin, 1927.

Hobsbawm, E. J. *Industry and Empire*. Harmondsworth, 1968.

Hoffmann, E. T. A. *Juristische Arbeiten*, edited by F. Schnapp. Munich, 1973.

Hoffmann, J. G. *Nachricht über die Vorträge und die Anordnung derselben des Dr J. G. Hoffmann*. Berlin, 1823.

Die Bevölkerung des Preußischen Staates nach den Ergebnissen der zu Ende des Jahres 1837 amtlich aufgenommenen Nachrichten. Berlin, 1839.

Das Verhältnis der Staatsgewalt zu den Vorstellungen ihrer Untergebenen. Berlin, 1842.

Hoffmann, L. 'Vorbericht', in *Polizei-Archiv für Preußen*, 1 (1817), 1–2.
(anon.) 'Etwas über Prügel', *Polizei Archiv für Preußen*, 3 (1819), 227–36.
Hofmann, W. *Die Bielefelder Stadtverordneten*. Stuttgart, 1964.
Hondrich, K. O. *Demokratisierung und Leistungsgesellschaft. Macht- und Herrschaftswandel als sozio-ökonomischer Prozeß*. Stuttgart, 1972.
Huber, E. R. *Deutsche Verfassungsgeschichte seit 1789*, vol. 1. Stuttgart, 1957. vol. 2. Stuttgart, 1960.
Dokumente zur deutschen Verfassungsgeschichte, vol. 1. Stuttgart, 1961.
'Zur Geschichte der politischen Polizei im 19. Jhdt', in E. R. Huber, *Nationalstaat und Verfassungsstaat*, pp. 144–67. Stuttgart, 1965.
Hübner, H., and Kathe, H. (eds.). *Lage und Kampf der Landarbeiter im ostelbischen Preußen (von Anfang des 19. Jahrhunderts bis zur Novemberrevolution 1918/19)*, vol. 1. Vaduz, 1977.
Janke, T. *Preußen 1807 und jetzt, oder: Was ist in Preußen seit dem Jahre 1807 ausgeführt, um den gesellschaftlichen Zustand zu verbessern und zu erheben? Eine kurze, den Freunden des Preußischen Vaterlandes geweihte Abhandlung*. Berlin, 1831.
Janowitz, M. *The Military in the Development of New Nations*. Chicago, 1964.
Jany, C. *Die Kgl. Preußische Armee und das deutsche Reichsheer 1807–1914*. (*Geschichte der Kgl. Preußischen Armee*, vol. 4). Berlin, 1933.
Johnson, H. C. *Frederick the Great and his Officials*. New Haven and London, 1975.
Jones, J. W. 'Law enforcement and popular disturbances in Wales, 1739–1835', *Journal of Modern History*, 42 (1970), 496–523.
Justi, J. H. G. von. *Grundsätze der Policeywissenschaft*. Göttingen, 1782.
Kaelble, H. *Berliner Unternehmer während der frühen Industrialisierung*. Berlin and New York, 1972.
Kampffmeyer, P., and Altmann, B. *Vor dem Sozialistengesetz. Krisenjahre des Obrigkeitsstaates*. Berlin, 1928.
Kamptz, W. von. *Der Dienst der Infanterie bei der Vertheidigung der Festungen gegen gewaltsamen Angriff*. Potsdam, 1855.
Kaufhold, K.-H. 'Das Gewerbe in Preußen um 1800'. Doctoral thesis. Göttingen, 1978.
Kehr, E. 'Zur Genesis der preußischen Bürokratie und des Rechtsstaates. Ein Beitrag zum Diktaturproblem', in E. Kehr, *Primat der Innenpolitik*, pp. 31–52, edited by H.-U. Wehler. Berlin, 1965.
Keinemann, F. von. *Das Kölner Ereignis, sein Widerhall in der Rheinprovinz und in Westfalen*. Parts 1 and 2. Münster, 1974.
Keir, D. L. *The Constitutional History of Modern Britain since 1485*, 6th edn. London, 1960.
Kermann, J. *Die Manufakturen im Rheinland 1750–1833*. Bonn, 1972.
Klein, E. *Von der Reform zur Restauration. Finanzpolitik und Reformgesetzgebung des preußischen Staatskanzlers K. A. von Hardenberg*. Berlin, 1965.
Klein, E. F. *Freiheit und Eigentum, abgehandelt in acht Gesprächen über die Beschlüsse der Französischen Nationalversammlung*. Berlin, 1790.
Kliem, M. 'Genesis der Führungskräfte der feudal-militärischen Konterrevolution 1848 in Preußen'. Doctoral thesis. Berlin, GDR, 1966.
Knapp, G. F. *Die Bauernbefreiung und der Ursprung der Landarbeiter in den älteren Theilen Preußens*, vols. 1 and 2, 2nd edn. Leipzig, 1927 (1887).
Knemeyer, F. L. *Regierungs- und Verwaltungsreformen in Deutschland zu Beginn des 19. Jahrhunderts*. Cologne and Berlin, 1970.
Knopp, G. *Die preußische Verwaltung des Regierungsbezirks Düsseldorf 1899–1919*. Cologne and Berlin, 1974.

Koch, C. F. *Allgemeines Landrecht für die Preußischen Staaten. Kommentar mit Anmerkungen.* Part 2, vol. 2. Berlin, 1854.

Kocka, J. 'Rezension zu: Koselleck, Preußen zwischen Reform und Revolution', VSWG, 57 (1970), 121–5.

'Preußischer Staat und Modernisierung im Vormärz. Marxistisch-leninistische Interpretationen und ihre Probleme', in H.-U. Wehler (ed.), *Sozialgeschichte heute.* Göttingen, 1974.

Koselleck, R. *Preußen zwischen Reform und Revolution. Allgemeines Landrecht, Verwaltung und soziale Bewegung von 1791–1848*, 1st edn. Stuttgart, 1967.

Kowalski, W. (ed.), *Vom kleinbürgerlichen Demokratismus zum Kommunismus. Die Hauptberichte der Bundeszentralbehörde in Frankfurt am Main von 1838 bis 1842 über die deutsche revolutionäre Bewegung.* Vaduz, 1978.

Kriedte, P., Medick, H., and Schlumbohm, J. *Industrialisation before Industrialisation.* Cambridge, 1981.

Kriminal-Ordnung für die Königlich Preußischen Staaten. Berlin, 1805.

Krug, L. *Betrachtungen über den Nationalreichtum des preußischen Staates und über den Wohlstand seiner Bewohner*, Part 2. Berlin, 1805. Repr. Aalen, 1970.

Abriß der Staatsökonomie. Berlin, 1808.

Krüger, H. *Zur Geschichte der Manufakturen und der Manufakturarbeiter in Preußen. Die mittleren Provinzen in der zweiten Hälfte des 18. Jahrhunderts.* Berlin, GDR, 1958.

Kuczynski, J. *Darstellung der Lage der Arbeiter in Deutschland von 1789–1849. (Geschichte der Lage der Arbeiter unter dem Kapitalismus.* Part 1, vol. 1). Berlin, GDR, 1961.

Kunze, P. *Die preußische Sorbenpolitik 1815–1847. Eine Studie zur Nationalitätenpolitik im Übergang vom Feudalismus zum Kapitalismus.* Bautzen, 1978.

Küther, C. *Räuber und Gauner in Deutschland. Das organisierte Bandenwesen im 18. und frühen 19. Jahrhundert.* Göttingen, 1976.

Kuznets, Simon. *Modern Economic Growth.* New Haven, 1966.

Laclau, E. 'The specificity of the political. The Poulantzas–Miliband debate', *Economy and Society*, 4 (1975), 87–110.

Lademacher, H. 'Der niederrheinische und westfälische Adel in der preußischen Verfassungsfrage', *Rheinische Vierteljahrsblätter*, 31 (1966–7), 442–54.

Lange, A. *Berlin zur Zeit Bebels und Bismarcks.* Berlin, GDR, 1972.

Lärmer, K. 'Maschinenbau in Preußen', *Jahrbuch für Wirtschaftsgeschichte* (1975/II), 13–32.

Lasker, E. *Zur Verfassungsgeschichte Preußens.* Leipzig, 1874.

Lasker, J. *Das Auge der Polizei. Aus dem Leben Berlins.* Berlin, 1844.

Laubert, M. *Die Verwaltung der Provinz Posen, 1815–47.* Breslau, 1923.

'Skizzen zur Posener Stadtgeschichte vor 100 Jahren', *Deutsche wiss. Zeitschrift im Wartheland* (1940), 68–128.

Lehmann, M. *Scharnhorst*, vol. 2. Leipzig, 1887.

Lehmann, R. *Quellen zur Lage der Privatbauern in der Niederlausitz im Zeitalter des Absolutismus.* Berlin, GDR, 1957.

Lenin, V. I. 'The agrarian programme of social democracy in the first Russian Revolution, 1905–1907', in Lenin, *Collected Works*, vol. 13, pp. 217–430. London, 1962.

Lennhoff, E. *Das ländliche Gesindewesen in der Kurmark Brandenburg vom 16. bis zum 19. Jahrhundert.* Breslau, 1906.

Leszcynski, R. von. *Fünfzig Jahre Geschichte des Kgl. Preuß. 2. Posensche Infanterie-Regiments Nr. 19. 1813–63.* Luxemburg, 1863.

Lévy-Leboyer, M. 'La croissance économique en France au XIXe siècle', *Annales*, 23 (1968), 788–807.
Lotz, A. *Geschichte der Deutschen Beamtentums*. Berlin, 1909.
Lowi, T. J. 'Decision-making vs. policy-making', *Public Administration Review*, 30 (1970), 314–25.
Lüdtke, A. 'Praxis und Funktion staatlicher Repression', *Geschichte und Gesellschaft*, 3 (1977), 190–211.
'The role of state violence in the period of transition to industrial capitalism: the example of Prussia from 1815 to 1848', *Social History*, 4 (1979), 175–221.
'Genesis und Durchsetzung des "modernen Staates". Zur Analyse von Herrschaft und Verwaltung', *Archiv für Sozialgeschichte*, 20 (1980), 470–91.
' "Wehrhafte Nation" und "innere Wohlfahrt": Zur militärischen Mobilisierbarkeit der bürgerlichen Gesellschaft. Konflikt und Konsens zwischen Militär und ziviler Administration in Preußen, 1815–1860', *Militärgeschichtliche Mitteilungen*, 30 (1981), issue 2, 7–56.
Luhmann, N. *Zweckbegriff und Systemrationalität*, 2nd edn. Frankfurt, 1973.
Macht. Stuttgart, 1975.
Lukes, S. *Power – A Radical View*. London, 1974.
Lüttwitz, Frhr von. *Über Verarmung, Armengesetze, Armen-Anstalten und insbesondere über Armen-Colonien mit vorzüglicher Rücksicht auf Preußen*. Breslau, 1834.
MacDonagh, O. *Early Victorian Government, 1830–1870*. London, 1977.
Machtan, L., and Milles, D. *Klassensymbiose und Bonapartismus. Zu einer materialistischen Analyse der gesellschaftlichen und politischen Herrschaftsverhältnisse in Preußen-Deutschland (1850–1878/79)*. Frankfurt, 1980.
MacPherson, C. B. 'Capitalism and the changing concept of property', in E. Kamenka and R. S. Neale (eds.), *Feudalism, Capitalism and Beyond*, pp. 104–24. London, 1975.
Mann, Heinrich. *Der Untertan*. Düsseldorf, 1984. 1st edn, 1914.
Margadant, T. W. *French Peasants in Revolt. The Insurrection of 1851*. Princeton, 1979.
Marquardt, F. D. 'Sozialer Aufstieg, sozialer Abstieg und die Entstehung der Berliner Arbeiterklasse, 1806–43', *Geschichte und Gesellschaft*, 1 (1975), 43–77.
Martiny, F. *Die Adelsfrage in Preußen vor 1806 als soziales und politisches Problem*. Stuttgart, 1938.
Marwitz, F. A. L. von der. *Lebensbeschreibung*, vol. 1, edited by F. Meusel. Berlin, 1908.
Marx, K. 'Contribution to the Critique of Hegel's Philosophy of Law', in K. Marx and F. Engels, *Collected Works*, vol. 3. London, 1975.
'The Eighteenth Brumaire of Louis Bonaparte', in K. Marx and F. Engels, *Collected Works*, vol. 11, pp. 99–181. London, 1979.
'Letter to Engels, March 25 1868', in *Marx–Engels Selected Correspondence*, pp. 188–200. Moscow, 1975.
Capital, vol. 1. Harmondsworth, 1976.
Marx, K., and Engels, F. *The German Ideology* (1845–6). London, 1965.
Manifesto of the Communist Party (1848). Moscow, 1967.
Mather, F. C. *Public Order in the Age of the Chartists*. New York, 1967.
Mayer, Arno. *The Persistence of the Old Regime. Europe to the Great War*. New York, 1981.
Mayer, G. 'Die Anfänge des politischen Radikalismus im vormärzlichen Preussen' (1913), in G. Mayer, *Radikalismus, Sozialismus und bürgerliche Demokratie*, pp. 7–107, edited by H.-U. Wehler. Frankfurt, 1969.

Medick, H. *Naturzustand und Naturgeschichte der bürgerlichen Gesellschaft.* Göttingen, 1973.

Meinecke, F. *Das Leben des Gen.-Feldmarschalls Hermann von Boyen*, vol. 2. Stuttgart, 1899.

Merker. *Handbuc für die ausübenden Polizei-Beamten.* Erfurt, 1818.

Die Notwendigkeit des Paßwesens zur Erhaltung der öffentlichen Sicherheit; zugleich ein Versuch, die Reisenden mit den Unannehmlichkeiten dieser Einrichtung auszusöhnen. Erfurt, 1818.

Merriman, J. M. *The Agony of the Republic. The Repression of the Left in Revolutionary France, 1848–51.* New Haven and London, 1978.

Mies, H. *Die preußische Verwaltung des Reg.-Bez. Marienwerder, 1830–70.* Cologne and Berlin, 1972.

Miller, W. R. *Cops and Bobbies. Police Authority in New York and London, 1830–1870.* Chicago and London, 1977.

Milward, A. S., and Saul, S. B. *The Economic Development of Continental Europe, 1780–1870.* London, 1973.

Minutoli, A. von. *Die Lage der Weber und Spinner im schlesichen Gebirge und die Maßregeln der preußischen Staatsregierung zur Verbesserung ihrer Lage* Berlin, 1851.

Mittelstrass, J. 'Über Interessen', in J. Mittelstrass, *Methodologische Probleme einer normativ-kritischen Gesellschaftstheorie*, pp. 126–69. Frankfurt, 1975.

Mittenzwei, I. *Preußen nach dem Siebenjährigen Krieg. Auseinandersetzungen zwischen Bürgertum und Staat um die Wirtschaftspolitik.* Berlin, GDR, 1979.

Mohl, R. 'Über die Nachteile des fabrikmßigen Betriebs der Industrie', *Archiv für politische Ökonomie und Polizeiwissenschaft*, 2 (1835), 141–203.

'Über Bureaukratie', *Zeitschrift für die gesamte Staatswissenschaft*, 3 (1846), 340–64.

Mohls, H. (ed.). *Generalfeldmarschall Alfred Graf von Waldersee in seinem militärischen Wirken*, vol. 1. Berlin, 1929.

Moore, B. jnr. *The Social Origins of Dictatorship and Democracy.* Harmondsworth, 1969.

Mooser, J. *Ländliche Klassengesellschaft, 1770–1848. Bauern und Unterschichten, Landwirtschaft und Gewerbe im östlichen Westfalen.* Göttingen, 1984.

Müllensiefen, P. E. *Ein deutsches Bürgerleben*, edited by F. von Oppeln-Bronikowski. Berlin, 1931.

Müller, H.-H. *Märkische Landwirtschaft vor den Agrarreformen von 1807. Entwicklungstendenzen des Ackerbaus in der zweiten Hälfte des 18. Jahrhunderts.* Potsdam, 1967.

Müller-Blattau, M. 'Die deutsche Polizei an der Wende vom Polizeistaat zum bürgerlichen Rechtsstaat', Doctoral thesis. Heidelberg, 1961.

Nipperdey, T. *Deutsche Geschichte 1860–1866. Bürgerwelt und starker Staat.* Munich, 1983.

Nollau, H. *Die Entwicklung der Kgl. Preußischen Polizei-Behörde zu Aachen 1818–1910.* Aachen, 1910.

North, D. C., and Thomas, R. P. *The Rise of the Western World.* Cambridge, 1973.

Obenaus, H. 'Finanzkrise und Verfassungsgebung. Zu den sozialen Bedingungen des frühen deutschen Konstitutionalismus', in G. A. Ritter (ed.), *Gesellschaft, Parlament und Regierung*, pp. 57–75. Düsseldorf, 1974.

Obenaus, W. *Die Entwicklung der preußischen Sicherheitspolizei.* Berlin, 1940.

Obermann, K. 'Die Arbeitermigrationen in Deutschland im Prozeß der Industrialisierung und der Entstehung der Arbeiterklasse in der Zeit von der

Gründung bis zur Auflösung des Deutschen Bundes (1815–67)', *Jahrbuch für Wirtschaftsgeschichte* (1972/1), 135–81.

Oertzen, P. von. *Die soziale Funktion des staatsrechtlichen Positivismus*. Frankfurt, 1974.

Offe, C. 'Klassenherrschaft und politisches System. Die Selektivität politischer Institutionen', in C. Offe, *Strukturprobleme des kapitalistischen Staates*, pp. 65–105. Frankfurt, 1972.

Berufsbildungsreform. Frankfurt am Main, 1975.

'Überlegungen und Hypothesen zum Problem politischer Legitimation', in C. Offe, *Bürgerlicher Staat und Legitimation*, pp. 80–105. Frankfurt, 1976.

Contradictions of the Welfare State. London, 1984.

Offermann, T. *Arbeiterbewegung und liberales Bürgertum in Deutschland 1850–1863*. Bonn, 1979.

Oldenburgh-Januschau, E. von. *Erinnerungen*, 2nd edn. Leipzig, 1936.

Ostermann, H. *Die gesamte Polizei-, und Militär-, Steuer-, und Gemeindeverwaltung in den Kgl. Preuß. Staaten*. Part 1. Coesfeld, 1836.

Pashukanis, E. *Law and Marxism*. London, 1978.

Paulizky, O., and Woedtke, A. von. *Geschichte des 4. Rhein. Inf.-Regiments Nr. 30*. Part 1, 1815–84. Berlin, 1884.

Payne, H. C. *The Police State of Louis Napoleon Bonaparte, 1851–60*. Seattle, 1966.

Pelger, H. 'Zur sozialdemokratischen Bewegung in der Rheinprovinz nach dem Sozialistengesetz', *Archiv für Sozialgeschichte*, 5 (1965), 377–406.

Pertz, G. H. *Das Leben des Feldmarschalls Grafen Neithardt von Gneisenau*, vol. 1. Berlin, 1864.

Peters, H. 'Erfurt im Jahre 1848', Doctoral thesis. Berlin, GDR, 1966.

Plaul, H. *Landarbeiterleben im 19. Jahrhundert*. Berlin, GDR, 1979.

Poestges, D. 'Die preußische Personalpolitik im Regierungsbezirk Aachen von 1815 bis zum Ende des Kulturkampfes', Doctoral thesis. Aachen, 1975.

Polanyi, K. *The Great Transformation*, 2nd edn. Boston, 1957. First edition 1944.

Pollard, S. 'Factory discipline in the Industrial Revolution', *Economic History Review*, 16 (1963), 254–71.

Peaceful Conquest. The Industrialization of Europe 1760–1970. Oxford, 1981.

Poulantzas, N. *Political Power and Social Classes*. London, 1973.

Preuss, H. *Die Entwicklung des deutschen Städtewesens*, vol. 1. Leipzig, 1906.

Preuss, U. K. *Legalität und Pluralismus*. Frankfurt, 1973.

Price, R. D. 'The French army and the revolution of 1830', *European Studies Review*, 3 (1973), 243–67.

Puhle, H.-J. 'Preußen: Entwicklung und Fehlentwicklung', in H.-J. Puhle and H.-U. Wehler (eds.), *Preußen im Rückblick, Geschichte und Gesellschaft*, special issue 6, pp. 11–42. Göttingen, 1980.

Quinault, R. 'The Warwickshire county magistracy and public order', in R. Quinault and J. Stevenson (eds.), *Popular Protest and Public Order*, London, 1974. pp. 181–214.

Radlik, U. 'Heine in der Zensur der Restaurationsepoche', in J. Hermand and M. Windfuhr (eds.), *Zur Literatur des Restaurationsepoche, 1815–1848*, pp. 460–89. Stuttgart, 1970.

Radzinowicz, L. *A History of English Criminal Law and its Administration from 1750*, vol. 4. London, 1968.

Redlich, F. 'Frühindustrielle Unternehmer und ihre Probleme im Lichte ihrer Selbstzeugnisse', in W. Fischer (ed.), *Wirtschafts- und sozialgeschichtliche Probleme der frühen Industrialisierung*, pp. 339–412. Berlin, 1968.

Reif, H. *Westfälischer Adel, 1770–1860. Vom Herrschaftsstand zur regionalen Elite.* Göttingen, 1979.

Riedel, M. *Bürgerliche Gesellschaft und Staat bei Hegel. Grundproblem und Struktur der Hegelschen Rechtsphilosophie*. Neuwied and Berlin, 1970.

Ristelhüber, J. B. *Leben und Schicksale zweier Strafgefangenen, nach der gekrönten Preisschrift 'Anton und Moritz' von L. P. de Jussieu frei Übersetzt.* Hamburg, 1836.

Robin, R. 'Der Charakter des Staates am Ende des Ancien Régime. Gesellschaftsformation, Staat und Übergang', in E. Schmitt (ed.), *Die Französische Revolution*, pp. 202–29. Cologne, 1976.

Ronge, V., and Schmieg, G. *Restriktionen politischer Planung*. Frankfurt, 1973.

Rönne, L. von. *Die preußischen Städteordnungen.* Breslau, 1840.

Das Staatsrecht der Preußischen Monarchie, 3rd edn. Part 1, vol. 1. Leipzig, 1869; Part 1, vol. 2 Leipzig, 1870; Part 2, vol. 2. Berlin, 1872.

Rönne, L. von, and Simon, H. *Das Polizeiwesen des Preußischen Staates*, vols. 1 and 2. 1840–1. *Die Verfassung und Verwaltung des Preußischen Staates.* Berlin and Breslau, 1840–56.

Rösen, H. 'Öl- oder Gasbeleuchtung in den Straßen Krefelds? 1837–47', *Die Heimat*, 35 (1964), 139ff.

'Der Aufstand der Krefelder "Seidenfabrikarbeiter" 1828 und die Bildung einer "Sicherheitswache" ', *Die Heimat* (1965), 32–61.

Rosenberg, H. *Bureaucracy, Aristocracy and Autocracy.* Cambridge, Mass., 1958.

'Die Pseudodemokratisierung der Rittergutsbesitzerklasse', in H. Rosenberg, *Probleme der deutschen Sozialgeschichte*, pp. 7–49. Frankfurt, 1969.

Machteliten und Wirtschaftskonjunkturen. Göttingen, 1978.

Rosin, H. *Polizeiverordnungsrecht.* Berlin, 1882.

Rumpf, J. D. F. *Handbuch für Landräte.* Berlin, 1835.

Rüfner, W. *Verwaltungsrechtsschutz in Preußen von 1749 bis 1842.* Bonn, 1962.

Rusche, G., and Kirchheimer, O. *Sozialstruktur und Strafvollzug*, 2nd edn. Frankfurt and Cologne, 1974. First edition, New York, 1939.

Saalfeld, D. 'Zur Frage des bäuerlichen Landesverlustes im Zusammenhang mit den preußischen Agrarreformen', *Zeitschrift für Agrargeschichte und Agrarsoziologie*, 11 (1963), 163–71.

Sammlung der für die Königlich Preußischen Staaten erschienenen Gesetze und Verordnungen 1806–1810. Berlin, 1822.

Sauer, W. 'Das Problem des deutschen Nationalstaates', in H.-U. Wehler (ed.), *Moderne deutsche Sozialgeschichte*, pp. 407–36, 544–50, 2nd edn. Cologne, 1968.

Saul, K. 'Der Staat und die "Mächte des Umsturzes". Ein Beitrag zu den Methoden antisozialistischer Repression und Agitation vom Scheitern des Sozialistengesetzes bis zur Jahrhundertwende', *Archiv für Sozialgeschichte*, 12 (1972), 293–350.

Schäffle, A. 'Die Stellung der politischen Verwaltung im Staatsorganismus aus dem Gesichtspunkt technisch zweckmäßiger Arbeitstheilung', *Zeitschrift für die gesamte Staatswissenschaft*, 27 (1871), 181–250.

Scheel, H. (ed.). *Das Reformministerium Stein. Akten zur Verfassungs- und Verwaltungsgeschichte aus den Jahren 1807/8*, vols. 1–3. Berlin, GDR, 1967–8.

Schissler, H. *Preußische Agrargesellschaft im Wandel. Wirtschaftliche, gesellschaftliche und politische Transformationsprozesse von 1763 bis 1847.* Göttingen, 1978.

Schläger, F. G. F. *Der Bußfertige. Ein Erbauungsbuch für Schuldbeladene, für Sträflinge in Gefängnissen und öffentlichen Zuchtanstalten.* Hanover, 1828.

Schlosser, J. G. *Briefe über die Gesetzgebung überhaupt und den Entwurf des preußischen Gesetzbuches*. Frankfurt, 1789.
Fünfter Brief über die Entwicklung des Preußischen Gesetzbuches. Frankfurt, 1790.
Schmidt, E. *Einführung in die Geschichte der deutschen Strafrechtspflege*, 5th edn. Göttingen, 1965.
Schmidt, F. *Untersuchungen über Bevölkerung, Arbeitslohn und Pauperism in ihrem gegenseitigen Zusammenhange*. Leipzig, 1836.
Schmidt, P. *Die ersten 50 Jahre der Kgl. Schutzmannschaft zu Berlin*. Berlin, 1898.
Schneer, A. *Über die Zustände der arbeitenden Klassen in Breslau*. Berlin, 1845.
Schoefert, J. G. *Der preußische Beamte oder die Kenntnis der preußischen Gesetze und Verordnungen über die Befähigung der höhern und niedern Verwaltungs-, Justiz-, Bau-, und Eisenbahnbeamten*, 2nd edn. Glogau, 1852.
Schofer, L. *The Formation of a Modern Labor Force. Upper Silesia, 1865–1914*. Berkeley, 1975.
Schrimpf, H. 'Die Auseinandersetzung um die Neuordnung des individuellen Rechtsschutzes gegenüber der staatlichen Verwaltung nach 1807', *Der Staat*, 18 (1979), 59–80.
Schück, A. 'Die Revision der preußischen Armengesetzgebung', *Archiv für Landeskunde der preußischen Monarchie* (1856), issue 4, 348–76.
Schücking, L. *Die Reaktion in der inneren Verwaltung*. Berlin, 1908.
Schwab, D. 'Eigentum', in *Geschichtliche Grundbegriffe*, vol. 2. Stuttgart, 1975.
Schweder, A. *Politische Polizei. Begriff und Wesen der politischen Polizei im Metternichschen System, in der Weimarer Republik und im nationalsozialistischen Staate*. Berlin, 1937.
Schwoerer, L. G. *'No Standing Armies!' The Antiarmy Ideology in Seventeenth Century England*. Baltimore and London, 1974.
Shelton, W. L. *English Hunger and Industrial Disorders. A Study of Social Conflict during the First Decades of George III's Regime*. London, 1973.
Siegrist, L. (pseud.). *Leben, Wirken und Ende weiland Sr. Exc. des Oberfürstlich Winkelkramschen Gen. d. Inf. Frhr. Leberecht von Knopf*. Darmstadt and Leipzig, 1969.
Siemann, W. 'Die Protokolle der Mainzer Untersuchungskommission von 1819 bis 1828', in F. Quarthal and W. Setzler (eds.), *Stadtverfassung–Verfassungsstaat–Pressepolitik*, Festschrift E. Naujoks. Sigmaringen, 1980, pp. 301–17.
Simon, Heinrich. *Aktenstücke zur neuesten Geschichte der Preußischen Polizei, gleichzeitig zur Grenzberichtigung zwischen Justiz und Polizei*. Leipzig, 1847.
Simon, W. M. *The Failure of the Prussian Reform Movement, 1807–19*. Ithaca, 1955.
Smith. A. *An Inquiry into the Nature and Causes of the Wealth of Nations*. London, 1776 (reprint, 1966).
Sohm, C. *Die unbestimmte Verurteilung in Preußen unter der Herrschaft des Allgemeinen Landrechts*. Leipzig, 1939.
Spitzer, A. B. 'The Bureaucrat as proconsul. The Restoration Prefect and the *Police Générale*', *Comparative Studies in Society and History*, 7 (1964), 371–92.
Spree, R. *Die Wachstumszyklen der deutschen Wirtschaft von 1840–1880, mit einem konjunkturstatistischen Anhang*. Berlin, 1977.
Stein, L. vom. *Geschichte der sozialen Bewegung in Frankreich* (1850). Reprinted Hildesheim, 1959.
Handbuch der Verwaltungslehre. 3rd edn, vol. 1. Stuttgart, 1888.
Stein, Frhr. vom *Briefe und amtliche Schriften*, vol. 6. Stuttgart, 1965.
Stengel, K. Frhr. von. *Die Organisation der Preußischen Verwaltung nach den neuen Reformgesetzen*. Leipzig, 1884.

Sterling, E. *Judenhaß. Die Anfänge des politischen Antisemitismus in Deutschland (1815–1850)*. Frankfurt, 1969.

Storch, R. D. 'The plague of the blue locusts. Police reform and popular resistance in northern England, 1840–57', *International Review of Social History*, 20 (1975), 61–90.

'The policeman as domestic missionary. Urban discipline and popular culture in northern England, 1850–80', *Journal of Social History*, 9 (1975–6), 481–509.

Strampff, H. L. von. *Kritische Briefe über den Entwurf des Strafgesetzbuches*. Berlin, 1844.

Stuckrad, von. *Geschichte des 1. Magdeburgischen Infanterieregiments*, no. 26, Part 1. Berlin, 1888.

Stürmer, M. 'Staatsstreichgedanken im Bismarckreich', *Historische Zeitschrift*, 209 (1969), 566–615.

Svarez, C. G. *Vorträge über Recht und Staat*, edited by H. Conrad and G. Kleinheyer. Cologne and Opladen, 1960.

Tenfelde, K. 'Ländliches Gesinde in Preußen. Gesinderecht und Gesindestatistik 1810–1861', *Archiv für Sozialgeschichte*, 19 (1979), 189–229.

Thompson, E. P. *Whigs and Hunters*. London, 1975.

Thun, A. *Die Industrie am Niederrhein und ihre Arbeiter*, vol. 1. Leipzig, 1879.

Tilly, C., Tilly, L., and Tilly, R. *The Rebellious Century, 1830–1930*. Cambridge, Mass., 1975.

Tilly, R. 'Protest and Collective Violence in Germany during Modernization (1800–1914)', mimeo. Münster, 1974.

Tilly, R. H. 'Capital formation in Germany in the 19th Century', in P. Mathias and M. M. Postan (eds.), *The Cambridge Economic History of Europe*, vol. 7, pp. 382–411. Cambridge, 1978.

Trapp, W. 'Volksschulreform und liberales Bürgertum in Konstanz', in G. Zang (ed.), *Provinzialisierung einer Region*, pp. 375–434. Frankfurt, 1978.

Über Militärwachen, Militärarreste und das Unterkommen der Militärsträflinge. Berlin, 1840.

Vaupel, R. (ed.). *Die Reorganisation des Preußischen Staates unter Stein und Hardenberg*. Part 1, vol. 1. Leipzig, 1938.

Vergleichende Suzammenstellung der Einwohnerzahl der Städte der Preußischen Staates von 1840–1855. Archiv für Landeskunde der preußischen Monarchie (1856), issue 4, 228 ff.

Vigier, Ph. *et al. Maintien de l'ordre et polices*. Paris, 1987.

Vincke, Frhr Ludwig von. *Die Tagebücher des Oberpräsidenten Ludwig Freiherrn Vincke 1813–1818*, edited by L. Graf von Westphalen. Münster, 1980.

Vogel, B. 'Die "allgemeine Gewerbefreiheit" als bürokratische Modernisierungsstrategie in Preußen. Eine Problemskizze zur Reformpolitik Hardenbergs', in D. Stegmann and P.-C. Witt (eds.), *Industrielle Gesellschaft und politisches System*, pp. 59–78. Bonn, 1978.

'Die preußischen Reformen als Gegenstand und Problem der Forschung', in B. Vogel (ed.), *Preußische Reformen 1807–1820*, pp. 1–27. Königstein, Taunus, 1980.

Vortriede, W. (ed.). *Bettina von Arnim's Armenbuch*. Frankfurt, 1969.

Vormbaum, T. *Politik und Gesinderecht im 19. Jahrhundert (vornehml. in Preußen 1810–1918)*. Berlin, 1980.

Wagner, A. *Grundlegung der politischen Ökonomie*, 3rd edn. Leipzig, 1892.

Waldersee, F. G. Graf von. *Der Dienst des preußischen Infanterie-Unteroffiziers*, 3rd edn. Berlin, 1848; 4th edn. Berlin, 1849.

Wallthor, A. H. von. *Die landschaftliche Selbstverwaltung Westfalens in ihrer Entwicklung seit dem 18. Jahrhundert.* Part 1. Münster, 1965.
Weber, E. *Die Mainzer Zentraluntersuchungskommission.* Karlsruhe, 1970.
Weber, M. *Essays in Sociology*, ed. H. H. Gerth and C. Wright Mills. Oxford, 1946.
Economy and Society, vol. 2. New York, 1968.
Wegmann, D. *Die leitenden staatlichen Verwaltungsbeamten der Provinz Westfalen 1815–1918.* Münster, 1969.
Wehler, H.-U. 'Symbol des halbabsolutischen Herrschaftssystems. Der Fall Zabern von 1913/14 als Verfassungskrise des Wilhelminischen Kaiserreichs', in H.-U. Wehler, *Krisenherde des Kaiserreichs, 1871–1918*, pp. 65–83. Göttingen, 1970.
Modernisierungstheorie und Geschichte. Göttingen, 1975.
Wehnert. *Über den Geist der preußischen Staatsorganisation und Staatsdienerschaft.* Potsdam, 1833.
Weidemann, F. *Oberschlesische Zustände in freien Rasirspiegel-Scenen.* Leipzig, 1843.
Wiemann, K. 'Bevölkerungsentwicklung und Frühindustrialisierung in Berlin, 1800–1850', in O. Büsch (ed.), *Untersuchungen zur Geschichte der frühen Industrialisierung*, pp. 150–90. Berlin, 1971.
Weitz, R. K. 'Der niederrheinische und westfälische Adel im ersten preußischen Verfassungskampf 1815–1823/24. Die verfassungs- und gesellschaftspolitischen Vorstellungen des Adelkreises um Freiherrn v. Stein', Doctoral thesis. Bonn, 1970.
Welcker, C. T. 'Belagerungszustand', in *Staatslexikon*, 3rd edn, vol. 2, pp. 448–83. Leipzig, 1858.
Wilfling, A. *Der administrative Waffengebrauch der öffentlichen Wachorgane und des Heeres.* Vienna, Leipzig, 1909.
Williams, A. *The Police of Paris, 1718–89.* Baton Rouge, La., 1979.
Willich, von. *Im preussischen Heere.* Mannheim, 1848.
Winter, G. (ed.). *Die Reorganisation des preußischen Staates unter Stein und Hardenberg*, Part 1, vol. 1. Leipzig, 1931.
Wirtz, R. 'Die Begriffsverwirrung der Bauern im Odenwald. Odenwälder "Excesse" und die Sinsheimer "republikanische Schilderhebung" ', in D. Puls (ed.), *Wahrnehmungsformen und Protestverhalten*, pp. 81–104. Frankfurt, 1979.
'Zur Logik plebejischer und bürgerlicher Aufstandsbewegungen. Die gescheiterte Revolution von 1848', *Sozialwissenschaftliche Informationen für Unterricht und Studium*, 8 (1979), 83–8.
Witzleben, A. von. *Grundzüge des Heerwesens und Infanteriedienstes der Kgl. Preuß. Armee.* Berlin, 1845.
Wolfe, A. 'New directions in the marxist theory of politics', *Politics and Society*, 4 (1974), 131–59.
Wolzendorff, K. 'Die Entwicklung des Polizeibegriffs im 19. Jahrhundert', Doctoral thesis. Marburg, 1905.
Die Polizeigedanke des modernen Staats. Breslau, 1918.
Wortmann, W. *Eisenbahnbauarbeiter im Vormärz. Socialgeschichtliche Untersuchung der Bauarbeiter der Köln–Mindener Eisenbahn in Minden-Ravensberg 1844–47.* Cologne and Vienna, 1972.
Wunder, B. *Privilegierung und Disziplinierung. Die Entstehung des Berufsbeamtentums in Bayern und Württemburg (1780–1825).* Munich and Vienna, 1978.
Wutzmer, H. 'Die Herkunft der industriellen Bourgeoisie Preußens in den vierziger Jahren des 19. Jahrhunderts', in H. Mottek *et al.*, *Studien zur Geschichte der industriellen Revolution in Deutschland.* Berlin, GDR, 1960, pp. 145–63.

Zachariae, H. A. *Deutsches Staats- und Bundesrecht*, 1st edn, vol. 2. Göttingen, 1842.
Zedlitz, Frhr. von. *Die Staatskräfte der Preußischen Monarchie unter Friedrich Wilhelm III*, vol. 2. Berlin, 1828. vol. 3. Berlin, 1830.
Zeller, P. *Systematisches Lehrbuch der Polizeiwissenschaft nach preußischen Edicten . . . sowohl zum Unterricht der Regierungsreferendarien . . . als auch zur Hülfe für die Kgl. Preuß. Regierungsräthe, Landräthe, Polizeipräsidenten, Polizeiräthe, Bürgermeister*, Part 1. Quedlinburg and Leipzig, 1828.
Ziekursch, J. *Hundert Jahre schlesische Agrargeschichte*, 2nd edn. Breslau, 1927.
Zimmermann, A. *Blüthe und Verfall des Leinengewerbes in Schlesien.* Breslau, 1885.
Zimmermann, C. W. *Die Diebe in Berlin.* Berlin, 1847.
Zimmermann, G. *Die deutsche Polizei im neunzehnten Jahrhundert*, vols. 1 and 2. Hanover, 1845; vol. 3. Hanover, 1849.
Zunkel, F. *Der Rheinisch-Westfälische Unternehmer, 1834–1879*. Cologne, 1962.
Zwahr, H. 'Ausbeutung und gesellschaftliche Stellung des Fabrik- und Manufakturproletariats am Ende der Industriellen Revolution im Spiegel Leipziger Fabrikordnungen', in W. Jacobeit, U. Mohrmann (eds.). *Kultur und Lebensweise des Proletariats. Kulturhistorisch-volkskundliche Studien und Materialien*, pp. 85–136. 2nd edn. Berlin, GDR, 1974.
Zychlinski. *Geschichte des Preuß. Inf.-Regiments Nr. 24*. Berlin, 1857.

Index

Alphabetical arrangement is word-by-word. Prepositions etc at the beginning of subheadings have been ignored in determining the alphabetical order of subheadings.